Thieves, Opportunists, and Autocrats

Thieves, Opportunists, and Autocrats

Building Regulatory States in Russia and Kazakhstan

DINISSA DUVANOVA

OXFORD
UNIVERSITY PRESS

OXFORD
UNIVERSITY PRESS

Oxford University Press is a department of the University of Oxford.
It furthers the University's objective of excellence in research, scholarship,
and education by publishing worldwide. Oxford is a registered trade mark of
Oxford University Press in the UK and in certain other countries.

Published in the United States of America by Oxford University Press
198 Madison Avenue, New York, NY 10016, United States of America.

CIP data is on file at the Library of Congress

ISBN 978–0–19–769776–4 (hbk.)
ISBN 978–0–19–769777–1 (pbk.)

DOI: 10.1093/oso/9780197697764.001.0001
DOI: 10.1093/oso/9780197697771.001.0001

Integrated Books International, United States of America

Contents

List of Figures

List of Tables

Acknowledgments

This book was long in the making and would not have been possible without the support I received from many different quarters. I owe enormous gratitude to my colleagues at Lehigh University for accommodating my numerous professional and personal needs and the warm collegial atmosphere that made my work on this manuscript most enjoyable. This book would have been much harder to complete if not for the dedicated assistance of Lehigh students Cun "Scott" Shi, Jae Choi, Rafael Hernandez, Tyler French, and Yuanyuan Xie. I would like to thank the Lehigh Humanities Center for organizing writing retreats and the Department of International Relations, specifically Norrin Ripsman, for organizing a manuscript development workshop to help me advance this book to publication.

Empirical research for this book was made possible by financial support from Lehigh University and a Fulbright US Scholar Teaching and Research Fellowship. I am most grateful to Bill Hunter from Lehigh, Harvey Palmer from SUNY Buffalo, and Timothy Frye from Columbia University for their encouragement and support of my Fulbright application. I thank the US Consulate in Almaty, Kazakhstan, and the rectorate of Alma University in Almaty for making my field work productive and enjoyable. My work on the manuscript was supported by New York University's Jordan Center for the Advanced Study of Russia. I am grateful to Josh Tucker for the opportunity to be a visiting fellow in such a vibrant intellectual community.

This book would never have been completed without the support I received from a large number of individuals in Russia and Kazakhstan who shared with me their valuable time, expertise, and resources. My writing was informed by accounts of real-world experiences of business owners, entrepreneurs, and public servants who shared with me their personal experiences and official positions. I am indebted to them for sharing my passion for the subject of this project and patience in answering my questions.

I owe enormous gratitude to Gulnaz Sharafutdinova, Peter Rutland, and John Heathershaw for reading earlier version of this book and sharing their insightful comments on the core theoretical ideas and empirical strategy of the book at the time I needed them most. If not for their ideas, criticism, and encouragement to think more critically about authoritarianism and state-building, this book would have been duller and narrower in its claims. I owe an important debt of gratitude to anonymous reviewers for reading the manuscript and criticizing it in the most constructive and insightful manner. I am grateful to Eve Baker and Leanne Rancourt for skillful copyediting.

Most importantly, I want to thank my children for accompanying me on my research trips, cheering me up, and learning to respect my research time. I am grateful for their patience and contagious optimism.

List of Frequently Used Abbreviations

BEEPS   Business Environment and Enterprise Performance Survey
CEO   chief executive officer
CPI   Corruption Perception Index
CPIA   Country Policy and Institutional Assessment, by the World Bank
DB   Doing Business Indicators, by the World Bank
EAEU   Eurasian Economic Union
EBRD   European Bank for Reconstruction and Development
EPC   Engineering Procurement Construction
FCI   Fixed Capital Investment
FDI   Foreign Direct Investment
GCI   Global Competitiveness Index
GDP   Gross Domestic Product
GI   Global Integrity Indicators
GLS   generalized least squares (regression)
HF   Heritage Foundation and Wall Street Journal Index of Economic Freedom
KZT   Kazakh Tenge
LIS   Legal Information System portal "Legislation of Russia" available from pravo.gov.ru
LLP   limited liability partnership
LRT   Light Rail Transport
OECD   Organization for Economic Cooperation and Development
RCLI   Republican Center for Legal Information, Kazakhstan
RIA   Russian Information Agency
SME   small and medium enterprises
USSR   Union of the Soviet Socialist Republics
WB   The World Bank
WEF   World Economic Forum

Note on Translation and Transliteration

I transliterated Russian and Kazakh words using the simplified Library of Congress system (diacritics and two-letter tie characters are omitted), except for names of well-known people where a different spelling has become conventional, for example, Yeltsin. I transliterated all Kazakh words from their Cyrillic spelling. Where Kazakh proper names are spelled differently in Russian and Kazakh, I transliterated from the Russian spelling. All translations from Russian and Kazakh original documents and records are my own.

Introduction

This book is about authoritarian state-building. It was finished at the time when the Russian war in Ukraine and its global ramifications drew the world's attention. With Ukraine's effective resistance against Russian aggression, many experts are desperately searching for signs of authoritarian Russia's economic decline, regime breakdown, and the downfall of President Vladimir Putin. In my home country of Kazakhstan, hope for political change following the alleged failed coup against President Kassym-Jomart Tokayev is guarded as the aging former President Nursultan Nazarbayev shields his clan against timid critics and holds high-profile meetings with Putin. It is unnerving to see dictatorships maintaining a strong grip despite economic hardship and international pressures. As the tensions mount, it becomes even more important to understand the sources of such disconcerting resilience of Eurasia's authoritarian states. This book is an attempt to understand how autocratic states have built resilient and adaptable instruments of survival into the very fabric of their regulatory institutions. My task is to uncover the logic underpinning the authoritarian structures of economic governance and connect these to the outcomes that have allowed Eurasian states to command resources necessary for their long-term survival and agility.

This book examines how two countries—Russia and Kazakhstan—have navigated the dilemmas associated with building mechanisms of state governance of the economy and society. These include institutions that define economic relations and are responsible for implementing state economic and social policy. These jointly constitute the "regulatory state." Though economic regulation is just one of many aspects of state operations, in modern capitalist societies it constitutes the core mechanism of a state interacting with the economy and conducting socioeconomic policy. Looking at Russian and Kazakh state-building through the prism of the regulatory state, this book attempts to understand how autocratic regimes balance between state

Thieves, Opportunists, and Autocrats: Building Regulatory States in Russia and Kazakhstan. Dinissa Duvanova, Oxford University Press. © Oxford University Press 2023. DOI: 10.1093/oso/9780197697771.003.0001

predation, corruption, and preferentialism on the one hand, and genuine improvements in state capacity and regulatory climate on the other.[1]

Building effective institutions of state economic regulation has been a political priority for Russia and Kazakhstan since the collapse of the Soviet command- and- control system. This priority still continues to affect the politics and economies of these countries. In December 2012, eight months after being elected for his third term in office, Putin discussed his political agenda with his most trusted electoral campaign associates. One of the 550 federal and provincial officials in attendance asked about a series of high-level corruption investigations initiated after the commencement of Putin's third presidential term. Putin's response made the day's headlines:

> This is by no means [just] a campaign. We must consistently fight to suppress and eradicate corruption.... In general, in a transitional economy, when all the requirements for market participants, for participants in social activities have not been formulated, this is not an easy task, but on the whole it can be solved. We need to fight corruption not only in the highest echelons of power..., we need to remember that people are pestered on the streets of cities and villages, when civil servants extort money. (Kremlin.ru)

The following year a number of privileged officials attending the December 2012 meeting were among those profiting from US$30 billion allocated by the state and state-owned companies for the 2014 Winter Olympics in Sochi.[2] Sochi holds the record for the most expensive Winter Olympics, with the final cost of its major infrastructure double or triple that of comparable international projects. Clearly, Putin's crusade against corruption did not extend to his cronies, but how successful was it at eradicating low-level graft and extortion?[3]

---

[1] Examples of Russia's 2019 "regulatory guillotine" that eliminated 3,003 mandatory business regulations (Analiticheskii tsentr pri pravitel'stve RF, 2019; Ministerstvo Ekonomicheskogo Razvitiia RF, 2021) and accelerated e-governance reforms of the late 2010s in Kazakhstan, discussed in Chapters 2 and 3, clearly indicate that autocratic regimes are able to govern well.

[2] This figure comes from the early investigation by Boris Nemtsov and Leonid Martynyuk (De Carbonnel, 2013). Later estimates by Navalny's Anti-Corruption Foundation give similar estimates.

[3] Over Putin's third term, Russia's corruption perception index (CPI) showed a modest improvement from 24 to 29 points, with 0 being highly corrupt and 100 being clean. Similarly, Russia continued to improve its international rankings in the ease of doing business and economic competitiveness. Still, in 2016 nearly 30 percent of public service users had paid a bribe in the previous 12 months, and in 2021 the country was ranked 136th in the world on government probity. Improvements in state governance remain nominal, with most Russians considering corruption an endemic and irremediable feature of public life.

Back in the early 2000s, Russia introduced a series of regulatory reforms aimed at addressing the notoriously high number of business regulations and stimulating small business development. It was expected that the move would reduce the regulatory burden and improve the business environment, but results were disappointing (Chazan, 2002). Despite an internationally acclaimed effort at reducing the number of regulatory procedures, the subjective assessments of the business climate by Russian enterprise managers hardly improved. According to a 2005 study conducted by the Center for Economic and Financial Research of the New Economic School in Moscow, following a series of deregulation initiatives, local authorities violated many guidelines spelled out in the laws and continued to impose regulatory hurdles.[4] While international development agencies recorded improvements in annual indicators of Russia's regulatory climate (World Bank, 2020a; Shwab and Zahidi, 2020), enterprise-level data and subnational analyses showed considerable inertia and continuing hurdles for business (Pyle, 2011; Karas et al., 2015; Yakovlev, 2006; Yakovlev and Zhuravskaya, 2013; World Bank, 2020b).

Despite deregulatory and civil service reforms, corruption and business hurdles persisted and became entrenched even deeper in society. Russian contemporary arts and literature have reflected on the perils of unconstrained power of state officials. The 2014 Oscar-nominated Andrey Zvyagintsev movie *Leviathan*, for instance, portrays how the power of regulatory enforcement in the hands of provincial officials could be used to acquire private assets and undermine the rule of law. The movie presents a gruesome account of state-enabled corruption, criminal extortion, and law-bending abuse at the hands of Russian public officials acting in tandem to enrich themselves and defend the powers granted them by their office. The film's title is a direct reference to Thomas Hobbes' *Leviathan*, a seventeenth-century treaty on the social contract with an all-powerful sovereign, the epitome of the emerging modern state. In the Russian film, the lives of ordinary people are crushed in the name of the state by state agents pursuing their personal interests. On the original cover of *Leviathan*, created by Abraham Bosse, hundreds of faces comprise the body of the Leviathan. The corrupt Russian state similarly has multitudes of agents who, in pursuit of

---

[4] The report states "registration frequently takes longer than the prescribed five days, firms are required to obtain [an] excessive number of permissive documents, and inspections are administered more frequently than is allowed and with violations of the law." In addition, about one-third of licenses were given "for types of activities that are formally not subject to licensing" (Shchetinin et al., 2005).

their personal interests, add to the state's corrupt power. This book is an attempt to describe the logic that holds these agents together.

Corruption, predation, and clientelism have become regarded as the core mechanisms of Russia's political rule and economic order (Hale, 2014; Dawisha, 2014; Aslund, 2019), and the notion of the dysfunctional state continues to dominate the way we think about post-communist political setbacks.[5] But herein lies a paradox: Why do the supposedly dysfunctional and failing institutions of the state persist and even strengthen the power of authoritarian rulers? In her meticulously well- documented account of the political career of Vladimir Putin and his inner circle of high-level officials, *Putin's Kleptocracy: Who Owns Russia?*, Karen Dawisha captured the massive extent of Russia's corruption, which includes standard extortion schemes by the major law enforcement and security agencies, routine buying and selling of legislative seats and government positions, and high-ranking state officials' connections to and patronage over organized crime.[6] Add to these direct political interference with the courts and law enforcement and disappearances, international abductions, and assassinations of businessmen and opposition figures, and we get the full picture of the operation of the Russian and Kazakh states.[7] It is hard to believe that these same states also were able to reduce the widespread gang violence rampant in the 1990s, modernize their military, considerably improve public service delivery, digitalize state agencies' workflows, and introduce strict professional criteria for entry and advancement in their lean and rationally regulated public administration. Neo-patrimonialism, predatory cabals, and patronal networks cannot explain the improved efficiency of autocratic states. By approaching this corruption/capacity paradox from the perspective of the regulatory state, this book attempts to understand how the Russian and Kazakh states have grown strong and resilient despite systemic corruption and debilitating cronyism.

---

[5] The announcement for the 2022 Association for Studies of Nationalities, virtual seminar on contested identities and state-making in the post-Soviet space reads "the state-making processes underway in the former [Soviet] republics are challenged by weak institutions, corruption, and complex relations with the Russian Federation." Accounts of post-communist state weakness tell us that politicians might not have full control over corrupt and predatory bureaucrats.

[6] Dawisha's research tapped into the Stasi archives, revelations of outcasted Russian elites, and Russian and Western investigative reports to bring to light Putin's hidden profile as one of the world's richest individuals. The book documents ways in which Putin and his St. Petersburg's associates enriched themselves by asset stripping, money laundering, illegal privatization and re-nationalization, and collaboration with criminal networks.

[7] For the case of Kazakhstan, see Sharipova (2018), Shkel (2019), and specifically Tutumlu and Rustemov (2019).

Why Russia and Kazakhstan?

Russia's recent experiences with regulatory reforms and autocratic consolidation make it an obvious case to investigate state- building, economic regulations, and authoritarian survival. The country's size, military might, and self-proclaimed special place in history contribute to the misconception of Russia's unique political path and institutional development. I counter this notion with a parallel presentation of another and very similar case of a neopatrimonial, personalistic, kleptocratic, and predatory regime supported by patron-client networks—Kazakhstan. I show that Russia shares with Kazakhstan not only the Soviet legacies, experiences of market reforms, predicaments of the resource curse,[8] and autocratic rule, but also many aspects of regulatory state development. Yet Russian federal structure provides an illustrative contrast to the centrally allocated administrative resources in Kazakhstan. This allows me to explicitly address the role of administrative resources, which despite increasing centralization still vary more profoundly across federal Russia as one of the building blocks of effective regulatory states. Because of these cases' stark similarity, however, it would be imprudent to draw any inferences from their comparative analysis, and I do not attempt that. Instead, I show that my proposed argument about the central role of regulatory state institutions in economic performance and regime survival is not idiosyncratic to Russia.

Following the collapse of the USSR, it seemed the countries' reform trajectories diverged. Kazakhstan reinforced its commitment to socially costly economic reforms and used early economic successes to legitimize autocratic consolidation (Kudaibergenova, 2015). Russia muddled through market reforms contested by competing elite and public demands (Shleifer and Treisman, 2000).[9] By the mid 2000s, however, it was clear that Russia had missed the window of opportunity for building democracy, but continued on the path of liberal capitalism (Aslund, 2007). Kazakhstan and Russia grew

---

[8] In the early 2000s, Weinthal and Luong (2001) argued that privatization in the natural resource sector had promised both countries an escape from the resource curse. It appeared that domestic ownership over natural resources in Russia had promoted the development of a more stable taxation regime, while foreign ownership in Kazakhstan contributed to the state's myopic oversight of tax reforms. Yet later developments had reversed these trends. Both states increased their direct and indirect ownership in the mineral sector, and the fusion of economic and political elites made private ownership irrelevant.

[9] Following Way (2015), I consider the 1990s' government in Russia as an unconsolidated electoral authoritarian regime that, due to the weakness of the party and state organization, had experienced "pluralism by default."

increasingly similar in their authoritarian politics and liberal economies. Both countries developed personalistic dictatorships (Frye, 2021) that tolerate personal freedoms but stifle free media, conduct elections but repudiate political opposition, and proclaim the rule of law but subvert constitutions. Both countries promoted integration into world markets and finance, allowing capital to flow in and out of their resource-rich economies. They also embraced deregulation of private enterprise and adhered to conservative fiscal and monetary policies. Following the energy price boom of 2000–2008, both countries accumulated large currency reserves, which were used to create state holdings and acquire private companies. The size of the state sector grew rapidly, but unlike in the Soviet times it was now managed—at least in principle—by the rules of the market.

Although corruption and fusion of political and economic powers goes back to the 1990s (Hellman et al., 2000; Holmes, 2006; Isaacs, 2014), the bulging state sector further compounded the sociopolitical costs of corruption and rent-seeking. The private capital flight of the 1990s turned into asset stripping of state-managed national wealth. Rapid social differentiation following the economic transition was a source of major grievances. Yet deepening economic inequality of the post-oil boom years caused even more resentment precisely because it was driven by the super-profits in the state-controlled sector. The billions of dollars made by oligarchs in the rigged mid-1990s privatization and the astronomical salaries and personal assets of managers of state companies made people question the legitimacy of private wealth (Frye, 2006) and disparage the kleptocratic regime.

This transformation naturally attracted keen scholarly interest. Because of its size and prominence in world politics, but also because of the shattered hopes for democratic development, Russia received the lion's share of attention. Driven by the desire to understand sources of Putin's political success and the state's increasing economic footprint that followed the 2008 financial crisis, political scientists delved into the nature of political rule in Russia. They proposed various frameworks to understand Russian politics and economy. Some suggested that Russia simply became yet another personalistic autocracy (Frye, 2021) or neo-patrimonial state (Robinson, 2011), similar to neighboring Kazakhstan and many other autocratic regimes around the world. Others concentrated on unique features of the Russian state and economy being ruled by "patronal" politics (Hale, 2014), a criminal kleptocratic cabal (Dawisha, 2014), or crony (Aslund, 2019) or "piranha" capitalism (Markus, 2016). In the time of the resurgence and entrenchment of authoritarianism around the world, research on Russian and post-Soviet politics made major contributions to advancing our understanding of authoritarianism. It showed, for instance, that authoritarian elections (Myagkov et al., 2009; Higashijima, 2022), media manipulation (Sharafutdinova, 2021), and party building (Reuter, 2017) had been used by post-Soviet rulers as effective mechanisms of authoritarian survival.

The earlier works on post-communist transitions had cast their theories in terms of institutional failures and subversions (Bunce, 1999; Treisman, 2001; Hellman, 1998). At the end of the 1990s, a review article by Cynthia Roberts and Thomas Sherlock concluded that state capacity lies at the root of Russia's "derailed" political-economic transition and called for "bringing the state back in" (Roberts and Sherlock, 1999). The subsequent scholarship, however, turned away from the state and towards the study of political regimes.[10] With the consolidation of authoritarianism and rising statism, issues of institution-building and political agency of societal actors[11] were relegated to the background. At the same time, scholarship made major advancement in the analysis of informal institutional arrangements that undermine the logic and function of formal institutions of the market economy, state administration, and political contestation (Ledeneva, 2013; Engvall, 2016; Taylor, 2018; Sharipova, 2018). These studies show that nepotism, clan politics, "blat" (informal networks), and bribery often take precedence over formal institutional means of resolving conflicts and coordinating exchange of resources. Advancement in understanding informal institutions came with decreasing attention to the development of formal state institutions. This volume remedies these oversights. It adds state regulatory institutions and formal rules governing the behavior of public servants to the list of authoritarian survival mechanisms. I demonstrate that autocratic regimes are able to build formal regulatory state institutions as effective tools for balancing domestic interests and ensuring their long-term survival.

The Russian and Kazakh cases are important examples of autocratic regimes' longevity and resilience to internal and external challenges. In the 2000s, scholars have linked Eurasian authoritarian entrenchment to improved economic conditions. Putin's popularity in the early 2000s was

---

[10] Some prominent exceptions are Taylor (2011), Way (2015), and Sharipova (2018). The concept of state-building also attracted the attention of international relations scholars (Busygina, 2017).

[11] In studying Kremlin politics, its "power vertical," and the erosion of regional political power, for example, the literature had to discount the importance of low-level bureaucrats who staff the regulatory state.

supported by an impressive economic growth that nearly doubled average incomes.[12] Much of this economic prosperity was due to the surge in global oil prices—an external factor of authoritarian resurgence. Kazakhstan's economic growth was also linked to the oil rents that allowed Nazarbayev's inner circle to co-opt or outmaneuver his political rivals and preempt social mobilization. Despite many hopes that the 2008 financial crisis and declining oil prices would weaken autocratic rule, the Russian and Kazakh regimes prevailed and even strengthened their grip on the economy and civil society. Both countries were able to avert long recessions and resume economic growth.

Further external threats did not make a dent on autocratic stability. The Russian annexation of Crimea in 2014, which was a blunt violation of international law and its own prior commitments, led to the imposition of international sanctions. Kazakhstan was affected, albeit indirectly, as a member of the Eurasian Economic Union. The 2022 invasion of Ukraine resulted in even more severe sanctions and economic isolation of the non-energy sectors of the Russian economy. As a member of the customs union with Russia, Kazakhstan suffered as well, struggling to maintain the value of its currency and coping with shortages and rising prices for essential goods.

The continuing resilience of Eurasian autocracies to economic hardship is quite paradoxical given the narrow social bases of support of autocratic rule. Domestic challenges to authoritarian regimes—the "vertical" challenges that come from society (Hanson, 2018)—also remain real and strong in Eurasian autocracies. A recent in-depth analysis of Russian labor relations by Crowley (2021) reveals that the fear of labor protests profoundly affects regimes' policy and institutional choices. Crowley argues that the need to cater to the interests of industrial workers has limited the economic reform choices for Putin, reinforcing the notion that autocratic survival continues to depend on popular support.

Mass protests and increasing use of oppression indicate that popular challenges to autocratic regimes are real. On January 2, 2022, in the west Kazakhstan city of Zhanaozen, protests broke out after a two-fold increase in the price of fuel produced by the state-controlled industry caused simmering social grievances to boil over (Kumenov and Lillis, 2022). The preceding month was marked by social mobilization against the so-called "automotive utilization collection"—a pseudo-tax on imported cars paid to Operator

---

[12] Treisman (2011) shows that economic performance has been a strong predictor of Putin's popularity.

ROP, a private company owned by Aliya Nazarbateva, the daughter of "the leader of the nation."[13] The Zhanaozen protests quickly spread to 14 major cities throughout the country. Soon, peaceful protests turned into violent clashes with the police. In the country's largest city of Almaty, law enforcement officers used stun grenades and tear gas but were overrun by tens of thousands of violent protesters, surrendering the city to looters and criminals.

Protesters shouted "Shal ket" ("Old man, out"), toppled statues of Nazarbayev, burned cars and government buildings, and looted banks and shopping centers (RFE/RL's Kazakh Service, 2022). In the western city of Atyrau, police fired upon and killed demonstrators. President Tokayev stated Kazakhstan was attacked by "international terrorist gangs" and called upon the Organization for Collective Security Treaty for security assistance. On January 7, Tokayev issued a "shoot to kill" order against protesters, and the insurrection was crushed with the help of "peacekeeping forces."[14] Later Tokayev declared the protests were part of the security forces' coup attempt, pledged to punish the terrorists and their accomplices, and announced reforms to scale back "oligopolistic tendencies." Criticizing the situation that gave rise to the popular uprising, Tokayev accurately summarized the workings of the plutocratic system he governed:

> The current system is focused mainly on serving large corporations on the principle: "To my friends, everything; to my enemies, the law." This system further strengthens the oligopoly in the economy. Large enterprises enjoy special privileges by suppressing competition and hindering reform. For example, the Development Bank of Kazakhstan has become a de facto personal bank for a select circle of individuals representing financial, industrial, and construction groups. We know everyone by name. Using access to high offices, they receive privileged conditions for the implementation of their projects. State resources, which could be used for the development of small and medium-sized businesses, are diverted to these projects (Tokayev, 2022).

---

[13] ROP stands for the rasshirennye obiazatel'stva proizvoditelei (enlarged producer responsibility), the 2016 government program for promoting local producers and surpassing environmentally damaging imports (Kapital.kz, 2022).

[14] The specifics of the deployment of "peacekeepers" and whether they were responsible for "clean outs" (zachistki) of the "terrorist" gangs remain undisclosed. There were hundreds of arrests and dozens of deaths after the peacekeepers arrived, and it remains unclear who was responsible for these.

In the subsequent weeks, Tokayev authorized the reorganization of the Samruk Kazyna sovereign wealth fund, the central institution of the quasi-governmental sector that accounted for about 60 percent of the national economy and that became synonymous with the Nazarbayev family's economic dominance (Akhmetkali, 2022). Tokayev also removed large-business owners from government positions and nationalized the controversial Operator ROP. Meanwhile, mass arrests did not spare even the seriously injured hospitalized protesters, and corpses of those killed in the clashes with security forces were stolen by unknown armed individuals from the morgues. A strikingly similar mixture of repression, cover-up, and appeasement was used by Tokayev's predecessor, Nazarbayev, in the aftermath of the 2011 oil worker strikes in Zhanaozen. Back then the protests were met by brutal police violence and the torture and imprisonment of activists and union leaders as well as cash payoffs, resettlement assistance, and reshuffling of government officials.[15]

Dawisha (2014) cited the principle mentioned by Tokayev—"To my friends, everything; to my enemies, the law"—to describe the system built by Vladimir Putin. The phrase is attributed to the Peruvian autocratic president Oskar Benavides and captures well the logic of bending the formal rules to accommodate one's cronies. The similarity between Kazakhstan and Russia does not stop there but also extends to the resilience of these crooked regimes against popular protests.[16] Russia's response to the anti-regime protests in 2011 and 2021 also used a mixture of police brutality, imprisonment of activists, and policy concessions to suppress and appease the disgruntled society. In 2022, the Russian autocracy confronted the public opposition to the war and grievances against sanctions-induced hardship with a combination of repression and appeasement. Anti-war demonstrations were met with unprecedented police brutality, intimidation of opposition, and criminalization of political dissent. Yet among the first governmental policies to address the effects of newly imposed sanctions were a package of measures for lifting regulatory oversight and tax burden on the small and medium enterprise (SME) sector. In March 2022, SMEs were granted interest payment deferrals, automatic business license extensions,

---

[15] On the 2011 Zhanaozen events, see *Nastoiashchee Vremia* (2019); Toyken (2021).

[16] Perhaps one important difference that sets these dictatorial regimes apart, though, is that in Kazakhstan, income streams of strategic assets predominately came under the control of Nazarbayev's family circle, while in Russia that circle comprises of the loyalists and strongmen from Putin's St. Petersburg days.

and a moratorium on all planned inspections (Government Decrees #337, #353, and #336). Between March 1 and September 1, 2022, Russian tax authorities also suspended regulatory compliance enforcement practices, such as freezing bank accounts, inspections of foreign currency transactions, and insolvency liquidations. Further SME support measures included freezing the property tax rates, simplifying commercial transport licensing, and suspending previously planned changes in product labeling. How does one reconcile these concessions to the small business sector with the notion that the regime cares only about the interests of crony elites?

If the Eurasian dictatorships are held together by informal patronage or cabals of security apparatus (*siloviki*) and criminals, one has to explain how spirals of predation, lawlessness, and perversion of legitimate state functions can coexist with growing state effectiveness, resilience, and continuing economic growth. How, despite declining natural rents and staggering inequalities, do the states continue to provide public benefits sufficient to maintain economic development and at least minimally satisfy public demands? To make better sense of these pressing questions, I turn to the analysis of institutional mechanisms through which states implement their economic policy. I focus my analysis on state agencies' powers over policy implementation and the political mechanisms to control it.

The Regulatory State in Autocratic Regimes:
Definitions and the Argument

Regulatory post-communist states emerged through a series of reforms that can be defined broadly and include economic policy, institutions, principles, and objectives, or, more narrowly, as the reforms of the mechanisms of state governance. The Organisation for Economic Co-operation and Development (OECD) defines regulatory reforms as including policies of price and trade liberalization, privatization, reforms of public administration, creation of new regulatory institutions, and market-oriented forms of regulation (OECD, 2005). Such a definition blends the concept of the regulatory state with the principles and objectives of a liberal market economy. Not all "transitional" economies, however, transitioned towards liberal economic ideals. In many post-Soviet economies, liberalization was uneven and at times reversed, but institutional mechanisms of state regulation continued to strengthen. To make the concept of the regulatory state useful for analyzing formal institutions of governance in the context of post-Soviet economies, I analytically separate government economic policy objectives (property rights allocation, redistribution, labor relations, trade, tax, and industrial policies) from the institutional mechanisms of state economic governance used to further these objectives. While the former may change with changing ideological preference or strategic considerations of political leadership, the latter often persist over time, are slow to change, and, if well designed, can apply themselves towards different policy objectives.[17]

I define the regulatory state as a mechanism of state governance of the economy and adjacent spheres (such as communal, personal, education, culture, and leisure domains), relying on state-recognized definitions of rights and obligations of individual, corporate, communal, and government actors monitoring and enforcing compliance with the state-defined rules of economic engagement. This definition allows me to concentrate on the state economic functions and power that are essential to understanding determinants of aggregate growth and individual wellbeing.[18] Defining the regulatory state in terms of the mechanisms of state intervention (legal frameworks, rational bureaucracy, courts, and law enforcement) rather than state functions or objectives of state policy has one crucial advantage: it provides for a clear analytical separation between institutional forms as they manifest themselves in interactions with state and non-state actors and stays away from ascribing specific logics or functions. This institutional, as opposed to functional, definition of the regulatory state, on the one hand, makes it possible to study how mechanisms of governance can be applied to different policy tasks. On the other hand, it recognizes that multiple institutional arrangements might lead to similar outcomes. Tax policy, for example, may serve multiple state functions, such as revenue generation, provision of public goods (including security), and resource mobilization against internal and external threats. Despite its multi-functionality, it is likely to be designed and implemented by the same set of state institutions and agencies. Defining the regulatory state through regulatory instruments aids in theorizing about institutional choices of state-builders.

---

[17] Eisner (2000) includes both policy and institutions in his definition of economic regulations, while Lehmbruch (1992) defines regulatory regimes as institutions and ideas of government policy towards industry.

[18] It should be recognized, however, that mechanisms and objectives of state economic policy spill into some non-economic spheres, such as family or non-profit organization domains, but may not spill over into other domains (e.g., military or counter-intelligence).

Regulations may take many institutional (statutory law, directives of the executive agencies, regulatory standards imposed by compulsory or voluntary professional or industry organizations) and organizational forms (administrative institutions, courts, the police, self-regulating organizations). All these affect economic outcomes by defining the formal "rules of engagement" and shaping the incentive structures of the relevant economic actors. Regulations on product safety, market entry, professional activities, business transactions, customer and worker protections, tax compliance, international trade, and many other areas affect the costs and benefits of alternative economic decisions and compliance strategies. They create obstacles and opportunities that cumulatively constitute the business environment and shape the nature of business-state relations.[19]

Empirical research finds a positive effect of light regulation on productivity, investment, employment, and skill levels (Loayza et al., 2009; Alesina et al., 2005; Cincera and Galgau, 2005; Bassanini and Brunello, 2007). Heavy-handed regulations stifle innovation (Cincera and Galgau, 2005) and increase poverty (Djankov et al., 2018). Other studies find that the positive effects of a lighter regulatory burden are not universal, but specific to certain economic sectors, development strategies, or structural conditions (Nicoletti and Scarpetta, 2003; Bosio et al., 2020). The diverging assessments of the net effect of state intervention often operate under the assumption that policies are carried out the way politicians formulate them

---

[19] Traditionally, government regulations are treated as costs on businesses that may stifle entrepreneurial innovation (Stigler, 1971; Peltzman, 1976). This approach associates lower taxes and fewer regulations with a business-friendly environment (i.e., stronger investment incentives), concluding that the state should withdraw from the economy for optimal economic outcomes (Noll, 1989; Li, 2006). Students of special-interest politics tell us that regulations often act as redistributive and rent-generating arrangements. A regulation often serves a set of particularistic interests at the public's expense, allocating resources away from efficient producers and hurting economic growth (Keeler, 1984; Weingast, 1981; Noll and Owen, 1983). Studies of rent-seeking link state regulatory intervention to preferentialism and corruption (Nye, 1969; Krueger, 1974; De Soto, 1990; Mauro, 1995; Acemoglu and Verdier, 2000; Djankov et al., 2002) and highlight the growth-inhibiting effects of large state bureaucracies (Ting, 2003), regulatory intervention (Kydland and Prescott, 1977), and state capture (Hellman, 1998). Moreover, according to Leff (1964), Huntington (1968), and Meon and Weill (2010), inefficient and burdensome state regulations necessitate corruption as an informal mechanism for improving economic efficiency. Unlike the neoliberal tradition's critical stance on state regulatory activities, transaction cost economics stress the benefits of well-designed regulatory institutions. This tradition places the state regulatory function at the heart of markets and development. North (1990), Scott (1998), and Bates (2010) posit that political institutions are inextricable from economic development, technological progress, and growth in productivity and efficiency. Evolution and development of state regulatory function is an intrinsic part of the economic system and the necessary foundation of markets. Scholars have explored ways in which well-designed regulatory regimes help attract investment and defy the predictions of the "race to the bottom" argument, which posits the global advantages of light regulatory burdens (Vogel and Kagan, 2004; Easson, 2004; Jensen et al., 2006).

and largely ignore discrepancies between their design and actual regulatory practices.[20] I challenge this assumption and scrutinize the independent effect the institutions of policy implementation have on economic outcomes.[21] State regulatory agents often possess the power to interpret regulatory policy freely. This power can be abused for personal enrichment and derailment of state policy. When bureaucrats are constrained to apply rules and regulations in a consistent and predictable manner, official regulatory policies directly translate into the regulatory climate experienced by economic actors. In contrast, when civil servants are able to exercise control over the application of rules and regulations, the actual regulatory policies are easily subverted. This argument is intuitive and finds support in other studies (Beazer, 2012; Bosio et al., 2020), but I also find it to be the key to understanding the institutional choices of state-builders.

Economic performance positively responds to well-defined and procedurally consistent regulatory regimes, making them the cornerstone for ensuring sustainable growth, economic power of the state, and wellbeing of the citizens. When institutional constraints on bureaucrats are lax and agency-level regulations are vague or silent on what and how state agencies are required to regulate, discretionary policy application leads to suboptimal economic outcomes, threatening popular support for the government. Democratic competition pressures politicians to formulate sound regulatory policy and create effective, publicly accountable agencies.

In the absence of political accountability, however, politicians may relinquish their power to discipline bureaucrats as a reward for their loyalty or to enable resource looting by regime cronies. In doing so they may risk damaging the overall health of the economy and provoke popular protests. Politicians' survival in office is predicated on the effective balancing of elite rent-seeking and public-benefiting economic growth—a task autocracies are

---

[20] For more on how empirical research has ignored the gap between official regulatory policy and the way it is implemented in practice, see Dellepiane-Avellaneda (2010).

[21] My insights come from the studies exploring issues of institutional performance as the central problems of public policy and economic development (Acemoglu and Verdier, 2000; Brown et al., 2009; Goldsmith, 1999; Frye, 2004). While a number of empirical studies find that inconsistent and poorly enforced economic policies undermine property rights, increase unpredictability, and generally destabilize the business climate (Frye and Shleifer, 1997; Tanzi and Davoodi, 2000; Djankov et al., 2002; Fisman and Svensson, 2007), other research stresses the benefits of bureaucratic autonomy and capacity to provide public goods (Brown et al., 2009; Scholz and Wang, 2006; Chaney and Saltzstein, 1998; Evans, 1995; Wade, 1990). Although different in their assessment of the role of the state bureaucracy, these studies clearly demonstrate that the mechanisms of policy implementation are not only important, but also independent from the content of economic regulations.

not well equipped to address. By suppressing civil society, the independent press, and freedom of expression, they disable the crucial "fire alarm" types of control over policy application. I contend that because authoritarian politics are inherently incompatible with the good governance mechanisms that rely on transparency and accountability, other mechanisms of controlling policy enforcement become paramount in autocratic regimes.[22] My exploration of how consideration of autocratic regime survival impacts the relationship between politicians, civil servants, and the private sector helps situate the distinctive features of Eurasian autocracies into the larger theory of institutional political economy.

My analysis zeroes in on the use of ex ante control mechanisms—formal regulatory legislation and administrative procedures that define the mechanisms of regulatory implementation. In autocratic states relying on cronyism and patronage for co-opting elites, formal mechanisms can be defined strategically to constrain or enable corruption, favoritism, and predation. I argue that more specific regulations, which decrease the extent of bureaucratic power to apply regulations selectively and positively impact economic performance, are used strategically by autocratic rulers to build more agile and resilient, but also repressive, unfair, and unequal, states. In this book I use the term "bureaucratic discretionary power" to label formal institutional arrangements permitting selective policy application by government agencies. I stress that "discretion" in this context refers to the formal institutional arrangements.

Discretionary power and corruption are not the same. The exercise of discretion and good judgment is often a prerequisite of public office. When acting in the interest of the public, discretionary policy application would mean flexibility in implementing principles of justice, equity, and public good. If, however, other motives, such as personal enrichment, professional

---

[22] This is not to deny the authoritarian regimes' use of government-organized participatory mechanisms of governance. The Soviet practices of managed and mandated participation in trade unions and professional, youth, and women's associations and tolerance of some types of public criticism highlight the regime-maintaining function of participatory authoritarian institutions. The modern types of authoritarian participation are less blunt but just as cunning. Owen (2020), for example, shows that "discourses of active citizenship and the legislative development of new government-organized participatory mechanisms in post-Soviet Russia and post-reform China" enhance authoritarian stability (p. 415). Government-controlled participatory institutions may minimize social discontent, reduce the risk of unmanageable civic activism, and demonstrate adherence to globally promoted good governance practices, but they hardly create real mechanisms of public oversight.

advancement, favoritism to friends and family, or promoting an agency's interests, are allowed to affect an official's judg-ment, the power to exercise discretion might lead to the neglect of public good and abusive policy application. The power to exercise discretion in policy application does not have to lead to corruption, but such power makes it easier to abuse public office for personal gains and helps hide such abuses from public scrutiny.[23]

Bureaucratic discretion is a powerful tool in the hands of autocrats. It acts both as a carrot and a stick. On the one hand it allows bureaucrats to derive personal benefits from their office and acts as a patronage mechanism. At the same time, by enabling corruption it helps establish a record of transgressions that can be used to blackmail officials into subordination to and complacency with the higher-ups. Zvyagintsev's central antagonist in "Leviathan"—a corrupt, tyrannical, and outright criminal mayor—is the embodiment of this logic. When a Moscow-based lawyer's investigation uncovered "*kompromat*," or incriminating evidence about the mayor's corrupt and criminal past, a local car mechanic asked, "Why isn't he in prison if you've got all this documented?" It is because "someone up top needs him," the lawyer responds. *Kompromat* makes it easier to compel officials to bend the law and use their power to promote the higher-ups' interests. Being part of this corrupt system in no way makes one immune from prosecution, and, paradoxically, such implicit and explicit threats help perpetuate corruption rather than deter it. As one anonymous retired official from a Kazakh state security agency reflected, "I am forever on a fishing hook (*ia na kriuchke*). They have my signature on so many documents authorizing things that can easily be questioned. It doesn't matter if I took bribes or not—I signed [the documents]" (Interviewer #19, May 2018). The same official reported that even in retirement he remains dependent on the patronage of his government associates and would consider any opportunity to leave the country.

---

[23] One way to highlight the difference between corruption and bureaucratic discretion is through the contrast between formal and informal relations. Helmke and Levitsky define informal institutions as "socially shared rules, often unwritten, that are created, communicated, and enforced outside of officially sanctioned channels" (Helmke and Levitsky, 2004). By this account, corruption is an informal institution, but the state-sanctioned freedom to allocate government administrative resources in a way that might please some clients and displease others—bureaucratic discretionary power—is a formal institutional feature. It might lead to informal practices of corruption or nepotism, but it might not. Discretionary policy application power is also not the same as the authority to formulate formal regulatory policy. Freedom over policy choices should not be conflated with freedom over policy application; hence, discretion does not equal "delegation."

Thieves and Autocrats

The title of this book features thieves, opportunists, and autocrats. In my story of regulatory state-building in Russia and Kazakhstan, the role of thieves is played by the state bureaucracies. I assume that they, when given the license to do so, generate red tape to increase the ease with which they plunder resources from businesspeople and average folk alike. I theorize that in doing so, they seek to increase their ability to extract bribes, favors, and economic opportunities from those who manufacture goods, provide services, or buy and sell. The thieves appreciate plundering opportunities and support the authority structure that allows them to do so. Their plundering also robs the economy. It reduces the amount of economic opportunities, dampens the overall efficiency of the economy, and disincentivizes productive economic behavior.

Of course, not all bureaucrats will become corrupt when opportunities arise. The history of the post-Soviet states is punctuated by examples of people like Alexey Dymovski, a former police officer, and Olga Kudeshkina, a Moscow judge, who exposed corrupt wrongdoings in the law enforcement community (Whitmore, 2010; Chazan, 2004). Also noteworthy are Grigory Rodchenko, the head of an anti-doping laboratory who, after participating in a doping cover-up, also exposed the Sochi Olympics doping scheme at great risk to his personal safety (Ruiz and Schwirtz, 2016); ex-governor and deputy prime minister Boris Nemtsov, who was assassinated outside of the Kremlin following his critique of Putin and Russian kleptocracy (Smith-Spark, 2015); and the countless honest public servants and politicians who have defied the "sistema" of telephone justice, corruption, and impunity. Still, my treatment of the civil servants responsible for enforcing policies of the state is akin to the Schumpeterian treatment of elected politicians as being innately selfish, power-grabbing "rascals" (Schumpeter, 1942). The same way the Schumpeterian procedural theory of democracy links positive outcomes of democratic politics to periodic competitive elections threatening to "throw rascals out," my theory of formal institutions of the regulatory state links greater efficiency and orderliness of state regulatory function to the institutional constraints on bureaucratic freedom to interpret rules and regulations. This book shows that even when a society does not have functioning institutions of public transparency and accountability—a situation we find in many dictatorial regimes—formal regulatory constraints effectively discipline the thieves in bureaucratic chairs. These regulatory constraints, however, cannot limit the autocrats, who are in charge of formulating the "rules of the game."

Initially I intended to put "crooks" in place of "autocrats" in the book title to follow the provocative slogan invented by Alexei Navalny during the 2011 Duma elections to describe President Putin's political guard, the United Russia Party (Navalny, 2011). Similar to Putin's "cabal" (Dawisha, 2014), President Nazarbayev, his family, and cronies also have been unequivocally linked to embezzlement, money laundering, and the use of state security services to intimidate and kill opponents and defectors (Cooley and Heathershaw, 2017). Focusing on the criminal and dishonest nature of Putin's or Nazarbayev's regimes, however, does not give justice to how effective they are in ruling their respective societies through the formal and informal hierarchical command order. Post-Soviet autocrats not only enable resource plundering by state officials, they also maintain the support of large segments of the population by disciplining the state officials' behavior and strategically punishing them when unchecked plunder wreaks havoc on the state's ability to satisfy popular demands. Calling these autocratic cliques "crooks" connotes the images of Huntingtonian political decay, or the erosion of a strong central state authority (Huntington, 1968), or Olson's "roving bandits" who neglect the future economic fortunes of societies they plunder (Olson, 2000). In reality, autocratic regulatory states are much more cunning, forward-looking, and robust, which means they might experience great longevity.

If the Russian or Kazakh states were ruled by gangs of thieves and crooks, they perhaps would be only a few steps away from economic decline, revolt, or total collapse. My book demonstrates that though the people who rule Russia and Kazakhstan might in fact be crooks, they are extremely well organized and strategic. They zealously guard their power and plan for future state plunder by improving the efficiency with which the public servants carry out their orders. With the same mechanisms of regulatory state-building, they amass obedient clienteles of state officials. These regimes have discovered the new combination in the toolbox of governance that allows them to effectively balance political loyalty and economic efficiency. In times of resource windfalls, the formal institutions of the regulatory state they have built over the past three decades have put looted and embezzled resources in the pockets of top-, medium-, and street-level officials. Corrupt methods to achieve this also conveniently plant "skeletons" in the officials' closets. When resource rents dry out, the mechanisms of formal rulemaking close up corruption opportunities by cutting back on the bureaucrats' freedoms to interpret formal regulations in favor of a ruler's private sector cronies. The formal institutional foundations of the state regulatory system I explore in this book allowed Russia and Kazakhstan to fine-tune the amount of resource plundering by state officials to balance the political loyalties of corrupt bureaucrats and economic elites on the one hand and economic growth and popular support on the other. These regulatory institutional innovations have produced much more agile autocracies than domestic democratic forces and the international community might have hoped for.

The Opportunists

The recipients of economic regulations are business owners, enterprise managers, self-employed professionals, employees, and consumers whose contracts, profits, incomes, and choices are being affected by the regulatory state's intervention. These are the "opportunists" from the book's title who respond to the incentives created not only by regulatory policies, but also by the laxity or rigidity of regulatory enforcement. They are the targets of extortion and official intimidation, but are also tax evaders, bribers, and interest peddlers eager to use opportunities presented by the state capture to get ahead of their business rivals. The way private economic actors respond to state regulatory intervention is central for understanding regulatory states. Entrepreneurs make critical choices of whether to comply with the regulator's requests or evade regulations trough bribery, collusion, or lobbying for changes in regulatory policy.[24] The opportunistic firm managers, company owners, accountants, lawyers, and taxpayers, in seeking ways to minimize the cost of compliance, enable the bureaucrats' rent-seeking behavior. The most resourceful of these also collude with autocratic state-builders to control the distribution of rents.

My theory of the regulatory state conceptualizes opportunistic business-people as being independent from the state. This might be objectionable in light of growing size of state ownership in Russia and Kazakhstan. Although in the 1990s both countries underwent privatization of state property, the trend reversed roughly at the turn of the century. By some accounts, before

---

[24] My 2013 book, *Building Business in Post-Communist Russia, Eastern Europe, and Eurasia*, delves into individual and collective business responses to the state's regulatory pressure.

the COVID-19 pandemic the Russian state controlled between 35 and 70 percent of its economy and accounted for 50 percent of employment (Aslund and Commander, 2016; Di Bella et al., 2019). In Kazakhstan, 750 of the largest quasi-public entities controlled by the government through state holdings accounted for nearly 40 percent of the GDP (Aubakirova, 2020). Such a heavy state economic footprint was achieved through the growing governments' stakes in publicly traded ventures and joint-stock companies or through the state ownership of land, buildings, and infrastructural facilities.

There have been different mechanisms through which post-communist autocracies have increased a state's share of the economy. The Russian state's share of the economy grew through several routes. Rostek (the State Corporation for Assistance to Development, Production and Export of Advanced Technology Industrial Product) and Rosnano (Russian State Corporation of Nanotechnology), for example, were formed in 2007 by a transfer of state property—research and development facilities—to carry out the government's industrial development program. Another vehicle of Russian state expansion has been acquisitions of privately owned corporate assets, which often took the form of shamelessly blunt expropriations from disloyal oligarchs. The state oil corporation Rosneft, for instance, became the world's largest publicly traded oil company after purchasing assets of Yukos while it was dismantled following allegations of illegal privatization and after taking over Russia's third largest and privately owned oil producer TNK-BP (Tyumenskaya Neftyanaya Kompaniya, Tyumen Oil Company) (Soldatkin and Callus, 2013). Many other publicly traded corporations, including Gazprom and Transneft, had grown their state-controlled assets after the early 2000s through re-nationalization, state-forced mergers, and murky cross-ownership schemes. In addition to controlling the shares of publicly traded companies, the Russian state also owns and manages economic resources directly, such as with Rosavtodor and Russian Railroads.

The Kazakh state economic footprint has remained relatively even throughout the independence period largely due to the slower pace of privatization, but also because of the early consolidation of economic assets in the hands of Nazarbayev's family and close associates. Kazakhstan largely avoided the massive economic elite turnover and oligarchic purges associated with the rise to power of Russia's second president. Still, the share of the state-controlled sector increased following the creation of Samruk-Kazyna, which was formed in 2006 as the investment-holding corporation for five national companies: the electric grid operator (KEGOC), Kazmunaigaz, Kazakh Railways, Kaztelecom, and the Kazakh Postal Service. Later, other state and state-controlled companies were transferred to Samruk-Kazyna, which expanded the state's share of the economy through its investment in profitable champions of national business. Spechler et al. (2017, p. 5) have characterized Kazakh state capitalism as a dual economy with "a recognized and growing periphery of market-based businesses besides strategic sectors that support the regime." This strategic sector—primarily hydrocarbon and mineral extraction and national industry champions—has enjoyed virtual immunity from the regulatory agency's oversight and interference.

One important reason to treat business as an independent actor is that the state-majority-owned enterprises and public economic entities in both countries are not ruled by the command-and-control methods of the Soviet era. Unlike in the socialist past, the states control these companies not through top-down day-to-day commands, but indirectly by influencing management decisions through CEO appointments and state holding companies' interference (Spechler et al., 2017). The states also use their regulatory policy to affect firms' operations, such as market access, export/import licensing, or tax obligations (Dawisha, 2014). Granting an export monopoly to Gazprom in 2006, for example,[25] was a formal state policy that significantly disadvantaged Gazprom's competitors. Coincidentally, this policy had not been enforced against the oil exports of TNK-BP for nearly a year. TNK-BP's violation of the Gazprom monopoly, however, was later used to force the BP subsidiary to sell its stock to Gazprom (Kramer, 2007). This clearly shows how institutions of discretionary policy application allow regulatory agencies to apply even the rigged rules selectively to further favor state-owned companies.

Although the state control of economic resources is essential for the continuing enrichment of autocrats' cronies, the preservation of the liberal economic order, markets, and private enterprise is essential for converting state resources to private wealth flows within and outside national borders. As statism has emerged in response to the regime-survival challenge, the growing economic role of the state does not diminish the power of private elites. The latter continue to enjoy access to economic rents in a crony-capitalist arrangement that preserves private enterprise and the neoliberal economic order as vehicles of elites' enrichment. Up to this date, a number

---

[25] Federal Law #117-F3 "On Export of Natural Gas."

of private companies (more than 50 percent private ownership) continue to occupy the top positions in the *Forbes* or RBK ratings of top-earning companies: Lukoil, Surgutneftegaz, Novatec, Tatneft, Evraz, and Nokilsk Nikel are the largest oil and metallurgical sector corporations remaining in private hands. Other large private corporations are retailers: X5, Magnit, and Megapolis Group. Privately owned leading companies of the telecom sector are Neon (formerly Vimpelcom) and MTS (Rosbizneskonsalting, 2021; *Forbes.ru*, 2021). The second, third, and fifth largest corporations operating in Kazakhstan are the joint-stock ventures Tengizshevroil, North Caspian Operating Company, and Karachaganak Petroleum Operating Venture, which are private subsidiaries assisting state-controlled oil exports (Mashaev and Veliev, 2021). The list of top-ranked Kazakh domestically owned private companies include, among others, the copper mining companies Kazakhmys and Kaz Mineral PLC; regional oil producers Kazpii Neft, South Oil, and Burgylau; retailers Arena-S, Tekhnodom, and Magnum; and construction companies Zhol Zhondeushi, Bazis, and Stroirekonstruktsiia (*Forbes.kz*, 2017). The continuing accumulation of highly concentrated private wealth has been achieved not despite, but in many respects thanks to, the growing state economic power of which the authoritarian regulatory state had been a central formal institutional mechanism.

Data, Methods, and Anecdotes

My approach has been both qualitative and quantitative. One specific obstacle in studying the regulatory state is the fact that in reality, regulatory state function often diverges considerably from the policy intentions of state authorities who formulate it. Authorities may try to simplify tax compliance, but regulatory agencies will create new paperwork to establish eligibility. Politicians may want to delegate regulatory functions to industry associations, but ministries will create convoluted procedures for associational accreditations. I turn this obstacle into an opportunity and adopt an empirical strategy that explicitly separates formal regulatory norms and informal practices. Data on formal characteristics of the regulatory climate–instruments of regulatory policy and documents controlling operations of regulatory institutions—help me capture the formal element of the regulatory state. Business surveys, indices of corruption, and anecdotal accounts of informal regulatory implementation practices capture the informal element.

Quantitative and qualitative data for this book were collected over the span of a decade. I interviewed entrepreneurs and state officials from regional procurator offices, arbitrage courts, and executive agencies from Kemerovo, Altai, Krasnodar, Novosibirsk, Perm, Penza, Kaliningrad, Almaty, and Pavlodar regions; and business owners, managers, and corporate attorneys from Yurga, Novosibirsk, Sochi, Moscow, Almaty, Kaskelen, Taldykorgan, Aktau, Uskaman, and Nursultan. Some of my private sector respondents were active participants in business associations and state-sponsored committees, working groups, and public consultative institutions. My contacts in the private and public institutions enabled me to attend public events hosting Kazakh ex-prime ministers and high officials from the Ministry of Industry and Infrastructure Development, Ministry of Finance, Ministry of National Development, and the Civil Service Agency of Kazakhstan. In Russia, I interviewed former ministerial officials, deputies of the State Duma, attorneys, prosecutors, and court officials. My access to these interactions was possible because of personal contacts and introductions by previous respondents. Others happened through the private and public social media accounts of state officials, which, as I discovered, are becoming increasingly popular among ambitious state officials and business circles in both countries.

In total I conducted 21 in-person interviews in Russia and interacted in person or online with 38 businesspeople, public officials, and local experts from Kazakhstan. About 40 percent of my respondents at some point occupied positions in the national or regional governments or state agencies, including courts or state prosecutor offices. About one-third had experiences in both the private and public sectors. Russian and Kazakh newspapers, websites of national and regional businesses and employers associations, blogs and social media profiles of state agencies, and information resources for business and legal professionals provided me with information about changes to regulatory policies and institutions, as well as the business community's responses to such changes. The newsletters of business associations, web-based legal services, and specialized periodicals such as *Zakon.kz* and *Kommersant* helped me identify aspects of regulatory intervention that were most harmful to business. Film and literature helped me appreciate ways in which state institutions permeate ordinary lives. They also provided an understanding of how ordinary people think about the state, economy, and bureaucracy and how much they know about and internalize the rules imposed on them by the state.

Over the course of their regulatory reforms, Russia and Kazakhstan maintained well-structured archival records of the official documents that enabled the change. To investigate connections between state regulations on business, development of state institutions responsible for policy enforcement, and the economic outcomes emerging from policy implementation, I utilize data based on these records. The quantitative data for Russia come from the Legal Information System (LIS) portal "Legislation of Russia" available from pravo.gov.ru, which contains documents issued by Russian ministerial and federal agencies (orders, resolutions, letters, and manuals), regional and local regulations, and decisions of the Higher and Federal Arbitration Courts. In March 2021, the database included 242,513 federal-level and 2,985,929 regional-level regulatory documents. I also analyzed a commercial GARANT dataset assembled from the archives of the Federal Ministry of Justice and regional governments. I relied on GARANT-provided classifications to identify documents pertaining to different spheres of economic activity. For the Kazakh case, I used the data from the Republican Center for Legal Information (RCLI) under the Ministry of Justice of the Republic of Kazakhstan (http://rkao.kz/), an official state legal information service based in Astana. In February 2019, the RCLI dataset contained 112,951 documents relating to economic relations. I supplemented these data with the international indices of state institutional performance and national and subnational economic statistics.

The Roadmap

The book is organized as follows. Chapter 1 lays out the theoretical argument and starts by distinguishing between the content of state intervention and enforcement practices, which are often conflated. I quarrel with the notion that rolling back regulations leads to improvements in the business climate by inserting the issue of regulatory enforcement at the center of the argument. Since the implementation of economic policy largely depends on the incentives and resources available to the state bureaucracy, I examine the nature of institutional constraints bureaucrats face when implementing regulatory policy. The existing theories do not fully explicate the mechanisms of political control and delegation in non-democratic regimes.

I bring together theories of regulation and bureaucratic politics in a framework that deliberately excludes public accountability as a mechanism for disciplining the executive agencies. I develop a theoretical argument that integrates the literature's conflicting expectations about the economic effects of discretionary regulatory policy implementation, along with the costs of regulatory compliance, into economic agents' utility function.

I turn to the analysis of the Russian and Kazakh regulatory states in Chapters 2 and 3. I trace the history of state regulation of these countries' respective economies since the collapse of the Soviet Union. In both countries, the 1990s were a time of major economic transformation that required rapid development of new regulatory approaches to the emerging market economies. The first wave of market reforms has exposed a business-incapacitating regulatory vacuum: much of the legal framework that would guide production, business operations, and business-state relations was missing and needed to be developed by the resource-stripped state institutions still organized on the Soviet principles of command-and-control interactions with society. The rules inherited from Soviet times were rapidly becoming outdated and largely irrelevant for the new market realities. I document the development of regulatory frameworks that were propelled by the substantive reforms spanning all the different spheres of economic relations, from banking to licensing, from drilling and mining to urban zoning and street vendor regulations.

Chapters 2 and 3 show that in the 1990s, policy inconsistency and a regulatory vacuum had allowed regulatory agencies to increase their influence over policy implementation and have an independent effect on the regulatory climate. Comprehensive regulatory reforms undertaken in the 2000s created more-disciplined regulatory agencies, facilitating economic recovery. Still, improvements in policy implementation remained limited. The logic of autocratic regime survival demanded that state agencies have discretion to channel economic rents to cronies and loyal supporters and that the bureaucrats engage in incriminating conduct that curtails their political ambitions.

Although many aspects of the state regulatory environment are linked to national-level political and economic arrangements, local authorities are often empowered to enact and implement regulatory policy of their own, contributing to subnational variation in regulatory regimes. I make use of such variation across 85 Russian regions and 14 Kazakh provinces. Unlike many other institutional constraints on capricious bureaucrats, statutory controls are nearly universal tools available in many different regime types. In Chapter 3, I use Kazakh subnational data to investigate statutory mechanisms for constraining bureaucratic discretion. In a unitary Kazakhstan, provincial authorities design some important aspects of local regulations, such as tax collection, zoning and land use, business licensing, and environmental regulations. At the same time, the country's political and administrative structures effectively rule out two confounding factors that can potentially affect the quality of the regulatory environment—electoral accountability and regional variations in institutional quality. I find that the lack of statutory controls undermines the efficient implementation of state regulations and dampens the growth of the private sector. This conclusion is supported by the examination of bureaucracy's impact on self-financed investment and small enterprise growth—economic indicators selected to avoid biases associated with the state sector rents.

While the Kazakh case allows me to hold constant the institutional aspects of regulatory bureaucracies, in federal Russia, regional administrative institutions vary across many different dimensions. Chapter 4 extends my analysis to two such dimensions: bureaucratic rulemaking (regulatory bylaws) and bureaucratic resources. I assess the effects of these characteristics on investment and small business performance across 85 Russian regions. I find that bureaucratic rulemaking compensates for the lack of statutory constraints on policy implementation and hence can act as one of the mechanisms for enforcing a uniform and predictable regulatory environment. Moreover, the way in which internal bureaucratic constraints affect economic outcomes largely depends on the underlying capacity of state institutions to provide public services. Quantitative analysis demonstrates that the positive effects of formal procedural consistency cannot be fully realized when bureaucracies are too small to effectively implement regulatory policy. The most favorable conditions combine well-staffed bureaucracy with detailed internal regulation of policy application. In addition to the quantitative analysis, the empirical chapters present a series of small case studies of various regulatory procedures to illustrate differential levels of discretionary power accumulated by regulatory bureaucracies.

In Chapter 5 I scrutinize the empirical implications of the logic of the autocrat's dilemma in promoting public or elite interests. With discretionary policy application benefiting the elites and growth-promoting institutional constraints benefiting the public, the national authorities strive for a balance that would keep them in power. Tracing the temporal change in the development of discretion-limiting formal regulations, I find that the regime survival calculus changes in response to the availability of natural resource rents used by the rulers of Russia and Kazakhstan to strengthen popular support for their rule. I find the fluctuations in oil rents of both governments over time to be a good predictor for the introduction of formal regulations. Moreover, at the regional level in Russia, mass protests that signal rising popular grievances reinvigorate regional discretion-constraining rulemaking.

Chapter 6 takes the analysis beyond the Russian and Kazakh cases and evaluates the economic effects of discretionary institutional powers in a cross-national comparative framework. Empirically, much of the existing research on regulations relies on governance measures that make government regulatory policy and its implementation virtually indistinguishable. This results in overlooking the importance of issues of implementation in studies of development and creates a void in understanding the efficacy of regulatory regimes. I fill in this gap by disentangling the effects of regulatory policy from those of regulatory implementation empirically and show that these have separate, albeit interactive, effects on economic performance. Using cross-sectional data covering 102 autocratic and democratic countries, I find that institutions enabling bureaucratic discretion render the state regulatory involvement largely irrelevant. Under high levels of bureaucratic discretion, the extent of state economic intervention has no effect on economic outcomes. This analysis confirms that institutions of regulatory implementation are dependent and consequential components of state governance.

Chapter 7 uses the results of my empirical exploration of the rise and development of the post-Soviet regulatory state to reexamine the state regulatory function. I reassess the regulatory roles of bureaucrats and legislators and discuss ways in which these actors shape the nature of industrial relations, markets, and states. The central finding emerging from this book is that the regulatory function has been the key element of state-building and regime survival in Russia and Kazakhstan. Looking at the institutional sources and economic effects of bureaucratic discretion, one is better able to understand the power relationships that hold these states together through the intricate, still robust mechanisms of bureaucratic control, access to informal sources of income and economic rents, and enforcement of loyalty through carrots of corruption and sticks of legal sanctions against breaking the formal rules. Returning to the question of what constitutes an effective and favorable regulatory climate, the chapter argues that strong legal constraints on the power of state institutions are a poor substitute for transparency and public accountability because autocrats can enforce their own rules selectively. Moreover, the rule-bound society is not necessarily more just, fair, and legitimate since the rulemakers can rig the entire playing field in their favor.

1

Regulatory State-Building and Authoritarian Survival

On March 25, 2018, a fire broke out in the Winter Cherry shopping mall of the Siberian city of Kemerovo, killing 60 people, including 37 children (*BBC News*, 2018). Eyewitnesses reported the building quickly became engulfed in smoke, the upper entertainment area cut off from safe exits. Terrified victims, trapped behind locked doors, made phone calls to their loved ones to tell them they needed help. Impassable fire escapes and fire code violations in the building design made it impossible for the firefighters to rescue them. The entire country was shaken by the tragedy, which many believed could have been avoided. While the flames were still burning, reports of corruption surrounding the renovation of the decades-old building housing the Kemerovo Confectionery Plant, which became Winter Cherry, made their way into the press. This event, the second deadliest fire in Russia's recent history, instigated a series of protests; the resignation of Russia's longest serving governor, Aman Tuleev; and a criminal investigation into the causes of the tragedy. Prosecutors convicted 12 individuals for violating fire safety rules, criminal conspiracy, negligence, and bribery. The investigation exposed the owners and top managers of the shopping complex for bribing Kemerovo officials to issue building inspection and fire safety documents for the mall that did not meet official safety standards (Voronov, 2020; *BBC News*, 2021).

Lax enforcement of regulations led to a national tragedy in Kazakhstan as well. Twelve people lost their lives on board Bek Air Flight 2100 on December 27, 2019. The Fokker 100 took off from the Almaty airport and crash landed in a field adjacent to the runway, sliding across the field until it slammed into the concrete fence of a two-story brick house. The impact shattered the front part of the airplane, causing the death of one crew member and 11 passengers (Rourke and Roth, 2019). The post-crash investigation revealed an egregious land machination scheme that local authorities developed to take advantage of patchy land-use regulations. Overlapping

Thieves, Opportunists, and Autocrats: Building Regulatory States in Russia and Kazakhstan. Dinissa Duvanova, Oxford University Press. © Oxford University Press 2023. DOI: 10.1093/oso/9780197697771.003.0002

jurisdictions and considerable discretionary power of rural administrators allowed them to profit from commercial and residential development in the restricted-use area. "If it were not for this scam, there would not be houses, and the plane would have glided safely through the snow and landed on its belly. People would be saved" blogged Bakhytzhan Bazarbek, a Kazakh attorney and land reform activist whose recommendations to abolish the unaccountable local Land Commissions were subsequently incorporated in the 2022 Land Code. In 2021, five local officials and one real estate agent were found guilty of illegal land sales and received three- to four-year prison sentences (Alkhabayev, 2021).

These tragic stories highlight the central importance of the state regulatory function not only for the economy, but also for society at large. State regulations are important instruments of government policy; they are part of the institutional foundation of economic systems and are key elements of state governance. That is why they figure prominently in studies of legislative processes, economic development, and institutions.[26] Although originating in the formal domain of the political process, in reality regulatory state function often diverges considerably from the policy intentions of the state authorities who formulate it. The incidents described above are tragic examples of this. Regulated entities pursue economic and political goals of their own and react to the regulatory policy by either complying with, evading, or influencing regulations. Moreover, administrative institutions implementing regulatory policies may have their own economic and political goals. If allowed to act with impunity, they may neglect, alter, or subvert the official regulatory policy for personal benefits. To make regulations effective, makers of regulatory policy must account for the potential strategic behavior on the part of businesses and regulatory agencies.

In what follows, I propose a theoretical framework for the analysis of state regulatory regimes as the outcome of strategic choices on the part of politicians, firms, and bureaucrats. Through this framework, I identify conditions that are essential for fostering effective regulatory states, as well

---

[26] For a discussion of different approaches to the regulatory state, see Moran (2002). The literature often distinguishes three types of regulations: economic (price and entry), social (environment, social cohesion, health, occupational safety), and administrative (government information collection). These regulations have different purposes but in practice are closely interrelated. For instance, the government may restrict entry into the chemical sector to better enforce environmental regulations, or it may impose price controls on the telecommunications industry in pursuit of its goals of social cohesion. Unlike other works that explicitly distinguish among these types, this analysis applies to all regulatory hurdles, regardless of their purpose.

as those that characterize or are most likely to result in corrupt, predatory, or haphazard regulatory states. I start by conceptually separating regulatory policy from regulatory implementation. Regulatory regimes consist of state policies towards economic activity, along with the institutions implementing these policies and ensuring compliance. Both policies and institutions are shaped by strategic interaction between the rulers and the ruled. I theorize how the logics of political survival, profit-seeking, and rent-seeking affect the choice of regulatory policy and regulatory implementation mechanisms, which jointly drive the outcomes of state regulatory activities.

Much of what we know about regulations does not explicitly account for the fact that objectives, constraints, and opportunities faced by the states, businesses, and bureaucrats in autocratic settings are different from those in democracies. It is impossible to link the content of regulatory policy to a regime type: regulations may be used to advance a wide range of government objectives, including but not limited to promoting growth, keeping the public safe, preventing economic turmoil, redistributing incomes, channeling rents, and securing political support. Both democratic and authoritarian rulers may pursue these objectives. Different political regimes, however, are built on somewhat different configurations of state institutions that are used to enforce a government's policy. This chapter shows that the lack of democratic accountability profoundly affects the nature of a state's regulatory process by restricting the rulers' choices over the composition of regulatory enforcement.

Separating Regulatory Policy and Its Implementation

The theoretical argument I propose starts with a simple proposition that the *de facto* regulatory environment experienced by the firm is shaped not only by the state regulatory policy or the content of regulatory regimes, but also by the policy implementation practices that may or may not be spelled out in the official regulatory norms.

Post-communist countries that have witnessed a diminished ability of their political authorities to control "subversive" (Bunce, 1999) state regulatory institutions provide multiple examples to illustrate the extent of discrepancies between the official regulatory policy's intent and how it is implemented in practice. For example, in the early 1990s, high rates of tax evasion, a large "shadow" economy, and collusion between businesses and tax authorities plagued Russia's transitional economy. Domestic and international observers blamed this on high taxes and complicated compliance procedures. In 1995, amid falling tax collection and a growing budget deficit, the Russian government introduced a simplified taxation mechanism aimed at increasing state revenue, improving the business climate, and stimulating domestic investment. Local governments were entrusted with implementing the law. Some local authorities, however, did not share the federal government's policy priorities and designed implementation mechanisms undermining the original policy intent. In St. Petersburg, for instance, authorities imposed an $8,500 fee on businesses that switched to the simplified taxation mechanisms (Murray, 1999). For many small businesses, this cost would not cover the benefits extended by the federal government under the simplified taxation regime. Because of these costly implementation mechanisms, a large number of St. Petersburg's small businesses were effectively denied access to the more liberal taxation regime, undermining the intent of the official regulatory policy.

To fight petty corruption and improve the quality of state service provision in Kazakhstan, in his 2004 presidential address to the nation Nursultan Nazarbayev announced plans for building electronic government platforms. Two years later, the first electronic government portal came to life to offer contact information of government agencies, copies of regulatory documents, and fee schedules for major government services. In 2010, the portal started processing electronic transactions for payment of taxes, fees, and fines, including traffic and parking tickets (Zaron.kz, 2012). Electronic transactions allowed millions of drivers to pay fines at bank-serviced payment terminals or by using their smartphones. No longer did they need to report in person to the district police departments. By removing the need to interact with the low-level police officials who processed the fines and cleared one's driving record, e-government applications and payment terminals significantly undercut corruption. As the online portals promoted legitimate fine collection, Almaty police started employing more traffic enforcement methods requiring face-to-face contact with motorists. Police officers started removing license plates from parked vehicles suspected of traffic violations. Although in 2003 the procurator general blocked the city ordinance allowing such a practice for parking violations (Informburo, 2010), it continued. The drivers could only collect their license plates from the officers in person, making it easier for the officers to solicit bribes.

Kazakh and Russian authorities continue to place high hopes on e-government portals as a mechanism for preventing street-level corruption.[27] My confidential interviews with Russian and Kazakh citizens, however, reveal that notorious "telephone justice" prevails despite e-government measures. Friends and "contacts" in police, immigration services, and tax agencies can help with "erasing" records in integrated government information systems. Those who have administrative access to such records may can remove traffic violations, "unfreeze" blocked accounts, and lift travel or asset transfer restrictions levied against those with unpaid taxes and fines.

These examples show that executive agencies implementing regulatory policy may have wide room for maneuver. Such free agency may come from various sources, such as budgetary autonomy, insulation from political appointments, internal personnel control, and freedom to exercise independent decision-making in areas that pertain to the agency's mission and operations. According to the standard analytical framework in the field of public administration, administrative agencies may perform rulemaking (administrative law), enforcement (monitoring or investigating compliance and prosecuting noncompliance), and adjudication (administrative justice) functions (Feldman, 2017). When politicians design administrative agencies, they empower bureaucrats to carry out regulatory policies by exercising these functions with a varying extent of autonomy or independence from political interference.

Agencies' independence in creating regulatory regimes, however, should not be conflated with the amount of regulatory discretion in policy implementation.[28] Discretionary power pertains to the regulator's capacity to interpret already defined regulatory norms freely and to make consequential decisions at the policy- implementation stage. Unlike the delegated autonomy that empowers the bureaucrats to influence regulatory regimes at the policy-formulation stage, discretionary powers increase bureaucrats' influence at the time of policy implementation.

---

[27] For the Russian efforts, see (d-Russia.ru, 2016; *Kriukovskie Vedomosti*, 2015).

[28] Francis (1993) specifically contrasts rulemaking and rule-enforcement functions of government agencies. He argues that the former should rest with the ministerial bureaucrats who design regulatory regimes. Ideally, implementation tasks should be carried out by specialized agencies, so rulemaking and rule implementation are not fused in one agency.

Bureaucratic Discretion and the Business Climate

Regulatory compliance is costly.[29] Emission fees reduce profits, overtime pay requirements increase wage bills, and product safety regulations require investments in new technology. The overall cost of compliance consists of the official costs—taxes and fees collected for the state coffers, as well as time and resources spent on harmonizing production and business practices with regulatory standards—and the costs of demonstrating compliance, which can include waiting time, queuing, paperwork, and legal fees. The latter types of costs—often called bureaucratic red tape—are an integral part of the regulatory regimes and are necessary for the bureaucrats to implement policy and sanction non-compliance.

Bureaucratic discretion in policy implementation allows civil servants entrusted with the application of economic regulation to influence firms' compliance costs. In the process of interpreting regulatory norms and designing mechanisms for monitoring compliance, bureaucrats might create additional hurdles for meeting policy-established criteria, demonstrating compliance, or correcting violations. Such ability to alter a part of the regulatory compliance cost may significantly affect the way in which economic agents experience regulatory policy. Moreover, because the red tape is not part of the official regulatory policy and can be "cut" by the bureaucrat without undermining the law, an agency's freedom in policy implementation may result in either greater favoritism or hostility to specific firms, locations, or sectors. According to Gordon and Hafer (2005, p. 245), "regulatory agencies impose costs and benefits tailored to individual firms through their discretionary enforcement activities." Effectively, the bureaucrats may increase or decrease the cost of regulatory compliance imposed on firms beyond those specified by the official regulatory policy. These bureaucratic decisions have the following implications for the business environment.

First, as discussed previously, inconsistent policy implementation makes the resulting cost of compliance and, by extension, the business climate less predictable.[30] Inconsistent implementation heightens the overall

---

[29] Clearly, state regulations have benefits too, but these are most often collective rather than excludable private goods. The benefits of regulations depend on collective rather than individual compliance and can be realized regardless of whether the regulatory costs were paid by the individual firm.

[30] See Beazer (2012) for a detailed account.

uncertainty, making it harder to plan for the future. Unless bureaucratic agencies can credibly signal their intent to apply policy in a stable manner, discretion generally reduces the predictability of the business climate, making companies more vulnerable to the whims of public officials. The lack of consistent enforcement may also promote greater risk-taking over regulatory compliance decisions and encourage noncompliance.

Second, the bureaucrats' ability to freely interpret regulatory norms in the process of their implementation makes regulatory agencies the targets of rent-seeking. Discretion allows bureaucrats to selectively apply regulations to reward those who return favors. Bureaucrats may be more lenient in enforcing regulations on some firms but not others. Selective lifting of the regulatory burden creates special benefits privileging certain firms over their competitors. Opportunities for preferentialism encourage rent-seeking on the part of the regulated business. Studies of bureaucratic behavior document "revolving door" personnel practices, nepotism,[31] and collusion between regulatory agencies and regulated industries. These practices allow the regulatory agents to derive pecuniary and non-pecuniary payoffs in exchange for selective non-enforcement of regulations.[32] In doing so, the bureaucrats undermine the goals set by their political principals and shirk in their capacity as regulators.

Third, the bureaucrats' ability to design regulatory implementation mechanisms is a key source of unnecessary bureaucratic red tape.[33] By obscuring the details of regulatory policy application, increasing the number of regulatory inspections, and multiplying the amount of paperwork, bureaucratic agencies may considerably worsen the firms' regulatory compliance burden. All other things held constant, additional red tape makes it costlier for the firms to comply with regulations. Although some administrative costs are

---

[31] For a recent study documenting this in Russia, see Szakonyi (2019).

[32] This kind of abuse of power has been famously labeled "corruption with theft" by Shleifer and Vishny's (1993). It entails payments for breaking the official rules and avoiding regulatory enforcement and leads to declining tax collection, under provided collective goods, and failing regulatory policy. In contrast, a more benign "corruption without theft" ' does not lead to violations of the official regulatory norms or underreporting of official fees and taxes—corrupt officials are simply cutting the red tape without compromising the content of regulations. Alternative models capture the same logic by distinguishing between ex post and ex ante corruption (Guriev, 2004) and bribery with compliance that exists in "corruption-tolerant" economies and bribery in the absence of regulatory compliance in "corruption-reliant" economies (Mendez and Sepulveda, 2010).

[33] Unlike studies that define red tape in terms of official routines, rules, or procedures designed by a benevolent political principal, I place the origins of red tape inside the bureaucracy (red tape has an operative rather than an economic rationale) and distinguish it from the principal-imposed regulatory policy. Such formulation allows for a clear theoretical distinction between principal- and agent- imposed costs of doing business.

often unavoidable, from the standpoint of economic agents these add up to an overall increase in the regulatory burden. A business paying 5 percent of its profit for an operating license and 1 percent of its profit in processing fees faces exactly the same regulatory cost as a business paying a 1 percent operating fee and a 5 percent processing fee.[34] "Cutting" the red tape selectively, for the firms willing to return the favor, may offer an additional stream of benefits for the corrupt bureaucrat. When relaxing the implementation rules they themselves create, bureaucrats may still pursue the regulatory goals set by their political principals and enforce regulatory policy.

The architectural masterpiece fiasco of the acclaimed Kazakh architect Shokan Mataibekov illustrates all three effects of discretionary regulatory implementation. In 2015, Mataibekov's "Slalom-house" residential building design earned the top prize at the World Architecture Festival. CNN and the *New York Times* called this artificial ski resort on a sloping roof of a 21-story residential tower to be constructed in the center of Astana (Nursultan, between 2019 and 2022) an architectural wonder (Slalom House: Ski Slope on Top of an Apartment Block, 2015; Huen, 2016). The innovative use of urban space, skiers, safety, unique appearance, and energy efficiency earned the architect the International Quality Summit gold medal for Leadership, Quality and Innovation (Kosenov, 2016). However, the *Financial Times* commented that award-winning architectural designs and Kazakh bureaucracy are incompatible and predicted Slalom-house would never be built in Kazakhstan (Miles, 2015).

Still, in 2016, the Astana-Gimaraty construction company had purchased 15 land plots designated for residential summer houses (*dachas*) and secured the land- use repurposing authorization from the city land- use committee. The city administration also approved the detailed architectural plan. Yet, in 2018, the prior approval was revised, and the design and financing documentation were sent to the state architectural expertise committee, which requested minor architectural amendments. Because of the sluggish bureaucracy, the amendment process took over two years. While the amendments were still pending approval, in 2020 the city administration modified the general architectural plan, proposing a new local road through the land parcel previously designated as a parking area for the Slalom-house.

---

[34] The fact that in the first case the official regulatory regime is five times as costly as in the latter case might be the single most important source of discrepancy between "objective" and "perception-based" empirical indicators of the business climate.

This modification meant the construction project would violate technical requirements and could not proceed. The city court confiscated the land plots under Articles 92, 93, and 94 of the Land Code for failure to develop. The developer appealed the court decision, citing changes in the city's general architectural plan as the force majeure preventing the commencement of construction. Despite the internationally acclaimed design and appeals of the CEO of Astana-Gimaraty V. Kim to Nazarbayev and Tokayev, the court ruled in favor of the city administration in 2022 (Informburo, 2022; *Kun.kz*, 2021). Inconsistency in approval decisions, sluggish implementation of regulatory compliance review, and the creation of new regulatory obstacles allowed city administration to kill the project.[35]

Jointly, these three elements of the bureaucratic power in policy implementation—inconsistency, non-enforcement, and red tape creation— shape strategic choices of firms, bureaucrats, and politicians motivated by profit, career, and political interests. Only the last element, red tape creation, is associated with true operational autonomy of bureaucrats from their political subordinates. Gaps in policy enforcement, or shirking, however, are not necessarily a sign of administrative autonomy. Self-serving bureaucrats can often disguise their intentionally sluggish or overzealous actions under the cloud of simple unprofessionalism or the lack of resources. I use the term "discretion" to refer to all types of bureaucratic action in exercising influence over policy implementation.

Business Responses

The private sector is not a passive object of the regulatory state; instead, it responds to the policy and institutional environment strategically (Gans-Morse, 2017a). Compliance, lobbying for deregulation, and market exit are examples of formal responses. Evasion, crime, or bribery are examples of informal responses. A long political-economic tradition in the study of corruption, which goes back to Krueger (1974), Shleifer and Vishny's (1993), and Rose-Ackerman (1999), bears out the notion that state regulatory

---

[35] The developer and the architect continue to appeal to the highest authorities: against haphazard application of rules to manipulate a desirable piece of real estate out of the hands of lawful owners. Even if presidential influence secures a favorable court ruling in the future, the circumstances in which it would be secured would mean the developer owes its right to continue construction to the benevolence of authorities and would be vulnerable to future attacks on the property rights.

activities are the largest culprit of rent-seeking behavior. Business influence over the nature of regulations is usually projected through high-level lawmakers and executives (Hellman et al., 2000; Szakonyi, 2021).[36] But the low-level bureaucrats who implement regulations may also influence the regulatory environment and hence become part of the firms' strategizing (Szakonyi, 2018, 2019).

The bureaucrats' power over policy implementation offers lucrative opportunities for informal engagement with regulated businesses. Discretionary power allows bureaucrats to negotiate compliance on a case-by-case basis and enables individual firms to seek preferential treatment. This creates opportunities for illicit dealings between individual firms and bureaucrats. If the bureaucrats are able to increase the cost of regulatory compliance faced by businesses, they can push up the upper limit of the bribe a firm is willing to pay for regulatory noncompliance or increase the number of firms willing to pay bribes. Assuming the bribery is not effectively deterred, discretionary power allows the bureaucrats to increase the potential payoffs of corruption by the predatory practice of escalating the costs of the regulatory burden.[37]

Cutting through the red tape in exchange for bribes—"corruption without theft" of public resources—does not lead to violations of the official regulatory norms or underreporting of official fees and taxes, and it will benefit businesses and bureaucrats with seemingly little damage to the official regulatory regimes.[38] Because it increases the overall cost of regulatory compliance, any additional red tape helps maximize bureaucratic rents

[36] When the bureaucrats are the makers of the regulatory policy, they may become the target of business influence the same way as politicians. Legally binding regulations enacted by administrative state agencies are known as administrative by laws and are the subject of more detailed analysis in the empirical chapters. Administrative by laws are formulated by high-level ministry or agency officials, who may become the targets of the aforementioned influence strategies.

[37] For an alternative theoretical model that links corruption to the discretionary use of resources, see Dal Bo et al. (2006).

[38] There is little reason to believe, however, that cutting the red tape in exchange for bribes precludes bureaucrats from engaging in "corruption with theft" or accepting bribes and favors in exchange for overlooking actual noncompliance. Manion (1996) presents a good illustration of this argument: "To avoid costly delays, applicants make corrupt overpayments to officials for enterprise licenses to which they are fully entitled. In making such payments, however, applicants do not know if bribes are overpayments or fees for valued services" (p. 170). Similarly to the framework developed here, Manion distinguishes formal (official) regulatory standards from operative standards devised by local bureaucrats. These operative procedures are responsible for much of the time costs, which, according to Manion, constitute "the greatest discretionary power that licensing officials possess" (p. 172).

under both types of corrupt transactions. If bribery allows the firms to cut the official processing time, any additional unofficial waiting time only increases the firms' willingness to resort to bribery and heightens bureaucratic rents. Bureaucrats may use their discretionary power over policy implementation strategically to extort higher bribes or greater favors from firms. By creating additional red tape that adds to the overall regulatory burden faced by the firms, bureaucrats create more opportunities for enriching themselves through the discretionary enforcement of regulations.

Not all bureaucratic agencies, however, may be able to engage in strategic manipulation of the regulatory environment. Formal constraints on bureaucratic discretion curtail bureaucratic rule-enforcing authority to the consistent application of existing regulations. The bureaucrats may not be able to alter regulatory procedures or selectively apply them. This system is not immune to corruption, insofar as the bureaucrats may still withdraw the enforcement of regulatory standards in exchange for bribes and favors. In the absence of discretionary power to interpret the content of regulations, define compliance criteria, and design enforcement practices, however, the bureaucrat cannot manipulate a firm's environment to entice corruption.[39] Economic actors' willingness to pay bribes rests on the expectation of economic gains associated with forgone regulatory obligations. Political and legal limitations on a bureaucratic agency's autonomy, therefore, make it impossible for the bureaucrat to add arbitrary regulatory hurdles and extort larger bribes.

The relationship between the official regulatory intervention and the maximum cost of doing business through legal compliance or corruption is illustrated by the left-hand graph in Figure 1. Under limited bureaucratic discretion, the maximum bribe extractable by a corrupt bureaucrat from a noncompliant firm does not exceed the official cost of regulations. Bureaucratic discretion considerably alters the dynamics of regulatory compliance. As the right-hand graph in Figure 1 shows, by creating red tape the bureaucrats can alter the total costs of regulatory compliance, enticing more firms to bribery as an alternative to compliance.

---

[39] It also becomes difficult for the bureaucrat to disguise wrongdoing in technical and clerical details.

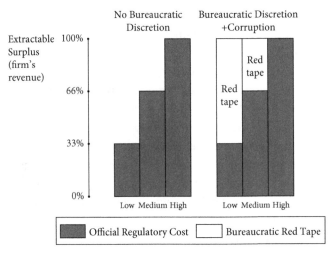

Figure 1 Regulatory Intervention and Regulatory Burden

Politicians' Dilemma

How does discretionary policy application affect politicians? Assuming that politicians are motivated to retain their office—a standard assumption consistent with the benevolent and predatory political rule and applicable to democratic and authoritarian politics—regulatory regimes present a set of choices. Good aggregate economic performance ensures that the state presides over an expanding economic pie and national economic wellbeing, which might improve a regime's legitimacy, whereas preferential treatment of special interests or core constituencies might be essential for maintaining their support and loyalty. These two considerations present politicians with a fundamental dilemma of how to allocate economic priorities between popular and elite interests (Geddes, 1994). Regulatory arrangements that promote aggregate economic performance might undercut the mechanisms for rewarding political loyalty. When politicians use regulatory regimes for channeling economic resources in exchange for loyalty, the aggregate economic performance is likely to suffer.

Numerous studies of this "politicians' dilemma" suggest that considerations of political survival are consequential for the choice of state economic policy and the institutional configuration of administrative agencies (Geddes, 1994; Bueno de Mesquita and Smith, 2012; Svolik, 2012; Egorov and Sonin, 2011; Frye, 2021). The literature, however, is less clear on the role or regulatory bureaucracy in the choice of economic policy.

Geddes (1994) sees administrative agencies' independence as an attribute of greater state capacity and competence and a potential countervailing factor against elites' influence. Gel'man (2017b), on the contrary, finds that the civil service's independence from political influence (the so-called "politics non-proliferation regime," p. 4) greatly undermines the effectiveness of economic policy implementation.[40]

One way to reconcile these contradictory treatments is to recognize that the state regulatory bureaucracy is an important political constituency itself and can act as a powerful interest group. Regulatory state bureaucracy often acts as a patronage network that channels access to economic resources to loyal regime supporters. Such resources may include salaries and employment benefits, control over state resources, and graft opportunities.[41] When the state cannot finance high salaries and does not control lucrative resources, the spoils of office may become the key mechanisms of rewarding political loyalty. For the rulers, bureaucratic corruption may not only be the mechanism of rewarding loyalty, but also a powerful tool to discipline implicated bureaucrats and economic elites.

There are numerous examples of autocrats' use of corruption allegations as a tool for silencing their opponents and delegitimizing their political aspirations. Mikhail Khodorkovsky, the Russian mining magnate, received lengthy prison sentences for tax evasion, corrupt privatization, and embezzlement after supporting pro-democracy initiatives (Sakwa, 2014). Kazakh prime minister Akezhan Kazhegildin and energy minister Mukhtar Abliazov were convicted of embezzlement, corruption, and abuse of office after founding political parties oppositional to President Nazarbayev (Cooley and Heathershaw, 2017). Viktor Babariko, a Belorussian banker and the main opponent to President Lukashenko, was arrested before the 2020 presidential election on corruption charges. In 2021, he was sentenced to 14 years in prison (Kiselyova and Tetrault-Farber, 2021). The ease with which President Medvedev sacked a powerful and reasonably popular mayor of Moscow, Yury Luzhkov, in 2010 further illustrates the expediency of corruption as a tool of political control. After the state-controlled media suggested Luzhkov's wife's nearly $3 billion fortune was connected to Luzhkov's 18-year mayoral tenure,

---

[40] The influence of powerful bureaucratic insiders, Gel'man argues, derails and hollows out important economic reforms aimed at reshaping business-state relations in post-communist Russia. Gel'man concludes that greater political control over bureaucracy would help streamline the reforms.

[41] Engvall (2016) explains that an expectation of discretionary opportunities to profit off public office motivates prospective civil servants to pay substantial bribes for being appointed to bureaucratic positions.

Luzhkov stepped down from his position without a fight (Harding, 2010). Corruption investigations and accusations have also been used by Russian authorities against middle-ranked officials (Fortescue, 2020).[42] Autocrats may prefer corruption to other more legitimate means of patronage because direct legitimate benefits extended via formal institutions instill a sense of entitlement on the part of state bureaucracy, making it politically risky to withdraw such benefits as a way of disciplining defectors.

As discussed earlier in this chapter, the value of bribes and favors the corrupt officials could potentially extract from regulated businesses is directly proportional to the costs of regulatory compliance. By varying these costs through official regulatory policy, politicians can manipulate the reward structure of loyal bureaucrats. High costs of regulatory compliance, however, may undermine the wellbeing of other important constituencies, presenting yet another dilemma: a heavy regulatory burden, if applied universally, may benefit corruption-prone public officials but harm economic elites. Discretionary policy application offers a convenient solution through creating the mechanism for selective enforcement of regulatory regimes. A high level of discretion in policy application, coupled with liberal regulatory policy, empowers the regulatory bureaucracy to prey upon disloyal businesses but spare those loyal to the political principals. The drawback is that once the bureaucrats have liberty over policy implementation, political principals lose control over the actual cost of regulatory regimes, rendering regulatory policy an ineffective tool of governing the economy.[43]

---

[42] Criminal charges are also used to silence political opposition. The well-publicized cases of the head of the Kazakh tax police and security services, Rakhat Aliyev (*The Guardian*, 2015), and the governor of Russia's Khabarovsk region, Sergey Furgal (*Aljazeera*, 2020), both accused of murder, suggest that this "political assassination" strategy is used against the most threatening political opponents.

[43] This logic echoes the theoretical work by Helmke and Levitsky (2004) on the relationship between formal and informal institutions. This relationship, according to the authors, is driven by the extent of congruence in formal and informal institutional outcomes and the effectiveness of formal institutions in constraining agents' behavior. A poorly formulated regulatory policy does not sufficiently constrain state agencies, resulting in ineffective formal institutions. When interacting with informal clientelism or corruption that benefits autocrats' cronies, weak formal institutions result in what Helmke and Levitsky call "substitutive" arrangements. In fact, autocratic states enable corruption through formulating poorly specified and hence unenforceable policy. Divergence of formal regulatory policy and informal corruption, however, occurs when the state is pressured to cater to the mass public demands for growth and effective governance. Under those circumstances, ineffective formal institutions no longer serve the state interests. By formulating more specific formal rules that constrain bureaucratic behavior, the state-builders may create what Helmke and Levitsky call an "accommodating" formal-informal nexus. Although informal institutional outcomes (corruption) still diverge from the formal policy objectives, the institutional nexus helps accommodate the interests of bureaucrats who are unable to openly violate formal rules and "enhance the stability of formal institutions by dampening demands for change" (p. 729).

Depriving the bureaucracy of its discretionary power would keep the politicians in charge of the direction of the regulatory policy but would shut down one effective and politically expedient way to redistribute resources to state and economic elites. Bureaucrats' independence in enforcing regulatory regimes, moreover, shapes businesses' political strategy. When the bureaucrats' hands are tied on regulatory enforcement, the official regulatory regimes become the primary nexus for rent-seeking, which results in politicians who are formulating the regulatory policy becoming directly involved in mediating between the elites and public interests. This potentially exacerbates political conflict among the elites and erodes the domestic legitimacy of the rulers. By divesting the control over regulatory regimes to bureaucratic rulemakers and discretionary enforcers, politicians may distance themselves from unpopular arrangements favoring special interests and gain political capital with the general public.

The politicians' dilemma, therefore, captures the conflicting incentives. On the one hand, there are benevolent policies of encouraging aggregate economic performance and disciplining the regulatory bureaucracy so it faithfully delivers the politician-imposed regulatory policies for the benefit of the mass public. On the other hand, there are incentives for rewarding elites' loyalty with rent-seeking and corruption opportunities created by poorly designed regulations and capricious implementation. These conflicting incentives are being addressed differently in different political regimes. But because they constitute the crux of state governance, modern regulatory states are the key institutional mechanisms for addressing the politicians' dilemma in ways that suit the regime-specific political survival logic.

The key differences between autocratic and democratic regulatory states are summarized in Figure 2. The regulatory state exists in the intersection of the political process that formulates regulatory policy, the economy that provides the state with material resources, and the administrative apparatus involved in economic policy implementation. Unlike in democracies, authoritarian political regimes do not have institutional mechanisms for separating or balancing political and economic power of the elites, leading to crony capitalist relations. Authoritarian regimes may tolerate corruption, preferentialism, or predation on the part of state administrative agencies in order to build clientelistic networks for supporting autocratic power through rigged elections, repression, or targeted giveaways. Systemic corruption facilitates the loyalty of the clientele not only because it guarantees access to economic rents, but also because it creates a credible threat of targeted

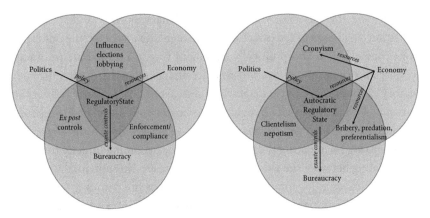

Figure 2 Graphical Representation of Theoretical Connections

Note: The democratic regulatory state (left) and autocratic regulatory state (right) emerge in the intersection of politics, economy, and administrative institutions.

criminal prosecution. While tolerating corruption, the autocrats are able to selectively prosecute it to punish insubordinate officials. Elite cronyism and widespread corruption, however, undercut the overall efficiency of the economy and may undermine autocrats' popular support. Hence, periodic rebalancing is needed to constrain the rent-seeking and predatory behavior of state officials.

State Control of Bureaucracy

Formal institutions both constrain and empower administrative agencies.[44] Institutional mechanisms of political control over public bureaucracies can be broken into two broad categories. Ex ante controls of bureaucratic behavior set up the scope of bureaucratic authority—an agency's composition, charge, and resources. These put constraints on bureaucratic behavior before the policy implementation decisions have taken place. Ex post controls include mechanisms for monitoring the work of bureaucrats as it takes place, as well as reflecting upon the outcomes of an agency's operations

---

[44] Federalism and centralization of executive power (Bardhan and Mookherjee, 2006) as well as internal organization of administrative agencies—the number of actors, levels of hierarchy, duplication of functions, and monopolization of decision-making—are believed to be consequential for an agency's policy-implementation autonomy (Mishra, 2006; Brown et al., 2009; Klitgaard et al., 2000; Lessmann and Markwardt, 2010).

(McCubbins et al., 1987; Galle, 2015). Both may significantly limit the freedom with which bureaucrats interpret the original intent of regulatory policies.

Ex post mechanisms of political control are usually associated with democratic political systems. Economic and political freedoms and an independent judiciary can constrain officials' rent-seeking and corruption (Mauro, 1995; Campos and Giovannoni, 2008; Sun and Johnston, 2010). Strong legal institutions are significant deterrents against abuses of public office (Treisman, 2000). Public scrutiny and reliable law enforcement impose considerable costs that outweigh any potential benefits of bribery and rent-seeking for bureaucrats and businesses. Independent media scrutiny and investigative reports are also important checks on government agencies in democracies. The transparency of an agency's operations and public oversight tend to limit red tape, preferentialism, and collusion (Jenkins, 2007; Klitgaard et al., 2000).[45] Luechinger et al. (2008) demonstrate that rents are lower in countries with an affordable independent judicial system and a long democratic track record. Clear channels of bureaucratic accountability and mechanisms of redress prevent shirking, so the low-level bureaucrats cannot misinterpret official regulatory norms with impunity. These deterrents mostly aim at changing the cost-benefit analysis but do nothing to address the underlying "ability" of bureaucrats to abuse office.

While the ex post controls largely mean sanctioning unwanted behavior, ex ante controls put the brakes on an agency's action by limiting what bureaucrats can do. Systems that limit a bureaucracy's independent action, prevent bureaucratic rulemaking or reinterpretation of existing rules, or specify the procedures of regulatory enforcement (Klitgaard, 1988; Lambsdorff and Cornelius, 2000; Dye, 2007) leave the "street-level" bureaucrats with little freedom for selective enforcement. Institutional constraints that force the bureaucrats to apply rules and regulations exactly as designed by the lawmakers create few opportunities for strategic manipulation of the regulatory environment. The major source of such constraints is the regulatory legislation that designs the nature of the regulatory process, including its content, mechanisms, and an agency's role in enforcing compliance.

Although in principle the reasons for controlling bureaucracy are not specific to a regime type—both the autocrats and democratically elected politicians might be affected by considerations of patronage, rent-seeking,

---

[45] For a thorough review of this literature, see Shah (2007) and Kunicova (2006).

and good economic governance—authoritarianism has fewer mechanisms for political control of a bureaucracy.[46] Despite their great diversity, all autocracies face the fundamental tension between state authority, on the one hand, and respect for civil liberties on the other. Authoritarian regimes tend to restrict the freedom of expression that undercuts citizens' ability to express their grievances against state institutions. Autocracies also are wary of powerful non-state institutions and a strong, organized civil society capable of imposing effective ex post constraints on discretionary bureaucratic behavior. Persecution of independent civil society actors makes it harder for the societal interest to countervail bureaucratic encroachment on the economy.

Investigating power relations in Nazarbayev's Kazakhstan, Tutumlu and Rustemov (2019, p. 8) concluded that in the authoritarian regime, "the fire-alarm approach[47] to oversight is pathologically flawed, because in the attempt to support competition and profit-maximization of internationally competitive domestic firms, this system of oversight cannot cope with . . . instruments of subversive bureaucratic practices." In the absence of public accountability, political turnover, and an independent press, state officials engage in patron-client relations, corruption, and falsification of economic performance indicators with impunity until popular protests "inspired by grave violations of economic rights by the bureaucracy" challenge the "rulers who vest their legitimacy in the building of a competitive market economy" (Tutumlu and Rustemov, 2019, p. 8).

Absence of the rule of law, which is a frequent feature of authoritarianism, is yet another constraint on the use of ex post controls of state bureaucracy. Independent courts are often incompatible with autocracies in which leaders and their associates are placed above the law. When the courts and law enforcement serve the powerful, they cannot be relied upon to act as the mechanism for fighting against the state authority and abuses of power by the state's agents. This precludes the development of effective "fire alarm" safeguards. In authoritarian regimes, ex post monitoring tends to rely upon

---

[46] Autocrats can always use more repression and violence, but the effectiveness of these instruments is predicated on monitoring the bureaucrats' behavior and performance. I concentrate on institutions that enable such monitoring.

[47] According to McCubbins and Schwartz (1984), the fire alarm is a type of political oversight over government agencies that allows citizens and interest groups to report on the issues of government performance. This type of ex post oversight is based upon freedom of association and expression, an independent press, and competitive elections, all of which compel politicians to act upon citizens' complaints.

deliberate actions of the state and may strain the resources of the legal system, police, and state audit agencies. Democracies, with their free press, organized interest groups, and civil society institutions, make the ex post mechanisms of redress, monitoring, and public accountability work effectively to control recalcitrant bureaucrats.

There is nothing about authoritarian regimes, however, that makes them unable to use ex ante mechanisms to incentivize better bureaucratic performance. Autocracies that enact regulatory law may delegate limited powers to the bureaucrats, directly determine the content of economic regulations, specify the details of enforcement, and delineate the scope of acceptable bureaucratic behavior. Such legal restrictions on the power of bureaucrats to influence the content and implementation of economic regulation are usually called statutory controls. Statutory controls may specify regulatory content, but unlike administrative (bureaucratic) law, which is the result of delegated regulatory authority, they solely rest with the political authorities. Statutory regulations may also design the specific mechanisms of regulatory implementation, delineating the exact steps a regulatory bureaucracy should take, such as the records it should keep, information it should solicit from regulated businesses, and penalties it should impose on violators. These ex ante mechanisms of disciplining the bureaucrats are not predicated on the existence of representative institutions, independent courts, the free press, or organized civil society and are available to any political regime presiding over a formally organized bureaucracy.

The more an autocratic regime is deficient in effective mechanisms of ex ante controls, the more important are the ex post mechanisms of constraining regulatory bureaucracy.[48] It is important to realize, however, that although all autocracies might have access to statutory mechanisms of constraining bureaucratic powers, the political benefits and drawbacks of delegation might be very uneven across a wide variety of authoritarian regimes. Bureaucratic preferences and behavior are likely to vary depending on elite cohesion, mechanisms of recruitment, extent of political competitiveness, and other regime features that may serve as a source of bureaucratic constraint in authoritarian regimes. Such political

---

[48] The best illustration of this point is the military and security service bureaucracies. It is precisely because these are closed to public scrutiny that strict adherence to the rules of engagement is key to organizational integrity.

considerations—although significantly affecting bureaucrats' utility—are too idiosyncratic to be accounted for at a theoretical level.

Empirical Implications and Hypotheses

The theoretical arguments presented in this chapter have several implications for the economic effects of regulatory policy, quality of governance, and political underpinnings of regulatory institutions. The links between regulatory institutions, corruption, and economic outcomes are not expected to be dependent on the political regime type. The importance of formal regulatory procedures for building effective regulatory institutions, however, is likely to be more prominent in autocratic regimes.

Regulations and Economic Outcomes

Much of the existing political economy research (Djankov et al., 2002; Fisman and Svensson, 2007; Wienekea and Gries, 2011) expects that economic regulations should have a negative effect on firms' expected profits, investment, and business growth. The theory of regulatory compliance suggests that this should only happen when a regulatory bureaucracy does not have the power to apply official regulations at its own discretion. Because of discretionary policy application, we should expect some discrepancy between the official and actual regulatory climate. Under a discretionary bureaucracy, the overall quality of the business climate is set by the official costs *and* unofficial hurdles imposed by administrative agencies. When the bureaucrats are free to interpret the official regulatory policies, the relationship between regulatory policy and the quality of the business environment can be rather tenuous. Light or heavy, the official regulatory policy is likely to be augmented by the bureaucrats to reflect their agency or personal incentives. Hence, the link between regulatory policy and the total regulatory burden experienced by private business should be conditional on bureaucratic constraints in policy implementation.

Hypothesis 1: *Other things held constant, when discretion is low, business-friendly regulations should improve economic performance; when discretion is high, regulations should have lesser or no effect on economic performance.*

Table 1 summarizes the empirical implications I test with quantitative data later in the book. Arrows denote causal directions. Interactive, or conditional, relationships are denoted by "×." The grayed out causal connection is not tested statistically but is explicated in the qualitative evidence presented in the book.

Regulations and Corruption

The strategic dynamics of regulatory compliance show that mechanisms of policy implementation have an important effect on whether the state regulations lead to bureaucratic corruption. The source of bureaucratic corruption lies in bureaucrats' power to implement regulations. Bureaucratic power to generate red tape creates additional, unofficial costs for economic agents, making them more likely to engage in regulatory evasion or corruption targeting bureaucratic institutions. Depending on the nature of bureaucratic power in interpreting the content of regulatory norms, there are different expectations regarding the relationship between official regulatory policy and bribery. Other things held constant, under limited bureaucratic discretion, more regulation generally leads to a higher bribe schedule. This is because the amount of a bribe the bureaucrat can expect from a noncompliant firm cannot exceed the overall regulatory cost a firm can avoid by bribing. Therefore, low levels of regulation should produce less bureaucratic corruption.[49] When bureaucrats are constrained in their rule-application capacity, high-cost regulatory regimes are more prone to bribery because at higher compliance costs, there is more to be gained by avoiding compliance. When the state bureaucracy cannot alter the cost of regulatory compliance, the cost of corruption should parallel the official costs imposed by state regulatory policy. Corruption, therefore, should be contained under a relatively light regulatory burden but be more costly under heavy regulation.

---

[49] Bribing the bureaucrats to reduce the amount of red tape or avoid noncompliance is not the only type of corruption. Influencing the formulation of regulatory policy (state capture) involves high-ranking civil servants and politicians, rather than street-level bureaucrats, and is usually considered evidence of political rather than bureaucratic corruption. In the empirical chapters testing my arguments, I use measures designed to capture bureaucratic, street-level corruption that arises in the process of policy application rather than policy formulation, avoiding measures reflective of the other forms of graft.

Table 1 Summary of Empirical Tests

Politics	Institutions	Implementation	Economy	Cases/Data
		Chapter 3		
	Elaborate formal regulations	→ Consistent implementation	Private sector performance →	Kazakh regional panel: RCLI and regional statistics
		Chapter 4		
	Elaborate formal regulations	× Bureaucratic resources	Private sector performance →	Russian regional panel: LIS and regional statistics
		Chapter 5		
Political Survival →	Elaborate formal regulations		Shrinking state revenue ↓	Russia & Kazakhstan time series RCLI, GARANT
		Chapter 6		
Economic Policy ×	Constrained Bureaucracy		Business-friendly climate →	102-country panel: GI, GCI, DBI, CPIA, HF, and economic statistics
Economic Policy ×	Constrained Bureaucracy	→ Corruption		

Note: The table references parts of the book containing empirical tests and illustrative examples. Relationships directly tested in the book appear in black font. A suggested, but not directly tested, link is in gray font. × — interactive relationship; → — causal relationship.

This logic, however, does not hold if the bureaucrats have ample discretionary powers in interpreting and applying regulations. Under discretionary policy application, bureaucrats largely influence the firms' cost of compliance. The official regulatory regime, therefore, has little effect on the actual costs firms pay to stay in compliance. The bureaucrats can use their discretionary power strategically to maximize their corruption-derived income by creating red tape and escalating the total cost of compliance. In other words, discretionary bureaucratic powers should render the official regulatory costs irrelevant in predicting the extent of corruption and regulatory noncompliance.

Hypothesis 2: *When bureaucratic discretion is low, the official regulatory burden has a direct positive effect on the cost of corruption. When bureaucratic discretion is high, the cost of corruption will not depend on the official level of regulatory burden.*

Administrative Resources and Economic Outcomes

As discussed earlier, different aspects of bureaucrats' independence from their political principals are expected to affect administrative quality in different ways. Theoretical arguments suggest that delegation of policymaking to well-incentivized regulatory agencies might be beneficial. Although it might be hard to speculate about what makes the bureaucrats prefer good economic outcomes, the regulatory compliance theory suggests one straightforward expectation. Given the major importance of regulatory enforcement mechanisms in connecting policy to economic outcomes, the lack of enforcement capacity should weaken the connection between regulatory policy and outcomes and undercut incentives for and the capacity of bureaucrats to develop technocratic expertise and design good policies.

Hypothesis 3: *When regulatory bureaucracies lack the enforcement capacity for their own regulatory decisions, bureaucratic rulemaking should have little effect on economic outcomes.*

Regarding discretionary bureaucratic powers, the regulatory state theory suggests that the effects of discretion are conditional upon the extent of the regulatory burden. This follows the argument that under a light regulatory burden, both favorable and unfavorable treatment by bureaucrats carries fewer economic consequences than under heavy-handed state involvement. Absent consistent and predictable policy application, the business environment should be seen as too risky for an average firm. Although there might be a non-zero probability that any given firm receives favorable treatment from a discretionary bureaucrat, administrative discretion carries the risks of unfavorable treatment and undermines the sense of regulatory stability.

Hypothesis 4: *Bureaucratic discretion should harm economic performance.*

Discretionary Power and Political Survival

Regulatory bureaucracies often function as political patronage networks, or the spoils system, in which politicians give government jobs to their supporters, friends, and relatives.[50] One important implication is that regimes relying on the political support of a state bureaucracy might be prone to heavy-handed regulatory policies. The costlier the regulations for economic actors, the more resources can potentially be channeled to bureaucrats through corruption. Costly regulations, however, might hurt powerful economic interests essential for politicians' survival in office. Discretionary policy application creates mechanisms for applying regulatory policy selectively, so both the bureaucrats and politically loyal firms receive rents. When considerations of political survival make politicians prioritize elites' loyalty over national economic performance, they will be more inclined to grant regulatory agency discretionary powers in policy implementation.

---

[50] Patronage in the top-level positions is often quite visible. In Kazakhstan, the members of President Nazarbayev's family were given key government positions. His older daughter, Dariga, was the head of the state news agency and the speaker of the Senate. One of his sons-in-law, Rakhat Aliev, was the chief of the Tax Police and deputy chief of the National Security Committee (the successor to the KGB); another son-in-law, Timur Kulibayevwere, served as a chair of the board of directors of Samruk-Kasyna state holding. Nazarbayev's nephew, Samat Abish, held the position of the first deputy chair of the National Security Committee. In Russia, President Putin's personal friend and judo partner, Arkady Rotenberg, among other executive positions led the state-owned vodka producer Rosspirtprom. Putin's residential co-op partners from the early 1990s held high-spoil positions. Vladimir Smirnov was a director of TENEX, the state-owned Rosatom foreign sales intermediary; Vladimir Yakunin was the deputy minister of Transportation; and Andrei Fursenko headed the ministry of Education and Science. Razman Kadyrov, the president of the Chechen Republic, appointed his 22-year-old daughter, Aishat, minister of culture. Kadyrov's cousin, Idris Baisultanov, is the minister of Education and Science of Chechnya, and Kadyrov's older sisters occupy positions in his administration. The mayor of Grozny, Khas-Magomed Kadyrov, is the president's relative.

Hypothesis 5: *The more value politicians place on the political support of the state bureaucracy, the more discretionary powers in policy application the bureaucrats receive.*

There will be times, however, when unsound management of the economy starts undercutting a ruler's ability to extract revenue. Limited resources make it impossible to satisfy the conflicting demands for rents and bribes on the one hand and improving economic conditions of the mass public. The decisions to balance elite and mass public interests "become more important during economic downturns when the ruler has fewer spoils to distribute to cronies and confronts an increasingly restive public" (Frye, 2021, p. 46). Economic crises that endanger politicians' chances to stay in office may press the rulers to invest in business-friendly regulatory regimes and scale down regulatory burden to stimulate the economy. When bureaucratic discretion is high, deregulation will not reduce corruption or improve the business climate. Low-cost official regulatory initiatives will be augmented by high-cost red tape and bribery, and predation will never be reduced by the leniency of the official regulatory policy. Realizing this, in times of economic crisis that call for more effective measures to reinvigorate the economy, politicians will scale back regulatory discretion in order to ensure their regulatory policies are not being eroded by faulty implementation.

Hypothesis 6: *In times of economic difficulties and shrinking state resources, politicians will be more likely to constrain bureaucratic discretion in regulatory policy application.*

Although these hypotheses apply to democratic and authoritarian settings, the lack of public accountability and an independent judiciary should heighten the importance of ex ante institutional control mechanisms. We can expect the empirical connection between formal institutional constraints of bureaucrats' behavior to be strongest in autocracies. Similarly, autocracies are more likely to develop such mechanisms when the rulers' political survival is threatened.

The hypotheses are formulated under *ceteris paribus* conditions, or holding constant the effects of all other economic, political, and institutional influences that might affect actors' considerations. Such factors include firm-specific variables that affect profitability, resource specificity, and political influence opportunities of firms. Macroeconomic conditions and political factors may create differential opportunities for engaging in rent-seeking, while levels of development may require different regulatory content and call for diverse implementation mechanisms.

The above hypotheses are largely formulated in terms of negative outcomes—declining economy, corruption, and instability. The opposite outcomes—economic growth, stability, and good governance—would be the consequence of limiting the discretionary policy implementation of regulatory bureaucracies. These same outcomes could be achieved through incentivizing more effective governance through channels of public accountability, independent oversight, and effective legal deterrence against the abuse of public office. These latter ex post constraints on bureaucratic behavior are largely unavailable in autocratic regimes. All political regimes, however, possess statutory mechanisms—legal proscriptions of regulatory content and implementation mechanisms—that can constrain bureaucrats in their capacity as regulatory enforcers.

Summary

Regulatory implementation mechanisms are important institutional conduits of regulatory policy. This chapter developed a theory of the regulatory state that explicitly focuses on the mechanisms of policy implementation. I argue that a thorough account of the economic effects of state regulatory involvement has to incorporate regulatory enforcement mechanisms that may alter the way in which state regulations are being carried out. Administrative agencies responsible for enforcing state regulatory policy have a profound effect on the business climate experienced by companies. Adding to the classical critiques of capricious rule enforcement as a source of regulatory failure (Kydland and Prescott, 1977; Hallward-Driemeier et al., 2010; Beazer, 2012), I theorize how the incentives for profit- and rent-seeking and political survival shape the strategic interactions between firms, administrative agencies, and political principals over the choice of regulatory regimes.

The theoretical argument I propose is simple. Formal rules that do not restrict regulatory agencies' discretionary authority empower state officials and low-level bureaucrats to make arbitrary regulatory decisions and selectively enforce regulatory compliance. When the bureaucrats engage in such behavior, the resulting regulatory regime often makes it costlier for the firms to comply with regulations. As the amount of red tape grows and costs of compliance increase, alternative strategies—collusion, bribery, and rent-seeking—become more attractive to businesses, which may dampen the overall effectiveness of economic regulations. Politicians may anticipate these effects and strategically empower the state bureaucracy with discretionary powers as a mechanism for rewarding political loyalty, or they may constrain the state bureaucracy's regulatory discretion to enhance economic performance.

The analytical distinction between the official content of state regulatory involvement and the way rules and regulations are applied by civil servants facilitates the inquiry into conditions under which state regulatory policy is more likely to affect the economic environment. This leads to a more nuanced theory, specifying how regulatory policy (economic regulations) and its implementation (bureaucratic environments, including corruption) interact in shaping the business climate. My arguments are consistent with the theories that trace growth-inhibiting economic and political behavior to the state regulatory function (McChesney, 1997; Huntington, 1968; Scholz and Wang, 2006; Stiglitz, 1999), but offer a more nuanced perspective on the issues of economic governance, further advancing the work that investigates how political institutions condition the effects of regulatory policy on economic performance (Hallerberg et al., 2010; Acemoglu et al., 2008).

The theory developed in this chapter suggests that we should modify the widely accepted premise that state intervention in the economy should determine the extent of bureaucratic corruption (Acemoglu and Verdier, 2000; Campos and Giovannoni, 2008; Djankov et al., 2002).[51] If firms engage in corruption to reduce the burden of their regulatory compliance, official regulatory requirements might be of little concern in systems where bureaucrats are free to interpret them and impose additional, unofficial regulatory hurdles (red tape). When the bureaucrats are constrained in their policy-implementation functions (so that little red tape is being generated), the official regulatory framework should more adequately predict the actual regulatory burden. When the bureaucrats are free to impose red tape, such a link should be tenuous or nonexistent. Because the official regulatory policy

---

[51] This belief goes back to Leff (1964) and Huntington (1968), who believed corruption exists to "grease the wheels" of over regulating bureaucracy. Although the subsequent research demonstrated corruption as an independent impediment to growth, but not the solution to business-stifling regulation (Mauro, 1995), many international institutions continue putting corruption and overregulation in the same category of business hurdles (World Bank, 2020a).

is only a partial reflection of the actual regulatory burden experienced by the firms, it should not be a good predictor of the levels of bureaucratic corruption. Instead, the amount of bribe the firm would be willing to pay should reflect the actual regulatory burden, which, in addition to the official burden of regulatory compliance, could include the cost of the red tape created by the bureaucrats.

This echoes some previous research implicating bureaucratic discretion as a culprit of regulatory malfeasance. According to Klitgaard (1988, p. 26), "corruption loves multiple and complex regulations with ample and uncheckable official discretion."[52] My analysis, however, goes beyond such classic "corruption equals regulation plus discretion" formula. The proposed mechanisms of strategic firm-regulator interactions over regulatory enforcement help reconcile theoretical arguments rooting corruption in state regulatory involvement (Treisman, 2000; Acemoglu and Verdier, 2000; Svensson, 2005; Campos and Giovannoni, 2008) with those linking corruption to institutional design (Mishra, 2006; Lessmann and Markwardt, 2010; Shah, 2007; Potter and Tavits, 2011). The theory of regulatory compliance shows that while economic performance, rent-seeking, and corruption are without doubt connected to the state regulatory function, mechanisms of regulatory implementation, rather than the regulatory burden per se, are the major culprits.

Lastly, this chapter offered few considerations for why politicians grant bureaucrats discretionary power and how they can impose stricter controls over policy implementation. Considerations of political survival may pressure rulers to sacrifice sound economic policy for economic rent opportunities extended to their political supporters. I argued that discretionary implementation mechanisms may help politicians balance the interests of politically loyal bureaucrats with those of powerful economic elites. Moreover, resulting corruption may act as an additional mechanism of ensuring political loyalties: powerful state and business actors become hostage to their corrupt past in that it restricts them from challenging the rulers. My discussion shows that although the logic of regulatory enforcement is not specific to a regime type—both autocratic and democratic states experience

---

[52] One prominent analysis of the origins of red tape remarks that "the problems with corruption and red tape in bureaucracy is that they cannot be treated independently... [E]xcessive red tape may emerge due to potential corruption; bribes may be extorted because of potentially high red tape" (Guriev, 2004). The causal argument presented here allows for the separation of these things analytically and situates the causal connection between the two in the strategic behavior on the part of regulatory agencies.

discrepancies between policy and implementation and are subject to corrupt enforcement—autocracies have access to fewer mechanisms of controlling discretion. Because of the inherent contradiction between freedom of expression and association, on the one hand, and authoritarian politics on the other, widely-advocated-for mechanisms of public accountability, transparency, and the rule of law as the checks on the state agent's regulatory decisions are problematic in autocratic regimes. There the major sources of constraints on bureaucrats are the institutional and material inputs into the regulatory process—statutory bases of bureaucrats' regulatory actions and the resources the bureaucrats have at their disposal to enable their monitoring and sanctioning actions.

2

The Evolution of the Russian Regulatory State

Regulatory Vacuum, Regulatory Maze, and Regulatory Guillotine

In this chapter I describe the development of Russian regulatory state institutions between 1991 and 2021. I trace the growth of these institutions through the corresponding development of legislation and executive-level binding regulations that are collectively known in Russia as the regulatory legal acts. Although informal practices have an important impact on state operations,[53] the most logical place to start the description of how the state implements its policies are the laws and official rules that establish formal institutions or governance and define their functions and chain of command, regulate recruitment and promotion of administrative personnel, establish rights and responsibilities of public office, allocate resources, and create oversight mechanisms. All these formally constraining factors are initiated, reformed, and terminated by formal actions of the state institutions—laws, decrees, resolutions, and standing orders—which are easily identified and quantified. To navigate my analysis of the formal aspects of the Russian regulatory state's functioning, I take a closer look at the formal rules and regulations issued by political and administrative institutions to formulate and execute state regulatory policy. I discuss how legislative statutes, presidential and gubernatorial orders, government resolutions, and ministerial and agency-level directives can be used as quantitative measures of regulatory complexity and mechanisms of political control over state bureaucracy.

From 1991 through 2021, Russian state regulatory functions underwent a tremendous transformation. The starting point was the Soviet "command-and- control" economy featuring five-year plans, state-defined performance targets, and the fusion of state bureaucracy and enterprise managers. Since

---

[53] See Ledeneva (2006, 2013) for a deep analysis of how informal practices combine and intertwine with formal institutions.

Thieves, Opportunists, and Autocrats: Building Regulatory States in Russia and Kazakhstan. Dinissa Duvanova, Oxford University Press. © Oxford University Press 2023. DOI: 10.1093/oso/9780197697771.003.0003

the start of the 2020s, Russia has had modern banking and financial systems, along with effective tax collection and state service provision; been a member of the World Trade Organization (WTO); and transformed institutions of corporate governance, with public sector institutions controlling the lion's share of corporate assets. The Russian "state capitalist" economy is regulated through an elaborate and extensive system of formal institutions and practices that control the flow of economic resources.[54]

During the 1990s, Russia experienced a "regulatory vacuum" created by a rapid economic liberalization and collapsing state. In the 2000s, it embarked on massive reforms of state economic and social policy and institutions that were interrupted by the 2008 financial crisis. While Russian economic policy took a sharp statist turn that disappointed the proponents of economic liberalism, state agencies continued the process of formal rulemaking, producing an avalanche of formal mandatory rules defining the state institutions' interactions among themselves and with the private sector.

In the 2010s, the state continued to reform its regulatory function to enhance compliance, curtail unnecessary regulatory hurdles, and improve the business climate. Every new policy initiative further contributed to the expansion of the regulatory maze, which grew to behemoth proportions at the time of an inward-oriented turn in the Russian economic development strategy. The latter was induced by Western sanctions following the 2014 internationally condemned annexation of Crimea. Throughout this period, the state improved the efficiency of its policy implementation and reduced the amount of discretionary power in the hands of low-level bureaucrats. To better understand the formal institutions that shape state regulatory policy and its implementation, this chapter combines descriptive qualitative and quantitative analyses of the formal regulatory corpus developed by the federal and regional institutions of government.

The rest of the chapter proceeds as follows. I first describe the mechanisms by which political and administrative authorities formulate, interpret, and implement socioeconomic policy in Russia. I describe the sources of data on the state regulatory corpus and present descriptive statistics documenting its temporal and regional variation. I then sketch the major turning points

---

[54] In *Seeing Like a State*, Scott (1998) argues that the building of state administrative capacity had historically aided these essential state functions of taxation, conscription, and prevention of rebellion. The Russian state struggled with all three in the 1990s, but regulatory state-building in the 2000s effectively enhanced its capacity to carry out all three of these essential functions by the early 2010s.

in the development of state economic policy and survey the milestones in reforming the institutional underpinnings of policy implementation. The development of the federal regulatory state does not account for all the state regulatory functions in Russia. The last two sections of this chapter discuss regional variation in the development of regulatory state functions and reasons for their variation. The chapter shows that the economic liberalization of the 1990s did not remove bureaucratic barriers for private business development, but instead empowered state institutions to create and use them in pursuit of their political and economic objectives. The repeated but modestly successful efforts to reduce administrative barriers I document in this chapter suggest that Russia's regulatory state balances between prioritizing effective, growth-promotive governance and preserving itself as a vehicle for patronage.

Formal Documents and State Regulatory Functions

Russia's regulatory environment is shaped by national and regional laws, executive orders, and institutions that enforce them through administrative action. Russia is a federal country with a functional separation of legislative, executive, and judicial powers. Both the legislative and executive branches can initiate legislation. Executive agencies, in implementing statutory law, issue bylaws that regulate corresponding aspects of social relations. Most regulations originate in the government and its administrative agencies.

In Russia, federal statutes (laws) have legal precedence over other regulatory documents[55] and constitute the foundation of the regulatory framework. The laws establish rules regulating economic and property relations. The semi-presidential constitutional arrangements dictate that the Russian federal legislature "exerts its influence upon policy making not so much by choosing the government, but rather through the exercise of law making"

---

[55] Russia's federal state empowers its provinces, republics, and autonomous territories to write and enforce their own regulatory frameworks through a series of subnational statutory and executive mechanisms. Following the adoption of the 1993 constitution, which failed to stipulate the exact division of responsibilities between the federal and regional governments, the regions negotiated a series of bilateral agreements with the center. These agreements contributed to the increasing autonomy of regional governments, who have the authority to enact laws and regulations of their own (Treisman, 2001). In the 2000s, the federal government pursued strong centralization policies. These moves, however, did not result in any significant reduction of the regional agencies' rulemaking initiative in economic and social policy domains.

(Shevchenko and Golosov, 2001, p. 239).[56] Between 1990 and 2018, Russian lawmakers produced 8,239 new statutes. The legislative output ranged between 34 and 575 laws per year, or 294.3 laws on average. By comparison, the Brazilian legislature produced 269 laws between 1985 and 1999 or an average of 19.2 laws per year (Neto and Santos, 2003). Between 1956 and 2001, Italy produced an average of 188.5 laws per year (Santoni and Zucchini, 2006), and Denmark produced an average of 35.9 new laws annually between 1992 and 2004 (Damgaard and Jensen, 2006).

The legislative output of the Russian State Duma is roughly comparable to the US Congress, which between 1991 and 2019 approved 6,767 bills, an average annual rate of 241.7 bills.[57] However, unlike the US Congress, where the number of passed bills declined from 804 in the 95th Congress (1977–1978) to 284 in the 112th Congress (2011–2013), the Duma's output rose. In terms of the overall volume of legislative work, Russia's record is rather modest. Federal legislators have contributed a net average of 110,536 additional words to the corpus of law per year, while for the US Congress this figure stands at around four to six million words per two-year legislative session. While the overall volume of legislative work reflected in the total number of words remains relatively constant in the US Congress (it produces fewer longer bills now than a few decades ago), the amount of regulatory detail found in Russian federal law has fluctuated significantly. Russian legislators were most prolific in 2001, when they added 597,602 new words of statutory regulation. In 1991, 2004, and 2006 the net addition to the statutory laws was under 10,000 words.

Russian civil servants' primary function is to enforce policy enacted by their political superiors and codified in law. The Russian law also gives administrative agencies the right to pass binding bylaws to develop specific mechanisms for implementing legislative statutes and executive orders. The small amount of regulatory detail contained in statutory regulations necessitates clarification and elaboration by the executive state agencies. In principle, bureaucratic agencies do not create regulations, but in practice, to facilitate the task of regulatory enforcement, administrative authorities pass binding orders. Ministries, agencies, and state commissions may clarify the content of the law or may establish mechanisms for enforcing laws or top

---

[56] For a thorough account of the legislative process in Russia, see Chaisty (2006).
[57] Averages are calculated by the author based on the legislative output reported at https://www.govtrack.us/congress/bills/statistics.

executive orders. In doing so, they create mandatory regulations, which are enforceable by law. These agency-level documents constitute the front end of the state regulatory system experienced by the citizens and corporations.

The federal arrangements tend to decentralize regulatory policy and its implementation and add another layer of regulatory rulemaking. Currently, Russia has 85 provinces, republics, and autonomous territories, and those governments have considerable independence from the federal government on socioeconomic issues.[58] Russian regions' legislative assemblies are popularly elected in partisan, often contested but rarely politicized, races.[59] They vary in size and internal organization. Regional legislatures issue statutes that take precedence over executive decisions of the governors.

The 1991 appointment of Boris Nemtsov as the governor of Nizhnii Novgorod by President Boris Yeltsin created the institution of a regional executive independent from the regional assemblies. Following the provisions of the 1993 constitution, between 1996 and 2005 chief regional executives—the governors, presidents of republics, heads of administrations, and mayors of Moscow and St. Petersburg (two cities with the status of a federal region)— were popularly elected in the regions. Governors of prosperous regions were also financially independent from the center and used their decision-making autonomy to pursue policies independent and sometimes at odds with the federal authorities. Starting in 2005, following President Putin's move to reduce regional independence,[60] the governors were elected by the regional assemblies on the recommendation of the president. This did not rein in the regional elites, but led to their consolidation (Chebankova, 2006), creating a moral hazard in cadre selection (Sharafutdinova, 2009) and exacerbating the autocrats' dilemma in forcing them to choose between political loyalty and economic performance (Reuter and Robertson, 2012).

In 2012, following a wave of mass electoral protests, the center restored popular gubernatorial elections (Moses, 2014a), but the 2015 federal law

---

[58] After the Soviet Union collapsed in 1991, the Russian state had 89 regions. Under President Putin's second term in office, several ethnocultural autonomies were administratively incorporated into other existing federal units. This reduced the number of regions to 83. After the annexation of the Crimean Peninsula, the Republic of Crimea and the city of Sevastopol were incorporated as two separate federal regions. The dataset of provincial regulations described later in the chapter traces administrative bylaws and legislative statutes of disembodied regions that remain in effect in parts of the newly created units.

[59] Research suggests that regional legislators may pursue their business interests rather than political interests in seeking office (Gehlbach et al., 2010; Szakonyi, 2018).

[60] Putin announced the new policy in September, and the State Duma adopted a corresponding law in December of 2004.

imposed term limits on gubernatorial offices. As the gubernatorial elections were reinstated, the mayoral and city council elections were eliminated, shifting the nexus of power to regional and federal politics (Moses, 2014b). Throughout their elected and appointed tenure, governors retained considerable power to shape state regulatory policy and implementation. They have allocated regional budgets, created and dismantled regional administrative agencies, and appointed regional officials. Governors and provincial administrations issue mandatory executive orders and decisions, contributing to the development of formal regulatory frameworks that govern regional state institutions and private entities. Although regional decisions cannot overturn federal regulations, regional authorities are free to interpret vague and unclear provisions of the federal mandates and "fill in the gaps" when federal policy is missing.

Regulatory Corpus

Russia keeps a good record of its regulatory corpus. The 1994 Presidential Decree #662 signed by Boris Yeltsin created centralized record-keeping and regular publication of all federal laws and executive-level decisions. Starting in 1994, all official documents issued by the State Duma, Council of the Federation (the upper chamber of the legislature), president, government, and prime minister are published at two-week intervals in the Collection of Legislation of the Russian Federation.

The Collection of Legislation classifies federal documents into "normative acts" (*normativnye akty*), which establish general, universally applicable mandatory requirements for indefinite or long-term duration; and other documents, including specific interpretations (e.g., technical standards for an industry) and case-specific (e.g., a ruling on a firm or institution) documents. Although all normative acts establish mandatory regulations, some non-normative documents (primarily those that provide further interpretation of the laws and executive orders) also create regulations. Statutory law, which is considered the original source of regulatory principles, is not interpretive (derivative) and cannot be case-based. Other federal documents fall into either of the two categories. Figure 3 graphs the annual output of federal-level rulemaking from 1994 to 2020. It shows a secular upward trend in the output of federal regulations. The legislative authorities produced more output in the 1990s. In the 2000s, the executive branch—primarily

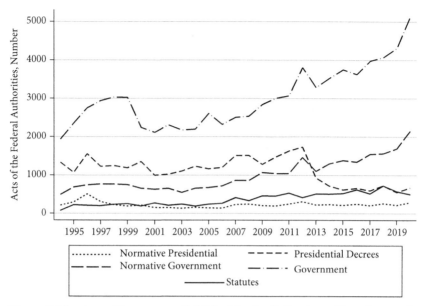

Figure 3 Number of Documents Published by the Collection of Legislation of the Russian Federation, 1994–2020

Source: Collection of Legislation of the Russian Federation provided by the Legal Information System portal "Legislation of Russia," available from pravo.gov.ru.

the government—became the most active contributor to the development of legally binding rules and regulations.

Federal legislation also requires regional authorities to use a systematic approach to publishing and archiving their regulatory documents. Although all official documents issued by the regional authorities had been officially published and recorded with local justice departments, such collections remained decentralized. Growing demand from the legal profession and company managers for easy access to regional regulations gave rise to private efforts to compile comprehensive datasets of all applicable regulatory documents. GARANT and *ConsultantPlus* are examples of such legal information services established in the early 1990s. In 2014, presidential decree #198, "On Publication of Laws and Other Legal Acts," established an official internet library of all legal documents issued by federal and regional authorities—www.pravo.gov.ru.

In addition to the digitized records of the official government documents published in the Collection of Legislation of the Russian Federation, the pravo.gov.ru digital library contains documents issued by ministerial and federal agencies (orders, resolutions, letters, and manuals), regional and local regulations, and decisions of the Higher and Federal Arbitration Courts. The database gives free public access to the full-text corpus of official documents, current or annulled by subsequent documents, tracing all amendments and changes of their legal status. The dataset was expanded over the years to include all recorded documents traced to the Soviet period (the earliest date back to 1937), standing at 242,513 documents by March 2021. The database of the regional and local (municipal) documents contains 2,985,929 documents dating back to 1936 (2,746,574 of those were adopted after 1991 and used in my quantitative analysis). All text from the regulatory documents and the quantitative data for the regional-level analysis presented in this book come from the pravo.gov.ru database.

Working with such a vast electronic archive is difficult. In 2019 I used a computer code to collect the full text of all documents available on pravo.gov.ru. The pravo.gov.ru database traces the timing of the documents coming into and out of force and does not double-count amendments as new regulations. I parsed out the document titles, issuing authorities, dates of enactment, amendments, and annulments. Doing this I was able not only to identify the rate of production of new regulations, but also the number of legal documents that were in force at any given time. Thanks to the uniformity imposed by the federal requirements, the document titles provided relatable information about their scope, origins, and legal status. However, the subject of the regulation and its relevance to the specific spheres of economic or non-economic activities could not be identified by computer processing. To get data on the subject area of federal regulations, I turned to GARANT, a prominent legal information service based in Moscow.

GARANT maintains an easily searchable and thematically organized comprehensive collection of legal documents issued by all Russian authorities. It was assembled from the archives of the Federal Ministry of Justice and regional governments and covers 145 thematic sections of federal and regional legislation as well as the decisions of the higher courts. I relied on GARANT-provided classifications to identify documents pertaining to different spheres of economic activity. At the time of data collection in 2019, GARANT had indexed over 118,000,000 documents produced by federal and regional governments, courts, self-governing semi-public organizations, trade unions, and professional and industry organizations. Of those, 214,330 documents were the federal regulations pertaining to commerce, entrepreneurship, labor relations, accounting and finance, subsoil resources, the environment, international commerce, customs, social policy, and administrative law. Of these, 1,089 were federal laws and 5,291 were specific instructions, technical standards (*tekhnicheskii eglament*), regulatory codes, and forms of documents. Other documents in the collection were executive decrees, ministerial orders, and agency directives. My analysis of federal economic regulations is restricted to these documents pertaining to different aspects of economic activity.

Time plots of the data show that the Russian regulatory framework expanded considerably over the analyzed period. Figure 4 shows that the growth of formal regulatory frameworks was relatively slow in the 1990s. The number of executive orders accumulated steadily in the 2000s. Starting in 2011, this process accelerated across all executive regulations and, even more dramatically, in the number of technical regulatory standards.[61] Graphs reveal a substantial discrepancy between the numeric count and cumulative length of the regulatory corpus, suggesting that regulatory detail is in fact not a simple corollary of the total number of regulatory documents. The introduction of regulatory detail, as measured by the overall length of regulatory documents, was initially more prevalent in statutory regulation, which by the early 2000s accounted for over 90 percent of the volume of federal regulatory text.[62] Since the turn of the century, the rate of growth of statutory regulations slowed considerably, and most of the growth occurred in the executive and technical regulatory spheres. In 2012, the total length of active executive orders surpassed that of the statutory law, and the cumulative length of technical regulations approached that of statutory law in 2017.

---

[61] The GARANT dataset allowed me to specifically identify technical regulations and standards that regulate application and implementation practices of federal laws, orders, and directives. These most directly capture the concept of formal constraint of policy application that I pursue in this book. These technical regulations are legally binding documents that provide very specific guidelines on regulatory enforcement and compliance, such as building codes, accounting manuals, or product and equipment certification guidelines.

[62] If the number and length of regulations are in fact important descriptors of state regulatory regimes, these measures should correlate with other indicators of regulatory quality and governance. My theoretical framework suggests that discretion-limiting statutory constraints should be inversely related to corruption but positively correlated with regulatory efficiency. To check if this is the case, I model the World Bank "Doing Business" indicators of Control of Corruption, Regulatory Quality, and Government Effectiveness as a multivariate vector autoregressive process with measures of bureaucratic discretion as an endogenous, and oil rents, government size, and GDP per capita as the exogenous covariates. I find that the number and length of all documents and documents that provide specific clarifying instructions on regulatory enforcement, which were in force in a given year, are positively correlated with the subsequent measures of Control of Corruption and Government Effectiveness. At the same time, I find that statutory regulations correlate with regulatory quality only. The second order autoregressive models produce similar results. See Appendix B for the results.

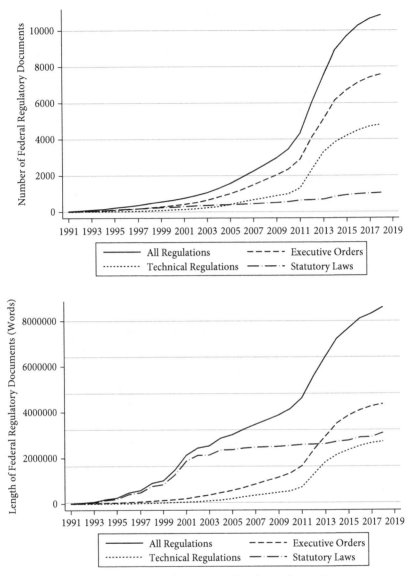

Figure 4 Number and Length of Russian Federal Regulatory Documents
Source: GARANT, 2019

The development of formal state regulations is intrinsically tied to economic and administrative reforms. The next section outlines major developments in the state regulatory policy and institutions, paying special attention to reform programs that defined the government's role in the economy and institutional changes in the mechanisms of regulatory policy implementation. Jointly, these describe the evolving nature of the Russian regulatory state and help us to understand the sources of discretion and constraint.

Russian Regulatory State

From the Soviet Union, Russia inherited an economy run by the bureaucratic command- and- control method and a public bureaucracy that many considered too extensive, politicized, and unprofessional (Bessinger, 1988; Aslund, 1995; Obolonsky, 1999). The collapse of the USSR ended the dual pyramid, or state economic management, in which the communist party intervened in enterprise-level decisions (Rutland, 2009). This resulted in a massive withdrawal of the state from economic management. Russia dismantled the central planning process, liberalized trade and capital flows, and privatized state property. Large-scale privatization and inconsistent liberalization created multiple opportunities for fast enrichment for enterprise managers and well-positioned government officials, leading to the rise of notorious "oligarchs" who amassed enormous ill-gotten riches and meddled in politics (Ericson, 2012; Schimpfössl, 2017; Novokmet et al., 2018). The "hard" structural reforms were stalled by the early "winners" of economic transition (Hellman, 1998) and the 1998 Asian financial crisis that brought Russia to default. The currency lost three-fourths of its pre-crisis value, which halted the imports of consumer goods and stimulated the development of domestic manufacturing. Inadvertently, the default paved the road to economic recovery and highlighted the urgency of structural reforms that would improve the business climate.

Appointed by Russia's first president, Boris Yeltsin, as prime minister in 1999, Vladimir Putin won the presidency in 2000, when the Russian economy was recovering from the 1998 crisis and grew 10 percent a year.[63] During Putin's first two presidential terms, high energy prices and conservative macroeconomic policy produced impressive economic improvements. Over that period, Russia's GDP increased 70 percent and per capita income doubled. Finance minister and presidential economic advisor Aleksey Kudrin and Minister of Economic Development and Trade German Gref spearheaded much-needed economic reforms (Rutland, 2008). This

---

[63] All economic data in this section are from the World Bank.

period was marked by important structural reforms and improvements in state capacity.

The financial discipline, improving investment climate, and economic boom of the 2000s did not safeguard Russia from the devastation of the 2008 financial crisis. Dmitry Medvedev, Putin's successor to the presidential post, managed a solid response to the crisis—Russia averted default and quickly resumed positive growth in 2010, but much of it was driven by recovering energy prices rather than modernization of the Russian economy (Robinson, 2013). Returning to the presidency in 2012, Vladimir Putin prioritized economic development through the strengthening state sector, improving investment climate, and continuing integration into the world economy (Kuz'minov and Mau, 2012). Russia joined the WTO, improving its banking regulations, tax code, and investor protection laws. Still, with the low world market prices on Russia's energy exports, the ambitious plans for economic modernization and improvement in living standards did not come to fruition. Moreover, the growth of the state sector did not break the backbone of the much-hated oligarchy, but simply reallocated the private wealth from Putin's political opponents to his cronies (Dawisha, 2014). The Russian super-rich did not become the champions of institutional guarantees for private property, contract enforcement, rule of law, and shareholder rights. Instead, they increasingly turned to foreign jurisdictions for adjudicating disputes and protecting their savings and investments (Sharafutdinova and Dawisha, 2017; Sharafutdinova and Lokshin, 2020). The Russian state has expanded its stake in the leading energy and industrial enterprises. According to the mainstream narrative, by the early 2010s the public sector grew to nearly 70 percent of Russia's GDP (Aslund and Commander, 2016), although more realistic estimates put it at 35 percent of the economy and 50 percent of total employment (Di Bella et al., 2019).

The 2014 annexation of Crimea, which was unrecognized by the international community, and subsequent Western sanctions put additional strains on the Russian economy. Russia responded by imposing countersanctions against imported goods. This helped boost the Russian agricultural sector and stimulate import-competing industries. The economic costs of sanctions and countersanctions were exacerbated by the nearly 70 percent drop in oil prices from 2014 to 2016. The Russian economy contracted by 2 percent, and the real incomes of the population dropped 7.1 percent in 2015 (OECD, 2020). The inflation-adjusted incomes continued to decline for six straight years until leveling off in 2019, 11 percent below the 2013 level

(*Moscow Times*, 2020). The estimates, however, suggest that the declining oil revenues were the major source of the drop in income.[64] The political leadership turned more firmly towards nationalism, announcing an import-substitution strategy and boosting agricultural production and exports of foodstuffs (Rutland, 2023). As a result of these policy changes, the state's role in the economy grew stronger, and Russia's reliance on Western trade and investment weakened (Connolly, 2018).

The COVID-19 pandemic had a relatively mild effect on the Russian economy due to the capacity of its large state sector to absorb the costs of limited lockdowns and carry out public policy. The retail and service industries, dominated by small businesses, suffered the worst. Russia's ability to produce the first COVID-19 vaccine, which, despite the controversial and politically motivated rushed approval, was proven safe and effective, gave the government carte blanche in pursuing a reckless reopening of the economy; it lifted most restrictions in the spring of 2021 (Nechepurenko, 2021). The government largely downplayed the severity of the public health emergency, refocusing the attention on the National Projects as the primary vehicle for addressing economic challenges (Aslund, 2020).

Economic Liberalization and the Regulatory Vacuum of the 1990s

In centrally planned economies, formal paperwork was the backbone of state control. The principle of state economic management, however, was not to design universally applicable rules of the game, but to send direct, specific orders allocating resources and production targets to specific industries, regions, and enterprises. Informal communication between the state and communist party officials and enterprise managers routinely accompanied official paperwork (Rutland, 2009; Ledeneva, 1998). When direct mechanisms for resource allocation were abandoned in the early 1990s, official regulations regarding product standardization, labor management, use of machinery and equipment, and many other aspects of production and commerce were slow to change (EBRD, 1999; Duvanova, 2013). Developed for the management of a centrally planned economy and with the central

---

[64] Sanctions accounted for only one-third of the drop in GDP (Gurvich and Prilepskii, 2015).

planners' goals in mind, these mandatory technical requirements often were poorly compatible with market-driven business and new technology.

Liberal reforms were introduced through a patchwork of laws and bylaws that redefined economic relations and required new instruments of state interaction with the economy. Liberalization did not void the Soviet-era technical and production process regulations, but it did add a new set of rules. These were often unclear, contradictory, and full of loopholes, allowing the winners of the rigged privatization to capture the rent of partial transition and stall further reforms (Hellman, 1998; Guriev and Rachinsky, 2005; Aslund, 2007). Pending the comprehensive institutional reforms of the state, regional authorities pursued independent economic policy[65] while the state bureaucracy resorted to numerous inspections to enforce the patchwork of rapidly changing and confusing regulations.[66] Opinion surveys of nascent entrepreneurs in the 1990s consistently ranked government regulations among the most critical issues of business operation. Excessive and confusing, regulations on business were considered the major obstacle to doing business (Frye and Shleifer, 1997; Johnson et al., 1998; Frye and Zhuravskaya, 2000) and gave rise to favoritism and widespread corruption by businesspeople attempting to navigate the field of bureaucratic obstructions (Boycko et al., 1995; Murray, 1999; Hellman et al., 2000; Radaev, 2000).

Not only were the regulatory frameworks of the 1990s poorly defined, but the effective implementation mechanisms were missing. Many well-intentioned policies were derailed at the implementation stage. Local bureaucrats' rulemaking was preserving low-level corruption opportunities and effectively undermining the central government's good intentions (Murray, 1999; Duvanova, 2013). Inconsistent regulatory enforcement by the local authorities was often identified as particularly problematic (Radaev, 1998). The local authorities' ability to alter the effects of regulatory policy initiatives of the central government continued into the 2000s (Yakovlev and Zhuravskaya, 2013).

The decade of the 1990s produced insufficient and largely unenforceable regulatory frameworks. The liberalization did not accomplish the task of promoting the development of a vibrant private sector. Instead, the state

---

[65] Chapter 5 discusses regional regulatory policy reforms in greater detail.
[66] Russian firms in the 1990s, for example, reported being inspected on average 21.9 times a year in Ul'ianovsk, 18.7 times in Moscow, and 15.3 times in Smolensk (Frye, 2002).

overburdened some aspects of business operation while completely ignoring the lack of regulatory frameworks desperately needed in business practices such as professional and personal services, real estate, the hospitality industry, and many others. The undefined property rights, complex taxation mechanisms, labor relations, and many sectoral regulations were particularly harmful for the small and medium enterprise (SME) sector. Surveying the impediments to SME growth, Radaev (1998, p. 276), identified the urgent need to develop further regulations on licensing, leasing, foundations, credit unions, and property rights as the necessary measures for stimulating the SMEs. In the 2000s, ambitious regulatory and institutional reforms attempted to close these regulatory gaps.

Successes and Failures of Alexey Kudrin's Reforms

Assuming the presidential post in 2000, Vladimir Putin promised to reform the state and the economy. His reforms aimed at creating a capable state; less cumbersome administration; effective policymaking and implementation; and much needed reduction of red tape, redundancies, and the regulatory vacuum. The comprehensive package of socioeconomic reforms inspired by the ideal of the modern rational state overseeing growth-promoting institutions of open economy came to be known as Kudrin's reforms, after the influential economic advisor to President Putin, economist Aleksey Kudrin (Pis'mennaia, 2013).[67] The 2001 "Law on Inspections," 2002 "Law on Delicensing," 2003 "Law on Simplified Taxation," and 2004 "Law on Registration" signaled that the reduction of regulatory hurdles was one of the first priorities of the government. These laws constrained the regulatory agencies to the maximum number of permitted inspections, reduced the number of business activities requiring licensing from 250 to 103, and introduced the "one window" (one-stop) processing procedure for business registration (entry regulations).

Other reforms updated the state policy in the areas of product and service certification, technical standards, accounting, banking, customs, and labor

[67] Kudrin was Russia's finance minister between 2000 and 2011. He is best known for his conservative macroeconomic policy and strict fiscal discipline. In 2000–2004 and 2007–2011, Kudrin served as deputy prime minister. Despite his dismissal from these top positions by President Medvedev, Kudrin has continued to be one of the primary economic advisors to the government. Since 2018, Kudrin has been the chairperson of the Federal Accounting Chamber, Russia's top audit institution.

relations. Despite a significant reduction of the official regulatory burden and continuing modernization of regulatory standards, businesses continued to struggle with bureaucratic obstacles. The results of the reforms were mixed: only half of the socioeconomic reforms of the 2000s were deemed successful (Rogov, 2010). Unlike with the case of the 1990s liberalization, the lack of progress cannot be attributed to state capture. High-profile cases of Yeltsin-era oligarchs imprisoned or driven into exile sent a powerful message about the state regaining its autonomy. The consolidation of Putin's political power might have diminished the impetus for reforms (Aslund, 2007), but the technocrat-reformers of the Kudrin-Gref camp had the upper hand in policy debates throughout the 2000s (Rutland, 2023). The logic of authoritarian regime survival might have prioritized political loyalty over technocratic expertise, making it difficult to reform institutions serving the entrenched bureaucratic and elite interests (Gel'man and Starodubtsev, 2014; Gel'man, 2017b). Much of the failure can be traced to the state's inability to reform its regulatory bureaucracy, which continued to freely interpret regulatory requirements and engage in preferential enforcement (Aidis and Adachi, 2007; Yakovlev and Zhuravskaya, 2013).

A few years after the roll out of the first round of Kudrin's reforms, the architects of the Russian regulatory state turned their attention to the issue of implementation. The official rhetoric in Russian political circles at the very top level draws a clear distinction between policymaking and implementation (administration).[68] To create a more capable administration, combat corruption and preferentialism, and modernize the way the state carried out its new regulatory policy, Russia implemented administrative reforms in 2005–2010.

Administrative Reforms

The 2004 law "On the State Civil Service (*O gosudarstvennoi grazhdanskoi sluzhbe*)" was considered a cornerstone of Kudrin's regulatory reforms because it was expected to create a modern, professional bureaucratic apparatus to implement substantive reforms of regulatory state function and

---

[68] Vladimir Putin sees the State Duma and his office as responsible for formulating policy and defining the "objectives of national development." The executive institutions, including the government, he declares, are responsible for the implementation of these priorities (TASS News Agency, 2020).

improve the overall quality of state administration in Russia. The law codified formal educational and experience requirements; competitive merit-based hiring and promotions; clear, hierarchically arranged and functionally defined positions; and institutional safeguards against undue political interference in public service. The law combined principles of rational Weberian bureaucracy and new public management approaches for targeting outcomes and performance-based assessments.

Much of the reform measures were directed at changing the institutional incentives faced by civil service personnel. In the 15 years since the reform's rollout, the civil service has transformed both in terms of the qualifications and operations of its personnel and in terms of its social prestige and desirability of employment. Compared to the pre-reform period, Russian bureaucrats have become more educated, better paid, more disciplined, and more professional (Kalgin, 2016; Kalinin, 2019; Fortescue, 2020). Recruitment to the civil service is guided by strict formal educational requirements, and most career bureaucrats in Russia (73 percent) now find their promotion and career advancement depending on the disciplined performance of tasks given to them by their supervisors (Gimpelson et al., 2009). The internal administrative regulations (*administrativnyi reglament*) assign specific responsibilities to public officials in different ranks and positions, which is seen as an essential mechanism for making them accountable to the higher-ups. While the low- and mid-level bureaucratic positions require civil service experience, and such officials rise through the ranks, at higher levels relevant experience outside of the state bureaucracy is deemed acceptable and is often encouraged.[69]

The central element of the reform was its attempt to separate policymaking, policy enforcement, and oversight functions in different state institutions. However, the subsequent executive orders retained with some ministries the service provision and enforcement functions, which the law intended to be performed by the state agencies and commissions. The Ministry of Education, for example, retained the right to manage the public property of education institutions, while the *RossStandart* agency both develops and

---

[69] Analyzing the biographical data on high-level ministerial officials, Fortescue (2020) finds that among the high-ranked ministry officials, nearly 37 percent had prior business experience, with the rest split between intra-agency and other agency backgrounds. Fortescue also finds no evidence of patrimonial networks that would likely produce cascading effects during times of personnel reshuffling or promotions. Although skeptical of the extent to which career paths and publicly available reports of corrupt behavior reveal the full picture, he concludes that "problem-solving officials have the strongest presence" in the high-level ministerial circles (p. 365).

oversees national standards and technical regulations (Kalinin, 2019). In other functional areas, such separation between policy, implementation, and oversight had been successfully accomplished. Financial, economic, and fiscal policy and implementation have been effectively separated under different institutional roofs.

Another element of reform was the introduction of performance-based assessment. Although those studying the Russian administration conclude that this had been one of the weakest links in the administrative reform (Malkov, 2010; Kalgin, 2012), the finding that Russian officials often manipulate their performance reports (Kalgin, 2016) suggests that official performance indicators are in fact consequential for rewards and promotion, which is incompatible with cronyism. President Medvedev, catering to the popular distaste for rampant corruption, continued the public service reform with popular albeit not necessarily effective measures of his own. These, among others, included a 100-fold increase in fines for bribery and personal asset disclosure requirements for public officials (*Gazeta.ru*, 2011). These and other mechanisms to enforce a code of conduct on Russian bureaucrats made their actions somewhat more transparent and accountable to the higher-ups, but not necessarily to the public (Klimenko, 2014).

The incremental reforms of the state regulatory function continued well into the 2010s. The May 16, 2011, government order #373, "On the Development and Approval of Administrative Regulations for the Execution of State Functions and Administrative Regulations" (amended on March 11, 2018), and the January 30, 2015, decision #83, "On the Assessment of the Actual Impact of Regulatory Legal Acts" (revised on August 29, 2018) required the federal regulatory authorities to develop their own assessment criteria. The Ministry of Economic Development was charged with overseeing the assessment. The government orders also required the regulatory agencies to publish their proposed regulatory initiatives on regulation.gov.ru and establish a public comment period. No specific guidelines for public hearings or discussion of comments, however, were established.

Civil service reforms went hand-in-hand with changes to regulatory policy. This often meant new regulatory functions and agencies were created in place of the old. Sometimes changes actually expanded the responsibilities and staff of regulatory agencies. The 2009 "Law on Retail Trade" illustrates this point. The law's objective was to protect smaller retailers from aggressive contractual practices of larger retail chains, prevent oligopolistic practices, and promote competition (Radaev, 2010). The reform increased state intervention in the private sector's contractual relations by enhancing the clarity of enforcement mechanisms and expanding the scope, budget, and staff of the Federal Service for Accreditation. That agency's staff nearly doubled, while regional agencies saw a modest reduction in staffing from 2,400 to 2,300 people between 2012 and 2017 (Radaev, 2018). Despite increasing the amount of state intervention, the new retail sector regulations contributed to a measurable reduction in the regulatory burden.

A detailed study compared survey responses of retailers and suppliers over the span of six years (2010, 2013, and 2016) and found no indication that the "Law on Retail Trade" has led to the reduction of contractual complexity. The author found only a very modest, if any, improvement for smaller suppliers, whom the anti-monopolistic spirit of the law aimed to protect. Up to three- quarters of the surveyed retailers and suppliers saw no changes in oligopolistic practices, but the surveys revealed a noticeable reduction in the reported frequency of inspections by the regulating agencies—local branches of the Federal Antimonopoly Service. The author found that the percentage of retailers reporting an increase in the frequency of all types of inspections declined from 25 to 16 percent among small retailers and from 21 to 10 percent among large retailers from 2013 to 2016, attributing the decline to the effects of the 2016 amendment that streamlined antimonopoly operations (Radaev, 2018).

According to the data from the State Statistical agency, through these reforms the Russian state bureaucracy expanded from 486,000 officials in 1999 to 828,000 in 2011, and then declined to 755,000 by 2014. These numbers did not include local and municipal-level employees. In 2020, according to gosstat.gov.ru, Russian federal and regional state institutions, local self-government bodies, and election commissions employed a total of 2,327,623 people. In comparison, 5.66 million people were employed by the French civil service in 2019 (Institute National de la Statistigue at des Etudeseconomiques, 2021), and Germany had 1.74 million high officials and judges and 3.19 million other federal and Länder-level employees in 2021 (Statistisches Bundesamt (Federal Statistical Office of Germany), 2021). Comparatively speaking, even with the recent expansion, the Russian civil service remains lean.[70]

---

[70] Cited numbers do not include the military and special security service personnel.

Continuing Simplification of Regulatory Procedures

The 2007–2008 financial crisis curtailed Russia's ambitious economic development plans, but the Russian government did not abandon its commitment to improve the business climate. At the start of his third term in 2012, Putin declared improvements in the business climate as one of the most promising directions of governance reforms. The problem of overregulation (*zaregulirovannost'*) was clearly stated not in terms of policy content, but in terms of the number and complexity of regulatory compliance procedures, amount of paperwork, and redundant bureaucratic tasks. The specific policy objective for the government was to improve Russia's position in the World Bank "Doing Business" (DB) ranking from 120th to twentieth in the world (Lomskaia et al., 2017; Kuz'minov and Mau, 2012). In 2013, Russia's rank was 92; in 2015—36. It then slid to the fortieth place in 2016, but by 2017 was again up to the thirty-fifth place and continued improving. According to the latest World Bank report, in 2019 Russia ranked twenty-eighth among 190 economies in the ease of doing business.

Between 2008 and 2020, the World Bank DB report identified 35 business regulation changes in Russia.[71] All but three positively contributed to the ease of doing business. For example, getting an electricity connection was simplified on five separate instances. Three times the government simplified the formal rules for obtaining electricity connection and two changes imposed time limitations on the official document processing period. Three of these changes in rules were also accompanied by drops in tariffs. Six regulatory changes pertained to construction permits. In 2008, the number of required documents to obtain construction permits was reduced. However, the 2008 construction permit regulations worsened the DB score because they simultaneously raised the relevant permit fees. The 2011 single-window land-use document processing requirements subsequently reduced the permit processing time. A number of incremental regulatory changes introduced in 2013, 2014, 2017, and 2019 reduced compulsory approvals and eliminated redundant technical requirements.

In the sphere of property registration, five different changes in regulatory requirements, primarily relating to the upgrades of cadastral registries,

---

[71] All data are from the World Bank DB annual reports (multiple years), available at https://www.doingbusiness.org/en/doingbusiness.

processing time restrictions, and title documentation, further eased the property registration procedures. Three regulatory changes contributed to the ease of obtaining credit: the establishment of the National Bureau of Credit Histories (2008) and collateral requirements regulations in 2016 and 2018. Four different regulatory changes contributed to the ease of international trade: the 2012 export/import document reduction, the 2014 digitalization of international trade transactions and the reduction in the number of physical inspections, the 2018 opening of an expedited processing import/export facility in the Gulf of Finland, and the 2019 reduction in time of the automated import/export clearance.

In the sphere of tax and tax administration, cuts in tax rates that went into effect in 2010, 2016, and 2019 and a series of measures that reduced the review window by tax authorities and introduced electronic tax and payroll preparation systems further improved the business climate. At the same time, one negative development—the 2012 increase of required social security contribution for employers—added to business costs. This tax increase followed the 2010 decrease in corporate taxes and was meant to compensate the government for the resulting revenue losses. Over the same period, Russia reformed its insolvency regulations, making it easier to close a business. Finally, Russia's record in terms of minority shareholders' protection—the poorest among all Russia's DB categories—saw improvements in 2017 (increasing shareholder rights) and 2020 (greater corporate transparency).

One highlight of the 2010s was the push for digitalization of federal state services. In 2012–2015, the Russian federal tax agency launched an e-government personal tax filing portal, gradually extending the list of federal fees, arrays, and taxes it collects electronically. Digitalization pursued the objective of making the taxation regime more transparent, understandable, and less burdensome for the taxpayers. Praising the e-government program in 2020, Putin said that it helped "organize the work (of tax authorities) so that taxpayers and the state were comfortable working together, so that they understand how this process is organized, pay taxes unobstructed, without unnecessary trouble and stress, without the state putting them each time under the different article (of the tax code)" (TASS News Agency, 2020). By 2020, the Russian federal bureaucracy was providing nearly 50 electronic services, including tax filing, online business registries, and federal unified civil registry (ZAGS).

Continuing Regulatory Failures

Despite ambitious deregulatory initiatives, the Russian state continues to produce unclear, contradictory, and insufficiently specific regulation. The post-annexation[72] real estate transactions freeze in Crimea, known as the land sales moratorium, illustrates the continuing reliance of Russian authorities on discretionary regulatory mechanisms (*RIA Novosti*, 2014). Soon after annexation, Crimean authorities were charged with overseeing the integration of Crimea's economy into the Russian economy and harmonizing local law and regulatory practices with Russian law.

Crimean residential and commercial real estate as well as its agricultural land were considered among the most lucrative opportunities for Russian investors. Historically, the peninsula had been a popular vacation destination and wine-producing region. Many Ukrainian citizens wished to dispose of their property in the occupied Crimea; others—mostly vacation property owners from Kyiv and other major Ukrainian cities—simply abandoned their houses. Initially, the housing market plummeted, but it was expected that Russians from more prosperous regions would soon drive the property prices backup. Discrepancies in land-use, lease, and ownership regulations would make many fall victim to scams (*RIA Novosti*, 2014a). In November 2014, to prevent an imminent housing bubble, Crimea enacted a five-year freeze on secondary residential real estate transactions.

Earlier in 2014, Crimea's legislature enacted provisions for granting Crimean residents suffering substandard housing conditions land plots for residential construction. Starting in May 2014, municipal authorities were allowed to privatize public property and distribute individual land plots free of charge to eligible citizens (Andreeva, 2014). The July 2014 law "On the Peculiarities of the Regulation of Property and Land Relations in the Territory of the Republic of Crimea" (38-ZRK) and January 2015 law "On the Provision of Land from State and Municipal Property" (66-ZRK) establish general principles for the distribution of residential construction plots. Development of technical regulations to implement these land distribution policies were delegated to municipalities. Many Crimean rural residents didn't hold property titles for their residences, many municipalities lacked land-use maps and land ownership records, and

---

[72] On March 16, 2014, Russia orchestrated a referendum over Crimea's joining the Russian Federation (Masters, 2014). On March 21, the State Duma passed laws incorporating Crimea and Sevastopol as the eighty-fourth and eighty-fifth regions of the Federation.

much of the housing stock was formally in summer house co-ops (*dachnye tovarishchestva*) and lacked individual titles. There was no clarity on what land was in municipal or private use. Municipal authorities were charged with developing land cadasters and zoning regulations and reviewing eligibility for land distribution.

A combination of the moratorium on individual land sales (including residential housing on those land plots) and municipal discretion in land distribution led to impassable gridlocks. Municipal authorities stalled the development of cadastral maps and land titles to entice desperate residents or enterprising developers to bribe their way into land ownership (Sukonkina, 2018). Corrupt judges in and outside of Crimea exploited legal loopholes to circumvent the Crimean moratorium. According to Russian law, the court may award real estate assets of litigants as a remedy for the injured parties in commercial or civil disputes. In many Russian provinces, attorneys of prospective house buyers and sellers bribed court officials to file fictitious commercial disputes. Complicit judges ruled in favor of Crimean property transfers as a form of compensation (Interviewee #038, March 2018). Such schemes initially were available in the southern provinces of Russia, but, as one of my respondents noted, "The farther you go from Crimea, the better off you [buyer or seller] are. It costs between 10 and 20 percent of [the] property value to obtain a [fictitious] court ruling, but the farther the judge is from Crimea, the less they know about [the] property's true value. It could be a house with a scenic view, or it could be in the middle of the city dump—they have no idea and no way of checking" (Interviewee #045, March 2018).

To further reinforce the ban on property sales, in 2017 the Crimean government enacted a moratorium on legalization of de facto residential property ownership, effectively stopping land title issue to long-time residents of individual houses and summer housing co-ops. According to the Minister of Property and Land Relations of the Republic of Crimea, Anna Anyukhina, "the decision to suspend the formal registration of rights to land plots was made in order to prevent errors in the preparation of documents, abuses and violations in the field of urban planning, as well as to ensure the streamlining and planning of the development of the territories of the Republic of Crimea" (Informatsionnyi portal stroitelnoi otrasli Kryma, 2017).

In 2018, Crimean investigative journalist Iuliia Sukonkina documented multiple cases of deliberate stalling of title issuance to long-term residents as well as the suspicious lack of progress in distributing free land plots to qualifying low-income residents. The journalist identified two factors that accounted for slow development of land management documentation, such as cadastral maps and municipal land-use masterplans: the lack of human resources in local bureaucracies and deliberate stalling by the authorities (Sukonkina, 2018). Authorities enjoyed a considerable amount of discretion in determining whether municipal land is appropriate for residential construction. According to Crimean attorney Shevket Mamutov, federal regulations empower them to deny land distribution requests under 25 various pretexts (Sukonkina, 2018). Commentators speculated that without clear masterplans and cadastral records it is easy to "hide" desirable land plots as lands inappropriate for housing until a bribe-paying investor is found. The 2017 title ban was the culprit, and authorities were pressured to reverse it later in 2018.

Land title and land-use regulations in Russia had been one of the areas in which a regulatory vacuum and inconsistency led to rampant corruption and dubious privatization schemes in the 1990s. The development of land cadasters and a series of land-use reforms in 2004–2006 closed some of those opportunities. The annexation of Crimea, however, created new opportunities for bureaucratic corruption, extortion, and collusion with private interests, which went far beyond the peninsula. The Crimean land resale moratorium is a vivid recent example of how the lack of well-developed formal regulations continues to cripple policy implementation and promote bureaucratic abuse.

The Regulatory Guillotine

The latest government initiative in administrative-barrier reduction was announced in the February 20, 2019, presidential address to the Federal Assembly. Putin condemned the existing regulations of business as cumbersome and outdated and called for a comprehensive review of the regulatory corpus. He tasked the government to review all federal mandatory business regulations, slash the redundant and outdated rules, and replace the patchwork of documents regulating similar activities with the new modernized regulatory norms by January 1, 2021 (*TASS News*, 2020; Ministerstvo Ekonomicheskogo Razvitiia RF, 2021).

The reform was referred to as a "regulatory guillotine," reflecting the government's promise to "slash all regulatory requirements impeding business growth" (Analiticheskii tsentr pri pravitel'stve RF, 2019). A comprehensive review of a patchwork regulatory system is not an original Russian idea. South Korea and Finland pioneered this approach in the mid-1980s, modernizing their otherwise overgrown and redundant regulatory frameworks. International consulting company Jacobs, Cordova, & Associates (http://regulatoryreform.com/) has advised over 100 governments around the world on developing the mechanisms and adopting the principles of similar regulatory reforms. Countries with different economic systems, regulatory policies, and levels of state economic intervention (examples include Great Britain, Egypt, Mexico, and Croatia) have all been advised by the firm. Post-Soviet Ukraine, Moldova, and Armenia also went through guillotine-like regulatory overhauls. One of the most successful programs has been attributed to Kazakhstan and its regulatory overhaul of the 2000s (Gin, 2019).

The government's review of the federal regulatory corpus and the development of new, modernized regulatory documents were carried out over the course of several months. Twin regulatory acts—"On State and Municipal Control (Supervision) in the Russian Federation (#248-FZ)" and "On Mandatory Requirements (#247-FZ)"—were proposed to the State Duma by the government and adopted on July 31, 2020. These established the legal foundation for the regulatory overhaul. The government and corresponding ministries drafted new regulations to replace those affected by the Regulatory Guillotine. In 2019–2020, the federal government adopted a number of resolutions annulling previous regulatory bylaws and introducing new ones. According to the Analytics Center of the Federal Government, the guillotine did not affect a single federal statute. The government slashed 15 of its orders and 577 resolutions and replaced these with two orders and 106 resolutions. About three-quarters of all slashed regulatory acts (2,411 out of 3,003) were ministerial and agency-level bylaws. These were replaced by 339 new bylaws (Analiticheskii tsentr pri pravitel'stve RF, 2019). After the target date of January 1, 2021, the federal government estimated that the reform reduced the total number of mandatory regulations by one-third, marking 2020 as the only year in the history of post-Soviet Russia when the total number of federal regulatory documents declined in absolute terms.

How did this regulatory shake-up affect the business climate? At the time of this writing, it is hard to assess how the harmonization of official regulations is starting to affect the way regulations are implemented. One aspect of the Russian regulatory state—its hierarchical and federal organization, in which the subordinate administrative institutions fill in the gaps in the orders and instructions they receive from the higher-ups—has not been altered. The new wave of regulatory innovations by the federal government required future regulatory rulemaking at the agency and regional levels. The Collection of Legislation of the RF, discussed earlier in the chapter, reveals that the overall rates of rulemaking by the Russian top federal state institutions did not decline but rather increased in 2020 and the first quarter of 2021. If the patterns of rulemaking observed earlier continue, the Regulatory Guillotine will produce a snowball of agency and regional-level bylaws.

On February 4, 2021, just a few months after the 2019 Mandatory Requirements law was passed, the minister of economic development, Maksim Reshetnikov, announced his plans for amendments to the law. Some of these were necessary to ensure the Regulatory Guillotine didn't undercut the state's ability to regulate the economy. Others were necessary for addressing changes in state regulatory activities during the 2020 pandemic. The minister reported that in 2020, only 790 inspections took place, a mere half of those planned under the guillotine reform. Impressed by the successes of e-inspections carried out in place of physical inspections due to COVID quarantine orders, Reshetnikov unveiled plans for further reduction in the 1.5 million inspections that the state regulatory institutions are expected to conduct annually under the Regulatory Guillotine reform. The government planned to expand e-filing, e-inspection, and e-complaint services because the pandemic experience demonstrated their effectiveness in maintaining regulatory oversight.

At the same time, the COVID-19 pandemic demanded an unprecedented volume of official regulatory documentation. Between January 29, 2020, the first time the state response to COVID-19 was discussed by Mishustin's cabinet, and the end of March 2021, Russian federal agencies issued over 2,000 pandemic-related regulatory documents. According to GARANT analytics, in less than 12 months there were four pandemic-related federal laws. Another 26 federal laws were amended with COVID-related provisions. GARANT identified 316 COVID-related regulatory acts of the government, president, and prime minister; 159 acts of the Consumer Protection Agency (*GosPotrebNadzor*); 151 of the Ministry of Public Health; 36 of the Federal Medico-Biological Agency; 199 by the Ministry of Education and Science and the Education Oversight Agency; 75 by the Ministry of Labor and Social Protection and the Federal Labor and Employment Service; and 190 by the Federal Tax Services. The Ministry of

Economic Development issued 90 regulatory documents, 19 of which were direct regulatory orders. The Federal Tourism Agency issued nine orders. Other federal government agencies issued another 862 official documents regulating transport, veterinary services, culture, sports, banking, and many other areas. All this expansive regulatory rulemaking took place amidst the guillotine's efforts to reduce the number of agency-level regulations. Ministerial and agency-level officials used the COVID-19 pandemic as an opportunity to introduce new rules and carve out some space for their discretionary enforcement, countervailing the Regulatory Guillotine's intent to undercut agencies' independent regulatory action.

In the aftermath of the Regulatory Guillotine, ministries and federal agencies have continued to issue orders and clarifying instructions in the areas subject to their regulatory oversight. For example, on February 24, 2021, the Ministry of Finance sent a letter to federal and regional state institutions clarifying the paperwork requirements established by the new federal financial oversight standard.[73] The letter responded to numerous inquiries from the federal and regional institutions by creating a new reporting document for the 2021 financial reports. In 1,203 words, the Ministry gives its interpretation of different aspects of the new regulation. This example shows that the state bureaucracy continues to define policy implementation procedures, defying state attempts to rein in its discretionary policy implementation power.

The business community has remained skeptical about the reforms. Small business advocate Kira Gin wrote in 2020, summarizing the widespread concerns: "As an attorney who daily deals with entrepreneurs' problems I see three problems [with the reform] that worries business. First is the impossibility to plan ahead; one time again everything is changing. Second, it is still impossible to defend the businesses' rights against bureaucrats in the court. Third, the reform does not address the lack of respect and protection of private property" (Gin, 2019). Other voices echoed this assessment. Rather than focusing on the unprecedented reduction in the number of federal regulatory documents, the pundits and business analysts placed much hope on the transparency requirement that became an integral part of the Regulatory Guillotine.

---

[73] The Federal Standard for Internal State (Municipal) Financial Control "Rules for Reporting the Results of Control Activities," approved by Decree of the Government of the Russian Federation from September 16, 2020, #1478 (Standard N 1478).

As part of the guillotine program, the federal government established regulatory transparency mechanisms (Resolution #1722 of October 22, 2020, and #528 of April 2, 2021) and a federal registry of mandatory regulatory requirements (Resolution #128 of February 6, 2021; the Ministry of Economic Development order #101 of March 5, 2021). If fully implemented, these will create a foundation for centralized ex ante administrative controls and curtail discretionary regulatory implementation at the level of federal ministries and below. The mechanism, although rather trivial, promises a clear basis for benchmarking the local practices against the government-formulated expectations. This can potentially close the gap between regulatory policy and its implementation. These mechanisms are still in the making, and it is too early to assess whether the federal regulatory registries will deter discretionary rule application as an ex ante mechanism for restricting discretion or will become the basis of ex post control via litigations and appeals of bureaucratic decisions.

Regional and Municipal Regulations

When the Russian Federation emerged as a new state on the ruins of the Soviet Union, 67 out of the then-89 regions did not have a single subnational-level regulatory document. In the Soviet period, regional authorities had the right to issue binding laws and orders, but these were few and limited in scope. The Legal Information System's systematic efforts to compile subnational regulations reveals that only 12—primarily the republics and autonomous regions—had statutory laws in 1990.

The Republic of Karelia in Russia's north, for example, had a constitution adopted in 1978, amended in 1984 with a 300-word addition, and again in 1989 with a 1,000-word, more substantive amendment. In 1990, two other 300-word amendments were introduced by the Karelian legislative assembly. Two additional amendments (1,028 and 1,770 words each) were introduced in 1991. These changed the political institutions in Karelia and its official name and status within the Federation, and it defined the rights of its citizens, including the right to use their native language. This Soviet-era document is included in the dataset because it was an active law on the start date of my analysis.

Regions issued laws and bylaws not only to reform their institutions and reaffirm their rights vis-a-vis the central government, but also to conduct socioeconomic policy of their own. To continue with the Karelian example, the first statutory policy documents passed by the Karelian legislature were the 1,393-word "Law on the Social Development of Rural Areas #XII-7/196," amended in 1993 and annulled in 2001, and the 1992 "Law on Adminis-trative Offenses" (4,237 words). The longest legislation adopted in Karelia in the early 1990s was the 12,781-word 1993 "Law on Subsoil Resources #XII-16/472" and the 29,631-word 1995 "Privatization Law."

While the federal arrangements empowered regional authorities to pursue economic policy of their own, unraveling political and economic reforms necessitated the development of regional legal frameworks and numerous executive and administrative orders, rulings, and directives. Following the adoption of the 1993 federal constitution, which failed to stipulate the exact division of responsibilities between the federal and regional governments, the regions negotiated a series of bilateral agreements with the center. These agreements and the center's diminishing capacity to deal with the economic meltdown of the 1990s contributed to the increasing autonomy of regional governments (Treisman, 2001). With the market reforms underway, many regional authorities aggressively developed a formal body of laws and bylaws, sometimes outpacing the federal government in their reform efforts. They also used their regulatory autonomy to limit the interregional movement of goods and services, charged duties on alcoholic beverages traded across provincial borders, imposed price controls on agricultural products and foodstuffs, protected the labor market from migrant workers, granted tax or credit preferences to local producers, and restricted licensing to suppress market entry (Broadman, 2001). Still, many regions largely depended on fiscal transfers from the center, which tempered the independence of their economic policy. Overall, the 1990s witnessed a very modest growth of a provincial regulatory corpus.

Figure 5 plots the average number of subnational laws and bylaws in force between 1990 and 2019. These are all archived legal documents, such as regulatory statutes and other normative acts, including regulatory documents produced by regional and local governments and their departments either to clarify or amend existing laws or create rules where none existed before. The municipal regulations are nested within the regional archives and often contain elaborate documents regulating aspects of urban development or commerce or targeting producers located within the municipal limits. Regulations adopted before 1990 and recorded as being in force by that year are included in the count. The figure shows that

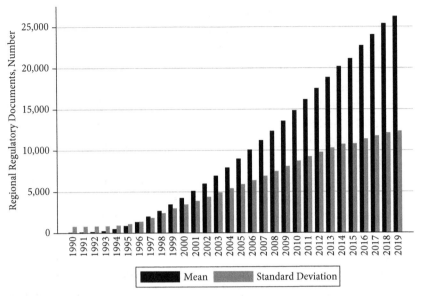

Figure 5 Number of Active Provincial Regulatory Documents, 1990–2019

Source: The Legal Information System portal "Legislation of Russia," available from pravo.gov.ru. Bars represent the average number and standard deviation of all provincial laws, executive orders, and administrative directives in effect between 1990 and 2019.

the dynamics of regional regulatory development were generally similar to that of the national developments. By the end of the 1990s, Vologda province in northern Russia had the largest number of provincial legal documents (80 legal documents). By 1995, every region except for war-torn Chechnya started formulating regional regulatory policy through laws, executive orders, and agency-level directives.

Regional regulations addressed areas most important to the local economies. The city of St. Peterburg and Krasnodar province developed many regulations on the hospitality industry because of their large tourist sectors. Cities and regions hosting large industries produced a larger than average number of environmental protection rules. Agricultural regions developed more agricultural regulations. Vologa, with its reputation of folk medicine traditions, features the "Ordinance on Streamlining the Activities of Traditional Healers" (# 621, December 29, 1992). Regional administrations vary, however, in the extent to which they use bureaucratic agencies' rulemaking authority in order to exercise control over these policy domains.

Despite the strong centralization policies pursued by the federal government in the 2000s, regional bureaucratic agencies continued to create and apply policy in a number of areas that shape business behavior, including market entry, land use, fees and taxes, and safety regulations (Salikov, 2005; Chebankova, 2008). Figure 5 shows that the growth of provincial regulations continued at a steady pace after the centralization reforms of the 2000s. In the 1990s, the development of regional regulatory frameworks was highly uneven. This is reflected in the large standard deviations in Figure 5. In later years, many underregulated provinces caught up with provinces that developed their regulations early on, leading to the declining standard deviation figures. Still, in 2019, the difference between the number of active provincial-level regulations was considerable: Chechnya had 4,722, while Smolensk had 64,254 active documents. The five most profusely rule-bound regions in 2019 were the city and province of Moscow, Krasnoyarsk territory, Tver', and Smolensk. Figure 6 breaks down the 2,746,574 regional laws and bylaws in force between 1990 and 2019 by province. On average, between 1990 and 2019, the most numerous regulations were in the city of Moscow; Krasnoyarsk territory; and Smolensk, Tver', and Leningrad provinces.

Sources of Variation in Regional and Municipal Regulations

Russia's autonomous areas, which are nested within other federal units (republics or territories), tend to have fewer regulatory documents. By 2018, the Chukotka and Yamalo-Nenets autonomous areas accumulated 6,979 and 10,743 laws and bylaws respectively. The country's average is 25,296.39 documents per region. Although the nested federal arrangement might be partially responsible—republican and territorial laws and ordinances also apply to their autonomous subunits—many republics also developed a few regulations. Ingushetiia, with its count of 8,202 documents, might have suffered from its proximity to the ethnic conflict in Chechnya and the corresponding disruption to its internal governance. Mari El, with its 9,143 documents, however, had little political unrest. The smallest number of documents by the end of the observed period can be found in Chechnya, Crimea, and the federal city of Sevastopol. The latter two started their rulemaking process anew after the 2014 annexation that took place in violation of Russia's previous international commitments. There are prominent underperformers among provinces as well. The Kurgan provincial regulatory corpus had only 12,045 active documents, and Volgograd had 13,736 in 2018.

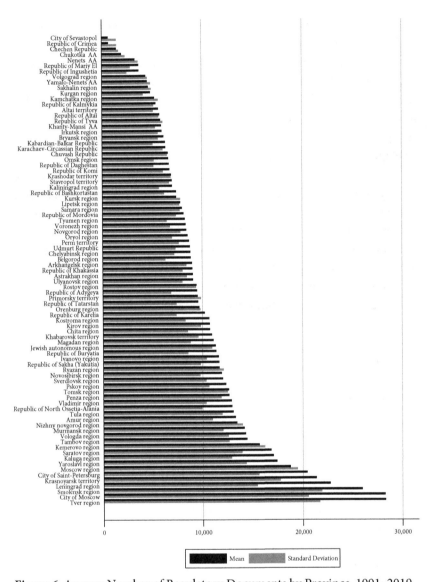

Figure 6 Average Number of Regulatory Documents by Province, 1991–2019

Source: The Legal Information System portal "Legislation of Russia," available at pravo.gov.ru. Bars represent the average number and standard deviation of all provincial laws, executive orders, and administrative directives for 85 provinces between 1991 and 2019.

Figure 7, which breaks down the total number of regional regulatory documents by type, may point towards an explanation. It distinguishes between statutory regulations issued by legislative assemblies, bylaws issued by provincial executive authorities and administrations, and other types of normative legal documents. The latter category includes documents issued by public institutions, such as trade unions and professional associations, technical regulations originating in the specialized (sectoral) agencies, and legally binding documents of the regional courts. Many outliers underperform in the number of statutory and specific technical documentation. If at least some bylaws and technical documents are written to clarify, apply, and enact statutory provisions, this might explain why regions with fewer statutory regulations also have a smaller number of executive ordinances and rulings.

The temporal snapshot of the document type in Figure 8 reveals trends similar to the federal dynamics. There were significantly fewer statutory documents than bylaws throughout the analyzed period. Up until the end of the 1990s, regions produced a minuscule number of technical and other documents. Unlike with the federal documents, the rates of growth of statutory regulations rose rather than fell from between 2000–2010. Also, after 2015, the size of the regional regulatory corpus stabilized with only a small year-to-year growth in the bylaw regulations.[74]

The development of laws and bylaws in the Russian regions is often instigated by the introduction of new statutory regulations at the federal level. For example, paragraph 3 of Article 227 of the 2000 Federal Tax Code established the way the income tax rate is cultivated for foreign nationals employed and self-employed in Russia:

> The amount of fixed advance payments is subject to indexation by the deflator coefficient established for the corresponding calendar year, as well as by the coefficient reflecting regional features of the labor market (hereinafter, the regional coefficient) established for the corresponding calendar year by laws of the subjects of the Russian Federation. In the event that the regional coefficient for the next calendar year is not established by the law of the subject [region] of the Russian Federation, its value shall be considered equal to one.

---

[74] The "regulatory guillotine" initiative, described earlier, may reinvigorate regional rulemaking, as the existing regional norms need to be harmonized with the national-level innovations.

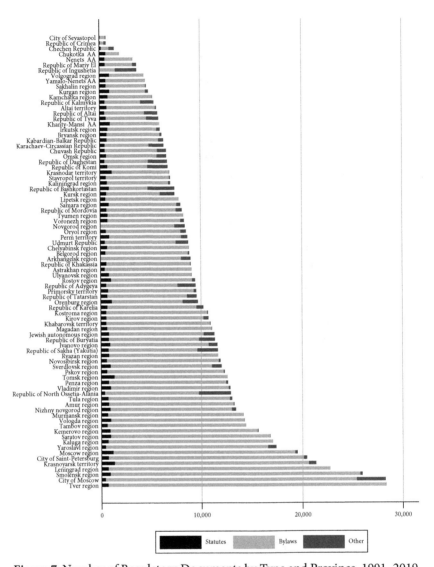

Figure 7 Number of Regulatory Documents by Type and Province, 1991–2019

Source: Legal Information System portal "Legislation of Russia," available from pravo.gov.ru. Bars represent the number of documents adopted by provincial legislative (statutes) and executive (bylaws) authorities, as well as other binding rules issued by judicial and non-state organizations between 1991 and 2019.

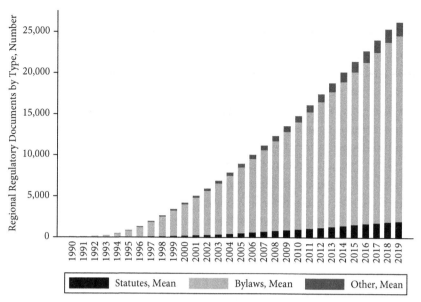

Figure 8 Number of Active Provincial Regulatory Documents by Type, 1991–2019

Source: The Legal Information System portal "Legislation of Russia," available from pravo.gov.ru. Bars represent the average number of provincial legislative (statutes) and executive (bylaws) authorities, as well as other binding rules issued by judicial and non-state organizations that were in effect between 1991 and 2019.

The federal law effectively empowered regional legislatures to pursue their own tax policy towards foreign nationals, with potential consequences for the labor market. In the absence of any labor market policy in this area, no regional documents were produced. However, some regions have used these provisions as a labor policy tool. The corresponding regional regulations are very short in length, as they only set one coefficient for tax calculation. For example, the 73-word "Law on Establishing the Coefficient Reflecting Regional Features of the Labor Market of the Republic of Karelia for 2016" reads:

> In accordance with paragraph 3 of Article 227 on establishing a coefficient reflecting the regional characteristics of the labor market of the Republic of Karelia for 2016, it was adopted by the Legislative Assembly on October 20, 2015 of the Tax Code of the Russian Federation to establish for 2016 a coefficient reflecting regional characteristics of the labor market of the Republic of Karelia, equal to 2.01. This Law shall enter into force on January 1, 2016.

This took the legislator 56 words in Russian. Karelia continued to use this tool to protect its labor market in 2017, 2018, and 2019 by passing corresponding pieces of legislation of comparable lengths. Although these laws established the coefficients only for the duration of one tax year, they were not annulled by the subsequent legislation and appear as "active" in the legal dockets. Because of their active legal status, in my database they continue being counted towards the total number and length of regulations in all subsequent years. Conceptually, they still impact tax liabilities and are the bases for audits and tax fraud investigations moving forward.

The texts of specific resolutions and rulings—those that go beyond budgetary allocations, elections, appointments, and dismissals—are usually a product of deliberate professional lawmaking that requires skills, experience, and analysis of the existing blueprints and alternatives. Local authorities often lack professional resources and organizational support available to the federal State Duma deputies through legislative committees and staff. Still, the local laws and executive orders are written in a standardized language and are often hard to distinguish from their federal counterparts. How did provincial officials do it? The close reading of the regional regulatory documents reveals a considerable amount of borrowing across the regions. The regional assembly deputies report the practice of hiring legal professionals from Moscow and other large cities who applied their previous experience drafting legislation and executive orders in the related fields.[75] Some regional regulations were informed by regulations developed in other regions and provided by the regional organizations, such as the Union of Russian Cities (Izotin, 2008), Association of Siberian and Far East Cities, and Association of Municipalities of Irkutsk Province (http://www.amoio.ru/about/). The former organization, for example, maintains a library of Russian and foreign legal documents, develops templates of different types of documents, and updates them in light of the requirements of the Ministry of Justice and the current federal legislation.

Regulatory Specificity

Figures 9 and 10 show that between 1990 and 2019, the overall length of the provincial regulatory corpus increased substantially from a few thousand

---

[75] According to Izotin (2008, p. 71), in 1993 a draft regional charter was priced at 130 million rubles by a Moscow-based legal consultant. Only regions with large budgets could afford this cost.

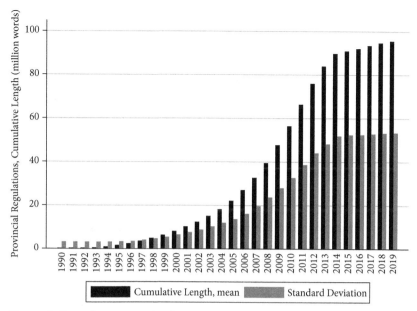

Figure 9 Cumulative Length of Active Provincial Regulatory Documents, 1990–2019

Source: The Legal Information System portal "Legislation of Russia," available from pravo.gov.ru. Bars represent the average cumulative length of all provincial laws, executive orders, and administrative directives that were in effect between 1990 and 2019, as well as the standard deviation.

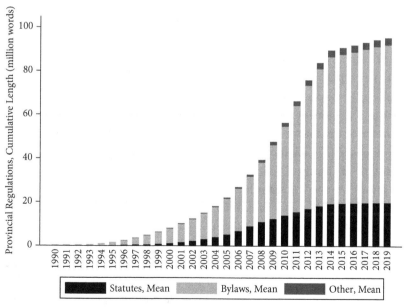

Figure 10 Cumulative Length of Active Provincial Regulatory Documents by Type, 1990–2019

Source: The Legal Information System portal "Legislation of Russia," available from pravo.gov.ru. Bars represent the average cumulative length of provincial legislative (statutes) and executive (bylaws) authorities, as well as other binding rules issued by judicial and non-state organizations that were in effect between 1990 and 2019.

words in the early 1990s to over 90 million in 2015. Until the late 1990s, the average overall length of provincial regulatory corpuses was just under a million words, but the standard deviation far exceeded the average as a few provinces started developing their regulatory frameworks earlier than others. Statutory regulations tend to be longer but cumulatively account for a small portion of a region's regulatory corpus. Much more numerous, the executive orders are usually much shorter in length and have a shorter lifespan.

Longer regulations often establish technical standards or develop specific regulatory frameworks that require enumeration of various categories and specific case-by-case decisions on the application of general regulatory principles. For instance, the January 9, 1995, order "On the Approval of the List of Territorial Public Highways of the Republic of Karelia" is 14,631 words long due to the inclusion of a long list of roads classified as public highways. The February 28, 1995, order "On the Allocation of Funds from the National Economy Reconstruction and Development Fund for the Purchase of Agricultural Machinery" contained only 363 words. The latter decree authorized spending without any description of the procedures to be used for identifying the supplier or specification of the machinery to be purchased.

The length of the documents appears to be non-trivial from the policy implementation standpoint. A significant number of executive decrees and agency-level orders enact detailed regulations formulated in separate documents titled *polozhenie* (regulation), *tekhnicheskii reglament* (technical regulation), *standarty* (standards), or *poriadok* (order). Others include these regulatory documents as appendices. The latter approach is exemplified by the order of the mayor of Tomsk, "On Approval of the Regulation on the Procedures for Concluding Long-term Contracts for the Municipal Needs of the City of Tomsk..." Of its 717 words, 96 constitute the actual order. The remaining 573 words (see the full text in Appendix C) constitute an appendix that (1) defines the types of municipal contracts the regulation covers; (2) establishes the "municipal legal act" as a type of standard contract; (3) defines specific elements of the "municipal legal act," including the planned results of the performance of work (rendering of services), description of the scope of work (services), deadline for the performance of work (rendering of services), and the maximum annual budget for a long-term municipal contract; (4) names the specific divisions of the city administration responsible for reviewing and approving these contracts; (5) establishes a specific format of two required supporting documents, that is, financial and economic project specifications and an explanatory note consisting of seven specific economic and technical parameters of the proposed project; (6) sets a 15-day deadline for the city departments to review applications according to four specified financial and economic criteria; and (7) references the corresponding federal regulation on matters not covered by the scope of the order.

A similar 2008 decree from the Arkhangelsk mayor originally used only 131 words to put its municipal contracting procedures into force. The original text of the decree contained a 54-word "Procedural Regulations" paragraph that did not contain the description of required accompanying documentation or clear sequencing of approvals from two different departments of city administration. Between 2008 and 2013, the lack of procedural clarity caused by the lower word count contributed to delays, business frustration, and allegations of preferentialism. In 2013, the decree was clarified by two executive amendments (#574 of September 4, 2013, and #618 of September 23, 2013), expanding its text to 650 words and clarifying the process for obtaining administrative approvals and the content of the required accompanying documentation. Because it took the Arkhangelsk city administration five years and two amendments to accomplish the same clarity as found in Tomsk's regulation, the private suppliers of municipal services for Tomsk faced fewer bureaucratic obstacles than in Arkhangelsk.

Conclusion

With the help of descriptive analysis of the archived official regulatory documents, this chapter described the development of the Russian regulatory state.[76] I sketched the major directions of Russia's economic policy from the

---

[76] The development of the Russian regulatory state, although necessarily influenced and constrained by pressing tasks of economic policy, should not be conflated with government-formulated economic targets. In 2006, President Medvedev introduced four national priorities (state programs) in health, housing, education, and agricultural development. In 2009 he launched the economic modernization program. In 2018 Putin unveiled an ambitious National Projects initiative for poverty reduction, economic modernization, diversification of the economy, and public goods provision (Pravitel'stvo Rossii, 2018). He dismissed previous national policy priorities and set 38 new socioeconomic targets (e.g., resettlement of decrepit housing and increasing life expectancy), 26 of which were considered implemented by 2020. The regulatory state has become increasingly instrumental in implementing government policy objectives; however, much of the institution-building of 2004–2012 and the subsequent incremental improvements in the administrative state capacity were not specific to the content of economic policy. Instead, the development of the institutions of the regulatory state laid the foundations for more effective implementation of specific policy targets.

early years of liberal market reforms of the 1990s, through the institutional modernization of the 2000s, to the continuing efforts to harmonize and streamline regulatory state function that culminated in Russia's "regulatory guillotine" initiative, which, for the first time in Russia's history, slashed a sizable number of regulatory documents.

A few conclusions are worth emphasizing. First, though it may seem obvious, it is often downplayed that formal regulatory documents are the major force behind the Russian state's socioeconomic policy, institutional change, and enforcement mechanisms. Regulations originate with the top-level state authorities, but when they are lacking, vague, or explicitly delegate decision-making, other federal and regional state institutions may step in and formulate their own formal rules.

Second, changes in the state's approach to regulatory policy—withdrawal, activism, and institutional and policy reforms—are clearly reflected in the quantitative data on formal regulatory environments. Over the analyzed period, the Russian regulatory state made a long journey from a patchwork of poorly designed rules missing crucial guidance to be filled in later by improvising regulatory agencies to an elaborate and discretion-limiting regulatory regime that heavily relies on codified principles, specific rules and requirements, and formal mechanisms of performance monitoring and oversight.

Third, throughout much of the recent history of Russian regulatory state-building, authorities waged a battle against bureaucratic barriers for business. Paradoxically, economic liberalization did not remove them but instead empowered the state institutions to create and use them in pursuit of their political and economic objectives. These bureaucratic barriers led to rampant corruption, were used as a mechanism of preferentialism and state predation, and served as a vehicle for patronage. The anti-barrier rhetoric appears constant, but the specific efforts to address the problem intensified and subsided and intensified again. The record of administrative reform suggests the authorities are engaged in a balancing act, making progress in some areas, such as improving bureaucrats' qualifications and career incentives and better monitoring their performance, but hesitating in areas of public accountability and oversight.

Lastly, the chapter demonstrated that regulatory documents are the source of formal institutional constraints of the policy implementation practices.

Legally binding documents establish the direction, principles, and mechanisms of mandatory regulations. The more elaborate formal rules provide a firmer foundation for implementation that is consistent with the intent of policymakers. Formal rules regulate not only companies and individuals, but also the bureaucrats who implement them.

3

Regulatory Details and Economic Development in Kazakhstan

In 1998, the year I left my home country of Kazakhstan, a film directed by Satubaldy Narymbetov premiered on Kazakh and Russian silver screens. *Ompa*, meaning luck in throwing dice, is an eclectic tale of Kazakh and Russian ex-military pilots who try their entrepreneurial fortune in a private Salam-Aleikum air carrier company operating a Soviet-made AN-2 biplane. The duo takes odd jobs, such as a ceremonial bride kidnapping, rural aerobatics show, and—as a sign of the tumultuous 1990s—fighting mafia hijackers. The pilots-turned-entrepreneurs encounter the state as a set of obstacles presented by air traffic control, border patrol, and local officials. They also experience a state authority void when dealing with cheating clients and criminals. The travels of the novice entrepreneurs end with a literal crash of the Salam-Aleikum business venture. The relentlessness of the self-employed "businessmen" determined to prevail against all odds is captured in the last scene of the movie as the main characters' despair turns into new hope with a lucky roll of dice.

The movie's protagonists, Russian-born Kazakh Daur and ethnic Russian Talalai from Kazakhstan, are emblematic of the shared experiences of two post-communist countries. Kazakhstan, a land-locked Central Asian country of 19 million predominantly Muslim inhabitants, is the world's ninth largest by territory. In the 1991 dissolution of the USSR, it became an independent unitary republic and joined the UN, the Commonwealth of Independent States, the Organization for Security and Cooperation in Europe, the Shanghai Cooperation Organization, the Collection Security Treaty Organization, the Organization of Islamic Cooperation, the Organization of Turkic States, the World Trade Organization, and the Eurasian Economic Union. Kazakhstan shared with Russia many challenges associated with the post-Soviet economic and political transition and, in 2002, acquired the status of a market economy under the US definition. With the world's eleventh-largest proven reserves in oil and natural gas, second-largest

Thieves, Opportunists, and Autocrats: Building Regulatory States in Russia and Kazakhstan. Dinissa Duvanova, Oxford University Press. © Oxford University Press 2023. DOI: 10.1093/oso/9780197697771.003.0004

uranium reserves, and hefty non-ferrous metal and other mineral reserves, the country's economy is heavily dominated by extractive and energy industries. The energy sector has fueled the country's steady economic growth. In 2006, it joined the ranks of the upper middle income countries. In 2021, Kazakhstan's GDP per capita stood at US$10,000.

Kazakhstan shared with its northern neighbor and other transitioning countries the tasks of redefining the state's relationship with the economy, rebuilding its institutions of governance, and promoting economic recovery and growth. Unlike in Russia, however, the Kazakh regulatory state did not face challenges associated with federal divisions of regulatory authority. The country had been stably authoritarian,[77] with an increasing concentration of central government authority and effective suppression of competing claims for power. Since its independence, Kazakhstan has witnessed fewer episodes of civil unrest than Russia and has not experienced open armed conflict. The Kazakh state retained control over the country's rich subsoil resources, which, coupled with a rather small population density, allowed it to generate revenue necessary to maintain and rebuild institutions of governance.

This chapter traces the development of formal state institutions regulating the economy and examines their effect on private investment activity and the performance of the non-state small business sector. I make use of the regional variation in economic performance across Kazakhstan to investigate connections between provincial regulatory frameworks that directly shape the street-level bureaucrats' regulatory activities. The chapter analyzes data on regulations enacted by elected provincial assemblies and provincial administrators appointed by the central government. The Kazakh case is particularly suited for the analysis of statutory controls on policy implementation because it lacks sensible mechanisms of public accountability and largely isolates local bureaucrats from local legislative oversight. This makes the statutory and administrative mechanisms of controlling policy implementation the primary formal means of controlling regulatory discretion. Moreover, because provincial executive authorities in Kazakhstan have political, organizational, and financial independence from provincial representative assemblies, I can investigate statutory and administrative regulations as separate causal factors. Moreover, Kazakhstan developed an entirely new body of regulatory codes after its independence in 1991. This conveniently resolves the issue of the possible irrelevance of old regulations.

---

[77] During the analyzed period, Kazakhstan had been consistently ranked "not free" by the Freedom House.

After describing the institutional make-up of the Kazakh state and its allocation of regulatory authority, I survey the major directions of economic policy and civil service reforms. I then turn to testing my hypotheses about economic effects of discretion in authoritarian settings. I scrutinize uneven development of regional economic regulations that may constrain the power of regulatory bureaucracy vis-a-vis private companies and economic performance in Kazakhstan between 1996 and 2018. Building on the work of Huber et al. (2001), who link agency discretion to the specificity of regulatory legislation, I conceptualize discretion as the flip side of regulatory specificity and approximate the latter with the lengths of regulatory documents. Using a newly assembled dataset containing information on the number, length, and types of all legislative statutes, executive orders, and bureaucratic bylaws adopted by the regional legislative and administrative authorities, I examine the effects of region-specific economic regulations on investment decisions and the development of the regional small and medium enterprise (SME) sector. The within-country comparison reduces the extent of unobserved institutional and cultural heterogeneity that often complicates cross-country comparative studies.[78]

My analysis shows that, generally, more-specific regulations positively impact capital investment and aggregate performance of small private companies. The statutory mechanisms for restricting bureaucratic discretion are no less effective than the administrative bylaws. This means that the regulatory specificity—but not the external (legislative) oversight—is the main mechanism connecting the development of formal regulatory norms to better economic outcomes.

Kazakh Regulatory State

The Kazakh regulatory environment is shaped by national and provincial institutions that codify regulatory norms in laws and enforce them through administrative action. Kazakhstan is a unitary country with a functional separation of legislative, executive, and judicial powers. The constitution empowers the president to appoint the prime minister, 17 members of

---

[78] For instance, concerns that unobserved heterogeneity across countries might bias results often loom large in such studies. Although within-country designs cannot eliminate these concerns completely, comparing across subunits of a single country such as Kazakhstan can dramatically reduce the scope of unobserved heterogeneity, since presumably all the cross-sectional units hold in common a number of shared historical and institutional factors.

the Council of Ministers, provincial governors, and city mayors (*akims*); select the Supreme Court judges; initiate and veto legislation, referenda, and constitutional amendments; and dissolve the national legislature.

In 2009, preparing for the transition of power to a loyal supporter, President Nursultan Nazarbayev[79] pushed through legislation perpetuating his control over the direction of state policy from the post of the permanent leader of the restructured Security Council (Chebotarev, 2018; elbasy.kz, 2021). This position gave Nazarbayev the power to veto important political decisions but kept him at arm's length from the more mundane tasks of running the country. In 2022, a national referendum terminated earlier constitutional provisions for the special status and powers of the first president but stopped short of stripping Nazarbayev of his lifetime immunity. The constitution was also amended to extend the presidential term to seven years without the right for reelection (Fremer, 2022).

Neither the president nor the chair of the Security Council have the power to appoint legislative branch officials at the national, provincial, or local levels. The bicameral legislature consists of the *Mazhilis*, which has 77 popularly elected members, and the Senate, which has 40 members elected by provincial assemblies and seven presidential appointees. Because of the prosecution of organized non-systemic opposition and masterfully manipulated national elections, the national legislature has not been a source of political opposition.

Currently, Kazakhstan has 14 provinces and three cities with administrative status equal to that of a region (cities of republican significance): Almaty, Astana, and Shymkent.[80] Almaty, the largest Kazakh city of about two million people, was the capital of the Kazakh Soviet Republic since 1929. In 1997 the capital was moved to the northern city of Akmola, which was renamed Astana, "capital" in Kazakh. Following President Nazarbayev's resignation in 2019, the capital was renamed Nursultan, a move reversed by President Kassym-Jomart Tokayev in 2022. The 1993 constitution created a unitary government but preserved local representative (legislative) institutions that existed under the Soviet rule and were regulated by the 1991 "Law on Local Self-government and Local Councils." Although the

---

[79] Nursultan Nazarbayev transformed his position of general secretary of the Kazakh Communist Party into a presidential post after Kazakhstan's independence in 1991 and retained that position through a combination of electoral manipulations, persecution of opposition, constitutional changes, and genuine popular support until the election of his loyal supporter and designated successor Kassym-Jomart Tokayev in 2019.

[80] Because Shymkent was part of the administrative center of the South-Kazakhstan province until June 2018, in my quantitative analysis I treat it as a part of that province.

1993 constitution granted local governments the right to make independent decisions, it did not clearly demarcate the jurisdiction of provincial, district, and municipal-level representative bodies (*maslikhats*) vis-a-vis the executive local authorities (*akimats*) (Makhmutova, 2001).

The 1992 presidential decree on "Improving the Organization and Activities of Public Administration Bodies Under the Conditions of Economic Reform" initiated the centralization of executive power, creating centrally appointed provincial, district, and municipal-level executives (*akims*) who became the agents of the central administration (national ministries) and were made directly accountable to the executive higher-ups (provincial and district-level *akims* and the president). As a result, the heads of the local executive institutions were transformed into local administrative institutions of the central government with few mechanisms of public accountability to the local population and the corresponding legislative bodies (Bhuiyan and Amagoh, 2011). Although starting in the mid-2000s Kazakhstan enacted a series of public service reforms that aimed at decentralizing public service provision, these failed to establish mechanisms of public accountability and retained the direct mechanisms of central control over regional and local authorities (Bhuiyan, 2010).

Both the legislative and the executive branches have the power of legislative initiative. Most of the enacted national laws, however, originate in the government or specialized agencies. Mandatory regulatory orders and directives of provincial and executive authorities often reflect changes in national regulatory policy initiated by the central executive institutions. Provincial administrative authorities, however, have more limited powers to introduce legislative proposals. *Akims* prepare regional budgets, submit zoning and land-use plans, and initiate provincial borrowing (January 23, 2001, law "On Local State Governance and Self-Governance in the Republic of Kazakhstan" #148-II). *Maslikhats* have substantial organizational resources to review and amend such proposals before approving them. Regional assemblies form permanent and ad hoc committees and employ professional staff. Provincial representatives receive monetary compensation. A large proportion of provincial legislation is initiated by changes in national law necessitating harmonization and local adaptation. Other statutory regulations are driven by local demands. The apolitical stance of provincial *maslikhats* is reflected in the technical language of their adopted statutes.[81]

---

[81] These are called "decisions," while the term "law" is reserved for the national-level legislative statutes.

A typical provincial regulatory statute has a long descriptive title and a preamble that stipulates the legal origins of the regulation with obligatory references to other national and regional statutes it replaces, amends, or clarifies. The preamble also stipulates the purpose of the regulation, but it does so in highly standardized legal language. Preambles appear to be the most uniform part of the statutes in terms of their form as well as their length.[82] The body of a typical regional statute is written in dry legal jargon. In the area of economic regulation, this mainly includes technical description of the subject, with explicit definitions for the terms included in the text. Lastly, with very few exceptions, regulatory statutes are concluded with a description of the implementation process. Some of this may be as short as "*maslikhat* charges [the executive branch institution] with the implementation of [this decision]," or they may contain a lengthy and detailed description of administrative procedures. Unlike the communist-era constitutions and some national-level post-communist laws used as outlets for political rhetoric, provincial economic regulations in Kazakhstan are not written as political statements. Their texts are dry, legalistic, and technical and often hard to comprehend for people outside of the legal profession.[83]

Despite the centralization and concentration of the executive power, local representative institutions continue to carry out their legislative functions and are responsible for over 65 percent of all statutory regulation passed in Kazakhstan since its independence. In contrast, executive orders issued by local *akims*, although more frequent, account for only 16 percent of all executive regulations. This highlights the fundamental difference between local executive (administrative) and legislative rulemaking. Lacking direct mechanisms of implementation, *maslikhats* have relied on the administrative resources of local executives (*akims*), but have faced the classical principal-agent problem stemming from their inability to discipline the discretionary behavior of the executive authorities. *Maslikhats* do not have other methods of disciplining regional *akims* besides statutory mechanisms.

---

[82] The length of a preamble does not increase with the total length of the regulation. The variance in the length of regional statutes, therefore, is not driven by the description of their expected merits or the legislators' political agenda. This makes the length of regulatory documents reflective of the amount of detail the legislators put into describing their content and implementation.

[83] Laws in the spheres of language use, education, civil society, media, and social policy that are more politically sensitive and symbolically important, on the other hand, tend to have a declarative nature. These are more likely to contain political rhetoric. Over the course of my field research, nearly one in three business owners I interviewed spontaneously ventured comments on the importance of legal training and expertise. To my follow-up questions, nearly all of these respondents referenced specialized legal language used in required business, tax, and compliance documentation.

By writing more-specific laws, provincial representative bodies create formal constraints that legally bind the behavior of regional regulatory officials. This potentially may restrict regional executive discretion. At the same time, *akimats* have produced numerous regulatory documents. Not being institutionally separated from the street-level bureaucrats who implement these bylaws, executive orders may or may not limit administrative discretion. By comparing the economic effects of administrative bylaws to those of local legislative regulations later in the chapter, I will shed more light on the issue.

Reforms of Economic Governance

Among the post-Soviet states, Kazakhstan stands as a case of rapid market liberalization and successful post-transition recovery. The country was the first of the former USSR countries to reform its pension system, successfully modernize its financial and banking systems, demonopolize public utilities, and cardinally reshape the state's role in the economy.[84] Kazakhstan's reforms of regulatory policy and governance institutions to a large extent were guided by the neoliberal and institution-building agenda of international economic organizations advocating "the best practice" institutions and policies to maximize the developmental objectives and minimize government involvement in the economy.[85] At the policy-setting stage, the central theme of the Kazakhstan 2050 Strategy, for example, was formulated around the developmental criteria of the World Economic Forum Global Competitiveness Index (GCI) and the World Bank Doing Business Index (DBI).

My analysis of legally binding official documents shows that the GCI and DBI became part of the Kazakh government's strategic planning process shortly after each index started issuing its ratings for Kazakhstan in 2004 and 2006, respectively.[86] From 2004–2007, government documents reference the GCI and DBI in terms of broad policy objectives. Starting in 2008, all

---

[84] Chapter 6 discusses Kazakhstan's record of economic reforms and surveys its major deregulation initiatives.

[85] Research on the politics of international rankings has identified several mechanisms of such influence, ranging from normative diffusion and social pressure to the rational strategies of dismissal, lobbying, or "teaching to the test"(Cooley and Snyder, 2015).

[86] In December 2019, the *zakon.kz* internet portal, which archives Kazakh news publications and officially published government documents, contained 7,468 entries for GCI and over 13,000 entries mentioning DBI.

economic strategic plans by the government formulated their performance goals in terms of the GCI and DBI indicators, setting these indices as objective targets for policy and institutional changes. In 2013, the government directly ordered regulatory agencies to follow specific policy and institutional targets deemed beneficial by the international developmental organizations, such as cutting the number of inspections, simplifying tax compliance procedures, and reducing the length of time to clear customs forms. In 2014, ministerial orders specified GCI and DBI rankings as the primary method for evaluating state executive agencies' performance. Starting in 2016, performance evaluation of various government agencies has been tied to the GCI or DBI in very specific ways, including formulas to incorporate error terms as part of targets set for the government agencies.[87]

In 2008, Prime Minister Karim Masimov assigned the responsibility for maintaining relationships with specific ranking and rating organizations to different state agencies. Twenty specific quantitative indicators were developed by the World Bank (WB), World Economic Forum, United Nations, Transparency International, Freedom House, Economist Intelligence Unit, Heritage Foundation, Reporters Sans Frontiers, and other international organizations. They were then divided among the Ministries of National Economy, Finance, Industry and Trade, Foreign Affairs, Interior, Justice, and Health; Civil Service Agency; Statistical Agency; Institute for Economic Research; Antimonopoly Agency; and others (Prime Minister's Order #162-p, December 6, 2008). A special working group that included officials from key ministries, quasi-governmental organizations, and private sector consultants, including those working on USAID-sponsored projects, was tasked with developing recommendations for state agencies. The resulting proposals became the basis for the government's directives to the ministries, agencies, and quasi-governmental organizations (Akorda.kz, 2017).

A 2013 interview with the chair of the Customs Committee of the Finance Ministry, Igor Ten (*Zakon.kz*, 2013), exemplifies ways in which bureaucrats embed international rankings in their administrative routines. In 2013, the prime minister issued five directives concerning customs regulations. The chief customs officer demonstrated a detailed understanding of research

---

[87] Kazakhstan is not the only country attempting to game the international economic rankings. An edited volume by Cooley and Snyder (2015) documents how countries around the world "teach to the test" in an attempt to acquire higher rankings and more favorable investment outlooks. The country of Georgia leaped from thirty-fifth percentile to the ninety-second percentile in DBI rankings between 2006 and 2009 and emerged as an absolute champion in "gaming the rankings" (Schueth, 2015).

methodologies underpinning DBI, GCI, and the WB Logistics Performance Index's three indicators assigned to his agency. He dismissed some international advice as unfair or unattainable but identified areas in which many quick and cost-effective changes would be achieved.

Strategic goals set in terms of rankings and ratings promote deregulatory initiatives, legislative changes, and improvements in policy implementation mechanisms. This often results in genuine reduction of the formal regulatory burden. Specifics of policy and institutional choices, however, often appear incoherent and fall short of improving the business climate. Despite continuing efforts, Kazakhstan's GCI and DBI scores fail to approach the levels of well-governed countries. In 2015, the Ministry of Justice's department of legal analysis concluded that while the deregulatory legislation improved the country's ranking, the perception-based indicators of business climate did not track deregulatory changes and depressed the country's overall rating (Ordabaiev, 2016).[88] Evidently, despite all the deregulatory initiatives, managers of Kazakh companies did not feel there had been significant improvements in the regulatory climate. Implementation of state regulatory policy continues to deviate from the stated policy objectives as the bureaucrats manage to hit the deregulation targets in areas least relevant to business operation.[89] While the deregulation reforms of the past two decades in Kazakhstan produced a more liberal, consistent, and formalized regulatory regime, the continuing regulatory hurdles and corruption point to poor enforcement and official abuse as the major problem. Quoting a female owner of a real estate brokerage firm from Taldykorgan, "We have good laws, the problem is they don't work" (Interview #17, July 2021).

In the words of well-known Kazakh legal expert and public activist Bakytzhan Bazarbek, "Two problems [exist]: underdeveloped legal norms, plus the difficulty in using the legal system to enforce existing legal norms." Bazarbek explains that in the area of land use and property rights, these two

---

[88] The GCI, for instance, is based on 114 different components, 34 of which are based on "hard" statistics, while the other 80 components, primarily assessing institutional and policy effectiveness, are based on expert opinion and surveys of top managers of large and medium enterprises operating in the local markets. On average, the GCI surveys cover 80–120 randomly selected Kazakhstani companies.

[89] A telling example is the outstanding progress made in streamlining maritime regulatory procedures, such as marine vessel title registration, certification, and inspection. However, for a landlocked country, low regulatory burden in maritime commerce is unlikely to constitute a noticeable improvement in the overall business climate. The country has lost its fishing and water transportation in the drying Aral Sea. It has only one Caspian port (Aktau) that does not freeze in winter, and the 12-vessel Caspian commercial fleet accounts for less than 1 percent of its freight volume (Sakenov, 2018).

problems undercut the interests of farmers, small business owners, and average citizens. Enforcement in the area of land use depends on litigation by the local *akims* who manage municipal and village property. However, *akims* are not interested in preserving communal land, but often advance the interests of private companies owned by their friends and relatives or bribe-paying outsiders. "Having formal regulations and the paper trail of administrative decisions allows us to rectify wrong-doing and restore illegally alienated communal property, so that corruption would not perpetually benefit the private interests," continues Bazarbek (*Kun.kz*, 2021).

To illustrate the importance of well-enforced laws and regulations, Bazarbek cited the stand-off between the residents of a new high-rise apartment building and Almaty Kasteev Art Museum. In 2020, the 16-story Central Esentai Residence apartment complex was built in the immediate proximity to the Kasteev museum, which was constructed in 1976. In the spring of 2021, the new residents complained to city authorities about noise produced by the museum's rooftop air conditioning unit. The Committee of Sanitary and Epidemiological Control determined the museum was violating safety standards and should remove its air conditioning unit from the rooftop (*Sputnik Kazakhstan*, 2021). The museum's authorities claimed the museum is not liable because the developer of the apartment complex did not follow the city's technical regulations on easements. The museum, they argued, is a monument of history and culture; therefore, according to the law, it should be surrounded by a 44-meter easement. The Esentai Residence apartment building was illegally constructed within a 38-meter distance from the museum. Corruption in the city administration allowed the developer to obtain the permit for illegal construction. The city authorities responsible for protecting public property not only allowed the wrongful action, but also intervened to violate legally protected rights of a public entity.

Administrative and Civil Service Reforms

Kazakh public administration has roots in the Soviet command-administrative bureaucratic apparatus. As one of the Soviet republics, the country had a hierarchically organized republican ministerial structure that largely paralleled the central bureaucratic institutions of the USSR (Olcott, 2002). The bureaucratic hierarchy was organized on territorial principles with provincial, district, city, and local (municipal or village) administrations reporting to the higher-level authorities, ministries, and central agencies. In the first years following its independence, Kazakhstan relied on the preexisting bureaucratic apparatus, making symbolic and personnel adjustments such as the introduction of Kazakh as the state language and the redrawing of administrative lines to reduce the number of provinces.

A plan for comprehensive administrative reform was first introduced by the president in 1997 in his ambitious and controversial "Strategy for the Development of Kazakhstan until 2030."[90] Item 24 of this long-term developmental program lists administrative reforms and modernization of governance as the nation's strategic priorities. The "Strategy" calls for the new civil service to be organized on the principles of "corporate governance," goal-oriented missions, transparency, and accountability. These goals closely lined up with the goals advocated by international organizations that took a keen interest in supporting the civil service reforms that followed.[91]

The first round of bureaucratic reforms created bureaucratic structures and redefined intra-bureaucracy relations. In 1998, a new administrative unit, the Civil Service Affairs Agency, was created to supervise the implementation of reforms and collect and analyze relevant information (Turisbekov, 2006). The "Law on Fighting Corruption" (1998) was the first in a series of normative documents signaling the government's intention to discipline its civil servants. In 1999, the special government committee on administrative reform introduced a bill that soon was passed by the parliament. The new "Law on Civil Service" established a gradation of administrative positions. Different categories required differential levels of education and experience. The law broke down bureaucratic offices into political (to be nominated by the political authorities) and professional (career bureaucrats to be promoted on a meritocratic basis). It focused on intra-bureaucracy issues, including recruitment and promotion criteria, principles of subordination and appointment, and legal rights of career bureaucrats vis-a-vis their political masters and the public. In reality, the principles of meritocratic promotion remained mere declarations until 2003, when the competitive examination was introduced to fill available

---

[90] The archived copy is available at http://portal.mfa.kz/portal/page/portal/mfa/ru/content/reference_info/strategy2030.

[91] See, for example, EBRD Transition Reports, 1996–2003, OECD public governance and management program overview http://www.oecd.org/topic/0,3373,en_2649_37405_1_1_1_1_37405,00.html, and a series of World Bank publications on the issue of public service available at http://web.worldbank.org/WBSITE/EXTERNAL/WBI/WBIPROGRAMS and http://www1.worldbank.org/prem/acr/ad.html.

civil service positions (Turisbekov, 2006). In 2005, the Bureaucratic Honor
Code codified the professional ethics principles without providing clear
institutional mechanisms for their enforcement.

The initial reforms did not accomplish their stated objectives. Career
bureaucrats continued to depend on the political appointees, bureaucrats'
performance was not judged on the basis of customer satisfaction, and the
inner workings of bureaucratic agencies remained closed to societal supervision (Kozhakhmetov, 2007). Despite the ongoing administrative reform,
Kazakhstan's ratings for governance and corruption control went down.
According to the World Bank, in the period between 1996 and 2004, Kazakhstan's accountability score dropped from −.93 to −1.03,[92] its corruption
control indicator decreased from −.92 to −1.17, and the regulatory quality
indicator decreased from −.35 to −.63. (See Figure 11).

The 2005 presidential decree and amendments to the "Law on Civil
Service" marked the second stage in the Kazakh administrative reform.

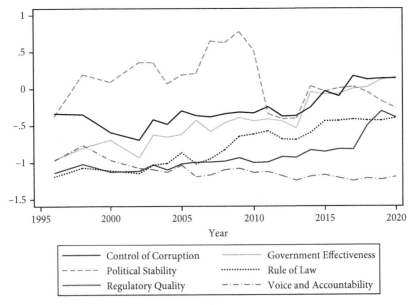

Figure 11 World Bank Governance Indicators

Note: The WB Worldwide Governance Indicators score six dimensions of governance based on
about 30 underlying data sources. The indicators for each dimension of governance range from
−2.5 to 2.5, with higher values corresponding to better outcomes.

---

[92] Ranging from −2.5 to 2.5, with the mean at zero. Greater negative numbers indicate worse
conditions.

International and domestic criticism of the increasing levels of corruption in Kazakh politics and public institutions reinvigorated the administrative reform efforts that now followed the anticorruption rhetoric. The 2005 amendments strengthened administrative and criminal penalties for corruption. Now, not only could persons found guilty of corruption no longer occupy political or administrative positions, but those who hired past offenders could actually be prosecuted. Critics saw these drastic measures as intended to increase the political control over bureaucracy on the eve of the approaching presidential elections (Kozhakhmetov, 2007). Many opposition leaders of that time held administrative positions in the past and might have built strong support in various echelons of state bureaucracy. Hence it was particularly important for the ruling elite to establish a strong control over civil service and deter the state bureaucracy from endorsing Nazarbayev's political rivals (Kyzylkulova, 2007; Ashimbaev, 2008).

Yet another component of the second-stage reform was introduced by the 2007 Presidential Order #372 "On the Status and Charge of Executive Secretary . . ." It created new mechanisms of interaction between political and administrative tiers of the executive branch. The new position of executive secretary was introduced in all ministries and agencies, to be appointed directly by the president. The responsibilities of the new executive secretaries included a broad range of issues of appointment, promotion, and material reward. Unlike the ministers and other political appointees, executive secretaries would not be required to resign at the time of governmental re-shuffles and would be answerable directly to the president. Closely resembling the Soviet-era party secretaries, presidentially appointed political secretaries were to fill key administrative positions in their corresponding institutions and agencies. The introduction of this new political position was rationalized on the basis of promotion of collegiality, professionalism, and reduction of nepotism, but in reality, it increased the number of bureaucrats directly appointed by the president and not subjected to the entrance exams, promotion rules, and other bureaucratic and public controls. It also placed career bureaucrats under greater dependence from the political authorities, thereby strengthening, centralizing, and personalizing the executive branch. Executive secretaries remained an effective mechanism of political control over the central bureaucracy until January 2021, when the position was abolished by President Tokayev's order #495.

Kazakhstan's administrative reforms of 1998–2007 resulted in an increasing concentration of the chief executive's power over bureaucratic hierarchy.

This was done through (1) a reduction of the number of bureaucratic agencies and reshuffling of their personnel, (2) the introduction of political appointees directly answerable to the president and possessing extensive powers over career bureaucrats, and (3) an increase in the severity of anticorruption measures that could easily be used to silence any dissent originating in the state bureaucracy. At the same time, there is little evidence that economic, societal, and political outcomes usually associated with the term "good governance" have followed the decade-long administrative reform. Civil service reforms have generally failed to build bureaucracies well equipped for serving the public. Although initially the reforms reduced the number of civil servants, according to the State Statistics Bureau, between 2016 and 2020 their ranks grew by 3 percent to 489,000 people.[93] The strengthening of the top executive's control of bureaucracy and further entrenchment of the Kazakh authoritarian regime was accomplished at the expense of public accountability, independence from political interference, legal protection of public officials, and professionalism. Paradoxically, these reforms promoted state-building and streamlined the system of public administration. However, they did it in a way that made public officials dependent on the central political power of the executive branch and promoted bureaucrats' political loyalty to the regime.[94]

Development of the Regulatory Corpus

The process of redefining the state's role in the economy was formally accomplished through redrawing the "rules of engagement" that define activities and powers of state agencies vis-a-vis companies and individuals and establish a legal foundation for economic activities. For Kazakhstan, the writing of new laws and setting up of new state institutions meant a validation of its

---

[93] This is a fraction of Russia's 2.3 million, Germany's 4.9 million, and France's 5.6 million civil servants. In per capita terms, for every 100 people there are 2.4 civil servants in Kazakhstan, 1.6 in Russia, 5.9 in Germany, and 8 in France.

[94] It should be recognized that some reforms are never intended to achieve their proclaimed goals. Popular rhetoric might conveniently mask unpopular initiatives or legitimate unacceptable costs. In this respect, the regime-sensitive definitions of state-building (Grzymala-Busse and Jones Luong, 2002) might offer a better analytical tool for making sense of the trajectories of authoritarian reforms. This conclusion generally follows Robinson's intuition that politicians often have other goals besides those they publicly proclaim, and it is important to take these goals into account (Robinson, 2003). It appears from this analysis that in designing bureaucratic reform programs, Kazakhstan's rulers were interested in building the state they want to govern but not necessarily a state that governs itself well.

claims for independent statehood. Shedding the old Soviet-era norms meant not only rewriting laws for the capitalist economy, it also meant writing new laws and regulations in the national language, which left the specialized agencies with some freedom to depart from Soviet-era patterns.

While regulatory policy principles were the purview of the government and legislatures, technical aspects of regulation were developed by the specialized state and commercial agencies with roots in the Soviet institutions. Design Institute Almatygiprogor-1, LLP—a successor to the Soviet-era design institute Almatygiprogor—exemplifies the origins of technical regulatory expertise in post-independence Kazakhstan. The State Design Institute Almatygiprogor was founded in 1967 to design standard architectural plans and develop norms and regulations for residential and communal construction and supporting infrastructure. The standard Soviet practice was for the same state-owned engineering organization to develop regulatory norms and design standard architectural plans. Almatygiprogor was the flagship organization in the capital of the Kazakh Soviet Republic. The institute was part of the all-Soviet network of similar organizations that designed detailed technical standards (*stroitel'nye normy i pravila*, or SNiPs). SNiPs were often developed in conjunction with and by the same engineers who produced standard construction blueprints for the Soviet construction industry.

With the collapse of the USSR, the network of research institutions disintegrated and the state financing of the Almaty institute came to an end. According to a retired division manager of the institute, technical documentation archives of Almatygiprogor were preserved thanks to the "professional duty of a handful of dedicated staff and the institute director, who survived the hungry 1990s by working odd jobs and renting out the institute's premises to commercial firms" (Interview #18, July 2021). The manager was in the middle of her career during the late 1990s. She reported receiving no salary for months at a time but showing up to work "because somebody needed to preserve technical documentation . . . , we knew it will be needed once construction projects resume." The dedicated staff of the Almatygiprogor were right about that. As the transitional recession turned into the construction boom of the 2000s, the institute reorganized itself as a private architectural design company. "Instead of three large [Soviet] construction companies with three architectural teams, there was now a dozen small firms trying to design buildings that would pass official code inspections. They all needed access to SNiPs and would pay good money for standard architectural designs." Such standard architectural plans could be customized to fit specific project requirements at a fraction of the cost for new engineering. "It was like the Klondike gold rush," she recollected; "I had to go to Astana and other cities to sell copies of our technical documentation on a regular basis."

At the same time, as the country's legislature started replacing Soviet-era laws and regulatory norms with the new legal corpus, the institute's archive became the major source of "new" technical regulatory norms. "We did a lot of translation to Kazakh from the old Soviet documents, modifying some outdated norms with references to modern equipment and construction materials. Our expertise was most needed for such work," said the Almatygiprogor manager (Interview #18, July 2021). Although the collapse of the USSR and rewriting of regulatory norms was a break from the past, the example of Almatygiprogor shows that the development of technical standards was incremental and drew heavily from the preexisting Soviet standards and technical expertise.

Quantifying Regulatory Change

With the help of the Republican Center for Legal Information (RCLI) under the Ministry of Justice of the Republic of Kazakhstan (http://rkao.kz/), an official state legal information service based in Astana, I traced the development of laws and other compulsory regulatory documents that formally redefined the relationships between state institutions and the economy from the early stages of privatization and economic liberalization to 2019. The RCLI maintains a comprehensive collection of legal documents issued by all public authorities in Kazakhstan since 1948. It was assembled directly from the archives of the Ministry of Justice, covering 37 thematic sections of national and local legislation. In February 2019, the RCLI dataset contained 112,951 documents classified as relating to economic relations. Of those, 111,190 documents originated in Kazakh institutions of power, and 1,761 were binding international regulations related to Kazakhstan's membership in the Commonwealth of Independent States, Eurasian Economic Union (EAEU), and other organizations.[95] Nearly all of these documents (98 percent) were adopted after 1991.

From the meta-data I identified 17,496 legislative statutes related to economic policy, including accounting, banking, and currency regulations;

---

[95] Documents in the areas of social security, education, constitutional law, state honors, defense, security, courts, criminal law, family law, natural disaster declarations, immigration, and culture

customs and export/import operations; securities regulation; use of residential and non-residential premises; utilities; land use; environmental regulations; natural resources; sectoral policy; labor relations; and "general" rules of incorporation, bankruptcy, and business licensing. The national legislature is responsible for 2,485, or 32 percent, of these laws, with the rest adopted by (elected) provincial, city, township, and village-level legislative assemblies or councils. The dataset also contains 34,573 executive orders. Of these, 28,799, or 83 percent, of all economic executive orders were issued by national-level authorities (the president, presidential administration, premier, cabinet, and ministries).

Chapter 5, which scrutinizes the political foundations of regulatory system development, presents data on the regulatory corpus developed by the Kazakh institutions of central government, including the president, national legislature, government, ministries, and specialized state agencies that jointly account for 53,828, documents, or 48 percent of the total number of economic regulations. The rest of the dataset's documents originated in the provincial-, city-, district-, and *auyl-* (village) level *akimats* or *maslikhats*. I nested the city- and district-level regulations within the corresponding provinces to account for the fact that some types of economic activities (industry, environment, agriculture, utilities) are regulated at the city or rural district levels. For the statistical analysis performed later in the chapter, I only consider regulatory documents issued by provincial, city, and administrative district authorities. Because I am not taking into account indicators of agricultural economic activity, I exclude village-level (*auyl*) regulatory documents. Moreover, administrative and representative authority largely overlap at the village level, which makes it harder to trace the separate effects of statutory and executive branch regulations. As a result, I empirically analyze 30,155 economy-related provincial, city, and district regulatory documents.

Of 30,155 legal documents issued by local authorities on subjects related to economic relationships, 2,481 pertained to general business regulation

were excluded from my analysis. Yet many documents are classified in ways that span at least two issue areas. Documents that regulate education, for example, may be included in the analysis if they also regulate licensing, building code requirements, or taxation of the institutions of education because such documents will also be classified as economic. To give a specific example, the April 26, 2006, decision of the *maslikhat* of Kostanai province, "On Approving the Regional Anticorruption Program in Kostanai Province for 2006–2010," had not been included in the database because it is classified as a criminal law and related to security. It did not contain specific economic regulations. The March 24, 2005, ruling of Ustkaman *akimat*, "On Approving the Rules for Accepting Waste Water in the Sewage System of Ustkaman City," is classified as housing and utilities and is included in my analysis because it regulates business access to city utilities. I also exclude regulatory documents of the EAEU because these are part of international law.

(rules of incorporation, licensing, bankruptcy); 15,121, accounting and finance; 5,936, labor relations; 1,592, agriculture-related activities; 1,150, housing and utilities; 1,087, environment and conservation; and 849, public health, veterinary, and sanitation requirements. In the provincial regulatory corpus, 600 documents regulated land use; 448, transport; 246, property rights (mostly privatization and communal property use); 207, the construction industry; 161, trade and food services; 79, subsoil resource use; and 44, industry. Given the fundamental nature of such regulation, the activities of regional authorities matter greatly for business actors.

The oldest subnational document recorded in the RCLI database was issued by the *akimat* of Zhambyl province in March 1997. The dataset contains not only the number of legal documents, but also the full text of each, which allowed me to quantify the amount of regulatory detail. Between 1997 and the beginning of 2019, subnational authorities added a total of 1,780 million new words to the regulatory corpus. I construct a panel dataset that records the number and length of various types of subnational regulations in effect in 14 Kazakh provinces and the two separately administered cities of Almaty and Astana in any given year. Figure 12 shows the variation in the average number and length of active regulations by province between 1996 and 2018. The distribution of regional statutory and executive regulations is highly uneven.

My field research revealed several possible sources of regional variation in legislative and executive rulemaking and regulatory specificity. Although executive provincial institutions are highly uniform in terms of their internal organization, provincial assemblies follow different sets of internal procedural rules that affect legislative output (author's interview with Abiken Toktybekov, director of the Institute of State and Local Government, Almaty, Kazakhstan, November 1, 2013). Two former regional *maslikhat* deputies commented on the different levels of sophistication of *maslikhat* deliberations in their respective provinces. Although my respondents were not aware of cross-provincial differences in lengths and details of regulations, they were eager to report that some provincial *maslikhats* produce "better" rulings because of the higher expertise of their deputies and staff and because of input from deputies who have personal stakes in specific areas of regulation. Less active and "conscientious" (*soznatel'nye*) deputies were seen as rubber-stampers for the executive branch initiatives (Interview #4, November 2013; Interview #21, December 2018). Figure 13 shows the overtime regulatory output by province over the analyzed period. Although the total output level

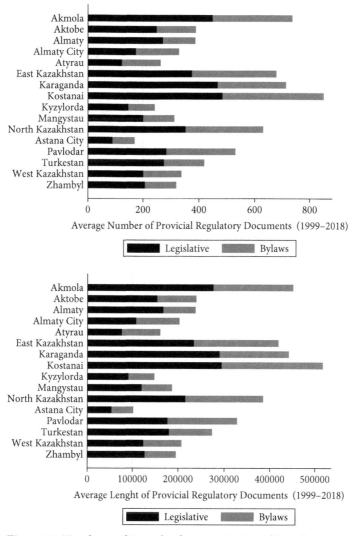

Figure 12 Number and Length of Active Provincial Regulatory Documents, 1996–2018 Average

Source: Republican Center for Legal Information (RCLI)

varied greatly across subnational units, most provinces experienced a rapid rise in regulatory output in the mid-2000s. This corresponds to the period of accelerated regulatory and civil service reforms.

The RCLI dataset records when statutory and executive regulations go into effect and when they are terminated. This allows researchers to consider only those regulations that are in force in a given year. Figure 14 documents a

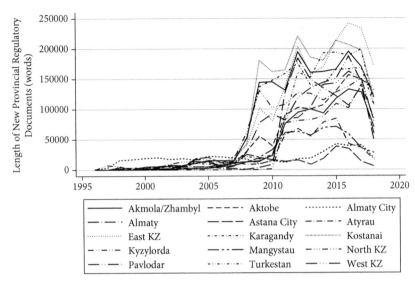

Figure 13 Total Length of New Regional Regulatory Documents in Words

Source: Republican Center for Legal Information (RCLI)

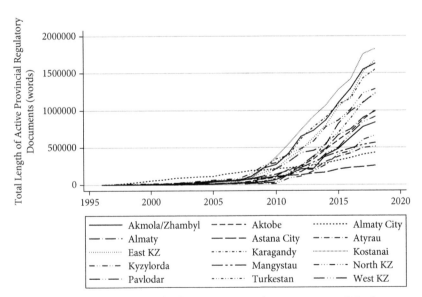

Figure 14 Cumulative Length of Active Regional Documents in Words

Source: Republican Center for Legal Information (RCLI)

steady growth of the compulsory subnational economic regulatory corpus. Consecutive waves of regulatory reforms did replace some of the older regulations, but more importantly, they significantly expanded the total number and length of formal state regulations of economic activity.

Assessing Bureaucratic Discretion

To capture the extent of bureaucratic discretion in implementing regulatory policy, I follow the empirical methodology developed by Huber et al. (2001) and Huber and Shipan (2002). These authors quantitatively analyzed regulatory statutes, arguing that detailed statutory law yields lesser discretion. In defending their methodology, Huber et al. (2001) made a convincing case, writing:

> It takes a great many more words for the legislature to specify who is to be covered, what sorts of enrollment techniques should be used, which procedures should be followed, and so on, than it does to simply ask the agency to "do something" without providing any additional instructions. Long bills with lots of words tend to specify these details, while short bills do not. More words imply more precise instructions to the agency, and thus less discretion (p. 337).

The same approach to measuring statutory constraint has led Randazzo et al. (2006) and Randazzo et al. (2011) to conclude that longer laws tend to reduce the extent of judicial discretion as well.[96]

This logic holds for Kazakh statutory regulations. Although the content of regulations I examine here is different from that studied by Huber and Shipan (2002), the mechanisms of regulatory frameworks generally follow the same patterns. The content analysis of Kazakh provincial and municipal regulations shows that longer laws contain more detailed descriptions of who should be subjected to regulations, how regulations should be applied, and what techniques should be used in the process. Detailed and specific legislative statutes make it more difficult for administrative authorities to enact

---

[96] Earlier works on public administration also used the count of statutory documents produced by government departments and number of pages of agency-created compulsory regulations as measures of bureaucratic output (Hood and Dunsire, 1981). Appendix D further investigates the construct validity of the proposed measure.

regulatory policies that differ from those that local legislators prefer. More concise regional statutes, on the contrary, explicitly or implicitly empower regulatory agencies to take an active role in designing and implementing regulatory policy of their own.

For example, one of the shortest regulations enacted in Almaty province is a 109-word regulation of gaming businesses. The law explicitly delegated the tasks of making and enforcing new casino zoning regulations to the executive agency. The lack of constraining details allowed the provincial bureaucrats to draft the boundaries of the newly established casino park in a way that closely traced the property boundaries of a well-connected land magnate, who used the newly acquired monopoly to drive competitors out of business (Mikhailova, 2006). An 11,082-word building code adopted in Kostanai, on the other hand, contains specific technical requirements that leave very little room for inconsistent interpretation and bureaucratic rulemaking.[97]

Even when a law does not explicitly empower the bureaucracy to engage in regulatory rulemaking, the lack of statutory detail often leads to ambiguities and confusion that necessitate the clarification of administrative bylaws. This not only empowers the bureaucracy to engage in administrative rulemaking, but also, in the absence of public accountability, may lead to bureaucratic preferentialism and corruption.[98] The 2010 building code enacted in the southern province of Kyzylorda is half the length of its counterpart regulation adopted in 2009 in the northern province of Kostanai. It concisely outlines the general regulatory guidelines and lacks specific standards and enforcement mechanisms. The details of construction regulations in Kyzylorda province are determined by administrative bylaws that were subsequently developed by the provincial bureaucracy. This gives provincial bureaucrats a lot of leeway in pursuing their own regulatory priorities.

---

[97] Section 2.8.2 (Construction site and materials transportation requirements), subsection 116, for example, stipulates "along the perimeter of the construction site the contractor should erect a fence made of unpainted horizontally profiled galvanized steel sheets, no less than two meters in height. The fence is to be constructed within one month of [executing] the contract of sale or land use and before the architecture and planning assignment." This detailed description rules out alternative interpretations of what makes an appropriate construction site fence and prevents regulatory agencies from imposing arbitrary, contradictory, or volatile standards. A shorter Kyzylorda statute, in comparison, contains no explicit requirements, but states "construction sites should be properly fenced."

[98] Reports indicate that "the most widespread form of corruption in Kazakhstan is administrative, including routine extortion and shadow control of companies by unelected officials" (Transparency International, 2012).

Another mechanism through which more detailed regulatory statutes can limit bureaucrats' power is by establishing unambiguous benchmarks for monitoring regulatory compliance. Detailed specification of regulatory standards, technical requirements, fee schedules, and compliance criteria can make it easier for the regulated firm to demonstrate compliance. A clear statutory norm detailing fee or tax schedules, containing a standard license application form, or specifying regulatory inspection procedures can alter the amount of power bureaucrats have vis-a-vis the firms. The more details the law codifies, the fewer ambiguities will result when determining whether the firm complies with regulations. Absence of clear implementation and enforcement procedures, on the other hand, creates a regulatory vacuum, which may lead to administrative impunity.

The 2003 Pavlodar "Law on Rules for Manufacturing, Exploitation, and Distribution of Heating Equipment and Energy," for example, codifies the maximum processing time for issuing manufacturing licenses, which effectively limits the regulator's ability to impose additional costs on businesses by delaying official authorizations. Article 3.11 states: "The license is to be issued no later than one month period, or 10 days for the subjects of small entrepreneurship, after the date of application supported by all aforementioned required documents."

It appears that long laws tend to limit bureaucratic discretion through two mechanisms. One such mechanism is that they offer bureaucrats fewer opportunities to engage in ad hoc rule interpretation that may alter a firm's regulatory environment. The other is that detailed statutes reduce ambiguity in regulatory implementation and establish clear benchmarks for determining regulatory compliance. The latter aspect makes it easier for the firms and state prosecutors to detect misapplication of regulatory policy by bureaucrats colluding with the industry or preying upon vulnerable businesses.[99] These considerations inform the decision to use the overall length of statutory regulations as a proxy for the amount of discretionary power they bestow on bureaucrats. Longer, more detailed laws are expected to (1) create fewer opportunities for the bureaucrats to engage in inconsistent rule application and (2) establish mechanisms of redress against bureaucratic misinterpretation and abuse of economic regulations.[100]

---

[99] This might not be of high relevance in common-law legal systems, where courts have greater freedom in establishing the legality of specific actions. In civil law, which Kazakhstan follows, the codified principles are essential in establishing administrative violations.

[100] One can think about statutory specificity through the logic of complete and incomplete contracting. At the most superficial level, specific statutes reduce the amount of incomplete information

Testing Economic Effects of Discretion

Hypothesis 4 in Chapter 1 posits a direct negative effect of bureaucratic discretion on economic outcomes. Conversely, the discretion-limiting features of a state regulatory system, such as detailed formal rules of engagement, should promote economic performance. Because the official regulatory system is shaped by statutory regulations as well as executive orders, I use the specificity of both to gauge bureaucratic discretion (constraint). As a result, I rely on a numeric count of regulatory statutes and administrative directives issued by the local representative and administrative authorities.[101] Although these local regulations constitute only a subset of all official regulatory documentation, the national-level regulations apply equally to all parts of the country and can be treated as having a more uniform effect. Because national-level policy initiatives may prioritize certain regions or regionally specific industries and exploit others, I have decided to concentrate my analysis on economic outcomes that are least location-specific: internally generated investment and SME sector development. Self-financed investment can be carried out by firms lacking access to external finance options, so it does not discriminate based on a firm's proximity to financial centers. The SME sector mostly serves local needs. When it comes to the region-specific effects, the SME-directed central government policy is more uniform than policy targeting the geographically concentrated agriculture-, energy-, or mining- sector firms. This further justifies my assumption about uniform effects of national- level regulatory documents.

In what follows, I conduct statistical analyses using a cross-sectional, time-series dataset of regional regulatory statutes, administrative directives, and economic indicators that are available for the 14 Kazakh provinces and special-status cities of Almaty and Astana. In addition to variation in the specificity of regulatory documents, provinces also display variation along

---

contracting. A more sophisticated analysis also would suggest they facilitate effective delegation and renegotiation of organizational responsibility and performance expectations. See Li, 2013 for a literature review on the topic.

[101] Clearly, a notion that more rules equal more constraints is an oversimplification. The content of regulations matters greatly, but variation in regulatory policy objectives and firm- and sector-specific conditions makes it hard to establish *a priori* expectations as to what regulations matter more. With no prior expectations about the types of economic regulations that affect firms the most, I make use of the total length of all economic regulations across various aspects of regulatory intervention. This broad measure contains a lot of noise and potentially biases the results in favor of the null hypothesis. Because I remain skeptical of the ability of local executive orders to constrain local regulatory implementation mechanisms, I split regulations into statutory on the one hand and administrative and executive (bylaws) on the other.

a number of economic outcomes, such as investment and development of the small business sector. These patterns of variation provide fertile ground for considering the relationship between the regulatory environment and business activity. In respect to the effects of discretionary bureaucratic power in implementing official rules and regulations, the theoretical argument developed in Chapter 1 allows me to evaluate the direction of bureaucratic discretionary bias empirically by observing whether $d \times c_r$—the actual cost of regulatory compliance, conceptualized as a product of the official regulatory burden (c_r) and discretionary application (d)—enters the aggregate economic performance function with a positive or negative sign. The theory suggests that the effects of discretion are conditional upon the extent of the regulatory burden; however, I lack subnational dynamic data accessing how liberal the regional economic policy was at different points in time. There are strong reasons to expect the overall direction of economic policy was more constant across regions and fluctuated with the changes in national policy, while the implementation regimes were more dependent on the lower-level subnational formal restrictions. In what follows, I use fixed-effect first- order autoregressive models to account for unobserved provincial-level effects and time dependence in dynamic series.

To capture provincial variation in economic performance, I consider investment in fixed capital and growth of small businesses. Capital investment and the small enterprise sector are central to the health of the market economy. The former indicator of economic performance reflects macroeconomic conditions. The latter reflects the micro-level environment. While capital investment is the engine of endogenous growth (Li, 2006), the small enterprise sector has been shown to be the engine of growth in employment and innovation (Storey, 1994). Theoretical arguments about the effects of state regulatory activity are of particular relevance to investment decisions and small enterprise development. Decisions to invest in fixed assets, as well as expand small businesses, reflect entrepreneurs' expectations about future macroeconomic performance and government economic policies and their expected effects. These are directly related to the official regulatory regimes and the ability of street-level bureaucrats to apply them in an effective and predictable manner.

In respect to bureaucratic discretion, the SME sector is a crucial case to investigate. On the one hand, the small business sector is extremely diverse, and its effective management may require specialized knowledge of local conditions and case-specific application of regulatory policy. This provides reasons for expecting that discretionary bureaucratic powers would positively affect the SME sector. On the other hand, SMEs are most vulnerable to any potential abuse of bureaucratic power. If bureaucrats choose to overstep their authority in a zealous pursuit of policy goals or reduce their workload by adopting half-measures, SMEs are the least likely source of trouble. High levels of fragmentation of managerial and financial resources makes a legal or political fight by SMEs against bureaucratic abuse less likely than in other sectors. Knowing that they can bend rules with impunity, bureaucrats might resort to corruption and predation to extort resources. Uneven enforcement may also prove destabilizing because it can give rise to regulatory uncertainty and hence impede establishment and development of SMEs.

In fact, SMEs' sensitivity to bureaucratic hurdles made them an economic priority of the government since the early years of independence.[102] The bureaucratic barriers on SMEs, nevertheless, continued to mount through the 1990s. In 2005, the government adopted "[t]he government program of accelerated measures for the development of small and medium-sized businesses in the Republic of Kazakhstan for 2005–2007" and allocated 29 billion Kazakh tenge (KZT) to support small businesses, 21,800 million of which were spent on direct financing of about 2,000 business projects. In 2010 and 2019 the government adopted comprehensive programs known as "Business Road Map 2020" and "Business Road Map 2025" aimed at improving the regulatory environment and reducing financial and infrastructural obstacles for SME development. Starting in the late 1990s, the SME development programs were implemented not by government agencies but by special government-financed foundations. These underwent several reorganizations in the 2000s.[103]

Despite Kazakhstan's dependence on natural resource sectors, the SME sector is extremely important for the health of the country's economy. According to the National Statistics Bureau, in 2020 it employed over

---

[102] On May 5, 1992, President Nazarbayev signed the decree "On the State Program for the Support and Development of Entrepreneurship in the Republic of Kazakhstan for 1992–1994," which was followed by the July 4, 1992 Law #1543-XII, "On the Protection and Support of Private Entrepreneurship."

[103] In 1997, to separate policymaking and policy-implementation authority in the SME sector, the government established the Small Business Development Foundation (Government Decree #665). In 2002, the foundation started a direct financial assistance program to support government initiatives in the SME sector. In 2006, the state-controlled joint stock company Kazyna Sustainable Development Foundation became a shareholder of the SME Development Foundation. Kazyna was later replaced by the national management holding company Baiterek. In 2007, it was renamed Damu (Growth) Entrepreneurship Development Foundation and continued to allocate direct loans to SMEs.

40 percent of the country's labor force, compared to 15 percent in the Russian Federation. In 2022 it also contributed 34.7 percent of the GDP (Satubaldina, 2022). SMEs dominate retail trade, some agricultural production, and personal services. Traditional bazaars to this date carry the lion's share of retail. The country's open-air and container markets are the major trade hubs of the Central Asian region. Small farmers and herders produce most food crops and meat. Personal service providers (nannies, drivers, barbers, and caterers) create the infrastructure for transforming oil rents into higher living standards of the population. SMEs account for the majority of preschool facilities. For the vast majority of Kazakh citizens, the health of the SME sector is of major economic consequence.

Modeling Fixed Capital Investment

I begin my empirical analysis by investigating how private investment in fixed capital responds to regulatory constraints. Domestic investment data are available for the following categories: government investment; investment financed by financial institutions, including domestic banks; and reinvested private sector profits, including previous savings generated by individual entrepreneurs. Private sector investment is captured by both financed and internal investments, but I choose the latter type of invested capital because it is a closer proxy for firms' confidence in the business climate. These data are measured in millions of current KZT.

Because investment in fixed capital depends on previous economic conditions, expected returns, and availability of complementary inputs, I control for several economic factors. Given the inverse relationship between consumption and investment, the "wealth effect" postulates that rates of investment often decline with wealth. As incomes grow, people prefer consumption over investment. Therefore, the model controls for regional per capita income (in constant KZT per capita). Inefficient and outdated technology may necessitate investment into the physical plant. To capture these concerns, the model includes the previous level of capitalization (cumulative past investment less depreciation). Central government investment in the regional economy increases the provision of public goods and may attract private capital to the region. To account for these confounding effects, the models include central government investment in the region. The structural composition of the regional economy may fundamentally affect investment patterns. To account for the potential trickling down of natural resource wealth, I include a measure of oil production (in thousand metric tons). I use the physical output measure because of its higher reliability.

I also control for the volume of regional trade, changes in unemployment, and the regional consumer price index (CPI). The number of university students controls for human capital and the quality of the labor force.[104] These controls capture conventional socioeconomic sources of business confidence: macroeconomic stability (CPI and unemployment), business opportunity (trade openness), and quality of human capital. Finally, I control for the number of operating businesses, which is based on the number of officially registered persons filing tax reports in a given year in a given region.

I consider two types of regulatory constraints: the total length of subnational legislative regulations and the total length of subnational executive and administrative regulations (bylaws). Both are normalized by the number of registered enterprises because a greater number of economic agents might require a more developed regulatory corpus. I also report models with nonnormalized measures of regulatory complexity. I model the relationships between regulatory detail and investment using province-level fixed effects and lagging all independent variables by one year. Longer lags do not change the results. Because current levels of investment are highly correlated with the previous levels, I model these relationships with a first-order autoregressive process. Table 2 contains the baseline results (controlling for the level of capitalization and oil economy only) in models 1 and 4, as well as full specification results. Results show that my measure of bureaucratic constraint (length of regulatory documents) has a consistently positive effect on self-financed private investment. The control variables enter the regression equation with the expected signs and statistically significant effects.

A 10-word increase in the length of the statutory regulation per firm produces a one-standard-deviation increase in capital investment. Only half of that increase in the length of bylaws would produce the same effect on investment. The results are robust to using the absolute values of the independent variable (not normalized by the number of firms). The estimated substantive effect of adding 100 words to regional statutory regulations, all

---

[104] A more conventional measure of human capital, university graduates, has major temporal inconsistencies. Because of the high concentration of four-year colleges and universities in the two major cities, I also estimate regressions with the number of professional school students and find similar results.

Table 2 Provincial Economic Regulations and Fixed Capital Investment, FE, RA(1)

	Regional Legislative Regulations			Regional Bylaws		
	Per Enterprise	Per Enterprise	Total Length	Per Enterprise	Per Enterprise	Total Length
	(1)	(2)	(3)	(4)	(5)	(6)
Specificity	4005	4542	.391	8801	9300	.707
	(1693)**	(1804)**	(.148)***	(2520)***	(2632)***	(.207)***
Length of regulations, words						
Natural Resource Wealth	77.111	52.753	53.076	78.115	54.045	53.071
	(5.952)***	(7.038)***	(7.034)***	(5.870)***	(6.926)***	(6.909)***
Annual oil production, 1,000 tons						
Wealth		51.505	82.754		62.665	97.913
		(50.213)	(53.952)		(49.787)	(53.439)*
Gross regional product per capita, KZT						
Size of Regional Economy		−.067	−.125		−.099	−.161
		(.074)	(.084)		(.074)	(.083)*
GPR, million KZT						
Fixed Capital Stock	92.244	79.781	80.801	89.383	80.069	81.542
	(9.926)***	(9.859)***	(9.743)***	(9.607)***	(9.584)***	(9.573)***
Fixed capital less depreciation, billion KZT						
Unemployment		32327	27709		29924	23959
		(15310)**	(15188)*		(15027)**	(15125)
% of labor force						
Regional Inflation		−2916	−3253		−3167	−3694
		(1512)*	(1522)**		(1490)**	(1516)**
Consumer price index, % to previous year						
Central Government Investment		.551	.609		.664	.702
		(.476)	(.477)		(.470)	(.472)
Million KZT						
Human Capital		−9.504	−8.856		−8.952	−8.391
		(3.813)**	(3.827)**		(3.769)**	(3.796)***
Number of university students						
Regional Wholesale Trade		.300	.308		.306	.316
		(.050)***	(.051)***		(.049)***	(.050)***
Million KZT						
Number of Operating Firms		−13.167	−14.099		−13.552	−14.389
		(7.025)*	(7.092)**		(6.871)**	(6.946)**
Constant	−444487	−73146	7006	−476436	−43214	78968
	(11057)***	(60686)	(59335)	(10581)***	(57801)	(57603)
N	212	196	196	212	196	196
R^2 within	.728	.827	.824	.726	.828	.824
R^2 between	.773	.755	.754	.776	.756	.758
R^2 overall	.595	.640	.635	.593	.633	.635
Autocorrelation ρ	.783	.714	.722	.797	.724	.731

Note: Dependent variable: fixed capital investment, million KZT. * , ** , *** significant at .05, .01, .001 level or better. Standard errors are in parentheses.

other things held constant, on average adds 39 million KZT in additional annual investment. Adding 100 words to regional bylaws increases investment by 70 million KZT. The lags and autoregressive error process methods presented in Table 2 help account for temporal dependence in the data. These results are robust to other standard ways of controlling for temporal dependence. When I substitute the length of regulatory documents with a one-year change in those variables, the results are similar.

Modeling Small Business Activity and Revenue

To see whether a discretionary regulatory environment impacts the development of the small business sector, I consider the total number of operating small businesses per 1,000 people. In modeling the effects of the regulatory environment on small enterprises per 1,000 people, I consider regional gross product, wealth, total investment in fixed capital, infrastructure development, human capital, inflation, unemployment, and natural resource wealth. When I regress the number of economically active small firms on measures of the regulatory environment, the results support my main argument. Specifically, Table 3 shows that statutory constraints have a consistent positive effect on the number of operating small businesses normalized by population size. The major drawback of this measure is that in many transitional economies, including Kazakhstan, workers unable to find gainful employment in larger firms often establish small businesses. A large number of private businesses, therefore, may indicate a poor, rather than a favorable, business climate. Regression results also show that larger regional economies tend to have lower turnover in the small business sector. Everything else being equal, regional gross product has a negative effect on total revenue and revenue per firm. This supports the notion that the small business sector develops when other economic opportunities are scarce.

Because of these concerns, I turn to the measures of small business turnover, or the amount of revenue produced by the small business sector. I consider changes in the aggregate and average annual revenues of firms employing less than 50 employees. These are defined by Kazakh statistical agencies as firms employing fewer than 100 people and having an operating budget smaller than US$250,000. Because many firms that fall in this category are family businesses or self-employed workers, who often cease economic activity without formally closing their business, I consider only

Table 3 Regional Economic Regulations and Small Business Activity, FE, RA(1)

	Legislative Regulations			Regional Bylaws		
	Per Enterprise		Total Length	Per Enterprise		Total Length
	(1)	(2)	(3)	(4)	(5)	(6)
Regulatory Specificity	.070	.066	7.83e-06	.149	.135	1.00e-05
Length of regulations, words	(.023)***	(.022)***	(1.79e-06)***	(.035)***	(.033)***	(2.51e-06)***
Natural Resource Wealth	.00009	.00007	.00009	.0001	.00007	.00008
Annual oil production, 1,000 tons	(.00008)	(.00008)	(.00008)	(.00008)	(.00008)	(.00008)
Wealth	.002	.002	.002	.002	.002	.002
GRP per capita, KZT	(.0006)***	(.0006)***	(.0006)***	(.0006)***	(.0006)***	(.0006)***
Size of Regional Economy	−.003	−.003	−.004	−.004	−.003	−.004
Gross regional product, billion KZT	(.0008)***	(.0008)***	(.0009)***	(.0009)***	(.0008)***	(.0009)***
Infrastructure Development	−.014	−.014	−.010		−.013	−.009
Fixed telephone lines, 1,000	(.004)***	(.004)***	(.004)**		(.004)***	(.004)*
Human Capital	.00006	.00006	.0001		.00007	.0001
Number of university students	(.00004)	(.00004)	(.00004)***		(.00004)	(.00004)***
Fixed Capital Investment	.0003	.0003	.0005		.0004	.0006
All sources, billion KZT	(.0008)	(.0008)	(.0008)		(.0008)	(.0008)
Regional Inflation	.053	.053	.011		.050	.010
CPI, % to previous year	(.016)***	(.016)***	(.012)		(.016)***	(.011)
Unemployment	.102	.102	−.024		.101	−.023
% of labor force	(.090)	(.090)	(.077)		(.088)	(.076)
Constant	11.651	7.665	11.368	11.467	7.566	11.351
	(.115)***	(.408)***	(.299)***	(.112)***	(.399)***	(.294)***
Obs.	228	226	241	228	226	241
R^2 within	.081	.179	.166	.120	.207	.196
R^2 between	.040	.077	.021	.045	.070	.014
R^2 overall	.021	.064	.010	.025	.055	.004
Autocorrelation ρ	.824	.798	.825	.827	.799	.823

Note: Dependent variable: per capita number of small operating enterprises. *, **, *** significant at .05, .01, .001 level or better. Standard errors are in parentheses.

Table 4 Economic Regulations and Small Business Revenue, FE, RA(1)

	Legislative Regulations			Regional Bylaws		
	Per Enterprise		Total Length	Per Enterprise		Total Length
	(1)	(2)	(3)	(4)	(5)	(6)
Regulatory Specificity	9.607	10.881	.0008	15.910	18.929	.001
Length of regulations, words	(3.797)**	(3.144)***	(.0003)***	(5.651)***	(4.676)***	(.0004)***
Natural Resource Wealth	.065	.030	.029	.066	.030	.027
Annual oil production, 1,000 tons	(.013)***	(.012)**	(.012)**	(.012)***	(.012)**	(.012)**
Wealth	.094	.070	.114	.108	.089	.118
GRP per capita, KZT	(.105)	(.087)	(.095)	(.103)	(.085)	(.095)
Size of Regional Economy	.0001	−.00006	−.0001	.00009	−.0001	−.0001
Gross regional product, million KZT	(.0001)	(.0001)	(.0001)	(.0001)	(.0001)	(.0001)
Infrastructure Development		−.882	−.752		−.826	−.706
Fixed telephone lines per 1,000		(.582)	(.595)		(.574)	(.596)
Human Capital		−.0001	.0004		.0006	.0007
Number of university students		(.006)	(.007)		(.006)	(.007)
Fixed Capital Investments		.0009	.0009		.0009	.0009
All sources, million KZT		(.0001)***	(.0001)***		(.0001)***	(.0001)***
Regional Inflation		.068	−.118		−.372	−.517
CPI, % to previous year		(2.495)	(2.512)		(2.488)	(2.524)
Unemployment		9.491	6.529		9.472	5.758
% of labor force		(14.631)	(14.556)		(14.654)	(14.555)
Constant	−635.571	−245.809	−208.298	−631.055	−221.672	−161.359
	(18.679)***	(64.576)***	(61.238)***	(18.740)***	(69.804)***	(61.670)***
N	212	211	211	212	211	211
R^2 within	.428	.624	.608	.443	.646	.611
R^2 between	.794	.807	.815	.796	.898	.821
R^2 overall	.519	.592	.590	.519	.593	.597
ρ	.841	.791	.803	.832	.771	.801

Note: Dependent variables: total and average annual revenue of small companies, million KZT. *, **, ***, significant at .05, .01, .001 level or better. Standard errors are in parentheses.

operating firms. These are companies that report economic activity and file tax forms in a given year. The models are specified the same way as in the case of small firms per capita.

Columns 1–3 in Table 4 report regression estimates for the legislative regulations and columns 4–6 for the bylaws. Results show that statutory constraints on regulatory policy application have statistically significant, but substantively weaker, effects on small business revenue. A one- standard-deviation increase in the length of statutory regulations per firm leads to a 6.5 billion KZT (.42 standard deviation) boost in small business sector revenue (Model 2), while an additional 1,000 legislative words increase revenue by 800,000 KZT per capita. The revenue increases produced by increasing the length of the bylaws are nearly twice as large.

Endogeneity

One potential challenge to this analysis is that economic outcomes could influence regulations. Discretionary regulatory frameworks may be designed to attract more investment and small business activity to low-investment regions, while more vibrant regional economies might require more detailed economic regulation. To check for the reverse causal link, I regressed the measures of regulatory environment and statutory constraint on the previous levels of investment and the small business sector size and revenue. Using the same set of controls as employed in the above analyses, I modeled the reverse causal relationships. Table 5 presents the results. The lack of statistical significance for the economic performance indicators rules out the reverse causal relationship, supporting the notion that regulatory specificity positively impacts the business climate, rather than the other way around. I experimented with the number of lags and various model specifications and found no statistically significant relationship between the indicators of economic performance and subsequent levels of regulatory discretion.

Streamlining Government Operations and Business Development

As discussed earlier in this chapter, many reform initiatives of the Kazakh government specifically targeted obstacles to SME development and attempted to limit local bureaucrats' freedom in interpreting business

Table 5 Endogeneity Check: Lagged Investment, Number of SMEs, and Small Business Revenue Do Not Affect Economic Statutory Regulations and Bylaws, FE, RA(1)

	Laws	Bylaws	Laws	Bylaws	Laws	Bylaws
	(1)	(2)	(3)	(4)	(5)	(6)
Fixed Capital Investment	4.74e-06	2.62e-06				
Million KZT	(4.82e-06)	(4.13e-06)				
Small Business Activity			.033	.139		
Operating SMEs per capita			(.206)	(.129)		
Annual SMEs Revenue					.003	.0005
1,000 KZT per capita					(.002)	(.001)
Natural Resource Wealth	−.0007	−.0005	−.0006	−.0005	−.0005	−.0006
Annual oil production, 1,000 Tons	(.0003)**	(.0002)**	(.0002)***	(.0001)***	(.0003)	(.0002)***
Wealth	−.006	−.004	−.005	−.004	−.007	−.004
GRP per capita, KZT	(.002)**	(.002)**	(.002)**	(.001)***	(.003)***	(.001)***
Size of Regional Economy	.02	.01	.01	.009	.01	.009
GRP, billion KZT	(.004)***	(.003)***	(.003)***	(.002)***	(.004)***	(.002)***
Fixed Capital Stock	−.0001	−.00003				
Less depreciation, million KZT	(.0004)	(.0003)				
Unemployment	−.287	−.231	−.005	.116	−.052	.497
% of labor force	(.627)	(.436)	(.242)	(.151)	(.638)	(.377)
Regional Inflation	.009	−.015	.042	.007	−.123	−.015
CPI, % to previous year	(.059)	(.043)	(.044)	(.028)	(.060)**	(.035)
Fixed Capital Investments			.002	.001	.003	.001
All sources, billion KZT			(.003)	(.002)	(.004)	(.002)
Central Gov. Investment	−.00003	−.00003				
Million KZT	(.00002)	(.00001)*				

Human Capital Number of university students	.0001 (.0002)	.0001 (.0001)	.00001 (.0001)	−.00003 (.00008)	.00006 (.0002)	−.00006 (.0001)
Regional Wholesale Trade Billion KZT	−.001 (.003)	−.002 (.002)				
# of Operating Firms	.0002 (.0003)	.00006 (.0002)				
Const.	12.480 (.921)***	14.631 (.689)***	19.718 (.576)***	17.277 (.352)***	31.517 (.943)***	19.366 (.506)***
N	191	184	222	222	184	191
R^2 within	.226	.166	.196	.227	.178	.255
R^2 between	.218	.311	.216	.427	.266	.326
R^2 overall	.041	.003	.079	.000	.022	.002
AR ρ	.902	.902	.930	.934	.902	.911

Note: Statutory and bureaucratic constraints are measured by the total length of regulatory documents. All independent variables are lagged by one year.

*, **, *** significant at .05, .01, .001 level or better. Standard errors are in parentheses.

regulatory frameworks. In 2010, the government introduced the "Business Roadmap 2020" program to revitalize the SME sector and promote exports through indirect subsidies and tax incentives (Government Decree #556 of July 10, 2010). The "Business Roadmap" lowers the effective interest rate on bank credit for capital improvements and market expansion projects from 19 percent to 7–10 percent and provides government-backed loans to Kazakh producers in 14 different sectors prioritized by the government. The initiative combined concessional lending with free professional consulting benefits for small and medium-size production firms. By clearly defining eligibility and performance criteria, it reduced official discretion in loan allocation and training. Moreover, it delegated credit approval to private domestic banks. Eligibility certification was delegated to the local chapters of the Damu Foundation, which was established by the government in 2007 to carry out government SME support programs. The commercial banks, now interested in government-provided financial incentives, were turned into the champions of SME lending. The Damu Foundation served as the government agent to guarantee loan performance. It also operated training and consulting programs for SME owners. In 2012–2014, 18 Business Service Centers were established in all regional centers and the cities of Semey and Turkestan.

According to Bakhytzhan Sarkeev, a senior official in the Ministry of Regional Development responsible for drafting the "Business Roadmap" programs and subsequently a member of the Damu Foundation board of directors, the document had to be a "crystal-clear manual" for any local official entrusted with program implementation. The architects of the program were specifically concerned with making the implementation mechanisms "clear and crisp" for commercial banks and municipal officials responsible for implementing SME support measures. They also needed to give SME managers a clear manual on how to apply for a loan, professional training, or consulting. The program would also need to be designed in a way that prevents collusion between banks and state bureaucrats and be impregnable to fictitious firms, bureaucratic embezzlement, or identity scams. The team considered the most serious obstacles in SME sector growth identified by the World Bank. Sarkeev stated, "We knew an average local bureaucrat had no interest in SME growth and would obstruct our plans if given a chance. So, the implementation plan had to be bullet proof against their usual conduct" (Interview with Sarkeev, July 2021).

Three years before meeting with Sarkeev, I had a chance to interview the owner of a medium-size packaging manufacturer from Almaty province, who had previously received consulting and lending assistance from the Damu program. He reported that obtaining a loan at a 6 percent annual financing rate was the best business expansion financing offer he received since he opened his business in the mid-2000s. All his previous investments were financed internally, because bank loans came with "monstrous" collateral requirements and double-digit interest rates. The businessman told me that "bank loans also are short-term, [so] they might be suitable for traders who buy and sell within a calendar year. In manufacturing we have long turnover. Long time passes between equipment order, delivery, assembly, tuning, production, shipping, and being paid. The banks want the loan repaid well before new equipment generates returns." (Interview #11, April 2018).

According to the plant's manager, working with the provincial administration to obtain the loan was easier than most government business. Eligibility criteria, a sample application letter, and the checklist of necessary documents were found on the local Damu chapter's website. The manager downloaded documents establishing the firm's eligibility from the e-gov.kz web application and submitted his application electronically. The manager suspected that his application was approved quickly because his firm is located in a rural area, not in a major city. He stated:

> One of the reasons I established my facility in Almaty province is because it is easier to deal with the local state authorities here. Officials here are not as spoiled by bribes and favors as in Almaty, they are also more appreciative of the tax-paying firms. Sometimes they get too intrusive, though . . . and I pull strings with my government contacts. But [the] Damu application was truly an exceptional case. I had no idea you can make Kazakh officials do what they are supposed to, but not what they fancy. (Interview #11, April 2018)

The procedural clarity, achieved by meticulously detailed policy documents, is the reason for such a favorable assessment.

Conclusion

This chapter described the institutional foundations of Kazakhstan's state regulatory system, identified causal mechanisms through which formal regulatory documents shape regulatory enforcement, and investigated how provincial regulatory documents affect economic outcomes. Economic transition and post-independence state-building lie at the foundation of the Kazakh regulatory state. Reduction of administrative barriers and civil service reforms implemented in the 2000s had been in line with international organizations' goals of promoting good governance and state capacity. However, many aspects of Kazakhstan's deregulatory and administrative reforms prioritized political centralization over effective governance and bureaucrats' loyalty over accountability. The emerging regulatory state was characterized by a strong developmental drive; agile, resourceful, and centrally controlled administrative institutions; and a nearly complete absence of mechanisms of political accountability.

Taking advantage of these features of the authoritarian regulatory state, I investigated whether statutory and administrative-level constraints on discretionary policy application influence the development of the private economic sector. I explored how the official regulatory documents written by representative institutions of provincial and local governments and administrative bylaws developed by provincial executive authorities affect the development of the private sector. I hypothesized that in the absence of public accountability, more detailed, longer regulations help constrain discretionary bureaucratic behavior in implementing regulations at the local level. Available data allowed me to investigate the effects of economic regulations originating in different branches of subnational governments and look into whether the more unaccountable representative institutions play a greater role in disciplining the "street-level" bureaucrats.

I suggested two distinct causal mechanisms by which detailed regulations lead to an improved business climate. First, detailed regulatory documents reduce ambiguity in determining regulatory compliance and deprive the local regulatory agencies of their power to apply regulations selectively. Second, more detailed regulations create an explicit benchmark for taking legal and administrative action against bureaucratic abuse.

To investigate whether more detailed regulatory statutes in fact improve the business climate and influence economic outcomes, I comparatively analyzed variations in legislative and bureaucratic rulemaking by Kazakh provincial authorities and provincial private sector performance. The single most important advantage of this approach is that it allowed me to hold constant institutional design, larger political and social environments, and the evolving policy priorities of government institutions. I utilized regional and temporal variation in the quantity and detail of regulatory norms and economic outcomes found in Kazakhstan, a country in which regional-level representative authorities formulate some regulatory norms while the centrally controlled bureaucracy is entrusted with their application. My empirical examination of cross-sectional, time-series data for 16 Kazakh administrative units reveals that in the period from the late-1990s to 2019, privately financed capital investments, as well as the size and revenue of the small business sector, positively responded to more detailed, longer regulations that constrain the implementation process.

The statistical tests presented in the chapter show that while controlling for observed socioeconomic conditions and unobserved province-specific effects, the overall length of statutory regulations and bylaws is positively correlated with three different measures of economic development: enterprise-financed investment, total revenue, and average revenue of the small business sector. The subnational research design and provincial fixed effects minimize the omitted variable concern. Lags and autoregressive error process methods helped account for temporal dependence in the data. The findings show that in the context of a publicly unaccountable regulatory administration, the formal constraints on policy implementation have positive economic consequences regardless of whether regulatory constraints originate in the legislative or executive institutions. This latter finding reinforces the notion that regulatory specificity, rather than separation of functions or legislative oversight, significantly affects the business environment.

4

Bureaucratic Discretion and State Capacity in Russian Regions

Is bureaucratic discretion a part of state capacity? So far, I have argued that bureaucratic discretion has a profound influence on the regulatory climate. However, other aspects of state administration also shape the quality of the regulatory climate and the ability of government agencies to carry out their functions. The literature conceptualizes these essential institutional characteristics as administrative (state) capacity to command resources and employ effective means to carry out state functions (Evans et al., 1985; Migdal, 1988; Fukuyama, 2004).[105] As this chapter will demonstrate, administrative capacity and administrative discretion do not necessarily go hand in hand. Discretionary power does not necessarily curtail an agency's effectiveness. In fact, well-functioning, effective state institutions may benefit from being able to make discretionary decisions. In other situations, discretion may enable corruption and undercut bureaucratic capacity to implement policy. I analyze 85 Russian provinces and find that administrative resources, statutory constraints, and intra-agency regulatory specificity are distributed unevenly, further reinforcing the notion that discretion should be analyzed as a separate aspect of the regulatory state. My investigation shows that formal constraints of the state bureaucracy are most beneficial for macro- and microeconomic outcomes under high-capacity settings. This means that institutional capacity and constraints are a separate but mutually reinforcing aspect of good governance.

Using an original dataset containing information on the number, length, and types of all legislative statutes and bureaucratic bylaws adopted in

---

[105] In their review of the state capacity literature, Enriquez and Centeno (2012) identify three theoretical traditions. The first roots state capacity in the state-society conflict, the second links capacity to the range and scope of state power, and the third sees capacity as a function of wealth and state revenue. I adopt the first approach, which is most closely related to the Weberian conceptualization of the state.

Thieves, Opportunists, and Autocrats: Building Regulatory States in Russia and Kazakhstan. Dinissa Duvanova, Oxford University Press. © Oxford University Press 2023. DOI: 10.1093/oso/9780197697771.003.0005

Russia's regions,[106] I examine the effects of state regulatory frameworks on regional investment and the development of the small business sector. Bylaws originating in the local executive agencies may both constrain and empower the bureaucrats. This chapter investigates how the provincial regulatory corpus in Russia may affect economic performance in the private sector. I find that the economic effects of bureaucratic regulatory specificity depend on the administrative capacity as measured by the size of the bureaucracy. Larger bureaucracy and regulatory specificity are positively associated with economic performance, but more importantly, when both are present, the resulting improvements in economic outcomes are amplified. I also find that in the grossly understaffed regional bureaucracies, additional rule specificity has the opposite effect and leads to deteriorating economic outcomes. This finding helps contextualize the role of discretion in the larger institutional context and highlights its possible limitations as an instrument of state control. Alternatively, the findings of this chapter may be interpreted as showing that the positive effects of regulatory specificity cannot be fully realized when bureaucracies are too small to effectively implement regulatory policy. The most favorable conditions combine high bureaucratic capacity with extensive (well-detailed) formal agency-level regulation.

State Capacity

In Chapter 1, I proposed theoretical arguments connecting the effectiveness of state policy to the motives and constraints of regulatory bureaucracy. Theories of delegation, rent-seeking, and regulatory consistency all point to discretionary policy implementation as an important factor affecting economic stability and growth. All these arguments, however, are built on the fundamental Weberian understanding of the state as an organization with the ability to make rules and implement its objectives (Evans et al., 1985; Geddes, 1994). In other words, they assume a certain minimal level of state

---

[106] Formally, Russia's subnational units are called "Subjects of the Federation." These federal subunits have unequal status within the Federation, enjoying varying degrees of autonomy from the center. Conventionally, the term "region," is used to denote all federal units, including 21 republics, 9 territories or *krays,* 49 provinces or *oblasts,* and 10 autonomous areas or *okrugs.* The Russian word *oblast* can be translated as either province or region. To prevent confusion, here I reserve the English word "province" for *oblast* and use "region" to refer to all federal units regardless of their Russian designations.

capacity to carry out its functions.[107] The delegation hypothesis, for example, rests on the assumption that bureaucrats are able to (1) develop special- ized expertise, (2) formulate independent policy preferences, and (3) steer policy implementation to the desired outcomes. It has been demonstrated, however, that when such assumptions do not hold, delegation loses its appeal as the mechanism for solving the credibility problem and enhancing stability (Huber and McCarty, 2004; Decarolis et al., 2019). Arguments linking bureaucratic independence to uncertainty and abuse also assume that bureaucrats act as gate-keepers who can effectively discriminate in favor of well-connected or well-paying clients (Djankov et al., 2002; Auriol et al., 2016). Such an assumption might not hold where bureaucratic agencies are disorderly, cannot effectively control resources, or have overlapping jurisdictions. The regulatory uncertainty argument, as well, makes an explicit assumption about state capacity—in this case low capacity—so that the lack of technocratic expertise, resources, and personnel makes it costly to monitor bureaucratic performance and serves as a convenient cover for uneven policy implementation. Overall, state capacity looms large in the theoretical arguments connecting state regulatory functions to economic outcomes, calling for an explicit empirical account of its effects.[108]

Although in most general terms state capacity has been associated with various aspects of state power, specific conceptualizations of state capacity employ various aspects, manifestations, and objectives of such power. This book conceptualizes the regulatory state in terms of institutional mech- anisms, rather than objectives, of state economic governance; hence, the capacity to implement state economic policy is the point of interest. The extant literature draws distinctions between "despotic" and "infrastructural" capacity (Mann, 2008), or extractive, coordination, and compliance capacity

---

[107] For a review tracing modern theoretical scholarship and empirical studies of state capacity to the classical Weberian notion of the state see Berwick and Christia (2018).

[108] The growing use of cross-national governance indicators in the political economy literature points to the emerging consensus over the institutional capacity of the state bureaucracy as an important explanatory variable affecting economic outcomes. Empirical research demonstrates the benefits of state capacity to provide public goods (Brown et al., 2009; Scholz and Wang, 2006; Kohli, 2010), emphasizes the positive role of bureaucratic competence (Best et al., 2017; Decarolis et al., 2019; Bosio et al., 2020), and singles out issues of institutional performance as the central problem of public policy and economic development (Mauro, 1995; Shleifer and Vishny's, 1993; Shleifer and Vishny, 1998; Djankov et al., 2018). The concept of state capacity has assumed a prominent role in the literature on Russian political economy, but the lack of consensus around what that capacity entails, had forced scholars to either conceptually distinguish state capacity and state quality (Taylor, 2011), concentrate on a specific aspect of state capacity (i.e., fiscal capacity, legal capacity) (Easter, 2012; Gans-Morse, 2017b), or evaluate competing conceptual definitions of state capacity (Berenson, 2018).

(Hanson and Sigman, 2021), and the capacity to infiltrate or penetrate civil society (Migdal, 1988; Scott, 1998). Such definitions of capacity focus on functional aspects of state operation—asking, what do states do?—but are less instructive in revealing specific mechanisms of state economic governance (what makes states effective?). To that end, conceptualizations of state capacity centered on resources—human, financial, material, coercive, and symbolic (i.e., legitimacy)—to get things done (Bratton, 1994) are more instrumental. Input-centered, rather than objective- or outcome-centered, conceptions of state capacity are more in line with the analytical separation of state economic policy and mechanisms of its implementation that have been central to the analytical framework of this book. Input- or resource-centered notions of state capacity correspond to the policy-implementation rather than policymaking aspect of economic state function. Following Fukuyama (2013), I reject the outcome- and objective-centered approaches to state capacity because they tend to blur policy and its implementation in empirical research, a point I discuss in more detail in the "Measuring Administrative Capacity" section later in this chapter. Reflecting upon the notion that "[t]he capacity to implement state-initiated policies depends . . . on the existence of effective bureaucratic organizations" (Geddes, 1994, p. 14), I conceptualize state administrative capacity as including administrative resources and professionalism of state bureaucracy.

Following Weber, who saw bureaucratic autonomy from societal forces as an essential attribute of a well-functioning modern state, some authors consider autonomous bureaucracy as a defining element of a high-capacity state (Weber, 1946; Mann, 1988; Migdal, 1988). Empirical research shows that greater autonomy incentivizes civil servants for better performance (Rasul and Rogger, 2016; Bandiera et al., 2019)[109] and makes the policy environment more predictable by insulating policy from major political changes (PRS Group, 2010). At the same time, scholars continue to highlight the growth-inhibiting effects of large state bureaucracies (Ting, 2003), discretionary regulatory intervention (Kydland and Prescott, 1977), and business

---

[109] Institutional accounts of economic development had emphasized the bureaucracy's position as a group of impartial technocrats who can effectively direct market forces and coordinate self-interested goals of private actors to achieve socially optimal outcomes (Rauch and Evans, 1999; Brown et al., 2009; Kohli, 2010). The literature on the political economy of export-led growth identified state economic policy together with the strength and autonomy of its regulatory bureaucracy as the catalyst of the East Asian economic miracle (Wade, 1990; Johnson, 1982).

capture (Yakovlev, 2006), which characterize overreaching powerful states. The simultaneous distrust and appreciation of state authority has permeated not only political-economic studies but also Russian sociopolitical discourse. As the mayor of Cherepovtsi, Viacheslav Pozgalev, remarked in mid-1990s:

> In general, in the country, I believe, a terrible contortion has occurred . . . public officials acquired an image of the enemy. But the word "chinovnik" (the official) is derived from "chin" (rank), and that implies "order." Without order, and without an official, no state can function properly.
>
> (Cited from (Chubanov, 1995))

One way to reconcile the contradictory accounts of effective, growth-promoting governance with those of state-enabled rent-seeking, resource misallocation, preferentialism, and corruption (Acemoglu and Verdier, 2000; Mauro, 1995; Shlapentokh, 2013; Radaev, 2018) is to reconsider state capacity and autonomy as two conceptually separate, but possibly reinforcing, features of institutional design. While the notion of state capacity concentrates on the *ability* of the government agencies to effectively formulate and implement social and economic policies (Evans et al., 1985), the concept of autonomy is focused on state actors' independent *agency*, which is enhanced with discretion and reduced by rules. It seems plausible that state capacity and autonomy might interact in enabling and facilitating the state's regulatory performance. It logically follows from the state-centered literature that state capacity enhances the efficacy of bureaucratic intervention. If bureaucratic autonomy in policy implementation is beneficial, higher levels of state capacity should enhance the effects of discretionary power. Assuming such an interactive relationship exists, this should be more visible in high-state-capacity settings, since these add *ability* to the independent agency. If, on the other hand, as I posited earlier in the book, formal constraints, rather than discretion, create a more beneficial business climate, discretion might not have much consequence in low-capacity settings. It would also follow that at the high levels of state capacity, the benefits of bureaucratic constraints would be the greatest.

To set up empirical expectations, the theories of delegation would indicate that diversity of business practices and volatility of economic conditions make bureaucratic discretion and expertise beneficial for both state capacity and the business environment. Empirically, this is consistent with the positive effects of state capacity and negative effects of discretion-constraining regulatory documents.[110] Bureaucratic predation and uncertainty arguments, on the other hand, would indicate unconstrained, unprofessional, and resource-deprived regulatory institutions as the most likely settings for regulatory abuse. Empirically, this is consistent with finding both capacity and regulatory constraints to have positive effects on economic outcomes. My argument about interactive effects adds to the latter the expectation that the magnitude of formal constraint on bureaucratic discretion should vary under different levels of state capacity. I expect that positive effects of bureaucratic constraint will be enhanced by higher levels of state capacity. The rest of the chapter puts these alternative expectations to the test by analyzing how aspects of state capacity and discretionary policy implementation interact in shaping economic outcomes.

Regulatory Burden, Administrative Capacity, and Business Climate

In Chapter 2, I documented how post-Soviet regulatory and civil service reforms substantially transformed Russian state governance. The threats to business also underwent a considerable transformation in post-Soviet Russia. The "wild" 1990s were notorious for their criminal racketeering, trading protective "roofs" for a regular "serfage," endless bureaucratic inspections, shameless bribe solicitations for questionable violations, and dysfunctional courts burying business disputes in mountains of paperwork (Frye and Zhuravskaya, 2000). In the mid-2000s, however, *reiderstvo*, or hostile takeovers, with the assistance of state security agencies replaced organized mafia (Markus, 2016). The courts were now in cahoots with political authorities. Bureaucratic extortion became much less overt and more targeted towards well-performing firms capable of generating a continuous stream of favors and payments rather than spontaneous bribes. Various sources of business threats also became more intertwined, and all

---

[110] In delegation literature, higher levels of autonomy may enhance state capacity through the development of specialized expertise and collection of accurate information about the underlying conditions. If bureaucrats are committed to the mission of their agencies, such technocratic expertise makes it possible to adapt policies to better meet economic needs. This would have a positive effect on economic outcomes. In this scenario, discretion and capacity are not independent factors that may reinforce each other, but rather are part of the same causal chain connecting autonomous policy implementation through increased state capacity to better policy outcomes. In this interpretation, state capacity becomes a rather inconsequential parameter, derivative of other underlying causes of performance.

threats now in one way or another entailed state institutions serving private interests of public officials and their private sector associates.

The case of an entrepreneur from Perm region well illustrates such fusion. In the late 2000s, the owner of a small business trading in construction materials made a decision to diversify. Together with his employee, who held an advanced chemical engineering degree, the businessman started small-scale production of a road deicing solution that instantly became very popular. The entrepreneur learned that the government of a major Russian city looked into reducing environmental and infrastructural damage caused by corrosive and soil-polluting deicing reagents. Salts of formic acid (sodium formates) offered many attractive properties. Formic acid, naturally found in ants and bees, melts ice at low temperatures, is non-corrosive, and is biodegradable. Perm region had several existing chemical plants suitable for production. The entrepreneur organized a new company, acquired an existing facility, imported needed foreign equipment, and developed a new proprietary product. In the initial years of production in Perm province, direct sales and large municipal orders indicated strong demand and growth prospects. The businessman stated, "The business was very competitive, everywhere people were eager to shift to environmentally friendly 'ant acid,' and we could grow big" (Interview #12, February 2015).

The use of formic acid for deicing in Russia goes back to the 1940s. In the United States, researchers recommended the use of this ingredient for road deicing as early as the 1960s (Boies and Bortz, 1965; Palmer, 1987). In Russia, the first patent for a deicing solution containing formic acid was registered in 1997. Reagents based on formic acid were approved by the Russian state technical standard and recommended by various research institutes. The Perm "ant acid" manufacturer enjoyed easy access to cheap suppliers and transportation infrastructure and could rely on the previously forged contacts with the local government. The entrepreneur felt optimistic and invested in developing attractive packaging and aggressive marketing. The business owner believed he obtained all the necessary patents, permits, and safety certifications. However, when his profits went up, managers of the regional industrial holding expressed their interest in the new product. Suddenly, the regional tax office and city administration initiated inquiries and an environmental inspection into the technical aspects of production and product safety. After encountering one bureaucratic hurdle after another, the entrepreneur learned that his business success made his firm a target of a hostile takeover attempt. After his company and personal resources were exhausted on numerous product tests and certifications, the owner found himself facing civil and criminal lawsuits over the alleged breach of contract and tax code violation. He learned that powerful economic interests were behind the lawsuits. In order to protect his other assets and avoid potential imprisonment, he gave up ownership of the deicing solution production facility and fled the country (Interviewee # 12, February 2015).[111]

The plight of the "ant acid" producer is not only emblematic of Russian start-ups and small business vulnerabilities against notorious *reiderstvo*, but also highlights the interplay between official predation and effective functioning of state institutions. Without their ability to effectively enforce decisions, state institutions would not have been able to pose an existential threat to the new business venture. Neither would they be seen as an attractive tool for carrying out the hostile takeover by a private competitor. Unlike in the 1990s, when businesses were threatened by criminal violence and haphazard regulatory enforcement, the more "orderly" 2000s brought about regulatory infractions and court litigations as major business threats. This story also demonstrates that greater institutional capacity not only enhances the state's ability to implement its policy, but also may further enhance its ability to advance special interests of economic and bureaucratic elites.

Economic Outcomes: Capital Investment and the SME Sector

To evaluate how bureaucratic regulatory specificity and state capacity interact in shaping the business climate in Russian provinces, I concentrate on two indicators: capital investment and SME development.[112] The former indicator of economic performance reflects macroeconomic conditions. The latter reflects the micro-level environment. Capital investment and the SME sector are central to the health of the economy: the first is the engine of endogenous growth, while the second is the engine of employment (Storey, 1994; Djankov et al., 2018) and innovation (Berry, 1998). Because both state regulatory functions impact private business decisions, capital investment

---

[111] All names and specific details are omitted to maintain confidentiality. I was able to independently verify the existence and continuing operation of the production facility as well as the dates of its initial establishment.

[112] In Russia, firms that employ fewer than 250 people or generate less than about $27 million in annual revenue are defined as SMEs.

and the SME sector growth are likely to be affected by the interplay between state capacity and bureaucratic regulatory specificity.

State regulatory activity directly impacts investment decisions and SME development. Decisions to invest in fixed assets, such as machinery upgrades, new facilities, expansion of operations, and capital renovations, reflect entrepreneurs' expectations about future macroeconomic performance and government economic policies. These are directly related to bureaucratic capacity and regulatory climate. Investment decisions are driven by expectations of future profits. Firms are likely to be sensitive to the subnational differences in regulatory climate that are the product of regional regulatory authorities' functions. The first points of interaction with regulatory agencies for most firms, regardless of the sector, are the regional tax, customs, labor code, environmental, and consumer safety officials. Regional offices collect federal and other taxes, enforce labor contracts, and inspect premises for sanitation and safety. Firm owners and managers should have firsthand experience in dealing with these "street-level" officials. Therefore, investment decisions by both small and large companies should be sensitive to the regional regulatory climate. In what follows, I separate fixed capital investment by sources and only consider the portion of total regional fixed capital investment that was reinvested from the firms' profits. In this way, investment decisions made by the state and financial sector actors are not included in my analysis.

Russian provinces have substantial variation in terms of the size, structural composition, level of development, and investment. Figure 15 plots the gross regional product per capita and private investment, excluding any attracted capital, for the period between 1999 and 2018 for the Russian regions.[113] Although 50 percent of province/year observations had only .03 million rubles per capita in private investment and 75 percent of observations had .05 million rubles, the graph shows that variation in private investment is similar to or larger than per capita income variation. Clearly, provincial economies differ in size, which affects both the supply and demand for investment. In the post-Soviet period, the smallest regional economy was that of the Republic of Altai, in southern Siberia, which on average was only a fifth of a percent of the size of the city of Moscow's economy, while its population was about 2 percent of that of Moscow.

---

[113] Total investment data are available starting in the mid-1990s. Earlier figures are inconsistent across different editions of statistical publications.

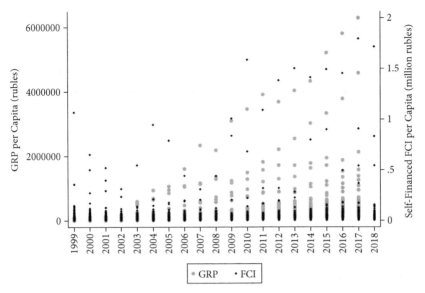

Figure 15 Gross Regional Product per Capita and Fixed Capital Investment from Firms' Internal Sources per Capita, Rubles in Current Prices
Note: Data from the Federal Statistical Agency. Dots represent provincial per capita figures.

In the statistical analysis presented in this chapter, economic indicators are normalized by the population size, but even accounting for the number of residents, volumes of investments vary tremendously across provinces and over time. Excluding oil- and mineral-rich regions, the per capita enterprise-financed capital investments were the greatest in Arkhangelsk, Lipetsk, and Tomsk provinces and Moscow city, and lowest in the North Caucasus, Ivanovo, Penza, Bryansk, and Jewish Autonomous Area. While the difference between the highest and lowest private-enterprise-financed fixed capital investment (FCI) volumes between the Republic of Ingushetiia and oil-producing Nenets Autonomous Area exceeds 455 times, the otherwise more comparable Lipetsk and Ivanovo provinces had a sixfold difference in private FCI per capita. The lowest average per capita total investment was in the Northern Caucasus; Republic of Tyva, Altai, and Adygea in southern Siberia; and Ivanovo, Penza, and Briansk provinces. The Republic of Komi; Arkhangelsk, Krasnoyarsk, Lipetsk, Orenburg, and Tomsk provinces; and Moscow city enjoyed the highest levels of FCI outside of the oil-rich regions.

Other indicators suggesting a beneficial business environment are new business formation and growth in output. Because of the centrality of the state regulatory involvement for business operation, organized economic interests are often heavily involved in the formulation of regulatory policy and may affect its enforcement. Studies of lobbying and state capture demonstrate that oftentimes the interests of powerful business actors are not only affected, but also help shape regulatory policy and institutions. This consideration presents significant challenges against attributing an independent effect of regulatory institutions on wealth and development of powerful business entities. The reverse causality poses a lesser problem when dealing with a disorganized and resource-poor SME sector; hence, instead of considering gross business formation and revenue, I concentrate my attention on the SME sector only.

Although the SME sector is believed to be more resilient to macroeconomic instability (Storey, 1994), there is a general agreement that it is highly dependent on the quality of infrastructure (Galbraith, 1985), favorable economic policy (McIntyre, 2003), and institutional environment (Welter and Smallbone, 2003). Successful development of a SME sector in transitional economies has been linked to favorable economic policy and the overall growth of the economy. Because SMEs are strongly dependent on public infrastructure, research and development, and economic performance of large companies, state capacity should be the most relevant source of the sector's good performance. When state capacity to provide public goods is high, SMEs can reap various benefits associated with improved infrastructure, law and order, and public sector development.

Two indicators of a business-friendly environment are relevant to the SME sector: business formation and small firms' revenue. Russian regions vary in terms of SME development across both dimensions. Figure 16 shows the dispersion of SME performance indicators over the analyzed period, and there are two trends. The number of SMEs increases over time from 5 per 1,000 residents in January 1996 to an average of 15.4 per 1,000 in 2016. By the end of the analyzed period, this indicator stands at 14.5 per 1,000 residents. While the average number of SMEs almost tripled, the standard deviation only doubled in two decades.

On average, between 1997 and 2018, the SMEs' revenue per capita increased from 1,642 rubles to 62,986 rubles in 1997 constant prices. The steady growth in per capita revenue receded in 2009 and 2010 and then again in 2015 due to the financial crisis and international sanctions. The standard deviation increased only threefold from 1,464 to 4,165 in 1997 constant rubles over the same period. The worst performing regions, both in terms of SME density and revenues, were the ethnic republics in the Caucasus,

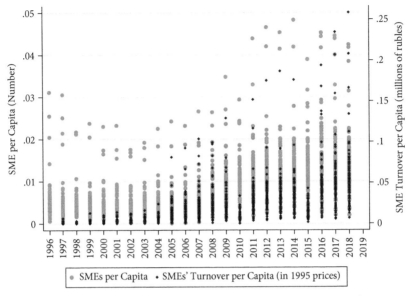

Figure 16 Small and Medium Enterprise Performance: Number and Turnover (Revenue) per Capita

Note: Data from the Federal Statistical Agency. Dots represent provincial per capita figures.

Tyva, and Kalmykia; Zabaykal'skii territory; and Kurgan province. The most vigorous SME sector is found in the cities of Moscow and St. Petersburg; Tyumen, Kaliningrad, Magadan, Novosibirsk, and Sverdlovsk provinces; and Primorskii territory.

Regional Variation in Regulatory Institutions

Chapter 4 has showed that in Kazakhstan, provincial authorities introduce some intra-country variation to regulatory institutions and put local bureaucrats under different formal constraints. Unlike the unitary Kazakhstan, where administrative resources are tightly controlled from the center, Russian federal units are not only free to develop their own statutory regulations, but also enjoy considerable independence in structuring their regulatory agencies. Russian regional executive agencies have more varying resources to support their function. At the same time, the overall direction of state regulatory function is shaped by the federal law. This presents an advantage from a methodological standpoint: unlike with cross-national comparisons, we are dealing with a regulatory system that is guided by the same general principles, so we are not comparing units whose state regulations pursue incompatible objectives. Diversity of regional policy and institutions on the one hand and unity of the regulatory system on the other make the Russian Federation a nearly perfect setting to investigate bureaucratic capacity and regulatory specificity as factors of economic performance.

The empirical approach makes use of regional variation in the Russian economy and bureaucratic structures described in Chapter 2. Statutory regulations place independent constraints on bureaucratic behavior. They are formulated by regional politicians and set institutional and legal parameters of agencies' behavior. The expectation is that statutory constraints are beneficial to the business climate and have a positive effect on investment and private sector development. Bureaucratic bylaws, however, are originating from within the same institutions that enforce regulations and hence might not in practice constrain bureaucratic action. The bylaws designed by the executive authorities may be used to the bureaucrats' advantage in allocating resources and defining priorities. In that sense, the bylaws may diverge from the statutory regulatory policy and empower the bureaucrats vis-a-vis regulated entities.

Yet it is possible that the mere existence of formal and elaborate agency-level rules and procedures may force bureaucrats to apply regulations and deliver public services in a uniform and predictable manner. Formal rules create explicit performance benchmarks, formalize regulatory procedures, establish implementation practices, and set explicit criteria to monitor bureaucratic performance. Hence, they routinize and constrain agencies' actions. Since, theoretically, both types of effects are possible, in what follows I empirically evaluate whether the amount of detail (captured by the total length) of executive orders, directives, decisions, and instructions has a positive or negative influence on economic indicators. I control for the separate and independent effect of statutory constraints as measured by the volume of regional legislation.

Measuring Administrative Capacity

There is no consensus on how to measure state capacity.[114] Some scholars concentrate on the "extractive" capacity, or the ability to collect tax revenues (Levi, 1988; Cárdenas et al., 2010; Berenson, 2018). Others measure capacity

---

[114] The literature theorizes several dimensions of state capacity, including extractive, technical, administrative, and political (Geddes, 1994; Grindle, 1996).

by public goods delivery. This includes the provision of law and order, quality regulatory institutions, and infrastructure (Kaufmann et al., 2009; Besley and Persson, 2009; Taylor, 2011; Gans-Morse, 2017b). Still others assess institutional features that enhance the "ability to perform basic administrative functions essential for economic development and social welfare" (Grindle, 1996; Rauch and Evans, 1999; Knack and Keefer, 1995).[115]

The extractive capacity underpins the ability to influence economic performance, though tax extraction may depend not only on government capacity, but also on its political preferences. Tax revenues are also influenced by economic performance, which raises further concerns about reverse causality. Public goods delivery is the central mechanism by which the state can affect economic outcomes. Still, the provision of public goods is predicated not only on the "ability" of the state apparatus but also on the political choices that reflect preferences. The *administrative* capacity is often assessed through the extent to which bureaucratic institutions approach Weberian ideal-typical bureaucracy. Empirical measures that gauge the structure of rewards and promotion, quantity and quality of administrative personnel, and technocratic resources at their disposal are based on this approach (Rauch and Evans, 1999; Evans, 1995; Brown et al., 2009; Goldsmith, 1999). One of the easiest ways to quantify the administrative resource as a whole is through the simple quantity of civil servants employed by the regional authorities. Such an approach avoids subjectivity in assigning qualifications, experience, or expertise to the administrative offices and is advantageous because it captures resources, which if not completely independent, are conceptually distant from indicators of economic performance.

All else being equal, larger bureaucracies that employ more personnel should have more administrative resources to implement economic policy and provide public services. Although a larger bureaucracy may mean more redundant tasks, such redundancy may in fact ensure a more precise application of economic policy. Brown et al. (2009) also suggested that larger bureaucracies might have less gate-keeping power and hence be less prone to corruption. Using firm-level data in a multilevel framework, Brown and colleagues find that firms that privatize within regions with relatively larger bureaucracies experience greater productivity than those where bureaucracies are smaller. They argue that this result is obtained because large

---

[115] See Fortin (2010) for an attempt to develop a quantitative cross-national measure of state capacity.

bureaucracies can better provide supportive infrastructure for the business environment and create competitive pressures that drive down the rents to be gained through bureaucratic corruption.

Bureaucracy size may be misleading as an indicator of technocratic resources. Recruitment and promotion rules may differ from one bureaucracy to another, leading to a different level of talent, expertise, and motivation on the part of civil servants. A few better-qualified bureaucrats may be more effective than more numerous but unqualified civil servants. To account for differing levels of expertise, all empirical models control for education levels in Russia's regions. Additionally, the uniformity of national standards of civil service guarantees comparable recruitment, promotion, and tenure rules across regional bureaucracies (Federal Law #58-FZ "On the System of State Service in the Russian Federation," May 27, 2003; Federal Law #79-FZ "On State Civil Service in the Russian Federation," July 27, 2004.)

I follow Brown et al. (2009) in operationalizing regional administrative capacity by the (logged) number of regional bureaucrats per capita. These data are available for 2000–2018 only, restricting all inferential analyses in this chapter to this period. Although a crude measure of administrative capacity, bureaucracy size has the advantage of being clearly distinct from the economic outcomes. Figure 17 summarizes the average size of regional bureaucracies.[116] The larger provinces tend to have a greater number of civil servants. The bars in Figure 17 represent the average size of regional bureaucracies over the analyzed period. These are sorted by the size of the regional population. Regions with larger populations tend to have more administrative divisions, render more services, and may have more diversified economies requiring more administrative agencies. Still, following Gehlbach (2008), I consider economies of scale when assessing the size of the bureaucracy. By analyzing the relationship between the size of the regional population and regional administration, I find that the per capita number of bureaucrats declines with an increase in population. In the panel of 85 provinces between 2000 and 2018, 67 percent of variation in per capita size of regional bureaucracy was attributed to economies of scale.[117] To model

---

[116] These include regional civil servants and bureaucrats working for the regional branches of the federal government. The numbers also include municipal bureaucrats, but not the manual workers employed by municipal service providers.

[117] I use the STATA -areg command to compute the adjusted R^2 for the panel data fixed effect models throughout this chapter.

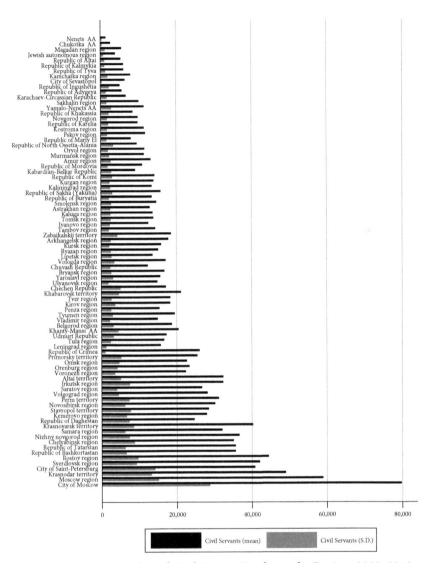

Figure 17 Average Number of Civil Service Employees by Region, 2000–2018

Note: Data from the Federal Statistical Agency. Bars are arranged by the size of each region's population.

this relationship, both the bureaucracy size and dependent variables in all models are normalized by population size.

If a well-staffed agency is an essential requisite for state capacity, we should expect bureaucracy size to be positively related to better regulatory enforcement and stronger economic performance. If, however, civil service produces patronage and rent-seeking opportunities, an oversized state bureaucracy can create additional hurdles for businesses. The bureaucratic discretion argument puts an interesting spin on these alternative visions of civil servants: bureaucracies may function differently depending on whether they are bound by rules or enjoy wide discretion. When lacking explicit rules and detailed procedures, bureaucracy may become an attractive patronage and rent-seeking institution, swelling in size, breeding redundancies, and confusing regulated entities. When, on the other hand, an agency is well organized but understaffed and resource deprived, it will not be able to enforce regulations effectively, posing no threat but not producing any value either. To see whether the effects of regulatory specificity depend on the size of regulatory bureaucracy, statistical models in Table 6 include an interaction between logged number of civil servants per capita and logged length of active bylaws normalized by registered businesses (excluding micro-enterprises and self-employed professionals).

Statistical Analysis

Modeling Fixed Capital Investment

According to *Rosstat*, the State Statistical Agency of the Russian Federation, the term "private investment" captures a mix of capital investment from enterprises as well as financial and banking institutions and federal and local governments. Since these are driven by different factors that might not necessarily reflect the underlying business climate—government investment may serve redistributive and developmental functions, while the availability of bank loans might be uneven due to unrelated institutional factors—I concentrate on investment originating from private companies and individuals. Conveniently, *Rosstat* reports these as "internal" investments, primarily consisting of companies' reinvested profits. Originally measured in millions of rubles per capita in current prices, this variable's distribution is extremely skewed. Using the regional consumer price indices, I convert these and all other monetary indicators into 1999 constant prices. I also transform the scale of the private investment variable by taking the natural log. Agency-level formal constraints are operationalized by the natural logarithm of the total length of bylaws per registered firm in a given region.[118] If agency-level regulations act as a formal constraint of bureaucratic abuse, we should see a positive effect of this variable on private investment. If, as discussed earlier, more detailed and lengthier agency-level regulations create additional hurdles for private activity, this variable should have a negative effect on investment.

Secondly, I investigate the effects of bureaucracy size by including a measure of the (logged) number of regional bureaucrats per capita. Reflecting the theoretical intuition that the economic effects of bureaucratic activities such as regulatory specificity depend heavily upon the administrative resources at agencies' disposal, I also include a measure capturing the interaction between bureaucracy size and bureaucratic regulatory specificity. Controlling for other important characteristics of regional business climates is necessary to increase the robustness of the results to other confounding factors. I add a battery of controls for factors that could be correlated with economic outcomes as well as with the number of bylaws and bureaucracy size.

As products of bureaucratic activity, bylaws are distinct from laws that originate from legislative regional authorities. Such laws and decrees often arise out of deliberative processes involving elected officials and remain conceptually distinct from bureaucratic bylaws. Because the existing body of legislative statutes might affect the extent of specificity of executive orders—most bureaucratic bylaws develop mechanisms for implementing legislative statutes—I control for the number of laws in a given region/year.[119] Since larger, more diversified economies might necessitate more developed statutory regulations, I normalize these by the number of registered companies. As I reasoned in previous chapters, a larger volume of regional statutes should create greater opportunity for legal protection against arbitrary actions of state bureaucracies. If a more developed body of regional law creates opportunities for redress against any bureaucratic misdoing, we should see a positive effect of the number of legislative statutes on economic outcomes. Because the measure of bureaucratic regulatory specificity and this control variable are both expressed in per firm terms, I also include the (logged) number of firms in a given region as a way to help account for economies of scale in regulation.

---

[118] Chapter 3 describes the regional variation in this measure in detail.

[119] Regional authorities are also constrained by federal laws. Because federal laws are constant across the country, I do not include them in my estimates of regulatory constraint.

The models control for several economic factors that may influence investment accumulation and co-vary with variables of interest. For example, if a large or growing economy requires a greater volume of bureaucratic regulation or a more extensive state apparatus, then one would want to control for these prominent drivers of investment. Accordingly, I measure the size of regional economies using gross regional product (in thousands of rubles per capita in 1999 constant prices) and their growth trends using year-to-year changes in regional gross product. To account for the effects of natural resource abundance on regions' investment environment, I measure mineral wealth by the production volumes of a region's mineral extraction industries. Due to the changes in industry classification methodology in the early 2000s, no continuous series capturing the mineral wealth are available at the regional level. Prior to 2005, the mineral wealth control variable included oil and natural gas production only.[120] Starting in 2005, the regional production volumes have combined all mineral sectors, including oil and gas, coal, metals, and other subsoil resources.

Prior investments in fixed capital may influence both the demand for investment and the availability of physical infrastructure that might increase the expected returns. Consequently, I add a control for the total capital stock of the region, measured in trillions of 1999 rubles. Likewise, high human capital within a region could potentially attract greater investment and provide the educated professionals needed to draft a large body of regulatory bylaws; thus, I control for the number of professional education graduates per 1,000 persons.[121] Finally, to capture regional variations in macroeconomic conditions that are likely to influence both the investment decisions and regulators' propensity to engage in regulatory activities, I include controls for the regional consumer price inflation and unemployment levels.

Because the data include regional-level observations over a period of 19 years (between 2000 and 2018), I model the relationship between regions' level of private fixed capital investment and bureaucratic regulation using regional-level fixed effects regressions. To account for temporal effects, the

---

[120] I compute production volumes for this earlier period using the reported physical production volumes and national price coefficients in the oil sector.

[121] It is customary to control for high (university) education graduates rather than less prestigious professional 2- and 4-year colleges. However, universities are unevenly dispersed across Russian regions, which biases the estimates in favor of the national centers of higher education. Professional education institutions are more likely to serve local rather than national needs, and their graduates are more likely to reside and seek employment in the given region. Regression results are robust to substituting university graduates for professional graduates.

dependent variable is lagged by one year. Before considering the joint effects of key independent variables of interest, I investigate the separate effects of institutional variables by entering them one at a time on the right-hand side of the regression model together with the full list of socioeconomic controls described above.

Column 1 in Table 6 reports the regression coefficients.[122] All institutional variables—the number of laws, length of bylaws, and size of bureaucracy—have a positive, statistically significant effect on private investment in fixed capital. These results are robust to the exclusion of the oil-rich regions, as well as the cities of Moscow and St. Petersburg. The positive coefficient on the legislative statutes variable confirms the findings from Chapter 3: more-developed statutory regulations improve economic outcomes. The positive effects of the length of administrative bylaws per firm suggest that bureaucratic regulatory specificity is likely to constrain and streamline policy application rather than create additional regulatory hurdles for private economic activity. The size of a regional bureaucracy also positively correlates with investment, which is consistent with the notion that increased state capacity promotes beneficial services and the regulatory environment rather than impedes the private sector.

Column 1 in Table 7 presents the results of the regression equation that includes all three of the institutional variables and all control variables. Column 2 adds an interaction term to the regression equation from Column 1.[123] Before discussing the effects of the key institutional variables, a quick discussion of the control variables is in order. Several economic predictors have statistically significant coefficient estimates that confirm general expectations. First, regions with many firms have higher levels of investment than those with fewer firms. Second, private investment tends to be higher in regions with higher levels of capital stock. Third, human capital, as measured by the number of professional-school graduates per 10,000 residents, is associated with higher levels of private fixed capital investment. Finally, higher levels of unemployment and inflation appear to be negatively correlated with fixed capital investment. It is worth noting that three variables—economic growth, per capita incomes, and natural resource

---

[122] Full regression results are omitted. These are available from the author upon request.

[123] For each of the three dependent variables I use in this chapter, Table 7 reports two models. One includes the interaction term between bureaucracy size and bureaucratic regulatory specificity, and the other does not. Estimates from the non-interactive models serve as a reference point, and my interpretation of the results focuses on the models that include the interaction term.

Table 6 Preliminary Estimates: Key Institutional Variables Estimated Separately

	Private FCI millions of rubles per capita (logged) (1)	SMEs number per capita (logged) (2)	SMEs' Revenue millions of rubles per capita (logged) (3)
Legislative Statutes			
Number of laws per registered firm	2.382 (.204)***	.694 (.157)***	1.814 (.314)***
Bureaucratic Regulatory Specificity			
Bylaws' length per registered firm (logged)	.484 (.022)***	.354 (.017)***	.494 (.036)***
Bureaucracy Size			
Number of laws per registered firm	1.473 (.073)***	.645 (.058)***	1.467 (.117)***
Obs.	1390 1390 1390	1389 1389 1388	1388 1388 1387

Note: Data taken from *Rosstat* and the Legal Information System. *** p<0.001, ** p<0.01, * p<0.05

Table 7 The Effects of Bureaucratic Regulatory Specificity on Regional Investment

	Private Investment millions of rubles per capita (logged)		SMEs number per capita (logged)		SMEs' Revenue millions of rubles per capita (logged)	
	(1)	(2)	(3)	(4)	(5)	(6)
Bureaucratic Regulatory Specificity	.329	.407	.331	.015	.351	.954
Number of bylaws per registered firm (logged)	(.023)***	(.076)***	(.018)***	(.059)	(.039)***	(.128)***
Bureaucracy Size	.911	1.121	.187	−.661	.930	2.550
Regional bureaucrats per 1,000 persons (logged)	(.074)***	(.207)***	(.058)***	(.161)***	(.126)***	(.352)***
Bureaucratic Regulatory Specificity × Bureaucracy Size		−.030		.123		−.234
Interaction term		(.028)***		(.022)***		(.048)***
Legislative Statutes	1.268	1.333	.043	−.220	.634	1.135
Number of laws per registered firm	(.175)***	(.185)***	(.138)	(.144)	(.300)**	(.315)***
Entrepreneurial Activity	.374	.362	.419	.471	1.065	.966
Number of registered firms (logged)	(.074)***	(.075)***	(.059)***	(.059)***	(.127)***	(.128)***
Natural Resources	.055	.048	1.020	1.040	.439	.386
Mining sector's production volume (trillions of rubles)	(.243)	(.243)	(.192)***	(.189)***	(.417)	(4.13e-07)
Fixed Capital Stock	.044	.040	−.145	−.131	−.093	−.118
Fixed assets' value (trillions of rubles)	(.026)*	(.027)	(.021)***	(.021)***	(.045)*	(.045)***
Economic Development	.0001	.0001	.0002	.00005	−.0007	−.0004
Gross regional product per capita (millions of rubles)	(.0001)	(.0001)	(.00009)**	(.0001)	(.0002)***	(.0002)*

	(1)	(2)	(3)	(4)	(5)	(6)
Human Capital	.004	.005	−.020	−.023	−.010	−.004
Professional education students per 10,000 persons	(.002)***	(.003)***	(.002)***	(.002)***	(.004)**	(.004)
Economic Growth	.377	.363	−.284	−.225	3.960	3.840
δ gross regional product, (trillions of rubles)	(.235)	(.236)	(.186)	(.184)	(.404)***	(.401)***
Unemployment	−.024	−.024	.002	.0003	−.051	−.047
Year average (percent of workforce)	(.004)***	(.004)***	(.003)	(.003)	(.007)***	(.007)***
Inflation	−.023	−.023	−.006	−.008	−.068	−.064
Consumer price index (percent)	(.003)***	(.003)***	(.002)***	(.002)***	(.004)***	(.004)***
Constant	−3.920	−4.387	−10.960	−9.067	−11.546	−15.158
	(.889)***	(.988)***	(.700)***	(.769)***	(1.524)***	(1.679)***
No. of Cases	1389	1389	1388	1388	1387	1387
No. of Groups	83	83	82	82	83	83
Adjusted R^2	.923	.923	.855	.858	.787	.791
Calculated by STATA -areg command						

Note: Data taken from *Rosstat* and the Legal Information System. *** $p<0.01$, ** $p<0.05$, * $p<0.10$. The model fit statistics are significant for all reported regressions.

wealth—do not have statistically significant effects. When these variables are dropped from the regression models, this has no substantive effect on the institutional variables of interest.

Turning to the variables central to this inquiry, models 1 and 2 provide evidence for positive effects of regulatory specificity and bureaucracy size. Because the sign on the interaction between bureaucratic regulatory specificity and bureaucracy size in Column 2 is negative and statistically significant, I reject the null hypothesis that the effects of these two variables on private investment are independent of each other. Separate from this interaction term, the coefficient estimates on either bureaucratic regulatory specificity or bureaucracy size by themselves tell us only about the marginal relationship between that variable and fixed capital investment when the value of the other variable from the interaction is zero.

With the two continuous variables' interaction, the direction and magnitude of joint effects can be hard to interpret. To ease interpretation, I reestimate the model from Column 2 with a series of dummy variables that dichotomize bureaucracy size. My first dummy takes the value of zero if the logged bureaucracy size is below the mean bureaucracy size, and it equals one if the bureaucracy size is equal to or greater than that number. I create similar dummies for values below two and one standard deviations from the mean in both directions. I run regressions substituting dummies for the continuous bureaucracy size variable and compute the marginal effects of bylaw specificity under small and large bureaucracy conditions when setting all controls at their means. If the effects of bylaw specificity vary depending on the levels of state capacity, we should see the varying slopes of marginal effect graphs.

Figure 18 shows that the relationship between bureaucratic regulation and private investment differs depending upon the size of the regional bureaucracy. It plots the marginal effects of bylaws' length in two different groups of region/years: one line shows the predictive margins for small bureaucracy size, the other for large bureaucracy. There are five different configurations separating "large" and "small." When separated at the mean, the effects of regulatory specificity are nearly identical for "large" and "small" bureaucracy sizes. Increasing the total length of bylaws one standard deviation above the mean (from 7.25 to 8.37 in log terms) corresponds to a 39 percent increase in region/years with fewer than 13 bureaucrats per 1,000 residents and a 38 percent increase in those region/years that have more bureaucrats.

Private Fixed Capital Investment per Capita
Predictive Margins with 95% Confidence Intervals

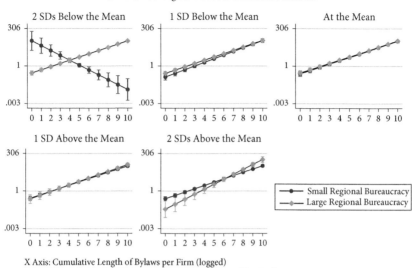

X Axis: Cumulative Length of Bylaws per Firm (logged)
Y Axis: Linear Prediction (FCI per capita, 1,000 rubles in 1999 prices)

Figure 18 Effects of Executive Regulatory Detail on Private CFIs Depend on Bureaucracy Size

Note: Data taken from *Rosstat* and the *Legal Information System*. The lines represent the predictive margins of interactive variable regression dichotomizing the bureaucracy size variable (regional bureaucrats per 1,000 persons, logged). "Small Regional Bureaucracy" corresponds to "0" when the bureaucracy size is below the mean value, as well as below two and one standard deviations above and below the mean. "Large Regional Bureaucracy" equals 1 otherwise.

At the more extreme values of bureaucracy size, however, we see larger discrepancies. An extremely large bureaucracy—two standard deviations above the mean in log scale, or 28.8 bureaucrats per 1,000 residents—outperforms a smaller bureaucracy when the specificity of bylaws is high and underperforms when specificity is low. A different logic appears to be at work in the smallest bureaucracies though. In regions where bureaucratic agencies are significantly understaffed compared to the national average (two standard deviations below the mean in log terms, or 5.9 bureaucrats per 1,000 residents), more wordy regulatory rules are associated with *lower* levels of fixed capital investment. The magnitude of the increase/reduction in this latter group is rather considerable: a one standard deviation increase in the length of bylaws leads to a 51 percent reduction in per capita private investment (from 263 to 128 rubles in 1999 prices) in regions with 5.9 or fewer bureaucrats per 1,000 population. The same increase in bylaw length leads to a 38 percent increase in per capita investment from 8,658 to 13,932 rubles in the rest of the cases. The confidence intervals of the negative effects, however, are much larger than those of the positive.

It appears that although both the regulatory specificity and state capacity work in the same direction to promote private investment, state capacity enables the positive effects of specificity. These results are also consistent with the claim by Brown and colleagues that the "helping hand" of larger bureaucracies serves to enhance the business environment. My analysis suggests that unless they coincide with a developed body of regulatory rules, bureaucracies that are large relative to their populations are not as beneficial as they might be under a more developed regulatory environment. A certain minimal level of state capacity is essential for the regulatory specificity to have any positive impact on economic performance.[124]

Modeling SME Development

To model the size of the SME sector, I use the same set of institutional and control variables. The dependent variable is the natural log of SMEs per 1,000 residents. The expectations regarding the length of bylaws and bureaucracy size are similar to the private investment models. Results are in Columns 3 and 4 of Table 7. Unlike in the previous estimation, the statutory regulations control does not have a statistically significant effect, and neither do the economic growth and unemployment controls. However, all other control variables, including the extractive industry production volumes, have the expected statistically significant effects. Fixed capital stock has a negative effect on SME density: quite expectedly lower levels of previous investment tend to shift economic activity to the less capital-intensive SME sector,

---

[124] If public investment is a substitute for private investment, one may find that the institutional variables have an effect that is directly opposite to that expected of their effects on private fixed capital investment. I carried out such an analysis and found that this is not the case. Institutional variables have similar impact on all levels of local/regional and federal government investment. The interaction effects, however, have a somewhat different configuration. Although the interaction effects are statistically significant across the entire spectrum of state capacity, when considering the regions with few public servants, state investment is not affected by changes in bylaw specificity. The specificity of bureaucratic rules becomes an important positive predictor of state and bank-financed investment only at higher levels of state capacity. These findings suggest that both state and private investment rise in response to a regulatory environment that is characterized by an increasingly comprehensive body of rules and agencies that are better staffed relative to the populations they serve. However, only private investment is deterred by the combination of low capacity and high discretion.

resulting in a large concentration of SMEs in regions with low levels of capitalization in other sectors.

Considering the model with the interaction term, the results are not as robust as with the private FCI estimation. Although the interaction term is significant, the bureaucratic constraint variable loses its statistical significance, and the bureaucracy size flips its sign. Still, the effects of bureaucracy size and the interactive term run in the opposite direction. I proceed to the visualization using the dichotomization approach described above.

Figure 19 plots the marginal relationship between bylaws per firm and number of SMEs per capita for varying sizes of regional bureaucracy. The graphs are very similar to those in Figure 18. When the sample is divided at the mean and one standard deviation around the mean bureaucracy size, the effects of regulatory specificity are nearly identical under the "small" and "large" bureaucracy settings. In both, an increasing specificity is associated with a greater number of SMEs. Only the extremely low levels of

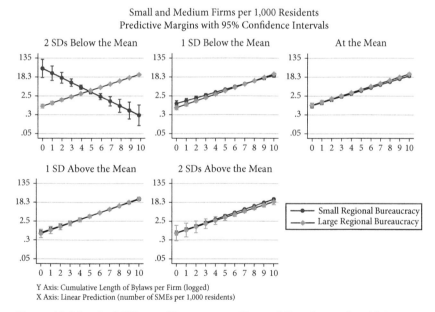

Figure 19 Marginal Effects of Bureaucracy Size and Regulatory Specificity on SME Sector Size

Note: Data taken from *Rosstat* and the *Legal Information System*. The lines represent the predictive margins of interactive variable regression dichotomizing the bureaucracy size variable (regional bureaucrats per 1,000 persons, logged). "Small Regional Bureaucracy" corresponds to "0" when the bureaucracy size is below the mean value, as well as below two and one standard deviations above and below the mean. "Large Regional Bureaucracy" equals 1 otherwise.

state capacity (regions with fewer than 5.9 bureaucrats per 1,000 persons, or two standard deviations below the mean) see the negative effects of specificity. There, a one standard deviation increase in bylaws corresponds to an estimated 42 percent decrease in SME density (from 1.2 to .7 per 1,000 residents). The confidence intervals around these estimates, however, are larger than for the rest of the sample.

According to Figure 19, in regions with more than 5.9 bureaucrats per 1,000 persons (about 1.8 in log terms), we see that bylaws have an unambiguously positive correlation with SME density. Taking the antilogs of corresponding values, a one standard deviation above the mean increase in the cumulative length of bylaws (2,892.5 words per firm) is associated with a 55 percent increase in the number of SMEs in well-staffed regions (from 9 to 14 per 1,000 residents). One substantive interpretation of these findings is that, rather than having a chilling effect on small business development, a growing body of regulatory codes can have a beneficial effect on entrepreneurial activity, conditional on the presence of a bureaucratic corpus that is large enough to oversee and administer regulatory bylaws properly.

Modeling Small Business Revenues

To bolster the confidence that the conditional relationship holds across different aspects of economic performance, I turn to an indicator that in some ways is closer to conditions for business on the ground: small business revenues. Measured in millions of rubles per capita, this dependent variable captures population-adjusted total revenues from small businesses within a given region. Regulatory conditions that hinder the development and operation of small business operations should correlate negatively with SMEs' revenues, while conditions that create a supportive environment should correlate positively. The last two columns in Table 7 report the statistical results of regressing this dependent variable on the measures of bureaucracy size, bureaucratic regulatory specificity, their interaction, and the battery of control variables discussed earlier.

The results resemble those from the models of private investment. Once again, all institutional variables are positive, and the interaction between bylaw specificity and bureaucracy size is negative and statistically significant, thereby rejecting the null hypothesis that bureaucratic regulatory specificity and bureaucracy size have effects that are independent of each other. To

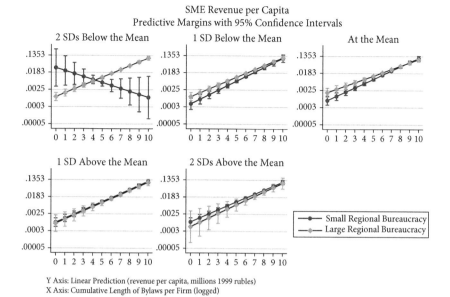

Figure 20 Marginal Effects of Bureaucracy Size and Regulatory Specificity on Small Business Revenue

Note: Data taken from *Rosstat* and the *Legal Information System*. The lines represent the predictive margins of interactive variable regression dichotomizing the bureaucracy size variable (regional bureaucrats per 1,000 persons, logged). "Small Regional Bureaucracy" corresponds to "0" when the bureaucracy size is below the mean value, as well as below two and one standard deviations above and below the mean. "Large Regional Bureaucracy" equals 1 otherwise.

interpret the substantive effects, I proceed with the dichotomized state capacity variable estimates. Figure 20 plots the estimated marginal effects of the interaction between bylaw specificity on the one hand and low and high levels of bureaucratic resources on the other under five different schemes to define the dummy variable. The plots illustrate how the estimated relationship between bureaucratic regulatory specificity and revenues of small businesses change given various sizes of regional bureaucracy.

Unlike private investment and SMEs per capita, at the mean levels (2.56 in log terms or 13 bureaucrats per 1,000) and one standard deviation (2.17 in log terms or 8.8 bureaucrats per 1,000) below the mean, larger bureaucracies outperform the smaller when regulatory specificity is low.[125] As the specificity of bylaws increases, however, small regional bureaucracy

---

[125] This result confirms the findings by Best et al. (2017) that bureaucratic expertise is most beneficial when bureaucrats have a lot of discretion. However, my other findings are not in line with such an interpretation.

settings benefit more from the additional regulatory detail. A one standard deviation increase in the logged word count above the mean leads to a 43 percent increase in revenue (from 27,796 to 48,368 rubles per capita) in small bureaucracies and a 35 percent increase (from 32,012 to 49,392 rubles per capita) in large bureaucracy settings. There is no difference between high and low bureaucratic capacity settings when regulations are the most highly detailed. At one and two standard deviations above the mean number of bureaucrats per capita, the differences are indiscernible due to identical estimates or overlapping confidence intervals.

Only the extremely low levels of state capacity present a different picture. In regions with 5.9 or fewer bureaucrats per 1,000 persons, a one standard deviation increase in bylaws per firm above the mean (a move from 7.25 to 8.37 in log terms) is associated with a 32 percent reduction in per capita revenue to small businesses (from 2,631 to 1,789 per capita). The confidence in the estimates of these marginal effects, however, is rather low, as the 95 percent CI bounds overlap at the highest and lowest values of the regulatory specificity variable. As the size of the regional bureaucracy increases, however, bureaucratic regulatory specificity takes on a positive association with SME revenue with tight confidence interval bounds. At 5.9 bureaucrats per 1,000 persons and above, a one standard deviation increase in bylaws over the mean corresponds with nearly a 40 percent increase in revenues to regional small business (from 28,990 to 48,070 constant 1999 rubles per capita).

Taken together, the three analyses provide a consistent result: the effects of regulatory detail on the business climate are conditional on the administrative capacity of the state. This is a more nuanced picture of economic regulation than is commonly found in the literature. In contrast to the unconditional expectations implied by the literature surrounding bureaucratic activism and regulation, I argue that the effects of key elements of the regulatory regime on the business environment are conditional and context-specific. Whether modeling private fixed capital investment, entrepreneurial activity, or revenues earned by small businesses, the results of the statistical analyses support these claims. As a whole, the analysis indicates that the way regulatory detail affects the private economy in large part depends upon the human resources the state agencies use to put those rules in effect. Without a sufficient staff to apply and implement adopted regulatory procedures, regulatory agencies may not be able to provide the predictability and efficiency associated with clear formal rules. In a similar fashion, my findings suggest a major qualification to the current understanding regarding bureaucracy size and its effects on business. Large bureaucracies alone are not enough to create a supportive regulatory environment; comprehensive and detailed regulatory specificity is necessary to clarify and reduce discretion for those applying the laws.

Conclusion

In this chapter I investigated how two aspects of state regulatory activity—bureaucratic capacity and the specificity of agency-level bylaws—affect macro- and microeconomic outcomes. I hypothesized that capacity and regulatory specificity should interact in influencing economic outcomes. Comparative research in this area is complicated by the fact that the regulatory tasks faced by state bureaucracies vary tremendously from one society to another, making it hard to assess the quality of regulatory institutions. To mitigate the effects of cross-national heterogeneity, I adopted a within-country research design. Examination of subnational variation in the level of bureaucratic regulatory specificity and the size of bureaucracy across regions of the Russian Federation supported my hypotheses. The way in which rule-generated bureaucratic constraints affect economic outcomes largely depends on the underlying capacity of state institutions to provide public services and enforce their own rules. This conclusion is supported by the examination of the bureaucracy's impact on regional private investment, development of the SME sector, and SME turnover, showing that my arguments are not specific to a single aspect of economic performance.

I evaluated two sets of theoretical propositions about the effects of bureaucratic constraints on business development. On the one hand, dedicated and well- intentioned regulatory authorities are believed to solve commitment, specialization, and stability problems and positively impact economic outcomes. On the other hand, equally plausible theoretical arguments and empirical evidence from developing and transitional countries suggest that independent and unaccountable bureaucracy may lead to predation, unpredictability, and inadequate policy enforcement. Empirical analysis presented in this chapter does not support the notion that the lack of agency-generated formal constraint is an institutional asset. Instead, I find that in well-staffed bureaucracies, lengthy, more detailed rules mean better economic outcomes. This result, however, does not hold for small bureaucracies. On the contrary, very small bureaucracies tend to become more burdensome when combined with lengthier regulations.

A different interpretation of these results is that regulatory specificity conditions the effects of the bureaucracy's size. In other words, bureaucratic constraint improves the performance of a well-staffed bureaucracy to a much greater extent than it improves the performance of an understaffed bureaucracy. While a growing number of unconstrained bureaucrats might not have a substantively significant impact on investment and small business turnover, a growing number of rule-bound bureaucrats may improve economic outcomes in a substantial way. This chapter speaks to the recent literature on state autonomy that finds discretion-reducing regulations promote economic outcomes in countries with low public sector capacity (Best et al., 2017; Bosio et al., 2020). Similarly to these studies, I find the effects of discretion to be conditional on state capacity. However, my findings show that the positive economic effects are limited at best. My investigation suggests that state capacity is the precondition and not a substitute for predation-reducing regulatory consistency. This chapter contributes to the studies linking better economic performance to resourceful bureaucracies (Rauch and Evans, 1999; Brown et al., 2009) by qualifying its conclusions with reference to other aspects of bureaucratic quality.

5
Institutional Controls and Autocratic Survival

Throughout this book, I have documented how regulatory implementation mechanisms act as important institutional conduits of regulatory policy in Russia and Kazakhstan. I conducted my analysis under the guidelines of the theory of the regulatory state that separates a state's regulatory policy and its enforcement mechanisms. Earlier in the book, I argued that the latter are independent and tremendously consequential for the regulatory climate and economic outcomes. My empirical investigation suggested that such effects are so profound that the rules and procedures of policy enforcement attract much scrutiny by the stakeholders and become frequent targets of institutional reforms. As Chapters 3 and 4 illustrated, discretionary policy application is often singled out as the primary reason of a state's failure to implement well-intentioned initiatives and a mechanism of predatory official corruption, clientelism, or state capture. Why do the repeated attempts to scale back, professionalize, and discipline the state bureaucracy continue to miss the often explicitly stated objectives of reducing bureaucrats' power? This chapter investigates macroeconomic conditions that might account for uneven development of the formal regulatory corpus and reduce discretionary policy implementation in authoritarian states.

Chapter 1 theorized how the incentives for profit- and rent-seeking and political survival shape the strategic interactions between firms, administrative agencies, and political principals over the choice of regulatory regimes. Discretionary powers change incentives and promote rent-seeking. Politicians may anticipate these effects and tolerate rent-seeking as a reward for political loyalty. Rent-seeking opportunities, especially those that unitize corrupt, illicit behaviors, not only reallocate resources to loyal supporters, they also undermine the development of rivals' political aspirations by putting proverbial "skeletons in the closet" of those with ill-gotten economic power and questionable links to the private sector.

Thieves, Opportunists, and Autocrats: Building Regulatory States in Russia and Kazakhstan. Dinissa Duvanova, Oxford University Press. © Oxford University Press 2023. DOI: 10.1093/oso/9780197697771.003.0006

Despite these political expediencies, discretionary policy implementation often results in suboptimal economic outcomes and, through the promotion of unfair rents, potentially incites social grievances. As a result, a ruler designing institutions of regulatory implementation faces the following tradeoff. On the one hand, constrained state agencies bound to formal interactions with regulated interests might be the optimal providers of public benefits, a predictable business environment, and the rule of law. On the other hand, state agencies with discretionary powers are most effective in channeling economic rents to the elites and regime supporters. This tradeoff, I argued in Chapter 1, is the key to understanding the mixed record of regulatory and civil service reforms in many authoritarian governments. Reforms that promote good governance practices might be initiated to improve autocrats' capacity, but they also might threaten autocrats' ability to stay in control. Formal rules granting or restraining discretionary policy implementation constitute a direct and convenient mechanism to rebalance special and general interest.

If discretionary powers do serve as a mechanism for rewarding loyal bureaucrats and economic elites, considerations for political survival may help explain variations in the discretionary policy application politicians are willing to tolerate. A more prosperous economy reduces social grievances and might lead to the rise of rival centers of wealth and power that politicians want to countervail with state preferentialism and targeted extortion. There-fore, we should observe much greater political tolerance of discretionary policy application in times of economic expansion and prosperity. When the state receives a windfall of revenues, rent-seeking becomes simulta-neously more tolerable and instrumental for redistributing resources to regime supporters.[126] There will be times, however, when the unsound management of the economy or exogenous shocks start undercutting rulers' ability to extract revenues. Economic crises that exacerbate competition for rents and aggravate economic grievances may necessitate fairer and more

---

[126] This logic also operates at a subnational level. With regional variations in levels of prosperity, political and economic elites in more prosperous regions may strengthen their local positions with popular electoral support, which may challenge the center's political power. Interestingly, a study of corporate raiding (*reiderstvo*) finds that Russia's regions experiencing more frequent raids are also more frequently engaged in electoral manipulations (Rochlitz, 2014). Rochlitz speculates that "the federal center may tolerate a certain degree of predatory activities by regional elites, as long as these elites are able to deliver a sufficiently high level of electoral support for the center." This is consistent with the logic of the autocrats' dilemma and a strategy of maintaining loyalty through the use of *kompromat*, or incriminating evidence.

predictable regulatory regimes and elimination of wasteful rents associated with discretionary policy application.

It is worth noting that the logic of political survival in the face of this trade-off might not explain economic liberalization or statist policy fluctuations. When bureaucratic discretion is high, a simple deregulation cannot reduce corruption or improve the business climate because more liberal official regulatory requirements could easily be augmented by high-cost red tape (Duvanova, 2014). This does not mean that economic crises do not influence the direction of economic policy.[127] In fact, crises often instigate the reexamination of existing policies and institutions. Some deep crises lead to significant policy and institutional innovations. Cutting back on rent-seeking, corruption, and elite-favoring preferentialism through greater formal control over bureaucratic function, however, does not require pivots in the state's economic priorities, creation of new institutions, or redefinition of business-state relations.

My argument accounts for an instrument of institutional control over state policy implementation that allows for a rebalancing of the interests of political patronage and economic efficiency without undermining the existing institutions of the state, changing the political priorities, or redefining business-state relations. One testable implication of this argument is that authoritarian regimes are more likely to scale back bureaucratic discretion when the economic and social foundations of their rule are shaken. Conversely, the windfall of economic resources politicians receive is more likely to empower state bureaucracy with discretion. In fact, it seems that corrupt patronage networks thrive as state budgets soar. The corrupt patronage networks of Yurii Luzhkov and Viktor Khrapunov, the mayors of Russia's and Kazakhstan's largest cities, grew quite large as rising oil prices fueled construction booms and infrastructure projects in the 2000s.[128] When the oil

---

[127] In Russia and Kazakhstan, the 2008 global financial crisis, for example, was not associated with a notable increase in state regulation or deregulation, but the 2014–2015 crisis was associated with growth in the number of regulatory documents. This suggests that economic crises in themselves do not explain variation in regulatory policy and institutions.

[128] Investigative reporters called Luzhkov "the chief of bribes" and claimed Moscow became the corruption capital in the 2000s (Noss, 2010). With the help of his wife's private companies, Luzhkov plundered the city's budget and extorted multi-million-ruble kickbacks from private contractors. When Luzhkov was sacked in 2010 for losing the president's confidence, his wife's estimated net worth of $2.9 billion made her the world's third-richest woman. The less internationally acclaimed but equally corrupt mayor of Almaty (1997–2004) and governor of East Kazakhstan province (2004–2007), Vikotr Khrapunon, was also assisted by his wife in making corruption the chief mechanism of local administration (Bland, 2018). For many years, both officials were allowed to plunder with impunity in exchange for their unconditional loyalty to Putin and Nazarbayev.

prices rose again following the 2008 financial crisis, Russia's corrupt officials financed the Adler–Krasnaya Polyana road in Sochi, the most expensive road in the world, and in 2013 the cost of the 168-meter-high Almaty Ritz Carlton Hotel exceeded the cost of building the 828-meter-high Burj Khalifa.

In "fat times," the resulting rent-seeking is not only beneficial for strengthening the elites' dependency on the state, but also may prevent the rise of independent economic and political elites. Luzhkov's and Khrapunov's corruption networks depended on autocratic regimes for protection against investigative media and opposition challengers. The autocrats' tolerance of corruption promoted state officials' loyalty and increased their stakes in maintaining political rule that covers up their past infractions and allows them to profit from public office. Such tolerance of corruption, however, may become too costly to afford in times of economic downturn, when any additional bureaucratic burden threatens to destabilize popular support for autocrats. This chapter tests this hypothesis (formally presented as Hypothesis 6 in Chapter 1) by investigating how the development of formal (both statutory and executive) constraints on regulatory implementation in Kazakhstan and Russia react to changes in oil revenues. I make use of the facts that these countries' governments derive a sizable share of their revenues from volatile natural resource sectors and that oil rents are largely exogenous of the state regulatory policy. Oil revenues grow in times of high oil prices in global markets and dwindle in times of oil price collapses. I also show that Russia's provincial regulatory policy responds with greater formal constraints to the popular unrest that challenges the political legitimacy of authoritarian governments.

The overall logic of the heightened need for regulatory efficiency in times of economic downturn might be regime neutral—both democratic and authoritarian leaders derive political dividends from public support. The expectation that bureaucratic discretion should be reduced in times of economic downturn, however, does not have to hold for democratic regimes. There, public scrutiny helps impede the use of bureaucratic appointments for political patronage, but more importantly, democracies possess a greater arsenal of tools for disciplining unruly administrators. With public scrutiny and transparency, democratic regulatory states do not need to choose between administrative flexibility (discretion) and efficiency. Here lies one of the most important contributions of this volume. While regulatory policy decisions are not specific to a regime type, when it comes to policy implementation, different political regimes rely on rather different configurations of state institutions to control the enforcement of regulatory policy. Given the lack of effective public oversight, autocratic regulatory states have to rely heavily on formal, statutory, and executive constraints. This means that the lack of democratic accountability profoundly affects the nature of a state's regulatory process.

The next section describes the discretion-limiting institutional reforms in Russia and Kazakhstan and develops testable implications of the political survival hypothesis. Both countries' lack of functioning institutions of ex post control of haphazard policy application and abuses by state authorities, such as free media, an independent judiciary, or strong civil society organizations, make the ex ante statutory and agency-level formal constraints the primary mechanisms of constraining discretion. I start by reviewing the national-level efforts to reform institutions of regulatory policy implementation in both countries. Such efforts proceeded under the banner of deregulation, modernization, and civil service reforms. In both countries, such reforms profoundly transformed the state regulatory functions but failed to eradicate preferentialism and corruption. Paradoxically, reforms created more effective formal and institutionalized mechanisms for perpetuating unfair advantage and power asymmetries.

To investigate whether the use of discretion-limiting ex ante controls follows the suggested regime survival logic, I analyze the temporal variation in the volumes of statutory and agency-level formal regulations. My empirical analysis shows that shrinking oil revenues are followed by growth in the overall length of laws and other official regulations imposing formal constraints on regulatory implementation. To further probe the suggested logic of a political tradeoff between discretion and efficiency, I also examine the relationship between regional protests and discretion-limiting regulatory detail in Russian provincial laws and bylaws. I show that protests intensify the subsequent efforts to reduce discretion but are not caused by unconstrained policy implementation.

Russia and Kazakhstan Between Discretion and Constraint

The patterns of regulatory and civil service reforms in Russia and Kazakhstan illustrate the political underpinnings of discretion-enabling or discretion-constraining institutional choices. In the early 2000s, these countries went through several waves of significant reforms of their regulatory policy and regulatory bureaucracy. These reforms were carried out in the name of improving the business climate. Russian regulatory reforms of the past two decades were praised for their notable reduction in official regulatory costs as well as for undermining some ubiquitous bureaucratic corruption opportunities. Kazakhstan carried out a comprehensive reform agenda, liberalizing its regulatory frameworks and improving its civil service through an early adoption of anticorruption, e-government, and transparency initiatives. Despite these far-reaching and multi-faceted reform initiatives, both countries' business climates are a far cry from fair and conducive to the ease of doing business. Why did the reforms miss their target? Were these reforms simply window dressing for predatory autocrats, or were they derailed by incapable state institutions and entrenched special interests? From the point of view of authoritarian regime survival, however, the outcomes of these reform efforts are hardly suboptimal. On the contrary, these countries' transformed institutions of governance have strengthened the regimes' ability to balance elite and popular support and effectively channel economic resources towards strengthening the authoritarian states. By building a more effective state apparatus, Putin's regime was able to improve government services and appease popular grievances. His state-building also helped him counter the political influence of regional leaders and use the support of corruption-implicated local officials to manipulate elections. Continuing patronage opportunities allowed Nazarbayev to command the support of state officials representing different regional clans, while the statutory specificity kept the same state servants in check through the fear of potential corruption investigations.

Kazakhstan

Economic reforms have been the top priority of President Nursultan Nazarbayev's regime since Kazakhstan's independence in 1991. After the economic meltdown that accompanied the disintegration of Soviet central planning and the breakdown of Russia-centered economic ties, the Kazakh economy faced the profound task of restructuring and economic recovery. In October 1997, Nazarbayev publicly presented the "Kazakhstan 2030" development strategy that was meant to unify the nation around the goal of long-term economic development towards the bright future of a safe, prosperous, and modern country. Absent the open political process, the program became the basis for economic policymaking by the government. The 1998 financial crisis delayed the program's implementation until 2001, when the government adopted the Strategic Development Plan of the Republic of Kazakhstan through the year 2010. The next stage in implementing "Kazakhstan 2030" was the Strategic Plan through the year 2020 (*Akorda.kz, n.d.*). In 2012, Nazarbayev announced the "Kazakhstan 2050 Strategy," which set priorities for future reforms and development.

So far, Kazakhstan has accomplished many of its stated reform objectives, including financial liberalization; small-scale and moderate large-scale privatization; tax, banking, pension, and civic service reforms; and a host of deregulatory initiatives aimed at reducing bureaucratic burden. The most recent developments in economic policy include subsidized credit to small producers, export promotion, and public-private initiatives to stimulate foreign direct investment (FDI). Much of the country's earlier economic restructuring and modernization was financed by the state's oil revenues. The 2007 economic crisis and declining oil revenues highlighted the need for attracting such foreign investment and building a small and medium business sector oriented for the domestic market. The 2017 National Investment Strategy aimed at increasing FDI by 26 percent from 2018–2022 via further improvements in the business climate. The Samruk-Kazyna state holding company was created as the key mechanism for reducing state ownership in the economy to showcase the government's commitment to market liberalism (*Astana Times*, 2017).

Kazakhstan's developmental drive also manifests itself in its industrial policy, which combined export promotion with subsidies to domestic small-scale producers.[129] Kazakhstan's developmental agenda is explicitly linked to the regime's survival. Nazarbayev's three-decade rule and the initial years of Tokayev's presidency have run under the banner of political stability, continuity, and, most importantly, improving the living standards of Kazakhstan's growing population. While Nazarbayev's immediate and extended family was plundering the country's energy and industrial assets throughout his time in office, the population was placated by the steady and rather modest improvements in living standards that, for the most part, were achieved through self-employment and entrepreneurial pursuits in service and retail sectors. Economic reforms have allowed the Kazakh state not only to more effectively exploit lucrative economic assets controlled by political elites,

---

[129] See the discussion of the "Business Roadmap 2020" program in Chapter 3.

but also, by limiting state social service obligations, preempted the popular claims on these resources. Unlike many other post-Soviet states, Kazakhstan was able to significantly downsize the state-financed social sphere and create regulatory frameworks enabling the population to engage in self-help, economic subsistence types of business pursuits.

Reform and deregulatory initiatives in Kazakhstan have largely been instigated by international economic crises: the implementation of Kazakhstan 2030 followed the 1997 financial crisis, and the 2010 reform program was formulated in the aftermath of the 2008–2009 financial crisis. Both are clear evidence that the norms and priorities of international development institutions—such as the reduction of regulatory burden and liberalization of regulatory policy—have made their way into Kazakhstan's public policy. Across government plans for privatization, demonopolization, and reduction of administrative barriers, the economic agenda of international development organizations looms large. Kazakhstan's technocrats are growing increasingly attentive to the international standards for evaluating economic outcomes. At the same time, it appears that deregulation and reforms of public administration have not stopped self-serving bureaucratic behavior.

According to Dosym Kydyrbaev, a long-time manager and consultant of state and private Kazakh corporations, the weakest aspects of state initiatives in promoting the country's private sector lies in their poor implementation by the mid-level career bureaucrats who have no stake in the outcomes but loyally serve their superiors (interviewed May 24, 2018).[130] Although the international rankings of the country's business climate indicate positive improvements, most local observers and business owners report a huge discrepancy between top-level reform initiatives and the "situation on the ground," which is often characterized by shady procurement contracts, convoluted regulatory procedures, and lack of proper and consistent regulatory enforcement. In Kazakhstan, regulatory reform necessarily crashes against two unassailable problems: the need to maintain patronage and the ability to use state institutions to channel economic rents. Because these had been

---

[130] Commenting on the career paths and incentive structure of Kazakh civil servants, Kydyrbaev echoes many observations made later by Fortescue (2020) about Russian civil servants. In Kazakhstan, political appointments at and above the level of department heads of corresponding national and provincial agencies are usually well-qualified and properly educated to perform their functions. Civil service, especially at the higher levels, is a prestigious, high-paying, and promising career path for the new generation of ambitious Western-educated Kazakhs. Although appointments and promotions follow the strict education and merit-based rules established by the 2015 law "On Civil Service" (416-V), political loyalty and cronyism continue to influence appointment decisions.

essential to maintaining Nazarbayev's family's rule, which by the accounts of many observers continues under Tokayev's presidency, regulatory and governance reforms fall short of creating effective mechanisms of transparency and public accountability of state agencies.[131]

A good illustration of such limitations is the public procurement scandal that unraveled in the midst of the COVID-19 pandemic. On July 10, 2020, the internet news portal Vlast.kz published a long list of public procurement contracts of the governments of Kazakhstani cities most severely affected by shortages of medical supplies, personal protective equipment, and hospital beds (Moldabekov, 2020). The report was based on electronic public procurement records from the e-government portal www.egov.kz, which started publishing procurement documentation in 2008. Daniyar Moldabekov, the author of the Vlast.kz report, questioned the priorities of the respective regional governments, which had allocated their budgets to cultural events, public relations, and non-critical infrastructure improvement projects, many of which would not be allowed to commence under the existing quarantine and social distancing requirements.

A group of civil activists who scrutinized the report and discussed it on social media brought to the public attention one highly questionable contract. On July 2, 2020, Almaty government's Department of Culture contracted the private vendor Vardi Asia for a NUR light 3D mapping show to be part of the annual Capital City Day celebration at a cost of 56.3 million KZT, or about US$140,000. Later reports give a slightly higher figure of 63 million KZT. The Capital City Day, a state holiday celebrated on July 6 (coincidentally the birthday of Nursultan Nazarbayev), had been traditionally celebrated by fireworks in all major cities of Kazakhstan. Due to the quarantine ordinance, the Almaty government canceled all public celebrations in the summer of 2020. Almaty residents were eager to attest to the fact that no fireworks or lasers lit up the skies above Almaty on July 6. The public outcry made its way to the official media. On December 7, 2020, the scandal culminated with Almaty's mayor, Bakytzhan Sagintayev, giving a live interview broadcast by the central communication services under the president of Kazakhstan. The mayor was questioned by state media journalists and admitted the show never took place and that the

---

[131] Although starting in the mid-2000s Kazakhstan enacted a series of public service reforms that aimed at streamlining public service provision, these failed to establish mechanisms of public accountability and retained the direct mechanisms of central control over regional and local authorities (Bhuiyan, 2010).

contract was authorized and executed in violation of the quarantine orders. On August 17, 2020, the city issued a payment to what turned out to be a private entity incorporated specifically for the purpose of securing the entertainment procurement contract for the services never delivered.

In a televised interview, Sagintayev expressed no remorse or even surprise, but rather downplayed the incident as a routine minor procedural mistake. No measures to investigate the incident were undertaken by the national officials to either punish the sloppy bureaucrats or recover the public funds. The mayor expressed the hope that the show would be staged sometime in the indefinite future. Activists posted social media messages deriding this incidence of corruption as yet another example of embezzlement of public funds through a murky one-day private company created for the sole purpose of securing the government contract, suggesting that this was not an isolated case, but just the tip of an iceberg that incidentally came to the public's attention.

It appears that the fireworks embezzlement was enabled by a Special (Simplified) Procurement Order (Resolution #127 by the Government of The Republic of Kazakhstan, March 20, 2020) that temporarily relaxed a highly regulated standard procurement procedure to speed up government functioning during the pandemic. In its own way, the Special Procurement Order increased the discretionary authority of low-level procurement officials and opened up corruption opportunities. The resolution was revoked by the end of 2020 to reimpose the elaborate ex ante control mechanisms of the actions of procurement officials. The embezzlement case likely came to the public's attention because pandemic-related shortages had heightened public interest in city finances. Against the backdrop of government failures to address the public health crisis, "the fireworks that never were" have intensified public grievances against self-serving officials. This case clearly illustrates how even modest transparency and public oversight mechanisms may undermine autocratic legitimacy, making the ex ante control of policy implementation an indispensable mechanism of autocratic governance.

Russia

The series of "hard" socioeconomic reforms of the 2000s in Russia—tax, land, banking, pension, civil service, and state budget reform, among others—have produced a system of governance that is much more formalized, rule-driven, and legalistic compared to the mid-1990s. Alexey Kudrin's reforms described in Chapter 3 created the institutional foundations of the Russian regulatory state. The Russian state transferred regulatory authority over many sectors to self-regulating organizations. Customs, registration, licensing, and bankruptcy procedures that stifled small business development throughout the 1990s were simplified and cut back. Economic reforms enhanced the procedural regulations (*reglamentatsiia*), standardized administrative procedures, eliminated many redundancies, and introduced a non-trivial degree of transparency in administrative institutions.

Regulatory reforms and Russia's "New Industrial Policy" were the logical extension of the liberal market reforms of the 1990s. Ambitious reform programs of Putin's first presidential term were very successful in improving areas of economic policy, while the reforms of social and administrative spheres fell short of their initial promises (Gel'man and Starodubtsev, 2014). The 2008–2009 financial crisis gave a new impetus to the economy-wide improvements in the investment climate. Deregulation proceeded not only as a top-down government initiative, but also accelerated through the state-private partnership with the aid of a special Agency for Strategic Initiatives (Freinkman and Yakovlev, 2015). International economic sanctions that followed the 2014 internationally unrecognized annexation of Crimea and Russian intervention in Donbas disrupted the inflow of FDI and largely removed the outward-looking rationale for improving the investment climate. Growing international isolation reoriented Russia's economic and regulatory policy towards domestic companies and investors, with no detriment to the priorities of simplified and efficient regulatory implementation. The Russian regulatory state continued to improve its policy implementation mechanisms aimed at better tax collection, regulatory oversight, public finance, and service provision. Between 2008 and 2020, the World Bank "Doing Business" (DB) project identified 35 new consequential business regulation changes in Russia. All but three of these had positively contributed to the ease of doing business.

Across Russia's extensive deregulation efforts, Russian reformers extensively relied upon ex ante mechanisms for cutting the red tape and removing administrative barriers. They painstakingly regimented the details of administrative processes, specifying the number of required documents, designing the paperwork templates, and setting time limits for how long officials could review and process applications. Deregulation and red tape reduction constrained the regulatory officials. Modernization of regulatory functions improved the business climate. Despite these measures, Russia continues to rank among the world's most corrupt countries according to the Corruption Perception Index and other perception-based indicators. Bad governance, rent-seeking, kleptocracy, and high corruption perception have been the consistent features of Russian politics, leading to repeated calls for deeper governance reform. Paradoxically, the growing record of positive, albeit somewhat short-handed, reforms of the regulatory state have coincided with the expanding state ownership of economic resources, market-defying monopolization in high-value economic sectors, and large-scale rents creation, allowing the ruling elites to concentrate an enormous amount of wealth and economic power in their hands (Markus, 2016; Aslund, 2019; Wood, 2018; Taylor, 2018).

The 2004 "Law on State Civil Service" (*O gosudarstvennoi grazhdanskoi sluzhbe*) laid down the formal framework for professional, merit-based, depoliticized, and performance-oriented public administration. Fifteen years down the road, Russian civil service looks much transformed both in terms of the qualification and operations of its personnel, but also in term of its social prestige and desirability of employment. The Russian bureaucracy now is more educated, better paid, and much more disciplined and professional (Kalgin, 2016; Kalinin, 2019; Fortescue, 2020). Although reforms went far in improving civil servants' qualifications and career incentives, they have generally failed in terms of replacing loyalty and patronage with performance-based incentives. External scrutiny of technocratic officials suggests that "poor bureaucratic performance is not to be explained by the widespread recruitment of unqualified cronies" (Fortescue, 2020, p. 380). Analyses of regional politics reveal that considerations of political loyalty compete with competence and good performance in the governors' appointment decisions (Reuter and Robertson, 2012).[132] Pockets of high-performance and effective public goods provision (Treisman, 2018; Taylor, 2018) suggest that continuing corruption is not a simple result of state failure to command its human and material resources towards prioritized issues.

Continuing frustration with corruption that persists despite bureaucrats' growing salaries, education, and professionalism, along with a clearer

---

[132] But see Reuter et al. (2016) on how local (mayoral) elections promote performance-based selection of local officials at the detriment of political loyalty.

definition of official functions, has brought reformers' attention to mechanisms of political accountability (Busygina and Filippov, 2013). Great hopes for eradicating inefficiency and promoting bureaucratic probity were placed on e-government and transparency. The "open data" (*otkrytye dannye*), "open budget" (*otkrytyi b'udzhet*), and "open government" (*otkrytoe pravitel'stvo*) initiatives promoted digitalization and modernization of government function (Kalinin, 2019). Since the mid-2010s, Russian government agencies have digitized most of their archives, workflow, and external reporting. They provided public access to business registries and procurement and budgetary records and expanded e-government service-provision platforms. Perhaps the most significant developments in the sphere of e-government and digitalization were the expansion of electronic tax and fee filing services, cadaster and enterprise registries, and public procurement records. These not only minimized the amount of personal contact with street-level bureaucrats, significantly curtailing their amount of discretionary bureaucratic power, but also promoted a better flow of information between society and government institutions.

The increased administrative transparency, however, presents a significant challenge for the Russian authoritarian state. While transparency may promote government effectiveness (Gorgulu et al., 2020), it also empowers society-based mechanisms of ex post monitoring of government operations. Digitization enables media investigations into bureaucratic malfeasance and scandals and may empower the public to place greater demands on the state. The rise of a new political movement led by Aleksei Navalny exemplifies the existential threats that government transparency and openness pose to the legitimacy of Putin's regime. Navalny's protest-inciting documentaries "He Is Not Dimon" (2017) and "Putin's Palace" (2021) exposed the lavish ill-gotten wealth of Dmitriy Medvedev and Vladimir Putin. As with many other investigative reports by Navalny, these documentaries were based on publicly available tax, property, and business contract records. Navalny's regime-threatening investigations in many ways were enabled by the profound modernization, formalization, and digitalization of the Russian state.

Despite the impressive deregulation and civil service reform, the Russian state retains its hostile and predatory nature. By no means, are the business-state relations emerging from the decades of deregulation fairer, more equitable, or more balanced. The corruption-ridden and patronage-promoting bureaucracy is cited as "an indispensable part of the mechanism of neopatrimonial governance within the framework of the power vertical"

(Gel'man, 2016, p. 461). The bureaucracy serves as a conduit of "crony capitalism" (Aslund, 2019) and the key mechanism of rent appropriation for well-connected and loyal officials (Burkhardt and Libman, 2018). The theory of the authoritarian regulatory state helps reconcile the track records of deregulation and civil service reforms with increasing statism and authoritarian cronyism. It appears that the Russian state is capable of achieving greater efficiency in directing and carrying out government functions. Still, reformers stop short of eradicating cronyism because, in the absence of good economic outcomes, the autocratic rule has to rely on the political loyalty of state officials and economic elites. Rewarding such loyalty comes at the detriment of good governance.

Discretion and Political Survival

Deregulation and reforms of governance in Russia and Kazakhstan created a peculiar type of regulatory state. Both countries rejected the heavy-handed state involvement in the economy as suboptimal: while favorable to the state bureaucracy that might convert regulatory hurdles into personal benefits, state involvement suffocates economic activity beneficial to private sector elites and the general public. Research shows that autocrats often benefit from institution-building that limits the state's power because such arrangements send a credible signal about the state's commitments to respecting private property and individual economic rights (Gandhi and Przeworski, 2006; Wright, 2008; Gehlbach and Keefer, 2012). Deregulation and modernization of state functions in Kazakhstan and Russia, however, did not reduce but rather increased the power of the autocratic states to control the private sector and the public bureaucracy. The easing of business regulations cleared further avenues for private enrichment of political elites. The administrative reforms improved the efficiency with which the state implements its policy but did not eradicate corruption and favoritism. Instead, reforms forged the ties between private and state sectors in ways that reinforce political loyalty and cronyism. In some areas, bureaucrats retained powers to engage in predatory behavior or apply regulatory policy selectively for the benefits of well-connected companies.

In the early 2020s, Russian and Kazakh state bureaucracies have become much more professional, disciplined, and efficient. Still, civil service continues to be the major vehicle of political patronage, personal enrichment, and resource redistribution. Regime survival in Kazakhstan, from the early days of independence through today, and in Russia increasingly from the late 2000s has relied upon the support of the state bureaucracy and regional government institutions. Does the lack of progress in eradicating bureaucratic corruption and building impartial institutions of effective governance stem from the desire to reward public servants for their political loyalties? Are the neo-patrimonialism and unruly bureaucracy a cost paid for the political survival of authoritarian regimes? An examination of formal constraints on the discretionary power of civil servants offers an empirical venue for testing implications of the politicians' dilemma as it applies to the task of building authoritarian regulatory states.

To maximize their time in office, autocrats face a choice between building an effective regulatory state on one hand and the political loyalty of public servants and business elites on the other. Bureaucrats and economic elites who provide support for the autocratic regime may personally benefit from economic policy that rewards particularistic interests, state-private collusion, and (or) opportunities to engage in corrupt practices at the detriment of the public. These elite-enriching activities directly undermine the foundations of an effective regulatory state, such as the rule of law, uniform enforcement, predictability, transparency, and bureaucratic probity. The autocrats' ability to commit to building an effective regulatory state, therefore, is limited by their interest in rewarding economic elites and public servants. Rewarding supporters with economic rents might become costly for autocrats with a compromised ability to satisfy economic demands of the public. When the overall size of the economic pie shrinks, economic conflict might make it harder for autocrats to tolerate bureaucratic predation and collusive arrangements that stifle business activity, entrepreneurship, and competition.[133]

It should follow that the more value politicians place on the political support of the state bureaucracy, the more discretionary powers, potentially convertible into personal enrichment, the bureaucrats receive. It would be hard to find direct evidence of growing autocratic tolerance for administrative self-serving or preferentialism that undermines public interest. In the absence of a robust independent press and independent judiciary, the lack of corruption prosecution, for example, cannot prove institutional probity.

---

[133] This reasoning holds constant other mechanisms of autocratic rule, such as coercive power and symbolic legitimacy.

On the contrary, it might mean that authorities are turning a blind eye on the abuse of public office. Preferential contracts or authority-sanctioned rents are usually granted behind closed doors, making them a hard target to investigate. The reverse causal link, connecting autocrats' growing concerns for public benefit provision to the crackdown on particularistic benefits, however, can have testable implications. When regime survival is threatened by the shrinking resource base of the state or growing social grievances, considerations of regime survival should require reduction of state bureaucrats' discretionary power. I hypothesized (Hypothesis 6 in Chapter 1) that in times of economic difficulties and shrinking state resources, politicians will be more likely to constrain bureaucratic discretion in regulatory policy application.

In fact, the development of the most detailed and discretion-constraining components of the regulatory state—technical regulations—lends support to this expectation. In Russia, the term "technical regulation" designates a system of legal norms that ensure the safety of products and services and their production, transportation, sale, consumption, and so forth. These contain not only the general principles, but detailed product specifications, quality standards, labeling, distribution, and other specific standards, as well as procedures for assessing standard compliance. Technical standards are explicitly designed to eliminate arbitrary interpretation by regulatory agencies. Ex-Soviet republics inherited from the USSR more than 100,000 technical regulation documents. Often contradictory and increasingly outdated, they were nearly impossible for enterprises to fully comply with. This, together with unclear structures of compliance-enforcing authority, contributed to widespread bureaucratic corruption (Kriuchkova, 2007). In 2003, the Duma passed the law "On Technical Regulation" as part of Kudrin-Gref deregulation reforms. It was supposed to create the foundation for the development of new, modernized technical regulation. In the period of high resource rents and rapid economic expansion, however, the development of technical regulation reform was stalled. Although agencies and industry association were able to propose over 200 regulations by 2008, only one new technical standard was officially approved. Only seven more came into force in 2008–2009 (Astakhova and Grozovskii, 2009). Collapsing oil prices that followed the 2007–2008 financial crisis, however, coincided with a new push for reform implementation. In the post-crisis years, dozens of new, lengthy, detailed regulations came into force, which significantly expanded the regulatory corpus.

Incentivizing more effective governance when the size of the economic pie shrinks can also be achieved through channels of public accountability, independent oversight, and effective legal deterrence against the abuse of public office. These ex post constraints on bureaucratic behavior entail the risks of empowering independent political actors. These risks may curtail the use of ex post constraints by authoritarian regulatory states. All political regimes, however, possess statutory mechanisms—legally binding documents defining regulatory content and implementation practices—that can constrain bureaucrats in their capacity as regulatory enforcers. Faced with the task of controlling the discretionary behavior of regulatory bureaucracy, autocrats may use statutory mechanisms and write more detailed regulations that codify specific bureaucratic actions, establish clear standards, and otherwise regulate policy implementation. The next section tests this proposition using quantitative data.

Data and Measurement

To empirically evaluate whether the logic of regime survival manifests itself in the formal development of regulatory frameworks, I make use of the fact that Kazakhstan and Russia have large oil-extracting industries that generate considerable flows of revenue into the government budgets. I use the World Bank's definition of oil rents. They are the difference between the value of crude oil production at regional prices and total costs of production. These were obtained from the World Bank's Changing Wealth of Nations database. Over the analyzed period, these range from 1.7 to 14.5 percent in the Russian Federation and from 1.4 to 26 percent in Kazakhstan. I use these as indicators of a regime's ability to satisfy popular economic demands, not only because they directly accrue to the government, but because even when in private hands, oil rents are easily taxable as countries' major exports. Larger oil rents open redistributive opportunities for appeasing popular economic grievances. Hypothesis 6 posits that declining oil rents should lead to the introduction of additional constraints on discretionary regulatory implementation.

The regime survival argument also implies that autocrats are sensitive to popular mobilization. Popular protests directly threaten authoritarian stability and call attention to underlying popular grievances. All things being equal, protests might tip the elite masses' benefit allocation equilibrium towards the provision of public goods. The implications of this proposition, however, are hard to test quantitatively, both because of the low frequency of nationwide protest events and the conceptual task of defining the level of mobilization that authoritarian regimes might perceive as a political threat. By focusing on the subnational variation in protest activity in the Russian Federation, I address both methodological problems. There is more temporal and cross-sectional variation in protest activity at the regional level;[134] regional protests do not need to be strong in order to undermine regional elites' positions vis-a-vis the federal government.

I conduct statistical analyses using the time series of the regulatory documents enacted by the governmental institutions and economic indicators for the Russian Federation and Kazakhstan between 1991 and 2018. The start date is the first year of independent statehood after the dissolution of the USSR. The end date is the year for which the complete annual counts of regulatory documents were available at the time of the original data collection in February 2019. This time period allows me to examine the growth and development of statutory, executive, and agency-level rulemaking in the early stages of economic liberalization, during the period of comprehensive regulatory reforms, and after the initial establishment of new regulatory systems. Chapters 3 and 4 described the sources and structure of the data. Because the argument about oil rents operates at the political regime level, I test it with national-level documents. For the analysis of regional protests, only regional-level documents are used.

In both countries, legislative statutes have legal precedence over other regulatory norms and constitute the foundation of the regulatory framework. National governments also issue binding orders that regulate economic relations and government institutions. Both statutory and executive regulations serve as conduits of state regulatory policy and institutional innovation. To facilitate the task of regulatory enforcement, administrative authorities (ministries and government agencies) have the right to pass binding orders. Such decisions may clarify the content of the law and establish mechanisms for enforcing compliance. In what follows, I analyze all regulatory documents produced by state institutions, as well as the documents produced by different types of government institutions.

---

[134] The empirical analysis in this chapter uses the Lankina Russian Protest-Event Dataset (http://eprints.lse.ac.uk/id/eprint/90298) to capture regional variation in protest activity.

The primary dependent variables in my analysis capture the overall cumulative length of regulatory documents that were in force in a given year. I use this as an indicator of ex ante formal constraint of the discretionary power of state bureaucracy. Chapters 2 and 3 establish that longer regulatory documents contain more detailed descriptions of who should be subjected to regulations, how regulations should be applied, and what techniques should be used in the process. These are the key ex ante formal mechanisms of constraining discretionary policy application. My analysis disregards the extent of regulatory fragmentation and does not distinguish between situations when the regulatory framework is defined by one comprehensive document or when it consists of a collection of shorter documents.

Kazakhstan

Data on the number and length of Kazakh national laws and administrative directives come from the databases of the Republican Center for Legal Information (RCLI) described in detail in Chapter 3. In what follows, I analyze 53,828 documents issued by national-level authorities. As Figure 21 shows, over time Kazakhstan accumulated a large corpus of laws, decrees, directives, and orders. The growth of all regulations, with the exception of presidential decrees, follows a linear upward trend.

Not all of the documents in the database, however, are economic regulations. The early years of independence are marked by an avalanche of laws and executive orders proclaiming new symbols of independence (the 1992 laws on the new flag, coats of arms, and national anthem, or the 1992–1994 laws renaming provinces, cities, and institutions). Some have strictly political purposes (orders and decrees appointing government officials), while others regulate social relations (i.e., language laws, new civil and criminal codes). In what follows, I analyze 27,703 national legal documents classified as relating to economic relations (53 percent of the total); 6,602 pertaining to general business regulation (rules of incorporation, licensing, bankruptcy, and taxation); 2,035 that regulated industry; 1,632, agriculture; 2,107, labor relations; 8,735, accounting and finance; and 674, subsoil resources. Tracing the dates these documents came into force and were annulled by subsequent regulations allows me to estimate the temporal changes in the number and detail of the country's entire regulatory corpus.

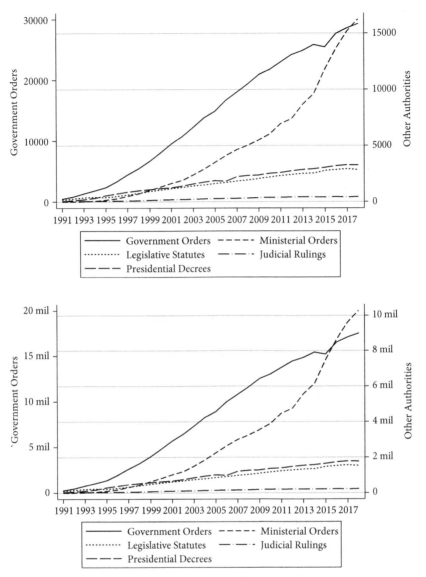

Figure 21 Total Number and Length of Kazakh National Regulatory Documents

Note: Number (up) and length in words (down) of legal documents in force in a given year by various Kazakh national authorities. Orders of the government are graphed on a separate scale.

Figure 22 graphically shows the annual rates of rulemaking across different spheres of economic activity.[135] The progress of new regulatory activity

---

[135] Different spheres of economic activity are defined by the Ministry of Justice for internal classification purposes.

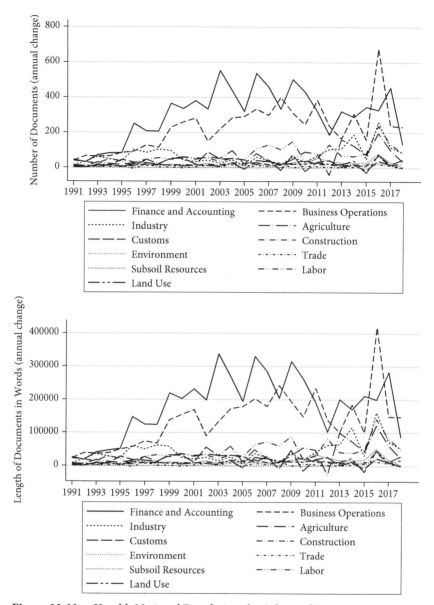

Figure 22 New Kazakh National Regulations by Sphere of Economic Activity

Note: Annual growth in number (up) and length in words (down) of legal documents across different spheres of economic activity.

was highly uneven across different spheres. Some spikes clearly overlap with high-level political development. Sharp increases in new regulatory documents coincide with the appointments of some prime ministers (Tokayev in 1999, Akhmetov in 2003), but not others (Tasmagambetov in 2002,

Masimov in 2007). The 2004 spike in financial and accounting regulations (the sphere with the most vigorous regulatory activity) is the direct result of the regulatory cascade following the introduction of a new tax code—a comprehensive reform that required major review and harmonization of bylaws regulating tax authorities, banking and financial transaction regulations, and accounting standards. The major economic event of 2015 was Kazakhstan's entry into the Eurasian Economic Union (EAEU)—a customs union with Russia, Belarus, and Armenia—which required comprehensive efforts to harmonize regulatory practices. Much of the regulatory innovation of 2015 is directly related to the demands of such harmonization, as well as the development of formal rules governing customs, EAEU trade flows, national industry and agriculture protection, and trade and labor market policies.

In addition to the thematic classification assigned by the Ministry of Justice, the dynamics of regulatory innovation differ by institutional origin. Using the metadata and keywords in the document titles, I classified documents into those originating in the judicial institutions (only the rulings of the Constitutional Court, and after 1995, Constitutional Council, were included in the original source), the legislature (the Supreme Soviet and unicameral Parliament from 1991–1995 and Majelis and Senate after 1995), and the executive institutions of central government. The latter include the top executive institutions—the president, prime minister, and cabinet (government)—and ministries and state agencies. Figure 23 summarizes the data.[136] The graphs show that legislative activism was on the rise in Kazakhstan in the 1990s and again in 2015. The government issued more new orders in the decade between 1999 and 2009 than in the previous and subsequent periods, while ministerial orders were on the rise throughout the entire period, with a one-year spike in 2015.

To test the hypothesis that authoritarian regimes implement formal regulatory controls to discipline administrative bureaucracy when the regime legitimacy (survival) is threatened, I rely on the total word count of regulatory documents in force in any given year. I expect that declining oil revenues make the autocratic government shift the regime survival strategy from distributing rents to promoting effective governance. This is when the autocrat is more likely to constrain a regulatory bureaucracy's discretionary power.

---

[136] Note that data on legislative statutes and judicial rulings are graphed on a separate scale.

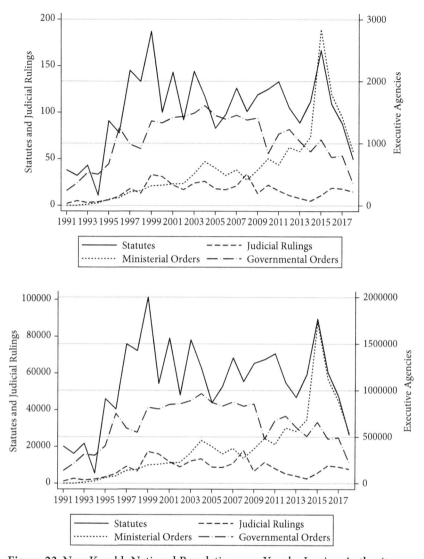

Figure 23 New Kazakh National Regulations per Year by Issuing Authority

Note: Annual growth in number (up) and length in words (down) of legal documents issued by various Kazakh national authorities. Orders of the executive agencies are graphed on a separate scale.

In Kazakhstan, the institutions of the executive branch are highly centralized and tightly controlled by the autocratic president, who can use his authority to appoint the government and reshuffle the heads of agencies to advance the regime's survival agenda. I expect the executive institutions to

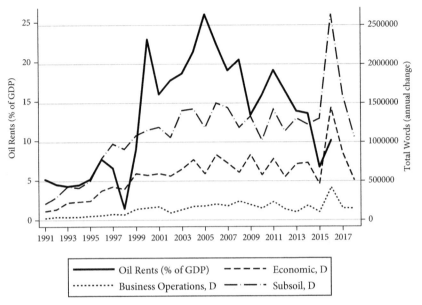

Figure 24 Oil Revenues and Annual Changes in the Total Length of Regulations

be the conduits of the regime's survival strategies and constrain or empower their bureaucratic subordinates through the use of discretionary policy application mechanisms. Because legislative and high judicial institutions are largely marginalized in Kazakhstan and do not preside over the dependent bureaucratic clientele, these are unlikely to be motivated by the political survival logic.

If, as my argument suggests, constrained policy application (more detailed regulatory norms) is driven by concerns for more effective management of the economy during times of declining mineral rents, the most immediate connection between regulatory detail and oil revenues should be observed in the sphere of natural resource management. To evaluate this expectation, I regress the annual changes in the length of regulatory documents pertaining to subsoil resource management on oil revenues' share of the GDP and a list of economic controls. To see if the logic of regime survival holds beyond the mineral resource regulations and applies to other shares of economic activities, I repeat the same set of analyses using the total lengths of all economic regulations. Figure 24 summarizes dependent and independent variables used for the analysis.[137]

---

[137] Most of the regulations' length series are non-stationary, but the Stata augmented Dickey-Fuller test rejects the unit root in their first-order differences. The oil rents variable is expressed as a GDP share and is a random walk with drift. I use it without a transformation.

Based on the time- series diagnostics, my regression specifications include the first difference (change) of the regulatory detail (length) variables, a linear time trend, and a dummy variable for 2015 to account for the exogenously induced spike in the rulemaking activity in that year. In addition to the standard macroeconomic controls (economy size, wealth, and growth), the size of the government, measured as the final central government consumption, is an important causal factor. Government consumption reflects the extent of government involvement in the economy and might demand additional rulemaking on how state agencies spend available resources. All independent variables are measured with one-year lags, but the size of the government is measured in the same year to avoid concerns over non-independence from oil revenues.

Regression results in Table 8 show that the rate of change in the total length of subsoil resource regulations declines in years following higher oil rents and grows in years following lower oil rents. Models 6–12 in Table 8 also show that the effects of oil rents go beyond the natural resource sector and affect the entire corpus of economic regulations. The latter results, however, are much stronger in the analyses of ministerial-level regulations than in the total corpus or the executive institutions.

To explore the differences across institutional origins and the thematic domain of the official regulatory documents, I perform a number of regression analyses following the same specification used in model 2 in Table 8, substituting the dependent variable with various permutations of policy domains and institutional origins of regulatory documents. Table 9 contains the coefficients and standard errors for the oil rents variable from these regressions. It shows that oil rents do not influence judicial decisions. Similarly, statutory laws, with the notable exception of trade sector regulations, also do not respond to oil rents. Surprisingly, oil rents are also inconsequential for the specificity of presidential orders. However, this might reflect the fact that most of the presidential decrees and decisions are of a declarative, symbolic, and course-setting nature and often call for the subsequent elaboration, implementation, and clarification by the government and specialized agencies.

Executive-level regulatory detail increases in the spheres of economy, business, industry, construction, and the environment in years following lower oil rents. The creation of ministry-level regulatory constraints in the regulation of subsoil resources is also sensitive to oil rents. One way to interpret the discrepancy between the results for governmental and agency-level regulations is to recognize that specialized agencies are more appropriate for the development of regulatory constraints in some domains but not others.

Table 8 Oil Rents Negatively Affect Formal Constraints on Regulatory Administration in Kazakhstan

| | Δ All Regulations | | | | | | Δ All Economic Regulations | | | | | |
| | All National Regulations | | Executive Regulations | | Ministerial Orders | | All National Regulations | | Executive Regulations | | Ministerial Orders | |
	(1)	(2)	(3)	(4)	(5)	(6)	(7)	(8)	(9)	(10)	(11)	(12)
Oil Rents	−29.42	−36.87	−28.29	−35.15	−18.90	−18.56	−13.55	−17.99	−13.21	−17.65	−9.08	−8.31
%GDP	(15.89)*	(16.74)**	(15.65)*	(16.59)**	(7.49)**	(8.45)**	(8.98)	(9.29)*	(9.03)	(9.30)*	(4.42)**	(4.96)*
GDP	−.005	−.008	−.005	−.008	−.002	−.002	−.002	−.005	−.002	−.005	−.001	−.001
Current USD, billion	(.003)*	(.003)**	(.003)*	(.003)**	(.001)**	(.002)	(.001)	(.002)**	(.001)	(.002)**	(.0007)**	(.001)
GDP per cap.	.09	.14	.09	.13	.06	.06	.05	.08	.05	.08	.04	.03
PPP (current USD)	(.03)***	(.04)***	(.03)***	(.04)***	(.01)***	(.02)***	(.02)***	(.02)***	(.02)***	(.02)***	(.008)***	(.01)***
GDP Growth	42.65	39.37	39.90	36.53	12.77	12.11	19.61	17.10	18.90	16.14	5.95	5.39
Annual %	(15.40)***	(17.00)**	(15.17)***	(16.85)***	(7.25)*	(8.58)	(8.71)**	(9.44)*	(8.75)**	(9.44)*	(4.28)	(5.04)
Govt. Size		−8.12		−9.43		−4.04		−7.92		−9.26		−4.07
Consumption, %GDP		(46.48)		(46.08)		(23.46)		(25.80)		(25.82)		(13.78)
Const.	601.34	482.12	514.29	424.62	−117.35	−67.02	243.40	203.88	227.18	201.48	−78.41	−16.03
	(243.29)**	(630.89)	(239.63)**	(625.50)	(114.59)	(318.46)	(137.55)*	(350.25)	(138.16)	(350.51)	(67.61)	(187.08)
Obs.	26	25	26	25	26	25	26	25	26	25	26	25
F statistic	8.12	7.05	8.17	6.87	26.61	17.1	8.44	7.68	8.2	7.56	25.48	16.31
R²	.67	.7	.67	.7	.87	.85	.68	.72	.67	.72	.86	.84
R²	.67	.7	.67	.7	.87	.85	.68	.72	.67	.72	.86	.84

Note: *, **, *** significant at .05, .01, .001 level or better. All economic data are from the World Bank.[a]

[a] Similar regressions were run on the document count and average document length. In earlier chapters, I discussed how the number of documents and the total length of the regulatory corpus are closely correlated. The count and total length of documents, unsurprisingly, respond to oil revenue similarly. Oil rents have no effect on the average length of regulatory documents.

Table 9 Regression Coefficients on "Oil Rents" Variable from the Difference Equations

	All	Economic	Business	Finance	Labor	Customs	Trade	Industry	Construction	Land Use	Subsoil	Environment
	(1)	(2)	(3)	(4)	(5)	(6)	(7)	(8)	(9)	(10)	(11)	(12)
Legislative	−1.728	−.420	−.091	−.347	−.041	−.021	−.027	.085	.033	.007	−.029	−.002
	(1.132)	(.524)	(.162)	(.385)	(.091)	(.041)	(.014)*	(.064)	(.023)	(.047)	(.021)	(.009)
Executive	−35.148	−17.646	−5.748	3.200	−.834	−.642	−.312	−4.384	−.784	−.641	−1.048	−.497
	(16.594)**	(9.298)*	(2.883)**	(3.405)	(1.354)	(.959)	(.233)	(1.379)***	(.268)***	(.438)	(.468)**	(.188)***
President[a]	−1.818	−.452	−67.746	−.061	.0002	−.020	−.027	−.036	.007	−.039	−.011	⋯
	(2.886)	(1.058)	(.292)	(.233)	(.488)	(.060)	(.026)	(.067)	(.048)	(.014.)	(2.886)	
Govt.	−14.766	−8.882	−1.406	.330	.247	.055	−.212		−.498	−.292	−.506	−.129
	(11.667)	(6.731)	(23.601)	(1.734)	(.812)	(.714)	(.225)		(.192)***	(.339)	(.367)	(.052)**
Ministry	−18.564	−8.312	−4.274	2.931	−1.081	−.863	−.073	−2.211	−.293	−.309	−.553	−.367
	(8.448)**	(4.963)*	(1.175)***	(2.329)	(.688)	(.584)	(.068)	(.870)**	(.161)*	(.142)**	(.160)**	(.146)**
Judicial	−.181	−.007	−.010		−.009		.002			−.005	⋯	.010
	(.349)	(.062)	(.015)		(.047)		(.009)			(.010)		(.008)

Note: Standard errors are in parentheses. *, **, *** significant at .05, .01, .001 level or better.

[a] The database contains no documents issued by the president on the matters of the environment. Judicial bodies did not rule on the matters of financial regulations, industrial relations, construction, or agriculture.

Consider, for example, that the construction industry is regulated by a patchwork of executive agencies, including the Committee for Construction and Housing and Communal Services of the Ministry of Industry and Infrastructure Development of the Republic of Kazakhstan; the government; the Institute of Standardization and Metrology; and provincial, city, and local representative (*maslikhats*) and executive (*akimats*) authorities. Since no specialized agency is vested with comprehensive control of the construction sector, the national government took the leading role in developing the implementation mechanisms for the July 16, 2001, law "On Architectural, Urban Planning and Construction Activities in the Republic of Kazakhstan." Industry relations, however, are regulated by the Ministry of Industry and Infrastructure Development (before 2014, the Ministry of Industry and New Technology). Much of the regulatory framework pertaining to the industrial policy and regulations had been developed by this specialized ministry.

Russia

Data on the number of federal-level laws and bylaws come from the databases of GARANT, described in Chapter 2. For the analysis, I use 214,330 documents identified as regulatory legislative and executive directives pertaining to commerce, entrepreneurship, labor relations, accounting and finance, subsoil resources, environment, international commerce, customs, social policy, and administrative law. Unlike in the Kazakh data, the Russian federal dataset allowed me to specifically identify technical regulations and standards that regulate application and implementation practices of federal laws, orders, and directives. These most directly capture the concept of formal constraint of policy application I pursue in this book. These technical regulations are legally binding documents that provide specific guidelines on regulatory enforcement and compliance, such as building codes, accounting manuals, or product and equipment certification guidelines. In the database, 3,043 documents were classified as pertaining to the national economy, entrepreneurship, and economic relations; 3,931 regulated finance; 1,309, customs; 523, the environment; 484, labor relations; 347, communal services; and 697, social welfare.[138] The dataset contains not

---

[138] Note that these categories do not overlap with those in the Kazakh regulatory documents. To check the robustness of my regression results, I also analyze the social policy documents and administrative regulations.

only the number of legal documents, but also the full text content, which allowed me to quantify the amount of regulatory detail.

The year-to-year differences in the detail of regulatory frameworks (Figure 25, left panel) reveal a few interesting patterns. Legislative

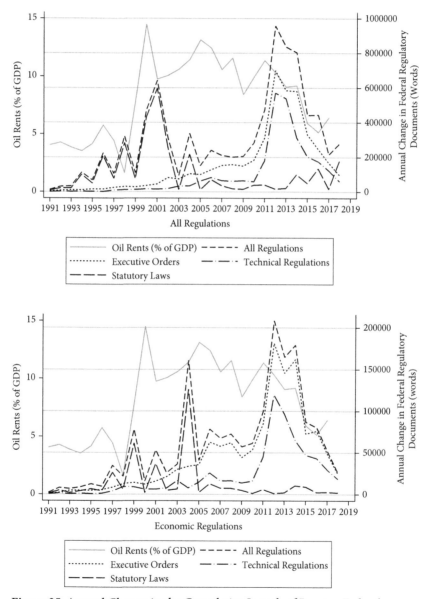

Figure 25 Annual Change in the Cumulative Length of Russian Federal Regulatory Documents and Oil Rents

productivity clearly drove the annual changes in regulatory detail in the 1990s, with minimal annual fluctuations in executive and technical regulations in that period. This was followed by a steady annual growth in technical and executive orders in the first decade of the twenty-first century and a rapid gain in the rates of change between 2009 and 2012. This period was followed by decreasing rates of change, which nevertheless exceeded those of the 1990s and early 2000s. The legislative constraint grew at a rather low rate between 2004 and 2012 but picked up after that. If restricting the analysis exclusively to the sphere of national economy and business regulations, the most dramatic expansion of statutory regulatory detail occurred in 2004, while executive and technical detail expansion peaked in 2012. Some of this growth coincides with the rollout of regulatory reforms, and some can be attributed to the explosion in federal rulemaking that followed the incorporation of Crimea as a subject of the Federation.

No clear pattern emerges from reviewing the time series of regulatory detail changes and temporal variation in oil revenue's contribution to Russia's GDP. The lack of consistency in the behavior of statutory and executive detail series, however, suggests that legislative and executive rulemaking follow different logic and might be differentially impacted by the availability of oil rents. I empirically test whether the declining oil revenues make the autocrats shift the regime survival strategy from distributing rents to promoting effective governance. This is when an autocrat is more likely to constrain a regulatory bureaucracy's discretionary power. To evaluate this expectation, I first perform time-series diagnostic tests to make sure I do not get spurious results.[139] I regress the annual changes in the logged number of different types of regulatory documents on changes in the oil revenue share of the GDP and the same list of economic controls I used for the Kazakh data analysis. The models also include a dummy variable that equals 1 in 2014, the year Crimea was incorporated into the Russian Federation.[140] All economic data are from the World Bank database, and the independent variables are lagged by one year.

Table 10 shows the regression results for two sets of dependent variables. The first set (models 1–4) contains those that aggregate all regulations that

---

[139] The regulation length series are not stationary and have a unit root in first difference. Logs of the regulatory length, however, exhibit stationarity in level and in difference. I chose the first difference of logged regulatory length variables as my dependent variables. The oil rents series are stationary in first difference.

[140] Results are robust when excluding the Crimea dummy, but modeling the incorporation of Crimea as a structural shift invalidates some results.

Table 10 Oil Rents Negatively Affect Federal Formal Constraints on Regulatory Administration in Russia

	Federal Documents				Economic Federal Documents			
	All (1)	Legislative (2)	Executive (3)	Technical (4)	All (5)	Legislative (6)	Executive (7)	Technical (8)
Oil rents, %GDP	−.084	−.080	−.097	−.033	−.045	−.042	−.037	−.046
	(.032)***	(.033)**	(.033)***	(.029)	(.019)**	(.024)*	(.014)***	(.021)**
GDP Trillion current USD	.638	.517	.605	.879	.320	.180	.415	.318
	(.449)	(.462)	(.464)	(.346)**	(.274)	(.344)	(.199)**	(.305)
GDP per Capita PPP 1000 (current USD)	−.077	−.072	−.069	−.081	−.043	−.037	−.047	−.040
	(.035)**	(.036)**	(.037)*	(.027)***	(.022)**	(.027)	(.016)***	(.024)*
Δ GDP Trillion current USD	−.204	−.190	−.046	−.408	−.020	−.020	−.067	.125
	(.403)	(.414)	(.416)	(.311)	(.246)	(.308)	(.178)	(.273)
Size of Government Final consumption, %GDP	−.106	−.097	−.119	−.121	−.031	−.009	−.060	−.013
	(.049)**	(.050)*	(.050)**	(.040)***	(.030)	(.037)	(.021)***	(.033)
Constant	2.680	2.533	2.847	2.825	1.088	.701	1.585	.739
	(.880)***	(.905)***	(.909)***	(.729)***	(.537)**	(.673)	(.390)***	(.597)
Observations	27	27	27	26	27	27	27	27
F statistic (6, 20)	3.357	3.406	3.023	2.901	2.761	2.138	4.873	1.881
R^2	.502	.505	.476	.478	.453	.391	.594	.361
Adjusted R^2	.352	.357	.318	.313	.289	.208	.472	.169
Durbin–Watson d	1.083	1.168	1.241	1.232	1.645	2.167	.871	1.523

Note: *, **, *** significant at .05, .01, .001 level or better. Standard errors are in parentheses.

may pertain to economic issues, including social policy and administrative law, but exclude criminal, procedural, judicial, and law enforcement codes. Model 1 presents the results for the entire corpus of documents pertaining to economic activities; Column 2, legislative statutes; Column 3, presidential decrees and orders and directives issued by federal ministries and agencies; and Column 4, technical regulations originating primarily, but not exclusively, in ministries and federal state agencies. I find that the total length of all federal economic regulations, statutory regulations, and clarifying bylaws are correlated with changes in oil rents. The second set of models presented in Table 10 includes regulations specifically classified as economic and business-related (models 5–8). This set also includes the results for statutory, executive, specialized technical, and the total number of regulations.

Negative and statistically significant coefficients on the oil rents variable mean that the Russian federal authorities are intensifying their rulemaking activities in times of declining oil rents, and such intensification is happening across the board. The results of the executive regulations variables are significant at the 99 percent confidence level and are highly robust to different model specifications. The legislative regulations are also affected by the annual changes in oil rents; however, these results are significant only at the 95 percent confidence level. Technical regulations respond to oil rents in the national economy sphere, but not at a more general level. In addition to the results presented in Table 10, I investigated how other categories of regulatory documents respond to changing oil rents. I found that executive-level regulations in the areas of finance, social, and labor policies experience growth in regulatory detail following drops in oil rents. Statutory regulations in these same areas either do not respond to oil rents, or, as in the case of labor policy, have the opposite of the expected effects. Other categories of the regulatory corpus are not statistically related to fluctuations in oil revenues. I conclude that Russian authorities enact more discretion-limiting documents in the statutory and executive realms in years immediately following shrinking oil rents.

Regional Protests in Russia

Turning to another threat to political survival—popular protests—I shift from the national to the regional level of analysis. Protests affect all regions of the Russian Federation, but there is considerable variation in time and geography of popular protests in the country. Some protests are instigated by region-specific or local issues (like the 2020 Khabarobsk protests over the conflict between Governor Sergey Furgal and the federal government), while others are part of nationwide waves of political (e.g., the 2011–2013 electoral protests) or economic (e.g., the 2004–2005 benefit monetization and 2018 pension reform) protests. Regardless of their specific grievance, protests threaten and undermine regional governments' positions vis-a-vis the center by either signaling the regional government's weakness and unpopularity or enticing the federal actors to interfere in regional politics. To appease the aggrieved population, regional authorities might attempt to streamline their governance, constrain corrupt or inefficient administration, and improve the efficacy of policy implementation and government services through formal constraints. In other words, the logic of political survival might operate at the provincial level. Provincial authorities may turn to formal aspects of constraining bureaucracy to improve governance when threatened by popular protests.

To investigate the use of regulatory constraints by regional authorities, I use data on protest events across Russian cities from the Lankina Russian Protest-Event Dataset. The data and methods are described by Lankina and Voznaya (2015) and Lankina and Tertytchnaya (2019). All but five regions had at least one protest episode over the period covered by the dataset. The Lankina dataset was merged with the regional data I analyzed in Chapter 4. The most protest-ridden years in Russia were 2009 and 2011. In 2009, Moscow city had its greatest number of yearly protests with 326, St. Petersburg had 156, Kaliningrad had 36 (its greatest number), and Primorskii Kraii had 35. Moscow province witnessed the greatest number of protests per year in 2011 with 39. The Lankina dataset codes protests based on their demands, which allows for the separation of political from economic and social demands. In what follows, I consider the annual count of all protest episodes in a region as well as the count of economic protests only.

I model the political survival logic in a panel setting and use a province-level fixed effects GLS estimation. The dependent variables are the first differences of cumulative lengths of regional regulatory documents, provincial laws, and administrative bylaws per capita. (I normalize by population size to account for the fact that more populous regions might require more elaborate administrative function.) I include economic controls from the oil rents equations because these are "the usual suspects" in predicting grievances and to maintain consistency with the national-level analyses. For this analysis, economic controls are measured at the regional level. Regressions include a quadratic trend variable because the regulation length series are trending upward over the analyzed period. Results are reported in Table 11.

Table 11 Regulatory Specificity Increases with Popular Unrest (Fixed Effects GLS)

	All Protests			Economic Protests		
	ΔAll	ΔLaws	ΔBylaws	ΔAll	ΔLaws	ΔBylaws
	(1)	(2)	(3)	(4)	(5)	(6)
Protests	69.533	15.673	52.898	226.436	42.918	178.998
# Episodes in a region	(29.950)**	(7.058)**	(24.280)**	(108.053)**	(25.483)*	(87.570)**
Government Size	−9537	−2431	−5669	−9367	−2382	−5548
Reg. expenditure/GRP	(6916)	(1629)	(5606)	(6919)	(1631)	(5607)
GRP	.007	.002	.005	.006	.001	.004
Current rubles	(.001)***	(.0003)***	(.001)***	(.001)***	(.0002)***	(.0008)***
GRP per Capita	−.016	−.004	−.012	−.016	−.004	−.012
Current rubles	(.002)***	(.0004)***	(.001)***	(.002)***	(.0004)***	(.001)***
GDP growth	−.002	−.0004	−.001	.003	.0005	.003
	(.003)	(.0007)	(.002)	(.004)	(.0009)	(.003)
Constant	−4.4e+08	−7.5e+07	−3.4e+08	−4.7e+08	−8.2e+07	−3.6e+08
	(1.5e+08)***	(3.6e+07)**	(1.2e+08)***	(1.5e+08)***	(3.6e+07)***	(1.2e+08)***
Observations	818	818	818	818	818	818
F stat. (7,727)	42.912	37.436	38.016	42.712	37.032	37.906
R^2 within	.292	.265	.268	.291	.263	.267
R^2 between	.353	.330	.371	.401	.381	.421
R^2 overall	.093	.085	.097	.100	.092	.104

Note: Fixed effects GLS. The protest variable is lagged by two years to account for the typical length of regulation approval. All other independent variables are lagged by one year. Regressions include a quadratic time trend. Standard errors are in parentheses. *, **, *** , significant at .05, .01, .001 level or better.

Across all models, regional protest episodes increase the rate of growth of regional regulatory detail. Such effects take into account regional economic conditions and are statistically significant and robust to dropping control variables and regions one at a time. Not only do the regions with higher incidents of protests produce more developed regulations—these effects could be due to regional sociodemographics unrelated to the economic conditions—they also tend to trail specific episodes of protests and hence cannot be reduced to time-invariant regional characteristics. The results are also substantively large, with one standard deviation increase in protests per region per year, resulting in 366 to 5,285 (or .5 standard deviations) additional words added to the regulatory corpus. One possible interpretation of the relationship observed in Table 11 is that popular dissatisfaction with a regional government might be related to changes in regional regulatory frameworks. In fact, protest activities tend to be more frequent in regions with more developed regulatory frameworks. The regressions might be capturing a causal relationship between the two but not necessarily in the correct causal order. As a quick check on reverse causality, I estimate whether the previous changes in the specificity of regulatory procedures lead to economic protests. Table 12 shows that when switching the key independent

Table 12 Popular Unrest Does Not Respond to Regulatory Changes

	Economic Protests		
	ΔAll	ΔLaws	ΔBylaws
Δ# Regulations	−.016	−.021	−.019
Words per capita	(.022)	(.069)	(.024)
Size of Government	3.506	3.486	3.433
Regional expenditure/GDP	(3.050)	(3.058)	(3.047)
GRP	−4.86	−4.81	−4.87
Million current rubles	(.410)***	(.403e)***	(.410)***
GRP per Capita	1.55	1.24	1.55
Million current rubles	(.988)	(.883)	(.982)
GDP Growth	.984	9.86	9.84
	(1.31)***	(1.31)***	(1.31)***
Constant	27021	37381	27093
	(73036)	(71491)	(72919)
Observations	808	808	808
F statistic (7,719)	30.606	30.519	30.612
R^2 within	.230	.229	.230
R^2 between	.741	.738	.742
R^2 overall	.088	.087	.088

Note: Fixed effects GLS. The regulations variable is lagged by two years. All other independent variables are lagged by one year. Regressions include a quadratic time trend. Standard errors are in parentheses. *, **, *** significant at .05, .01, .001 level or better.

and dependent variables, the relationship does not hold. The preceding changes in regulatory specificity do not correlate with the subsequent protest events. Changing the lag specification from one to two years, or including multiple lags, does not change this result. Although this analysis does not rule out the possibility of some long-term feedback effects, direct reverse causal effects are not detected.

Conclusion

This chapter investigated the possible explanations for the expansion of formal regulatory detail governing bureaucratic institutions. Unlike some other components of the regulatory state, statutory and agency-level controls can lead to a better quality of regulatory governance even when the traditional mechanisms of democratic public accountability are absent. Reflecting on the notion that clear and detailed regulations can discipline the public bureaucracy and positively affect the business climate, this chapter examined constraints and opportunities for building sound regulatory states by the autocratic regimes. I suggest that the conflicting incentives of the autocratic leaders can affect the extent to which the state relies upon statutory controls as the means of promoting regulatory efficiency. By treating the institutional mechanisms of state regulatory actions as dependent on the specific strategies of regime survival, this chapter advances a more nuanced and compelling theory of how the nature of authoritarianism shapes economic outcomes.

I investigated whether the autocrats' dilemma that ties the regime's survival strategy to two mutually exclusive priorities of catering to elite or public interests explains the use of ex ante constraint on regulatory discretion. For that purpose, I surveyed the development of national-level regulations in Kazakhstan and federal and regional-level regulations in Russia. These countries are particularly suited for testing my hypothesis because (1) they lack reliable mechanisms of public accountability and (2) theyrely upon oil revenues as an exogenous source of rents and public benefits. I found that in times of economic difficulties and shrinking oil rents, Russian and Kazakh national authorities are more likely to produce more elaborate and lengthy regulations, including those that constrain bureaucratic discretion in regulatory policy application.

I argued that in times when considerations of political survival make politicians prioritize national economic performance over elite enrichment, discretionary policy implementation is likely to be scaled back with the adoption of detailed statutory, executive, or agency-level regulations. The large-N quantitative data analysis reveals that accelerated development of discretion-constraining regulatory detail generally follows periods of declining oil rents, and at the regional level in Russia, periods of heightened protest activities. These results are consistent with the implications of the political survival thesis, but due to the methodological limitations associated with the analysis of short data series, they cannot serve as the ultimate "proof" of the validity of my hypothesis.

My arguments linking the amount of formal constraints on state regulatory agencies to the logic of political survival do not rule out the fact that oftentimes politicians respond to adverse economic conditions or social unrest with substantive policy changes—they often do. But when social and economic conditions call for recalibrating the balance between loyal bureaucrats and economic elites on the one hand and the general public on the other, formal mechanisms of policy application serve as a valuable tool of improved governance. Such mechanisms appear to function as a direct and flexible element of state regulatory function. They lie solely within the formal powers of the government institutions and do not require cooperation of the non-state actors. They directly redistribute the flow of economic resources without committing any additional budgetary funds. Finally, and most importantly, they allow the politicians to enhance the efficiency and effectiveness of institutions of governance without the risks associated with the development of societal oversight over government resources.

6

Bureaucratic Discretion and Business Climate around the World

One of the larger takeaway points of the theory of the regulatory state is that policy implementation matters. The purpose of this chapter is to validate the notion that mechanisms of regulatory policy application are consequential for regulatory outcomes beyond the context of transitional economies and autocratic politics. Using cross-national aggregate and enterprise-level data, this chapter demonstrates that patterns of regulatory enforcement influence whether state regulatory intervention will positively or negatively affect the business climate. State regulations affect the nature of economic coordination, security of property rights, domestic and foreign investment, competition, and time horizons of economic actors. It is logical to expect that these outcomes jointly shape perceptions of how business-friendly a regulatory regime is. Such logic, however, only holds insofar as the regulations are in fact being enforced to produce the intended effects on economic activities. When state regulatory agencies entrusted with regulatory implementation employ their discretion, as I argued in the previous chapters, the link between policy and intended outcomes might break. Does the discretionary bureaucracy in fact attenuate the link between regulatory policy and the business climate?[141]

In this chapter I assess three propositions pertaining to the role of policy implementation in the economy. All three are not specific to autocratic politics and help establish the general significance of institutional constraints

---

[141] By concentrating on the expert-based indicators of the business climate instead of economic performance (growth, productivity, investment), I mitigate the concerns over a reverse causal link between economic development and institutional quality. There are strong reasons to believe that regulatory policy and states' enforcement capacity are affected by their macroeconomic performance. Critics of institutional explanations of economic development have argued that most indicators of institutional quality, including state regulatory policy and capacity, are influenced by past and present levels of economic performance. Industrialized wealthy nations have more resources to invest in building better regulatory institutions (Kurtz and Schrank, 2007; Glaeser et al., 2004). Chapters 4 and 5 investigate direct and indirect effects of discretion on economic performance indicators, such as levels of investment and small business development.

Thieves, Opportunists, and Autocrats: Building Regulatory States in Russia and Kazakhstan. Dinissa Duvanova, Oxford University Press. © Oxford University Press 2023. DOI: 10.1093/oso/9780197697771.003.0007

on bureaucratic behavior. Hypothesis 4, as proposed in Chapter 1, postulates an independent direct effect of unconstrained policy implementation on the business climate. I argued that because it entails greater uncertainty and ambiguity in the regulatory process, discretionary bureaucratic power should negatively impact the business climate. To test this, I turn to two different types of data that capture the concept of discretionary policy application—macro-level indicators of functioning oversight of governance institutions and micro-level experiences with regulatory implementation.

Hypothesis 1 postulates that discretionary bureaucratic power attenuates the link between the state regulatory policy and resulting business climate by diminishing the effectiveness of loosely interpreted and misapplied state regulatory policy. In other words, the link between what is believed to be a set of business-friendly state regulations and the overall quality of the business climate should be stronger in discretion-free settings and weaker under discretionary policy implementation. I test these hypotheses with the help of widely used indicators of regulatory burden and the attractiveness of business operation conditions.

Hypothesis 2 captures the empirical implications of the causal mechanism that suggests corruption is being enabled by discretion. Corruption is an important reason the official regulatory norms are of little effect when the institutional frameworks enable discretionary policy application. I argued that high levels of bureaucratic discretion boost the creation of bureaucratic red tape. Such bureaucracy-imposed regulatory hurdles, I argued, allow corrupt officials to maximize the proceeds from corruption and influence-wielding. In what follows, I put this causal mechanism to the test by investigating how regulatory implementation attenuates the link between regulatory policy and corruption.

This chapter is based on a cross-national comparative analysis that covers developed and developing economies with different levels of state engagement in the economy, political systems, and institutional structures. It also uses available business survey data to verify that the results hold at the micro level, capturing actual experiences of running a business. While the survey data are clearly "closer" to the theoretical logic of my arguments, a cross-national panel has two advantages. The first is purely methodological. A diverse sample helps rule out regional or country-level idiosyncratic features as alternative explanations and increases confidence in the results. Testing my hypotheses against a diverse set of countries helps rule out idiosyncratic features of post-Soviet politics and the economy as alternative explanations for the discrepancy between formal regulatory policy and actual implementation practices. Most alternative accounts explaining why official institutions and policy radically depart from the actual practices of business-state interactions highlight the peculiarly intertwined formal institutions of the modern state and informal clienteles of economic and political support.[142] For the most part, they concentrate on idiosyncratic features of Russian and post-Soviet political regimes, social institutions, or historical legacies. By testing my arguments against countries of the West, East, and Global South, I show they hold despite these idiosyncrasies. Also, sample heterogeneity serves as an additional guarantee that the empirical results are not the product of selection of relevant institutional, political, or economic variables that may affect the business environment.

The second advantage is more theoretical. By demonstrating that my analysis holds for the more diverse set of cases, including those that do not fit the patrimonial, crony capitalist, patronal, or "bad governance" frameworks, I advance a more universalistic argument. The argument about the consequential nature of regulatory implementation is not predicated on a specific configuration of economic and political institutions—it applies to unitary and federal states, democracies and autocracies, and developed and developing nations. Unless empirically evaluated against a diverse sample of countries, the universal significance of discretionary administration cannot be established. If discretionary policy application is found to affect economic outcomes outside of the Russian and post-Soviet economies, my arguments would not be specific to the transitional or statist context, and discretionary policy application is likely to shape the business-state relations as these economies further diverge from their common Soviet past.

The chapter is organized as follows. I first discuss the country-level empirical measures of discretionary policy application. Given the fact that public administrations vary greatly in their structures, resources, and tasks entrusted to them, there is no surprise that assessing discretion at the national level presents considerable research challenges. Next, I describe the indicators of regulatory policy and the business climate. There is no lack of reputable sources of cross-national data to measure the extent of the regulatory burden or quality of the business climate based on business

---

[142] Patrimonial capitalism (Robinson, 2011), "piranha capitalism" (Markus, 2016), "states as investment markets" (Engvall, 2016), and crony capitalism (Aslund, 2019) help us understand the governance failures and suboptimal outcomes of a state's management of the economy.

surveys, expert assessments, or national economic statistics. The task for me is to pick those that capture the conceptual distinction between regulations as they exist on the books and the assessment of how beneficial for business growth is the actual environment these are meant to create. After describing the data and explaining my modeling choices, I present the results of my cross-national panel analysis. I then present some additional analyses of business survey data that corroborate my findings. I conclude the chapter by testing the empirical implications of the causal mechanisms, linking discretionary policy application and corruption.

The central message of this chapter is that the effect of regulatory procedures on the business climate is attenuated by the institutions responsible for policy application. Institutions that put a check on the behavior of state administrative agencies are generally beneficial for business confidence and strengthen the link between liberal regulations and conducive business climate. Institutions that enable bureaucratic discretion help account for large discrepancies between the regulatory policy and the quality of the business climate. By investigating the hypothesized connections between regulatory policy and the business environment through the prism of policy implementation mechanisms, this chapter subjects the theory of bureaucratic power to yet another empirical test. The empirical evidence presented below also supports the notion that a capricious bureaucracy exacerbates regulatory hurdles and creates opportunities for corruption even under otherwise unlikely conditions.

Macro-level Measures of Discretion, the Business Climate, and Regulations

Discretion

Measuring discretion is not a straightforward task, especially in cross-national applications. Discretionary powers might be concentrated at different levels of regulatory bureaucracy and might be unevenly distributed across policy domains. Some policy application tasks may be inherently associated with greater discretion, such as in awarding public contracts to private vendors, rather than enforcing strict eligibility criteria or as in granting import permits or professional licenses. To complicate the matter, different countries have different priorities concerning the nature and extent of their regulatory intervention—some are more proactive in certain sectors than others—as well as changing policy priorities that might shift the burden of regulatory activity from one sector to another, depending on political and economic conditions. With these considerations in mind, one should look for macro-level indicators to capture the institutional design factors associated with greater or lesser reliance on discretionary mechanisms of policy implementation.

On the conceptual level, the task of measuring bureaucratic discretion also has to take into account the fact that the political regime type, degree of federalism, and diversity of public sector management strategies may potentially bias our measures of bureaucratic quality. No direct cross-national macro-level measure of discretion has been constructed. However, the Global Integrity (GI) international think tank coordinated the efforts of researchers and journalists to compile indicators of institutional structures and performances for about 120 countries and territories around the world with a specific focus on openness, accountability, and orderliness of government institutions. I use the organization's country-level ranking of the effectiveness of supreme audit institutions as an instrument for bureaucratic constraint.[143]

Since bureaucratic discretion may originate from different institutional, economic, and political factors, the GI ranking of the effectiveness of the supreme audit institution, auditor general, or equivalent agency takes into account a range of potentially relevant sources of constraint. The GI report assesses the effectiveness of the supreme audit institution based on whether (1) it is covering the entire public sector; (2) it is legally protected from political interference; (3) in practice, the head of the agency is protected from removal without relevant justification; (4) the agency has a professional, full-time staff; (5) agency appointments support the independence of the agency; (6) the agency receives regular funding; (7) it makes regular public reports; (8) the government acts on the findings of the agency; (9) the agency is able to initiate its own investigations; and (10) by law, citizens can access audit reports, (11) doing so in actual practice within a reasonable time period and (12) at a reasonable cost. The GI aggregates across these components and produces the overall effectiveness score, which in my analysis serves as an instrument for measuring institutional constraints on bureaucratic power

[143] Global Integrity 2006, "Global Integrity Indicators" [online database], http://www. globalintegrity.org/, accessed May 2010.

to apply policy freely. I reason that strong and effective audit institutions constrain state bureaucracies in ways that make discretionary policy application less likely. In fact, previous research has shown that independent and resourceful supreme audit institutions effectively uncover fraud and corruption in public institutions in Europe, North America, Russia, and China and can deter corruption by public officials (Dye, 2007). There is also clear evidence that investigations by state audit institutions have led to successful prosecution of corruption in Zambia, Poland, Hungary, South Korea, and other countries (Evans, 2008).

The original measure of audit effectiveness was collected for 25 countries in 2004. The countries were assigned scores between 0 and 7, with high audit corresponding to low discretion. The subsequent ratings ranged from 0 to 100, with each of the evaluation categories mentioned above weighted equally in the total score on supreme audit effectiveness.[144] Forty-one countries were ranked in 2006 and 52 in 2007. In 2008, 46 countries were assigned scores, and in 2009–2011 the dataset included 31 countries. Starting in 2014, the GI refocused their mission on the African continent and continued to use their methodology for scoring institutional quality with a sample of 54 African countries. This meant that some previously ranked countries were dropped from the dataset, while new countries were included. In total, 119 countries/territories received GI scores. With gaps between the surveys and countries moving in and out of the dataset, there are 525 country/year observations between 2004 and 2018. Table 13 lists the 102 countries included in my analysis and the number of available early observations. Belarus, Central African Republic, Comoros, Republic of Congo, Djibouti, Equatorial Guinea, Eritrea, Guinea-Bissau, Niger, Libya, Kosovo, Iraq, Virgin Islands, Vanuatu, Togo, Sao Tome and Principe, and Papua New Guinea are excluded from the regression analysis because of missing data of covariates.

Across 525 total available observations (including countries and territories for which the corresponding macroeconomic covariates are unavailable), the minimum score for the "Effectiveness of Supreme Audit Institutions" is 20, the maximum score is 100, and the mean is 63.6 points. The changes in sample composition over time are reflected in the considerable variation of the mean scores from one installment to another. While the mean supreme audit score in 2004, when the sample included a

---

[144] I rescaled the 2004 data to make them comparable to the subsequent scores.

Table 13 Countries Included in Cross-National Analysis and Number of Repeated Observations

Albania 1	Georgia 5	Nepal 4
Algeria 2	Germany 2	Nicaragua 4
Angola 7	Ghana 10	Nigeria 10
Argentina 5	Guatemala 3	North Macedonia 3
Armenia 3	Guinea 5	Pakistan 4
Australia 1	Hungary 2	Panama 1
Azerbaijan 5	India 5	Peru 2
Bangladesh 3	Indonesia 5	Philippines 5
Benin 6	Ireland 1	Poland 2
Bolivia 5	Israel 1	Portugal 1
Botswana 5	Italy 4	Romania 4
Brazil 2	Japan 3	Russia 5
Bulgaria 4	Jordan 3	Rwanda 6
Burkina Faso 6	Kazakhstan 3	Senegal 6
Burundi 6	Kenya 11	Serbia 4
Cabo Verde 5	Kuwait 3	Seychelles 5
Cambodia 1	Latvia 1	Sierra Leone 9
Cameroon 8	Lebanon 3	South Africa 10
Canada 3	Lesotho 5	Spain 1
Chad 5	Liberia 9	Sri Lanka 1
Chile 1	Lithuania 1	Tajikistan 3
China 4	Madagascar 5	Tanzania 8
Colombia 4	Malawi 8	Thailand 1
Congo, Democratic Republic 5	Malaysia 1	Timor-Leste 1
Costa Rica 1	Mali 5	Tunisia 5
Cote d'Ivoire 5	Mauritania 5	Turkey 4
Czech Republic 2	Mauritius 5	Uganda 10
Ecuador 2	Mexico 5	Ukraine 4
Egypt 9	Moldova 3	United States 5
Eswatini 5	Mongolia 2	Venezuela 3
Ethiopia 8	Montenegro 2	Vietnam 3
France 1	Morocco 7	Yemen 3
Gabon 5	Mozambique 7	Zambia 5
Gambia 5	Namibia 7	Zimbabwe 9

large number of high-income countries, was 89.7 (rescaled scores), when the 46-country sample was expanded in 2008 to include a large number of low-income nations, the mean dropped to 71.7 points. From 2014–2018, when the sample consisted of African countries only, the mean supreme audit institutions score did not exceed 48.6 points, reflecting the continent's lower levels of institutional constraint on state bureaucracy.

To give some indication of how this measure of the strength of audit institutions fares across countries, the People's Republic of China received an average of 80.6 points across its four repeated annual observations,

Austria was scored at 97.2, and Egypt had a mean of 39.1 across nine observations (Figure 26). This book's reader would perhaps be more interested in the distribution the GI supreme audit institutions measure across East-Central Europe and the USSR successor states. In this group of countries, the lowest average (across three observation points) is found in Tajikistan (54.86 points), a country with low levels of economic development, authoritarian rule, and a history of violent civil conflict. Serbia, a country in the upper middle-income category, but with divisive politics and persistent mismanagement of government institutions following the dictatorial rule of Slobodan Milosevic, has an average score of 56.95 points across four observations. Serbia's and Tajikistan's levels of top-level institutional constraints are lower than most African countries, including the world's poorest, Sierra Leone, with its 65.8 average score.

At the higher end of this scale are Latvia (94.79 points), Bulgaria (94.44 average over four observations), Poland (92.59 average over two observations), Albania (91.66), and Hungary (90.29 points). Russia stands at an 88.11-point average over five observations, in close proximity to Ukraine (89.82 points over four observations) and Romania (84.5-point average over four observations). Outside of the region, Turkey, with 84.25 points over four observations has a comparable score to Russia. Audit effectiveness scores for Lithuania (82), Czech Republic (79.68), and Georgia (78.67 average over five observations) are close to those of the People's Republic of China (80.57 average over four observations). Armenia, Kazakhstan, and Azerbaijan fall slightly below that level with averages of 77.43 and 75.97 over three observations for Armenia and Kazakhstan and five observations for Azerbaijan.

The supreme audit effectiveness measure varies widely not only across but also within many countries, capturing temporal changes in the formal rules and practice of governance. The pooled sample standard deviation is 23.4 points, while there is a standard deviation of 19.2 points across Sudan's six annual observations. Ghana's score ranges between 55 and 96.88 and Venezuela's between 76.73 and 94.04, while the Philippines' lowest and highest scores are 38.7 points apart, or more than one standard deviation, ranging between 57.3 and 96 points. In East-Central Europe, Serbia has the largest variance across its supreme audit scores, improving from 43.75 points in 2009 to 68.75 in 2011 (a 25-point improvement). Georgia improved by 22.62 points between 63.84 in 2008 and 86.46 in 2011, while Tajikistan's score rose 18.06 points from 44.79 in 2004 to 62.85 in 2011.

The GI index also documents declines in the strength of top-level institutional constraints on state agencies. Ukraine's score declined 15.18 points,

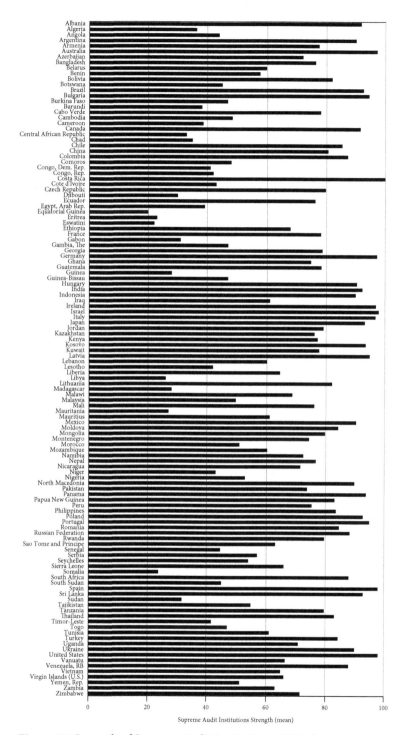

Figure 26 Strength of Supreme Audit Institutions, GI Indicators

Note: Data from GI, multiple-year averages.

from 96.43 in 2004 to 81.25 in 2011; Russia's score declined 17.2 points, from 97.62 in 2004 to 80.47 in 2008; and Kazakhstan experienced the largest decline in the post-Soviet space, dropping 43.75 points, from 93.75 in 2007 to 50 points in 2010. Although much of the intra-country variation in the supreme audit institutions score can be linked to political changes, even countries with a considerable level of institutional stability exhibit non-trivial temporal variation in their GI supreme audit rankings because these integrate the assessment of actual practices that go beyond *de jure* authority. Overall, in the sample, the standard deviation for repeated within-country observations ranges from 2 to 21 points.

For clarity in interpreting the results of interactive variable regression, I create a binary variable distinguishing between "high" and "low" levels of discretion. I code a country/year observation as a "low" discretion environment if the GI score described above exceeds 70 points. A country would need to exhibit a considerable extent of audit electiveness across a majority of GI subindicators, and the majority of countries that pass the 70-point mark would be considered as having effective formal constraints on the arbitrary actions of civil servants. Still, the 70-point cut-off mark is low enough to include well-governed, non-Western, low-income countries, as well as those countries that are not fully democratic. The coding of 1 on this binary variable corresponds to higher scores on the effectiveness of supreme audit institutions with high bureaucratic constraint or low discretion, while 0 corresponds to the low effectiveness of supreme audit institutions, or high discretion. The resulting binary variable codes 229 observations as "high" quality of supreme audit institutions, or "Low Discretion." At the same time, 296 country/year observations are coded "High Discretion." Thirty-three countries included in the analysis have experienced changes in this coding—either improvement or deterioration in the audit quality—over different installments of the GI reports.

Business Climate

A number of reputable organizations routinely rank countries on the ease of doing business, quality of governance, political risk factors for investment, and the overall quality of the business climate in a given country. These ratings—regardless of whether they are based on expert- or business-based surveys or "hard" data on measurable conditions—reflect specific assumptions about what constitutes a "good" business climate. One of the most common assumptions is that any type of state regulatory intervention decreases the attractiveness of the business climate. However, we know from a plethora of research that regulations may make a situation more conducive to private investment, growth, and development. The World Economic Forum (WEF) Global Competitiveness Index (GCI) minimizes the neoliberal bias against regulations by assigning positive weights on economic and social institutions regulating labor, finance, and corporate spheres. Accommodating the notion that state regulatory involvement may constitute a business asset rather than a liability, the GCI adds infrastructure, macroeconomic stability, health, education, skill levels, technological readiness, business sophistication, and innovation to the standard mix of market-friendly policies and institutions.

The methodology of aggregating across these different dimensions does not follow a one-size-fits-all approach. Instead, it attempts to weigh different aspects of the business environment differently, as "they will matter differently for different countries, depending on their particular starting conditions or stage of development" (Lopez-Claros, 2006, p. xiii). Departing from the heavy reliance on subjective expert- and survey-based ratings, the GCI introduces a number of "hard" data measures to evaluate the quality of the labor force, infrastructure, research and development, and macroeconomic stability. The GCI ranks national competitiveness on a scale ranging from 0 to 6, with high values corresponding to greater competitiveness and a more favorable business environment. This reflects the average levels of operational and strategic sophistication of companies operating in a given country and the overall quality of the national business environment, accounting for the limitations associated with differential levels of national wealth and the composition of the economy.[145]

Regulations

Similar to business climate, there are many alternative options for assessing the official regulatory burden. The problem is that the most widely used measures of regulatory quality and regulatory burden are based on perceptions, not on "hard" data. Survey responses of business leaders and

---

[145] Later in the chapter, as a robustness check, I also consider a more traditional neoliberal operationalization of the overall favorability of the business environment based on the Heritage Foundation (HF) and *Wall Street Journal* Index of Economic Freedom. Since 2013, however, HF changed its methodology and used the World Bank DB data discussed below as the basis for their business freedom score. The business freedom subindicator is computed based on the cost, time, and freedom to open, operate, and close a business and get electricity. While previously the HF relied upon the Economist Intelligence Unit data for this subcategory, currently it borrows from the DB measures of regulatory burden.

country experts, however, are likely to reflect the *actual* level of regulatory burden experienced by businesses, not the official state regulatory policy. This, according to the argument advanced in Chapter 1, comprises the official costs of regulatory policy (the quantity of interest) as well as the unofficial costs, including the cost of the red tape created by bureaucrats in order to extort more bribes and favors. For the "well-connected" firm, on the contrary, the reports of their environment can look rosier than the official policy. If the regulatory agencies apply regulations selectively, such firms are likely to receive "special treatment" and introduce discrepancy between the official and actual regulatory burden they experience. Most perception-based measures of regulatory burden do not allow for the differentiation of the official and actual regulatory costs.

To capture the extent of regulatory burden attributable solely to official regulatory policy, I turn to data measuring the number of regulatory procedures faced by businesses around the world. The "Doing Business" (DB) project by the World Bank is the source of data on the number of regulatory procedures involved in (1) starting a business, (2) dealing with construction permits, (3) getting electricity, (4) registering property, (5) getting credit, (6) protecting minority investors, (7) paying taxes, (8) trading across borders, (9) enforcing contracts, and (10) insolvency.[146] Following the research methodology pioneered by Djankov et al. (2002), the World Bank identifies the number of regulatory procedures from official government publications, reports of development agencies, and government web pages, which makes the data reflective of the official, rather than unofficial, regulatory practices. These data were first collected in 1999 by Djankov et al. (2002) in a pilot study. In 2002, based on Djankov's research methodology, the World Bank started a systematic collection of direct measures of official regulatory burden and gradually expanded the number of included countries from 133 to 190. The data I use cover the period between 2004 and 2018.[147]

---

[146] DB data are available at http://www.doingbusiness.org.

[147] In 2021, the World Bank suspended its annual DB publication after an external audit found the bank's senior officials pressured the staff to alter data in the 2018 and 2020 report installments. Reuters reported ratings were altered to benefit China, Saudi Arabia, and other countries. Critics called for stopping the World Bank's practice of selling consulting services to governments aimed at improving their scores. To restore the credibility of the DB report, the bank announced it will improve the transparency of its sources and put more weight on survey-based indicators (Shalal, 2021). In the following analysis, I only use the survey-based components of DB data—the average number of regulatory procedures reported by the surveyed managers of firms sampled by a random stratified method. These measures are verifiable aggregations of the published World Bank Business Environment Surveys and are not subject to data manipulation.

In what follows, the stringency of regulatory regimes is operationalized in terms of (1) the total number of all regulatory procedures available between 2004 and 2018 and (2) the official number of regulatory procedures required to open a new business (regulations of entry).[148] Since the extent of economic integration, structure of the economy, levels of productivity, and other economic characteristics are likely to make various types of regulations differentially relevant under different conditions, I computed a summary measure by a simple summation across different categories of regulations. These include regulatory procedures for starting up a business, construction permits, registering property, enforcing contracts, and trading across borders because these were part of the early installments of data collection and have the longest available time series. Later in the chapter I refer to this variable as "Economic Regulations." "Entry Procedures" is an alternative way to operationalize regulatory burden that is based on the indicators for ease of opening a new business. Unlike other types of DB indicators (e.g., export/import procedures, construction permits), entry regulations are likely to have more universal significance across countries at various levels of income, productivity, infrastructure development, and openness to foreign trade. Unlike the alternative instruments for assessing the difficulty of doing business, these data are designed to capture the "objective" burden of the official regulatory intervention that affects firms in different lines of business.

Data Analysis

Assessing the Direct Effects of Discretion

In the panel of 102 countries, the proposed measure of country-level discretionary policy application—the GI Supreme Audit Institutions Index—is positively correlated with indicators of the business climate and governance quality. Controlling for a nation's wealth, the size of its economy, and oil rents in a random effects panel data analysis, the lagged values of the Supreme Audit Institutions Index have a sizable, statistically significant effect on all six components of the World Bank good governance indicators (see Table 14). The GI supreme audit index also correlates with a number of relevant World Bank Country Policy and Institutional Assessment (CPIA)

---

[148] For methodological details, see http://www.doingbusiness.org.

Table 14 Effects of Supreme Audit Institutions on World Bank Governance Indicators

	Voice & Accountability	Political Stability	Government Effectiveness	Regulatory Quality	Rule of Law	Control Corruption
Audit Strength	.002	.004	.003	.004	.002	.002
GI score	(.0006)***	(.001)***	(.0005)***	(.0006)***	(.0006)***	(.0006)***
Obs.	462	462	462	462	462	462

Table 15 Effects of Supreme Audit Institutions on World Bank Country Policy and Institutional Assessment Indicators

	Business Regulatory Environment	Public Sector Management and Institutions	Quality of Public Administration	Transparency, Accountability, and Corruption
Audit Strength	.002	.002	.004	.006
GI score (0–100)	(.0008)***	(.0008)***	(.001)***	(.001)***
Obs.	227	227	227	227

indicators compiled by the bank annually for 73 low-income countries eligible for the international development association programs. The CPIA consists of 16 indicators grouped into four categories, including economic management, structural policies, policies for social inclusion and equity, and public sector management and institutions. Table 15 presents the regression coefficients on the supreme audit index obtained from the panel regressions controlling for wealth, size of the economy, and oil and mineral rents. I select the most relevant CPIA subcomponents. Business Regulatory Environment is one of three subcomponents of the Structural Policies cluster. Quality of Public Administration, and Transparency, Accountability, and Corruption are two relevant components of the Public Sector Institutions cluster. I also use the entire Public Sector Management cluster score.

Table 16 reports the coefficients on the GI supreme audit variable obtained from the panel multiple regression on the HF and *Wall Street Journal* Index of Economic Freedom and some of its subindicators.[149] Controlling for the size of the economy and wealth, the overall economic freedom score; property rights; and the judicial effectiveness, business, and financial freedom scores

[149] The HF Economic Freedom Index is computed since 1995 and currently includes 12 components. Property rights, judicial effectiveness, and government integrity constitute the rule of law factor. Tax burden, government spending, and fiscal health subcomponents measure the size of the government. Business, labor, and monetary freedoms measure regulatory efficiency. Trade, investment, and financial freedom subcategories assess market openness.

Table 16 Effects of Supreme Audit Institutions on Heritage Foundation
Economic Freedom Indices

Economic Freedoms	Overall Score	Property Rights	Judicial Effec- tiveness	Business	Labor	Trade	Invest- ment	Finance
Audit Strength	.028	.082	.341	.018	.025	.031	−.065	.072
GI score	(.012)**	(.031)***	(.072)***	(.024)***	(.023)	(.023)	(.035)*	(.023)***
Obs.	438	444	103	445	445	443	443	438

are strong correlates of the GI supreme audit index. The HF ratings for
tax burden; government spending; fiscal health; and monetary, labor, and
trade freedom, reflective of the policy choices, however, are uncorrelated
with audit strength. This is consistent with theoretical expectations. Such
indicators are heavily dependent on the government's fiscal, monetary, trade,
and labor policy choices and might only marginally reflect implementation
practices. Interestingly, investment freedom is negatively affected by audit
institutions' strength. However, the Audit Strength variable has a stable,
positive, substantive, and statistically significant effect on the foreign direct
investment (FDI) flows. A 10-point increase in the GI audit score adds the
FDI equivalent of between .5 to .6 percent of a country's GDP. This result is
robust to the inclusion of standard economic (wealth, growth, economy size,
mineral rents) and institutional (political stability, rule of law) controls.

It appears that the GI index of top-level institutional constraints that
I interpret as the opposite of discretionary administration has an expected
positive effect on the widely accepted indicators of good regulatory climate
and good governance.

Discretion and Business Climate

I argued that bureaucratic discretion attenuates the link between state intervention and the resulting business climate (Hypothesis 1). In theory, regulatory procedures should have a strong effect on the regulatory environment only when applied consistently. Capricious, discretionary policy
implementation, however, should render the effect of official regulatory costs
less consequential for the quality of the business environment. To test this
conditional relationship, I estimate a series of panel regression models that
interact the bureaucratic constraint variable with measures of regulatory

interference. Appendix E presents model specifications and regression result tables. In what follows I discuss the results of my empirical tests and their graphic representation.

I start by evaluating independent effects of discretion (constraint) and regulatory interference. Bureaucratic constraint, measured by the GI index of supreme audit institutions, has an expected positive effect on economic performance, but such effect does not produce substantial improvement in a country's GCI. One standard deviation increase in audit effectiveness improves the 6-point GCI score only by .02 points. Regression analysis does not decisively reject Hypothesis 4, postulating that bureaucratic discretion should harm economic performance. Still, my results suggest that discretion in itself is not particularly detrimental to the business climate. Regression analysis also shows that separate effects of entry regulations are negative, which lines up well with notions that regulations are harmful to business. One standard deviation increase in the number of entry regulations lowers the country GCI score by .18 points. In themselves, these effects are statistically significant from zero, but not substantively large.

When interacted in the regression model specification, however, discretion and regulation variables produce an interesting picture. When discretion is high, the effects of entry regulations are not statistically significant from zero. In other words, in high-discretion regimes, regulations do not matter. When discretion is low, however, regulations become important negative predictors of a country's GCI score. Such effects become much larger in substantive terms, compared to the regression equations that estimate separate independent effects of regulations and discretion. Figure 27 graphically represents this difference. It plots the predicted values of the GCI score from the regression equation that interacts discretion with the number of entry procedures from the World Bank DB project (model 3 in Table 20, Appendix E). The lines correspond to predicted values of GCI under two alternative regulatory enforcement regimes after setting the control variables at their means. While the relationship between entry regulations and business climate is negative in the low-discretion regime, it is nonexistent in the high-discretion settings. These results are robust to the inclusion of the political (regime and stability) and additional economic controls (growth, oil rents, or FDI).

To check if my results hold against alternative ways to measure the extent of the regulatory burden, I substitute the number of regulations of entry that usually act as obstacles to starting a business with the count of regulatory

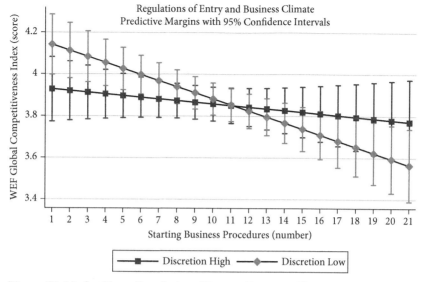

Figure 27 Market Entry Regulations Hamper Business Climate in Low-Discretion Settings Only

Note: Data from the World Bank, GI, and WEF. The lines represent the predictive margins of the random effects regression analysis. "Discretion Low" corresponds to the rating of supreme audit institutions of 70 points and above on a 20–100-point scale. "Discretion High" corresponds to scores below 70 points.

procedures required for property registration, construction permits, contract enforcement, paying taxes, obtaining electricity, and trading across borders. The GCI responds positively to the total count of regulations in these categories (see model 4, Table 20 in Appendix E). One interpretation is that the GCI assigns higher scores to the countries with more developed business infrastructure, more rule-bound business practices, and public goods. Larger numbers of regulatory norms in the above mentioned categories, therefore, might be indicative of better economic governance structures and more competitive economies. The discretionary policy application, however, continues to render regulatory procedures irrelevant in predicting the business climate.[150] Substantively, under a constrained bureaucracy, one standard deviation increase in the count of regulatory procedures leads to a .08-point increase in the 6-point GCI score. This effect is statistically significant at the .001 percent confidence level. Figure 28 illustrates these effects

---

[150] The signs of the interaction term coefficient in model 4, Table 20 in Appendix E, flip as well, meaning that effects of regulations are dampened by bureaucratic discretion.

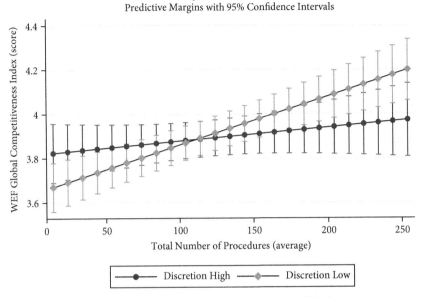

Figure 28 Developed Regulatory Frameworks Improve Global
Competitiveness Index in Low-Discretion Settings Only

Note: Data from the World Bank, GI, and WEF. The lines represent the predictive margins of the random effects regression analysis. "Discretion Low" corresponds to the rating of supreme audit institutions of 70 points and above on a 20–100-point scale. "Discretion High" corresponds to scores below 70 points.

with predicted values from the regression that operationalizes regulatory burden with a more inclusive set of regulatory procedures. The predicted values of the *All Procedures* variable are plotted against regulatory burden for low- and high-discretion cases and holding the control variables at their means. When discretion is high, regulations have no effect on the business climate.

These results are robust to a different way of measuring the outcome variable. When I measure the business environment by the HF Index of Economic Freedom instead of GCI, regulatory intervention factors negatively into indicators based on a more conservative, neoliberal methodology (model 5 in Table 20, Appendix E). Results of this analysis suggest that more numerous regulations (the more inclusive measure of regulatory burden) are associated with a less business-friendly climate. This gives further credence to my speculation that positive effects of regulations on the GCI are the product of the WEF's methodology of accessing the quality of the business environment. What remains unchanged across all regression models, however, is the interaction effect. Regulations have no effect on the business environment under a high-discretion bureaucratic environment. In the low-discretion environment, however, the effects of regulations are statistically significant from zero and negative. One standard deviation increase in regulatory procedures under a disciplined bureaucracy leads to a 5.35-point decrease in the 100-point Economic Freedom Index. Figure 29 plots the predicted values for economic freedom under low-discretion and high-discretion regimes, holding the control variables at their means.[151]

Overall, the analysis is consistent with the notion that bureaucratic discretion conditions the relationship between regulatory policy and the regulatory environment experienced by businesses. Regulatory intervention affects the overall quality of the business environment only when bureaucrats

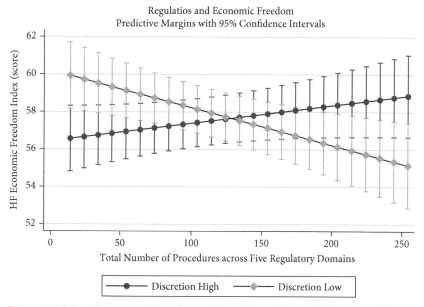

Figure 29 More Numerous Regulatory Procedures Hamper Indicators of Economic Freedom in Low-Discretion Settings Only

Note: Data from the World Bank, GI, and HF. The lines represent the predictive margins of the random effects regression analysis. "Discretion Low" corresponds to the rating of supreme audit institutions of 70 points and above on a 20–100-point scale. "Discretion High" corresponds to scores below 70 points.

---

[151] Since 2013, its subcomponent—index of business freedom—is not constructed independently from the DB indicators; hence, I interpret this analysis with caution, only as an additional robustness check.

have limited discretionary power in interpreting and carrying out regulatory policies. When such powers are not restricted by oversight institutions, the extent of the official regulatory involvement is not a good predictor of the quality of the business environment.

Additional Evidence from Business Surveys

Examination of survey data adds more support to the notion that discretionary policy application impacts the business climate.[152] In 1999, to document the progress of market reforms, the European Bank of Reconstruction and Development conducted a Business Environment and Enterprise Performance Survey (BEEPS) of business owners and executive managers in the transitional economies. In subsequent years, the survey methodology was perfected and expanded to become the World Bank Enterprise Survey project, reflecting firsthand business experiences with the business environment, enterprise performance, and regulatory climate. Among other things, the representative sample of business owners and managers reports the percentage of senior management's time per year spent in dealing with business regulations. The answers ranged from 0 to 95 percent. This survey question became the standard way of assessing the actual (official plus informal) burden of regulatory compliance (Schwab, 2010).

Several early installments of the BEEPS also contained the following question: "If a government agent acts against the rules, I can usually go to another official or to his superior to get the correct treatment without recourse to unofficial payments." This question is likely to reflect discretionary powers of "street-level" bureaucrats. It would be reasonable to expect that for bureaucrats whose misdoings are likely to be rectified by other bureaucratic authorities, the level of discretion is lower compared to those whose decision is unlikely to be challenged by the superior authorities. Respondents agreeing with this question are likely to face less discretion. Unfortunately, from 2009 on, this question was dropped from the enterprise surveys, so only three survey installments can be used to track discretionary policy application. For the empirical test, I merge the firm-level survey data reflective of the individual-level experiences of the regulatory environment and discretion with the contemporaneous country-level measures of the

---

[152] This section is based in part on Duvanova (2014).

number of DB regulations of entry. As an additional robustness check, I also consider the estimated length of time it would take an average firm to officially register (enter the market). The 1999, 2002, and 2005 installments of BEEPS are merged with the 2003, 2005, and 2007 DB indicators respectively.[153]

The 1999 BEEPS survey included 3,953 firms in 24 post-communist countries (Albania, Armenia, Azerbaijan, Belarus, Bosnia, Bulgaria, Croatia, Czech Republic, Estonia, Macedonia, Georgia, Hungary, Kazakhstan, Kyrgyz Republic, Latvia, Lithuania, Moldova, Poland, Romania, Russia, Slovak Republic, Slovenia, Ukraine, and Uzbekistan). A total of 6,153 firms were covered by the survey in 2002 and 9,098 enterprises were covered in 2005. These were located in 26 countries, the BEEPS 1999 countries plus Serbia and Montenegro and Tajikistan. The firms participating in the survey represent different sectors and industries and are of different size and ownership type.

To test Hypothesis 1, I again use a regression model with interacted variables. I construct a binary variable that takes the value of one if a respondent answered "always," "mostly," or "frequently" to the question about availability of "correct treatment" to address bureaucratic wrongdoing. Responses falling in the "sometimes," "seldom," and "never" categories were coded as zero. Because I merge the firm-level (discretionary regulatory application and actual regulatory burden) and country-level (official regulatory burden) variables, I use the country-level fixed effects estimation.[154] With the data at hand, I am able to control for firms' size, type of ownership, incorporation history, and longevity; managers' confidence in the ability of the legal system to enforce contracts and protect property rights; and the availability of information on rules and regulations affecting one's business. Dummy variables are used to account for sectoral effects. At a country level, the GDP per capita, EBRD transition index, and Polity IV political regime variables capture the macroeconomic and political environment.[155] Regression results can be found in Table 21, Appendix E.

---

[153] These provide the closest temporal match with an appropriate lag. DB 2003 was collected in 2002, DB 2005 reflects the number of regulatory procedures that were in place by the end of 2004, and DB 2007 indicators were collected in 2005.

[154] Note that only the country-level variables form a true panel. Only 18 percent of firm-level data constitute repeated observations.

[155] Bosnia and Herzegovina has not been rated by Polity IV in the analyzed years and was excluded from the analysis reported below. Because of missing data for some variables, only 28 percent of the 1999 sample yields complete data. Seventy-three percent of the observations from the 2002 survey and 75 percent from the 2005 survey were included in the analysis.

Results are consistent with those of the country-level panels analysis. The number of entry procedures and days required to register a business positively correlate with the actual burden of regulatory compliance. The regression results support the notion that discretion and regulatory burden interact in a non-trivial manner. When bureaucratic discretion is low, one standard deviation increase in the number of official regulatory procedures results in a 31 percent increase in de facto regulatory time burden on the manager, or an increase of .83 percentage points. Holding all other things constant and averaging across the fixed effects, at the maximum number of entry procedures, firms spend about four times as much time on ensuring regulatory compliance compared to firms operating under the minimum number of regulatory procedures. Under the high-discretion bureaucratic regimes, however, the effects of entry regulations are not statistically different from zero. The official time requirements for business registration have similarly increased the actual regulatory time under a non-discretionary bureaucracy; however, when bureaucratic discretion is high, the effects of the official entry time are not statistically different from zero.

As yet another robustness check, I use a different survey question to operationalize the dependent variable. I use an ordered scale variable constructed by combining survey answers that identify tax administration, licensing, and permits; customs and trade; and labor regulations as the most problematic "for the operation and growth of business." The resulting scale variable ranges from 0 to 16, with a mean of 8.1 and standard deviation of 3.1. The question was part of the 1999 and 2002 surveys only, so the 2005 data are dropped.[156] I find that official regulatory procedures have the expected positive effect on the actual regulatory burden. The interaction hypothesis also finds support. In a low-discretion regime, an increase in the official business regulations tends to lead to a higher level of dissatisfaction with the regulatory environment. However, under a discretionary bureaucracy, the effect of the official regulatory procedures is not statistically different from zero. All in all, the analysis of business survey data from the 1990s and 2000s shows that the official regulatory burden positively affected the actual costs of running a business only under low levels of bureaucratic discretion.

---

[156] Column 5, Table 21 in Appendix E, contains the results of the baseline model. Column 6 reports the results of the interacted variables' regression specification. These analyses use country-level random effects.

Causal Mechanism

In Chapter 1, I discussed preferentialism, inconsistency, and red tape creation as potential mechanisms for the discrepancy between the official regulatory regimes and business environment in action. These discrepancies account for the gap in the measures of the official cost of complying with regulations and the actual costs of doing business.[157] I suggested that high levels of discretion invite a predatory behavior by the regulatory agencies—red-tape creation—that would allow the bureaucrats to extract additional bribes. Although corruption often accompanies heavy government involvement in the economy, I reasoned that places with low regulatory intervention but high discretion might experience corruption as well. This corruption would be linked to discretionary policy application, as predatory bureaucrats may use the red-tape creation as a mechanism for extracting more bribes. The data at hand enables the testing of this causal mechanism.

Hypothesis 2 posits that discretion might attenuate the standard link between higher regulatory burden and the prevalence of corruption. Discretionary policy-implementation power allows the regulatory agents to augment light compliance costs with the red tape, driving up the demand for corruption and increasing the size of bribes.[158] If this mechanism is in place, one should see corruption increase with the regulatory intervention in low-discretion regimes only. High discretion should make the official regulatory burden an irrelevant factor for explaining corruption. To test this, I return to the panel of 102 countries.

To measure the extent of corruption, I use the Control of Corruption indicator from the World Bank World Governance Indicators database. It is based on the aggregation of various perception-based data reflective of various types of corruption, abuse of public power, and state capture and ranges between −2.5 and 2.5 points, with negative numbers corresponding to more pervasive corruption and positive numbers corresponding to more effective control of corruption (https://info.worldbank.org/

---

[157] An influential political economic argument links bureaucratic corruption to burdensome economic regulations (Shleifer and Vishny, 1998; Mauro, 1995; Djankov et al., 2002). The harder it is to comply with regulations, the more attractive are the corrupt ways for avoiding compliance.

[158] Elsewhere (Duvanova, 2014) I analyzed data covering 25 post-communist economies between 1999 and 2005 and found that unofficial regulatory hurdles, rather than the official regulatory policy, contribute to the firms' owners' higher perceived levels of corruption. This means that corruption is driven not by the extent of state regulatory intervention, but by the aspects of its implementation, which under a discretionary environment are likely to incorporate preferentialism, inconsistency, and red tape.

governance/wgi). Regulatory intervention is again measured by the number of official regulations of entry, property registration, construction, contract enforcement, paying taxes, obtaining electricity, and trading across borders. Effective law enforcement might deter public officials from corruption and make them less likely to exercise regulatory discretion to alter official regulatory burden; hence, I make sure that all regression results are robust to the inclusion of the World Bank World Governance Indicators Rule of Law control variable. Regression coefficients can be found in Appendix E, Table 20, models 6–8.

My investigation reveals that audit effectiveness is positively correlated with Control of Corruption. One standard deviation increase in the continuous Audit Effectiveness variable contributes to a .05 improvement in the Control of Corruption index, which is equivalent to the effect of switching from a high- to low- discretion regime in model 7. I also find that more numerous official regulatory procedures have a negative effect on the Control of Corruption indicator. One standard deviation increase in the count of regulatory procedures (38.6 regulations) leads to a .02-point drop in the Control of Corruption index.

Interaction analysis shows that in fact discretion impacts the connection between regulations and corruption. When bureaucratic discretion is high, regulatory burden has no statistically significant effect on corruption. When bureaucratic discretion is low, regulatory burden has a significant negative effect on the Control of Corruption indicator. In other words, a heavy regulatory burden leads to more corruption. The effect of one standard deviation increase in regulatory procedures results in close to a .04-point drop in the Control of Corruption index. This effect is twice as large as in the model without the interaction term.

Figure 30 plots the predicted values for the Control of Corruption variable against the number of regulatory procedures for discretionary and constrained bureaucracy cases, holding all other variables at their mean values. It can be seen that the darker line representing cases of high bureaucratic discretion is nearly horizontal, reflecting no relationship, while the lighter line for low-discretion regimes declines in the number of procedures. This supports the notion that the regulations lead to more corruption with an important caveat: such a relationship exists only when regulations are applied without discretion. Such results hold when regression models include standard economic and political controls, such as the size of the

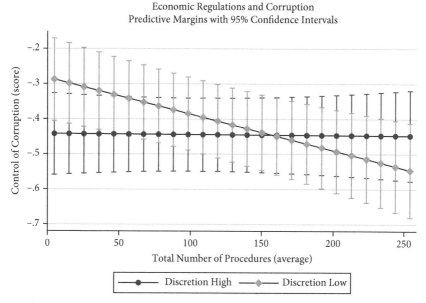

Figure 30 More Numerous Regulations Breed Corruption in High-Discretion Settings Only

Note: Data from the World Bank, GI, and WEF. The lines represent the predictive margins of the random effects regression analysis. "Discretion Low" corresponds to the rating of supreme audit institutions of 70 points and above on a 20–100-point scale. "Discretion High" corresponds to scores below 70 points.

economy, growth, FDI, natural resource rents, political freedoms, stability, and the rule of law.

Conclusion

This chapter investigated the empirical connection between the formal aspects of state regulatory involvement and the resulting business climate, which is a summary assessment of the overall favorability of the country's conditions for business activity. Statistical analysis of a panel of countries representing all of the world's geographic regions, political regimes, and levels of development reveals that institutions of governance that enable discretionary policy application might affect the business climate directly, but more importantly, they affect it indirectly by weakening the link between the official regulations and business climate in which firms operate. In other words, economic regulations shape the business environment only when they are not subject to discretionary policy application.

This conclusion is intuitive and follows a theoretical distinction between regulatory policies and institutional mechanisms of their implementation. Yet it runs contrary to the conventional practice of ignoring such an effect as trivial. This chapter shows that bureaucratic discretion is an important institutional factor that conditions the effects of regulatory policy on the business environment. By allowing the regulatory bureaucracy to interpret regulatory frameworks freely and to apply them capriciously, bureaucratic discretion makes the official regulatory policy a largely irrelevant factor in shaping the business environment.

In examining the causal mechanisms implicit in the theory of discretionary policy implementation, I found that more interventionist regulatory policy translates into heavier corruption pressures in systems with limited bureaucratic discretion. Under a high level of bureaucratic discretion, by contrast, I observe no relationship between the extent of official regulatory involvement and the level of corruption. My analysis connected constrained policy application to a conventional marker of good governance—bureaucratic probity. These results corroborate other research on how quality of governance conditions economic outcomes (Loayza et al., 2009; Shlapentokh, 2013; Gel'man, 2017a,b). The evidence presented in this chapter further elaborates the details of these effects by showing that a specific component of regulatory enforcement—bureaucratic discretion—makes the official regulatory policies an irrelevant factor in shaping the business climate.

One caveat to this logic is that economic policy may be endogenous to institutional arrangements that shape its implementation.[159] If politicians are aware of the nature of regulatory enforcement, they may not only consider institutional means of limiting bureaucratic discretion (Baum, 2007), but they could also formulate regulatory policies in ways that make these less vulnerable to bureaucratic discretion. In Chapters 2 and 4 I discussed the politics of regulatory policymaking and demonstrated that in fact much of the regulatory policy innovation is done in response to the existing implementation practices, traditions, and material constraints. The

---

[159] Acemoglu et al. (2008, p. 355) explain: "one would not expect a society with a functioning system of accountability and with checks on politicians to be pursuing highly distortionary policies in the first place."

bureaucratic institutional environment is implicitly or explicitly taken into account by policymakers. Although inextricably linked in practice, policy formulation and policy implementation remain conceptually distinct, and empirical analysis of this chapter shows that much can be learned from the analytical separation of political (policymaking) and bureaucratic (policy implementation) functions.

The interactive relationship between regulatory policy and its enforcement means that the institutional mechanisms employed in economic policy implementation are not of lesser importance than the regulatory policy itself. An alternative view has been that bureaucratic autonomy is an institutional asset (Huntington, 1968; Evans, 1992; Piore, 2011; Bosio et al., 2020). When bureaucratic autonomy (discretion) is used wisely, some studies suggest, it can diminish the onerous effects of the official regulatory burden (Rasul and Rogger, 2016; Bandiera et al., 2019; Decarolis et al., 2019).[160] A more responsible application of discretionary power, however, necessarily depends on the structure of bureaucratic incentives and is shaped by the larger institutional environment.

This chapter largely ignored differences in the political underpinning of such institutional constraints. I adopted a regime-neutral notion of discretion that does not distinguish among constraints originating from the political control of bureaucracy, public accountability, or bureaucratic resources (staffing, *esprit de corps*, funding, etc.) Although this politically neutral approach to policy implementation enabled me to compare societies with different types of political regimes, relationships between branches of government, levels of economic development, and technological sophistication, it misses important variations in the origins of bureaucratic constraint that I tried to explore at length earlier in the book. As my other empirical chapters demonstrated, the political regime is crucial for arriving at a better understanding of the regulatory state. The origins of bureaucratic constraint are linked to the political regimes and institutional choices of state-builders. The rule of law, regime type, and public accountability factor into the state agency's policy implementation incentives.

---

[160] Such interpretation is in fact generally consistent with this chapter's finding that high levels of bureaucratic discretion (or autonomy) may mitigate the negative effect of entry regulations.

7

Towards a Theory of the Authoritarian Regulatory State

What can the story of regulatory authoritarian state-building tell us about the evolving role of the state in the contemporary economic order? In this book I have tried to reconcile the conflicting evidence of simultaneous improvements in Russian and Kazakh state governance characteristics (Gorgulu et al., 2020; World Bank, 2020a) and unmistakable signs of growing predation, systemic corruption, and cronyism (Hale, 2014; Dawisha, 2014; Cooley and Heathershaw, 2017; Aslund and Commander, 2016). To better understand the political economies that have combined features and outcomes usually seen as fundamentally incompatible, I turned to the issue of state regulatory intervention, which is the central mechanism of state economic policymaking in modern capitalism. I argued that regulatory state-building by authoritarian rulers made the Russian and Kazakh states simultaneously more formally rule-bound and clientelistic.

In Chapter 1, I theoretically scrutinized institutional mechanisms of economic policy implementation. Economic and social consequences of state policies have long been the focus of the political economy literature, including the literature on post-communist states, but institutions of policy implementation, which are an equally important aspect of regulatory state function, often receive less rigorous treatment. There, in the specifics of the institutional state policy-implementation arrangements, we find the roots of ineffective governance: preferentialism, corruption, red tape, and state predation. Underperforming regulatory enforcement institutions are often responsible for large discrepancies between top-level officials' promotion of anti-corruption and good governance on the one hand and practical implementation of these policies and reforms by self-serving bureaucrats. Did the architects of deregulation reforms lack the correct "recipe" for building effective regulatory regimes? Was the deregulatory policy a Potemkin village intended to fool foreign investors and international institutions? In other words, did the reforms fail by omission or by design?

Thieves, Opportunists, and Autocrats: Building Regulatory States in Russia and Kazakhstan. Dinissa Duvanova, Oxford University Press. © Oxford University Press 2023. DOI: 10.1093/oso/9780197697771.003.0008

Analyzing discrepancies between policy and its implementation, I argued, is the key to understanding post-Soviet governance. I suggested these discrepancies are enabled by intentional institutional policy choices that grant state administrators and street-level officials leeway in deciding how to enforce regulations. This leeway allows high- and low-ranking officials to extract rents through threats and favors, leading to uneven enforcement of official state policy, growing business risk and uncertainty, and poor economic performance.

I proposed a political theory of the authoritarian regulatory state, in which politicians use institutions of the state they have at their disposal as a means to balance conflicting elite demands for economic rents and popular demands for public goods and economic growth. An effective balancing of the two would ensure long-term regime survival by preventing elite subversion and popular revolt in the short run and by ensuring continued access to economic rents that would be undermined by overgrazing elites in the long run. I proposed that vague, less-detailed, and nonspecific regulatory instructions initiated by statutory laws and agency-level bylaws grant the state bureaucracy discretionary power to design specific aspects of policy implementation and enable extralegal preferentialism, informality, corruption, and outright predation.

My theory suggested that the bureaucratic power over policy implementation should allow a simultaneous pursuit of the politician-initiated, growth-promoting, formal economic policies and their selective elite-benefiting deviations. By building strong state institutions that can then selectively enforce economic regulations, the post-Soviet states could arrive at seemingly impossible combinations of growing regulatory effectiveness and corrosive corruption. I also reasoned that when the logic of political survival requires the autocrats to dial back on predatory abuse of bureaucratic power, autocratic regimes could not use the standard ex post control of bureaucratic abuse, such as transparency and public accountability, because these are incompatible with autocratic politics. Hence, the instruments of ex ante control of bureaucratic behavior—formal regulatory documents containing very specific rules of policy application—should rise as the primary mechanism of controlling state predation and ensuring economic growth. Because this theory is built on a long chain of logical arguments, no single empirical test could falsify it in its entirety. Therefore, I identified and subjected to empirical tests several testable implications of these separate logical connections.

In the empirical chapters, I examined a unique set of data quantifying the details of evolving economic regulations in Russia and Kazakhstan. These data span nearly three decades of sweeping regulatory changes in these countries and track sub-national variations in the regulatory climate. Such data were not previously available and are based on the content and meta-analyses of nearly a million regional regulatory statutes and regulatory bylaws enacted in Russia and Kazakhstan between 1990 and 2020. I also considered qualitative evidence of bureaucrats' role in state regulatory enforcement. The empirical tests of my theoretical propositions targeted three logical connections: (1) between institutional constraints on policy implementation and the gap between policy and outcomes, (2) between the amount of detail in regulatory policy documents and economic performance, and (3) between economic resources at autocrats' disposal and the use of discretion-limiting formal institutions. For my theory to be valid, all three connections had to be verified.

In Chapters 2 through 4, I documented the development of regulatory regimes in Russia and Kazakhstan—countries that experienced a tremendous shift from a command-and-control program to the condition of regulatory states over the past decades. Using their subnational variation in the development of formal regulatory mechanisms, I presented qualitative and quantitative evidence on how the lack of consistent and effective policy implementation contributes to poor economic outcomes. I made the case for a clear analytical separation of regulatory policy and the institutional mechanisms of its implementation and argued that ex ante statutory and administrative mechanisms of bureaucratic control are key to understanding contemporary post-Soviet regulatory states. Contrary to most of the literature on policy delegation, my investigation concluded that discretionary power in applying state regulations leads to suboptimal outcomes: in the absence of effective mechanisms of public accountability, discretionary bureaucracy breeds preferentialism, corruption, and an unstable and insecure business climate. More importantly, my empirical analysis found that in the absence of the traditional mechanisms of public accountability, state bureaucracies can positively affect the private economy when operating in the confines of clear and detailed statutory and administrative regulations.

Much of the empirical analysis in this volume investigates the plight of opportunistic businesspeople through the lenses of economic performance indicators that, in my opinion, best reflect the true health of the private economy. I stayed away from the performance indicators that focus on the "national champions" because these could overstate the overall health of the economy.[161] The aggregate growth indicators also might paint a distorted picture. In Russia and Kazakhstan, they are driven by super profits in sectors and companies controlled by the small cliques of plutocrats. Oil and mineral rents contribute large shares to foreign exchange, which makes trade indicators equally suspect of missing the true picture of the health of the economy. In Chapters 3 and 4, I concentrated on three indicators reflective of the plight of the entrepreneurial class not belonging to the circle of super-rich cronies of autocratic regimes. I focused on the reinvested firms' profits, the growth of small and medium-size firms, and these firms' cumulative revenues. In doing so, I attempted to stay away from the indicators driven by state sector development and large firms enjoying state patronage.

Chapter 5 examined how political considerations affect the use of institutional constraints on bureaucratic power. Unlike resource-based hard constraints, the statutory law and executive directions are deliberate policy choices of politicians and policymaking state authorities. In Chapter 5, I tested whether the use of statutory, executive, and administrative constraints might be driven by the autocrats' dilemma in balancing collective goods and particularistic benefits and found that a more active use of bureaucracy-constraining ex ante mechanisms intensifies in the periods of declining natural resource rents and heightened mass protest activity. This supports the notion that discretion-limiting formal constraints are deliberate political mechanisms of shaping regulatory outcomes rather than incidental byproducts of the political process. Effectively, this analysis traced the origins of good economic performance to the state institutional structures that are shaped by structural constraints and autocrats' desires to secure their power in the times of economic adversity.

I concluded the empirical validation of my arguments with the analysis of a global sample of autocratic and democratic regimes to establish that institutional constraints of bureaucratic action can in fact limit the

---

[161] Researchers have doubted the extent to which the FDI flows—a universally accepted indicator of a growth-conducive business environment—are indicative of the overall health of post-Soviet economies, suspecting that much of the FDIs to Russia, for example, are the returned capital outflows (Sharafutdinova and Dawisha, 2017) whose owners resorted to institutional arbitrage to secure the property rights abroad. The lion's share of FDI in Kazakhstan flows to the large companies managed by Samruk-Kazyna state investment holding, which was formed in 2006 and now controls all natural resource monopolies; Kazmunaigaz, the largest Kazakh oil and gas company; Kazatomprom, the atomic energy company; and Tauken Samruk, the non-ferrous metal mining company.

discrepancy between formal policy and its actual implementation. Because cross-national data on the quality of institutional constraints are hard to come by and because institutional quality is endogenous to bureaucratic performance and regulatory quality, Chapter 6 instrumented the bureaucratic constraints with an index of formal and exercised power of central audit institutions to investigate administrative agencies, command resources, and prosecute offenders. This instrumentation, although not perfect, has allowed me to isolate the effects of formal institutional constraints from informal practices and connect the lack of the former to the larger gaps between economic policy objectives and the actual regulatory environment. Because the data capture the resulting strength of discretion-constraining audits, but not regime-specific mechanisms for controlling discretion, I did not limit the analysis to autocratic regimes. Instead, my aim was to validate the overall premise that discretion plays an important role in explaining the gap between policy and economic outcomes.

In this final chapter, I return to the theoretical foundation of my research and connect the theory of the authoritarian regulatory state to the larger themes in the study of post-Soviet politics, economic development, authoritarianism, and state governance. Reflecting on the fundamental notion that states' control of economic resources is essential to their very survival (Tilly, 1993; Scott, 1998; North et al., 2009), I discuss how regulatory state-building in post-Soviet cases can explain ways in which modern authoritarianism oscillates between repression and appeasement, personal freedoms and state control, and between the embrace of the neoliberal economic order and the statist economy.

The two states I analyze in this book have built formal and informal institutions of state control and economic order that have promoted and preserved authoritarian politics. Although their authoritarian political trajectories cannot be reduced solely to the economic causes, institutions of regulatory enforcement these countries developed were an integral part of the political processes leading to their authoritarian consolidations. In this chapter, I argue that the logic of regulatory state-building in Russia and Kazakhstan sheds light not only on these states' relations to economies and bureaucracies, but also the very nature of post-Soviet authoritarianism. The development of the state regulatory function is instrumental in defining the way in which the Russian and Kazakh states have maintained access to economic resources. It also builds a foundation for a robust and adaptable form of authoritarianism that is capable of withstanding windfalls and shortages of economic rents and can balance elements of liberal and statist economic orders. My hope is that this research can help reconcile somewhat contradictory, stylized facts about post-Soviet politics and economies and help us better understand how improvements in state capacity can be compatible with state predation and how deregulatory initiatives can coincide with a deteriorating business climate.

This chapter also discusses how the analytical framework I propose for understanding business-state relations goes beyond the post-communist context. The history of regulatory state-building is largely a history of state-building in the contemporary world. I believe this book has contributed to the state-building literature by describing an expanded toolkit of authoritarian institutional innovation and adaptation. On one hand, this expanding toolkit has contributed to greater state efficiency; ability to balance economic interests and priorities; and adaptability to the unprecedented acceleration in the pace of technological, political, and socioeconomic change. On the other hand, the innovative tools have allowed authoritarian states to survive and strengthen despite the accelerated rates of inequality, growing polarization, and retrenchment of civil society.

I start by discussing how my analysis of authoritarian regulatory state-building in Russia and Kazakhstan contributes to the study of these countries' politics and economies. I then examine the role of regulatory state function in building the kinds of agile and adaptable authoritarian regimes that are able to balance popular demands and systemic cronyism, and I speculate about larger implications of regulatory state function for the survival and development of authoritarian rule. I discuss how the authoritarian regulatory state theory can account for various economic, political, and social developments in modern authoritarian regimes, including their ambivalent relationship with corruption and the rule of law, and their selective embrace of neoliberal and developmental agendas. By piecing together different aspects of the regulatory environment analyzed throughout the book, this concluding chapter puts the state regulatory function at the center of the authoritarian state-capacity-building project. I stress that the building of the state capacity achieved through the vehicle of the authoritarian regulatory state is limited to political systems constraining freedoms, political competition, and/or civil society's autonomy and hence provides asymmetric benefits that prioritize the interests of the autocrats and economic elites over ordinary citizens. The chapter concludes by discussing political-economic limitations of authoritarian regulatory states.

Regulatory State and Eurasian Autocracies

My focus on the authoritarian regulatory state—the formal regulatory instruments for conducting state economic policy and exercising control over bureaucracy for political reasons—has allowed me to address the parallel and interdependent processes of state-building and regime-building.[162] Research on Russian and post-Soviet authoritarianism over the past decade has made a valuable contribution to the study of authoritarianism.[163] Scholars have also continued to problematize post-Soviet state-building efforts (Taylor, 2011; Sharipova, 2018). This volume bridges studies of authoritarianism and state-building by adding state regulatory institutions to the list of authoritarian survival mechanisms. It shows that autocratic regimes are able to build formal regulatory state institutions as effective tools for balancing domestic interests and strengthening their power to affect social and economic outcomes. Building on the literature that considers various ways in which political regimes constrain policy and institutional choices (Egorov et al., 2009; Egorov and Sonin, 2011; Gehlbach and Keefer, 2011), my theoretical argument links the use of institutional instruments of policy implementation to the political survival strategy. In doing so, I have contributed to the literature on Russian and post-Soviet business-state relations (Frye, 2017; Markus, 2016; Berenson, 2018), state institution-building (Taylor, 2011; Gans-Morse, 2017b), and institutional accounts of corruption (McMann, 2014; Holmes, 2006; Zaloznaya, 2017). By addressing institutional sources of regulatory effectiveness, this book explores not only the economic consequences but also political underpinnings of institutional choices affecting policy implementation. By problematizing issues of policy implementation, I build upon and extend the line of political economy research examining how post-Soviet institutions produce policy (Wilson-Sokhey, 2017; Treisman, 2018; Szakonyi, 2020, 2021; Gorgulu et al., 2020).

The empirical analysis in this book demonstrates that formal mechanisms of policy implementation profoundly influence post-Soviet regulatory policy outcomes and should be more closely integrated into the research tradition that explores the quality of governance (Taylor, 2011; Easter,

---

[162] I follow Hanson (2018) in distinguishing regimes, which are "the set of formal and informal rules that identify who holds power" (p. 18), from the states, which are more permanent coercive, administrative, and revenue collection institutions of power that often transcend specific political regimes.

[163] See, for example, Hale (2014), Way (2015), and Reuter (2017).

2012; Gans-Morse, 2017b; Berenson, 2018). The perspective adopted sharply departs from the increasingly popular "unique history" and "extraordinary personality" explanations convincingly criticized by Frye (2021). Similarly to Engvall (2016) and Hale (2014), my approach zeroes in on the problem of subversive behaviors on the part of state agents that often undermine the official functions of state institutions. However, this book differs from many influential accounts of corruption, nepotism, and informal power relations by its emphasis on the formal institutional mechanisms that underpin informal power relations. Without denying the importance of informal institutions and practices, the theory of the authoritarian regulatory state presented in this book reclaims the centrality of formal institutions. It explains how formal institutions may permit and bolster informal power relations and details the features of formal institutional arrangements that suppress or enable preferentialism, nepotism, or corruption.

Substantial growth of state ownership had been a defining feature of the Russian and Kazakh economies. Does this diminish the importance of state regulatory policy as the mechanism of economic governance? In this book I justified the analytical separation between state (autocrats' political objectives and state bureaucracy's self-serving objectives) and private economic interests because "with the return … to state capitalism, the state nationalizes the risks but continues to privatize the rewards to those closest to the president in return for their loyalty" (Dawisha, 2014, p. 2). The fact remains that profit-seeking and private enrichment, rather than service to the state, continue to be the primary motives even for those economic elites whose fortunes are closely tied to the states' favors. Their service to the state, if any, was instrumental to the task of multiplying the privately controlled wealth. The latter incentive, which had shaped the partial liberalization and privatization initiatives of the 1990s, drove Russia's and Kazakhstan's integration into the global economy, prompted state-building institutional reforms of the 2000s, and facilitated the subsequent turn towards statism and economic nationalism. As long as private enrichment continues to motivate economic elites, statism can easily be reverted to a more liberal economic arrangement if it promises more lucrative private gains. The latter could come from opportunities associated with bringing genuine FDI into the elite-controlled ventures,[164] or from the international decriminalization of

---

[164] One could argue many of Kazakhstan's large private companies survived because of foreign co-ownership.

ill-gotten private assets. There have been signs of pending liberalization in the Russian Ministry of Finance program to reduce the number of majority-state-owned companies in 2020–2025 and the government's 2019 plans to privatize 293 state-owned enterprises (Gordeev, 2020; *RIA Novosti*, 2019), but with the war in Ukraine, the state sector is likely to remain strong.

Speaking to a reporter in 2005, Putin insisted that officials heading state-controlled companies do not become oligarchs but only serve the interests of the state, saying, "They do not own these companies' shares, do not receive dividends or salaries" (*Lenpravda*, 2005). However, Putin was concealing the truth. In 2020 the same issue came to the fore, and unable to deny the astronomical compensations of the CEOs he appointed to control state corporations, Putin resorted to the "capitalism" defense: "A corporation has to compensate their international specialist at international market prices . . . Bosses have to be paid more because they are bosses" (Poliakova, 2020). This anecdote further reinforces the notion that modern state capitalism primarily serves the interests of economic elites, rather than the state interests broadly defined (Bremmer, 2009, p. 52).

This book's parallel investigation of the centrally administered Kazakhstan and federal Russia has implications for the research on Russia's center–regional power dynamics. Curtailed by Putin's power centralization reforms,[165] Russia's federalism has become a topic of close scholastic scrutiny (Sharafutdinova, 2013; Libman and Rochlitz, 2019). Most experts believe that Russia now is more centrally administered than ever. Should Russian federalism be discounted? My analysis of regional economies and regulatory institutions in Russia and Kazakhstan helps put the Russian federalism debate in a larger comparative perspective. It shows that despite the continuing authoritarian encroachment on regional autonomy, Russia's center–region dynamics remain strikingly different from those of unitary Kazakhstan. Empirical analysis presented in this volume indicates that despite Putin's centralization campaign, Russian regional authorities continue to exercise independent agency and carry administrative responsibility for policy outcomes.

---

[165] The major centralization efforts included the transfer of regional administrative authority to the "federal districts" created in 2000 and cancellation of electoral mechanisms for selecting regional and local government officials in 2005–2011.

Bureaucratic Discretion, Autocratic Impunity, and Grand Corruption

This book's focus on regulatory policy implementation made me concentrate on micro-level mechanisms of bureaucratic decision-making, street-level administrative actions, and formal regulatory constraints on routine bureaucratic functions. Still, the logic of authoritarian regulatory state-building gives us a useful analytical tool for understanding instances of grand corruption and resource stripping by the autocrats, whose rent-seeking depletes national wealth. The discretionary power enables state officials not only to marginally affect the intended policy outcomes, but when unchecked, allows them to divert government resources to the pockets of well-connected private contractors, banks, and intermediaries. Discretionary powers of government officials enable not only small-scale bureaucratic corruption hidden from public scrutiny, but also leads to large-scale international corruption scandals.

In 2005, President Nazarbayev gave the Astana city administration carte blanche to build high-priority light rail transport (LRT) infrastructure. City officials were tasked with setting the project objectives, securing investment, and awarding construction contracts. In 2006, the *akim* of Astana, Umirzak Shukeev, presented a $1.5 billion proposal for 61 kilometers of elevated LRT. Shukeev's successor, Askar Mamin, did not share Nazarbayev's fascination with the LTR and abandoned the project in 2008 in favor of cheaper and more practical bus transit. Nazarbayev soon replaced Mamin with Imangali Tasmagambetov, who shared the president's weakness for grandiose futuristic city planning. Tasmagambetov helped Astana LRT LLP, solely owned by the city government, secure a grant from the French government and contract a French and two domestic companies to carry out the project. In 2011, the expected construction costs rose to $2.3 billion, and on his birthday, which also happens to coincide with the Astana City Day celebration, Nazarbayev publicly commenced construction (Sorbello, 2021).

By 2013 no actual LRT construction work had been carried out though, and LRT LLP asked for additional funds. President Nazarbayev and Karim Massimov allegedly pitched the project to China's President Xi Jinping during his 2013 visit to Astana, with no immediate success. The following year, the new *akim*, Adilbek Dzhaksybekov, terminated the LRT project after the Asian Development Bank issued an unfavorable investment report. At that time, the National Bureau of Corruption Prevention reported that

Astana LRT LLP had embezzled $2 million. An additional $48.7 million was reportedly lost to mismanagement and corruption in 2015.

In 2015, after Prime Minister Massimov's visit to Beijing, Nazarbayev and Xi signed an Engineering Procurement Construction (EPC) LRT contract, which became part of the "One Belt One Road" initiative. The consortium of Chinese companies pledged to provide LRT engineering and construction services worth $1.6 billion. The China Development Bank extended a loan to the Kazakh government to cover 80 percent of the proposed costs, and the Kazakh government pledged the remaining 20 percent. Contrary to its standard practice not to finance non-Chinese companies, China Development Bank transferred the funds directly to Astana LRT LLP. Nazarbayev's grandson, Nurali Aliev, who at that time was appointed deputy mayor of Astana, pledged to finish construction in time for Astana Expo 2017. The length of the proposed track was reduced to 22.4 kilometers, one-third of the initial plans. In 2016, however, shortly before the release of the Panama Papers incriminating Aliev and his father in corruption and money laundering, it was announced the LRT project would be delayed again.

Aset Isekeshev, who was appointed *akim* of Astana in 2017, unilaterally revised the EPC contract and dismissed the CEO of Astana LRT LLP, Talgat Ardan, over outstanding liabilities. The Chinese consortium complained about contract revisions, but in 2017 commenced the project anyway, building 1,974 augured piles, 143 foundation grills, 38 supporting structures, and six prefabricated girders. This amounted to 15 percent of the contracted work (Koskina, 2019). No work on the project has been done since 2017. Thirty-eight Y-shaped structures in the streets of Astana stand as a hideous memorial to Kazakh grand corruption.

By the end of 2017, Chinese Development Bank had allocated $343 million to Astana LRT LLP; of this amount, only $86 million was paid to the Chinese contractors. The Astana government subsidiary generated $203 million in debt (Sorbello, 2021). Despite clear signs of corrupt dealings, the national budget of Kazakhstan allocated an additional $87.5 million to LRT LLP in 2018 (Koskina, 2019). Later that year, $258 million of LRT LLP funds were frozen in the company's bank accounts. Seven government officials and private sector contractors were arrested and charged with corruption, including Rashid Amanzhulov, the head of Astana Department of Passenger Transport and Highways; Zhanat Nurpiisov, the secretary of the Astana city *maslikhat*; and Ulukbek Achilov, the CEO of NurTrade LLP, a local contractor (Vaal, 2021). International arrest warrants were issued against two alleged organizers of the corruption scheme: Ardan and Kanat Sultanbekov, the deputy mayor of Astana in 2009–2014. No top-level decision-makers in the city government responsible for reviewing and awarding private contracts have been charged in the embezzlement scheme. The press speculated that prosecutors scapegoated relatively unimportant figures to cover up more senior officials (Kazakhstan2.0, 2021).

To fully repay the loan to China Development Bank, Astana LRT LLP issued bonds in the amount of $1.5 billion. People's Bank of Kazakhstan purchased $400 million worth of these securities. The remaining bonds were purchased by Baiterek National Management Holding, a government-controlled conglomerate of financial institutions. In effect, the Kazakh government absorbed all corruption-related losses (Koskina, 2019). In 2021, the LRT LLP, renamed City Transportation Systems, issued public tender for a $1 billion loan (*Esquire.kz*, 2021). Despite this hefty infusion of funds, *akim* Altai Kulginov was still unable to produce any evidence that actual construction work had resumed (*Informburo*, 2021).

The Astana LRT scandal is a perfect example of the expediency of discretionary power of state officials in channeling state resources to the pockets of high-ranking economic and government elites controlling private contractors, banks, and state subsidiaries. Six rapidly succeeding *akims* used their power to define the project parameters, timing, and implementation to orchestrate large-scale corruption and embezzlement schemes with impunity. Astana city authorities assumed no responsibility for tens of millions of dollars of embezzled FDI and government investment. The autocratic leader directly granted city officials discretionary power over the LRT infrastructure development project, which allowed members of his family and his personal political appointees to make decisions that allowed millions of dollars to flow into private hands. Thieves, opportunists, and autocrats were the major culprits of the Astana LRT corruption monument.

Beyond the Russian and Kazakh Cases

Although the book's empirical analysis centered on Russian and Kazakh regulatory state-building, the theory I proposed to guide my exploration is more general in linking state development to the constraints and objectives of authoritarian political regimes. With its federal arrangements, evolving regime time, and fluctuating mineral rents, the development of the Russian regulatory state allowed me to test multiple testable implications of the theory. The parallel presentation of the Kazakh case has shown that the Russian regulatory state, however complex, is not unique in its development. Scholars of post-Soviet politics will make parallels to the patterns of business-state relations, informal elite influence, and formal legal and administrative processes found not only in the Azeri and Uzbek cases, but also in the more competitive and participatory settings of Kyrgyzstan, Armenia, or Ukraine. Current research on Chinese politics has documented the rise of the dynamic Chinese-style regulatory state (Pearson, 2005; Jones and Hameiri, 2021), which shares many features with the cases I analyzed in this book, including cronyism in business-state relations (Pei, 2016), officials' "considerable discretion to advance allied business interests" (Zhang, 2010, pp. 53–54), policy implementation "outcomes that are often at odds with what top Chinese leaders anticipated or desired" (Jones and Hameiri, 2021, p. 21), and political efforts "to rein in subordinates, clarify guidelines or recentralize authority" (Jones and Hameiri, 2021, p. 13). Although different institutional mechanisms may be used to enable these regulatory state dynamics,[166] I believe that the theory of regime-contingent regulatory state development could help scholars analyze institutions of modern regulatory states built by autocrats around the world.

Political Regimes and Regulatory States

The autocrats' dilemma, I argued in Chapter 1, underpins the development of the regulatory state. Although the problem of balancing special and general interests is not unique to autocracies, autocratic regimes face regime-specific constraints in that the potent mechanisms for ensuring effective enforcement of government policies and adequate provision of collective goods—transparency and accountability—threaten autocrats' monopoly on information and political expression and require independent courts and civil society. Autocracies cannot rely upon such ex post mechanisms of controlling administrative state institutions because these undermine the very nature of dictatorial rule. Instead, autocrats have to put more emphasis

---

[166] Jones and Hameiri (2021), for example, identified party doctrine; vague policy; coordinating institutions; fiscal and policy concessions; and the appointment, appraisal, and discipline power of the Chinese Community Party as five key institutional mechanisms operating in China.

on statutory controls to discipline bureaucracies.[167] Kazakh and Russian regimes exhibit a number of standard characteristics of authoritarian rule, such as the prominent position of the presidency, lack of judicial independence, underdeveloped institutions of civil society, repression of free press, and restrictions on political competition. These characteristics impose limitations on the use of standard democratic principles of transparency and public accountability.

Autocratic regimes are extremely diverse both in terms of their social bases of support and economic resources at their disposal, but also in terms of the policy and institutional choices they make and challenges they face in domestic and international political arenas. How can my theory inform the analysis of regulatory states under different authoritarian arrangements? Let us consider a few important dimensions across which regimes might differ. The first is the size and composition of autocrats' "selectorate," with the resulting arrangements ranging from populist to personal (sometimes called sultanistic) autocracies. Populist autocracies may be expected to distance themselves from any policy choices that distribute rents to special interests. To preserve the legitimacy of their claims for power, populist regimes cannot openly promote elites' interests. They may want to keep the policy-enforcing regulatory authorities at arm's length. If the autocrats want to engage in clandestine elite-benefiting activities, such as allocation of government contracts, granting monopolistic rights, public subsidies, or privileged access to public finance, ineffective state governance might be the modus operandi for the regulatory regimes they build. In such arrangements, discretionary policy application can serve as a firewall between the central government and failing state bureaucracy, which can be blamed for the exacerbation of social inequalities, underprovision of public goods, and illegal enrichment of the elites. Weak regulatory institutions would enable avenues for elite enrichment without assigning the responsibility for unjust social outcomes to the autocrats.

The People's Republic of China can serve as a good illustration of this logic. There, the central government has been successfully deflecting public

---

[167] Egorov et al. (2009) argue that delegation of decision-making authority to bureaucrats may pose a threat to the autocrats' political power. Independent decision-making in the power vertical might erode loyalty and syphon the resources away from autocrat-controlled institutions. Delegation of decision-making power, however, should not be conflated with discretionary powers in executing political decisions. Hence, throughout the book I used the term "discretion" rather than "autonomy" or "independence" to describe the bureaucrats' ability to alter regulations on a case-by-case basis without deliberate delegation of authority and administrative responsibility for consequences.

disdain for the widespread corruption, self-serving officials, and glaring gap between the rich and the poor. The central organs of the Communist Party will not benefit from building a disciplined civil service and bridging the gap between economic policies and their practical implementation because this would only highlight the contradictions and limitations of a dual economy, lack of property rights, and neglect of public interests. Civil service reforms aimed at increasing probity, if successful, would also close off the blame deflection channel, making the central government the target of popular grievances. In light of the theory of the authoritarian regulatory state, all these considerations suggest that the truly predatory autocrats presiding over complex, hard-to-control economies cannot commit to regulatory institutions that would limit capricious policy application. The logic of authoritarian regime survival makes autocrats do three things: (1) invest in building regulatory institutions that they can freely interpret; (2) laxly apply economic policy; and (3) forgo effective, predictable, and corruption-free institutions associated with better governance.

Another dimension across which autocracies differ is the size of the state bureaucracy.[168] In autocratic regimes employing larger bureaucracies, regime survival depends more on the bureaucrat's support. This can be bought by formal entitlements, such as pensions, benefits, or in-kind privileges or, as explicated in the theory of the authoritarian regulatory state, through informal "grazing rights" to skim off private sector resources for bureaucrats' personal benefit. Discretionary policy application conveniently creates the types of grazing opportunities that can be easily rolled back in retaliation for disloyalty or regime-threatening political ambitions. Informal grazing rights created by the loosely defined regulatory frameworks are also more advantageous for the rulers than formally defined patronage benefits because they do not create entitlements often associated with formal reward mechanisms. When withdrawn, they leave the public sector employees with no legal recourse against autocrats' disfavor. From this standpoint, bureaucratic authoritarianism of the mid-twentieth century could have benefited

---

[168] Large state sectors often translate into large civil bureaucracies, but as seen in Russia and Kazakhstan, this might not always be the case. Russian federal and regional bureaucracy by the end of 2019 accounted for about 10 percent of total employment, which is only 67.1 percent of the US figure and about half of the OECD average. According to the OECD data, it is less than Mexico's 11.8 percent, Brazil's 12.5 percent, Argentina's 17.2 percent, and Panama's 19.8 percent (OECD, 2020). In Kazakhstan, according to the Bureau of National Statistics, the state bureaucracy in 2020 accounted for only 5.6 percent of total employment, on par with Japan's 5.8 percent last recorded by the OECD in 2017, but smaller than Korea's 8.1 percent (2019), the Philippines' 8.5 percent (2016), and Indonesia's 8.9 percent (2016) (OECD and Asian Development Bank, 2019).

from the laxly defined regulatory frameworks that created extensive patronage networks in the public employment sector. Because they enable predatory behavior of state officials, vaguely defined and laxly enforced laws can be used to economically repress ethnic minorities and political opposition entrenched in the private sector.

Yet another point of variation in the authoritarian regimes is the extent to which they are integrated into the international economy. Political pressures from trading partners, dependence on foreign finance, product markets, or developmental assistance have been pushing autocracies around the world to embrace the tenets of the Washington consensus and lower the amount of state intervention in the economy. Neoliberal economic doctrine spreads either directly through the International Monetary Fund, World Bank, or European Union pressures, or through the "race to the bottom" set off by international competition for FDI. In terms of the model developed in Chapter 1, global economic pressures constrain the politicians to lower the official cost of doing business as reflected by the formal requirements, regulations, and legal norms. One way to satisfy the conflicting expectations of the global actors for liberal regulatory regimes and national elites' protectionist pressures is through permitting and enabling lax regulatory policy application of officially liberal regulations. Instead of being dubbed as stubborn interventionists, the autocrats can reform formally, score points with international financial institutions, and improve their global ratings, all while building lax enforcement institutions that allow policy subversion at the implementation stage. Then, citing the unruly petty bureaucrats' derailment of the top-level neoliberal initiatives, politicians may seek international assistance for institutional "capacity building."

In Chapter 5, I made use of Russia's and Kazakhstan's resource dependency to test implications of authoritarian regulatory state regime survival logic, which dictates a balancing of broad-based economic growth and parochial elite interests. In resource-rich autocracies, of which both Russia and Kazakhstan are good examples, the state often distributes the resource rents to win popular or elite support. In Russia, the thrust of Putin's state-capacity-improving efforts clustered in the periods of low oil prices and international sanctions that put strains on state finances. The change from the populism of the early 2000s to the statism of the 2010s, which accompanied declining oil revenues and slowing rates of growth, exacerbated the political competition for resources and put more pressure on the state bureaucracy to engage in arbitrary policy enforcement. That helps explain the push for the "regulatory guillotine" at the end of 2019. Rising energy prices prompted by Russia's war in Ukraine are unlikely to create budgetary surpluses. International sanctions and cuts in natural gas supplies to Europe will dampen the budgetary receipts from oil and gas exports in Russia. As a result, the Russian regime continues to face strong pressures to discipline its regulatory bureaucracy and clamp down on corruption.

Kazakhstan's early caving under Nazarbayev's rule to the outside pressures for liberalization has brought about a combination of accelerated economic transition and spiraling corruption, nepotism, and resource-stripping. The moves towards bureaucracy-constraining civil service reforms, the 2022 reforms for reducing private rents, and the plans for reinstalling local elections in 2023 under Tokayev's lead coincide with the declining natural resource rents and growing popular resentment against corrupt officials competing for shrinking private sector profits. Although the energy prices rose in 2022, oil revenues are still insufficient to compensate for the costs of trade and financial disruptions associated with the country's continuing membership in the Eurasian Economic Union, which ties it closely to the sinking Russian economy.

These accounts suggest resource-dependent autocracies, or more generally autocracies vulnerable to fluctuating sources of government finance, might be particularly attracted to structuring their political support clienteles along the lines of discretionary policy enforcement.[169] Autocratic regulatory state institutions could provide stability as the sources of clientelistic rents dry out because the preceding accumulation of clientelistic rents immobilizes any significant elite opposition, ensuring no challengers to an autocrat's power can rise in the ranks of state officials or privileged economic elites.

This brings me to yet another consideration in the regime survival strategy: the strength of the political opposition. As the strength of Russian and Kazakh opposition forces eroded with forced exiles, assassinations, electoral fraud, and imprisonments of regime opponents, the benefits

---

[169] Globalization might precipitate autocratic breakdowns in the small economies with more modest prospects for rent generation and strong popular mobilization, such as Tajikistan, for example. In such regimes, opportunities to expatriate economic rents diminish the necessity to invest in public goods, state-building, and economic development. International economic isolation sets the opposite pressure: unable to freely expatriate their economic rents, the autocrats and their cronies should be more interested in promoting growth and ensuring popular support for their rule.

of using discretion-inviting vague policy formulation to encourage self-incriminating corrupt dealings also declined. The decline of opposition in the 1990s in Kazakhstan and in the 2000s in Russia also decreased the attractiveness of using lax policy implementation to reward and intimidate the patronage networks of state officials. Consolidation of authoritarian regimes makes them less vulnerable to the competing regional elites as well. Although this might mean that increasing concentration of power might promote a more disciplined and orderly regulatory state, by no means are more powerful autocrats less interested in using lax policy enforcement to promote select elite interests.

Seemingly, the logic of blame avoidance for the domestic policy outcomes and the inability to build effective institutions of governance could apply to participatory competitive democracies as well. Kyrgyzstan had experienced external pressures for economic liberalization and reforms of state regulatory function because the clan-based political competition periodically reshuffled the state bureaucracy, and the use of state offices for personal gain was enabled by the considerable laxity of policy implementation. Further, the state bureaucracy lacked clear procedural guidelines, skill-based personnel recruitment, and promotion and disciplinary measures (Engvall, 2016). Through this disorderly and corrupt civil service, the Kyrgyz state mitigated the external pressure to improve the business climate with the demands for clientelistic rent distribution. However, the availability of ex post mechanisms for punishing corrupt officials—an independent press, viable political organizations, and repeating episodes of mass mobilization against predatory officials—have undermined the necessity of ex ante formal mechanisms for controlling bureaucracy. Faced with greater uncertainty about their prospects to retain power, Kyrgyz presidents were eager to reward the allied clans with grazing rights, rather than discipline them with formal procedures. With more fire alarms embedded in society, presidential clans had greater opportunity to learn about disloyalty or grave abuses of their political allies, which further devalued the ex ante control mechanisms. Paradoxically, greater competitiveness and openness of Kyrgyz politics forestalled efforts to establish effective, formal, rule-based mechanisms for disciplining state officials, resulting in less capable and orderly state institutions. The greater competitiveness promoted the "roving bandits" political dynamic in which access to predatory official positions is sold/purchased/won through the political struggle of regional clans.

Corruption by Design

This book's analysis of the development of the authoritarian regulatory state sheds an interesting light on the problems of high-level (political) and low-level (bureaucratic) corruption. Political corruption features prominently in academic and journalistic accounts of Russian and Eurasian politics. Insinuations, speculations, direct accusations, and prosecution of corruption have become so ubiquitous it is hard to find a prominent Russian or Kazakh politician who is immune to this curse. The list of high-ranking officials fleeing corruption investigations or serving sentences starts with Kazakhstan's ex-premier Akezhan Kazhegildin and Saint Petersburg's ex-mayor Anatoly Sobchak, both unsuccessful presidential candidates. The list also prominently features other former high-ranking politicians: Almaty mayors Yuriy Khrapunov and Zamanbek Nurkadilov; regional governors Alexander Khoroskavin (Sakhalin), Vyacheslav Gayzer (Komi), Nikita Belykh (Kirov), and Vitaliy Nakhlupin (Crimea); ex-ministers Aleksey Ulyukaev (Ministry of Economic Development), Mikhail Abyzov (minister without portfolio), Viktor Ishaev (Minister for the Far East Development and ex-governor of Khabaovsk); legislators Vadim Belousov and Rauf Arashukov; and many others (*MBKhMedia*, 2020). Many of these cases have clearly been politically motivated. The high-profile cases of Mukhtar Ablyazov, Rakhat Aliyev, Mikhail Khodorkovskii, and Sergey Furgal show that authorities frequently use criminal investigations of fraud, tax evasion, embezzlement, and even murder to silence those who challenge their monopoly on power. Still, many known loyalists are also accused of corruption, such as with the arrest of the Penza governor and member of the United Russia Party, Ivan Belozertsev. Appointed to his position by President Putin in 2015 and reelected in 2020, Belozertsev was believed to be a protégé of State Duma Speaker Vyacheslav Volodin and Defense Minister Sergey Shoigu (*Deutshe Welle Russia*, 2021). At the time of his arrest, it was not clear why he was targeted while other equally corrupt officials were not.

Prosecuted corruption cases are the tip of the iceberg. A large number of high-profile corruption cases have been dropped or never went to the courts, including the "Kazakhgate" investigation of oil contract kickbacks to Nazarbayev (Solash, 2010), exuberant UK property buying spree of Goga Ashkenadze (Gauhar Berkalieva) (Burrell, 2011), "Xerox affair" of the 1996 Russian presidential elections, Mabetex Kremlin renovation case implicating Yeltsin's family, "food for oil" corruption scheme of Putin and Sobchak in the early 1990s, "Three Whales" case leading to high-level officials in the Customs Committee and Prosecutor's office (*Novaia Gazeta*, 2002), and the "Duck House" and Gelendzhik palace properties of Medvedev and Putin, to name a few. Systemic corruption, extensive ties between state officials and organized crime, and the use of political offices for private enrichment had been the prominent characteristics of post-Soviet politics. Although the optics of Putin's era might seem different from turbulent and pluralist Yeltsin's Russia, detailed accounts of Putin's associates' activities in the 1990s clearly show a striking continuity in the mechanisms and methods of appropriating state assets, creation of exclusive lucrative business opportunities for political cronies, and the instrumental use of legal improvisation to enable corruption on a massive scale (Dawisha, 2014).

Ministerial and regional-level corruption does not make as many headlines as do high-profile political cases, but this type is widespread and costly. In 2019, RIA Federal Press reported a 3.6 percent increase in the number of economic criminal cases (primarily corruption and embezzlement) from the previous year, including corruption in the Federal Security Services (Cherkalin's case), Russian bar association (Gogolev's case), Ministry of Internal Affairs (Melnikov's case), Ministry of Culture (Molosolov's case), Federal Tax Services (Rodionov's case), and Investigative Committee for the Sverdlovsk Region (Busylko's case) (*RIA Press*, 2019). Corruption-related criminal cases, prosecuted in Russia as business-related fraud or bribery, often target regional legislators, department heads of federal and regional agencies, regional and district-level police, and election officials (ITAR-TASS, 2021). In Russia, corruption penetrates all levels of public administration, including the street-level bureaucrats, such as traffic police officers, university admissions clerks, or rank-and-file tax inspectors. Frivolous policy application, contradictory rules, lack of procedural clarity, and proliferation of alternative interpretations of rules often lie at the root of low-level corruption (Duvanova, 2013). Still, lax regulations in themselves do not equal corruption. Countries with common law legal traditions rely upon discretionary decisions of judges and regulators to make well-informed public service decisions. There, a combination of discretion, professionalism, and career motives produces variations in rule application that often help promote public interest rather than breed corruption and self-dealing. In the authoritarian regulatory state, however, the use of formal rules encouraging discretion—those that are vague and do not contain regulatory detail—enable corruption and abuse of office.

In the authoritarian regulatory state, the unscripted bureaucratic improvisations in regulatory policy implementation, as well as private sector rent-seeking, helps the authorities establish useful *kompromat* that can later be used selectively to silence dissent, punish disloyalty, or preempt independent political aspirations. The history of political scandals, including the character assassination of prosecutor general Yurii Skuratov, imprisonments of Khodorkovski and Navalny, and the Interpol arrest warrant for Mukhtar Ablyazov, shows that when it is lacking, the *kompromat* can easily be created by the autocrat's security services. Still, for the fabricated evidence to be convincing, there has to be a track record of multiple public officials breaking the law. Selective use of discretionary regulatory mechanisms has enabled the post-Soviet autocrats to build well-controlled clienteles of officials and private sector cronies at all levels of the state hierarchy by exchanging lucrative rents for the *kompromat*-enforced loyalty. As the "Golden Pretzels of the United Russia" affair illustrates,[170] lax rule enforcement—in this case the legal prohibition on commercial activity by the State Duma deputies—could easily be reversed to purge the ranks of the autocrat's clients (the United Russia deputies) at times when the autocrat needs a boost of popular legitimacy or cronies' loyalty. Against this backdrop, authoritarian prosecution of corruption is always politically motivated. Either it is used to eliminate a political opponent or to boost loyalty and popular appeal.

Authoritarian Regulatory State and the Rule of Law

The use of formal legal documents to advance the autocrats' objectives highlights the dangers of treating legality and legalism as a shorthand for the rule of law. In this book I documented the autocratic regimes' increasing use of formal rules and codified procedures as a mechanism of economic control. Supremacy of law, however, entails the legal and constitutional constraint of the rulers, not the use of the law to maintain their rule. In the absence

---

[170] In 2012, the State Duma deputies Dmitry Gudkov and Ilya Ponomarev published a blog post titled "Golden Pretzels of the United Russia." The publication revealed extensive commercial activities of the United Russia Duma deputies. Russian federal law strictly prohibits Duma members' engagement in business or commerce and prevents them from assuming positions on the governing boards of commercial organizations. According to the law, all implicated Duma deputies were subject to an early termination of their legislative mandates. The United Russia deputies, however, continued to serve in the Duma because the federal prosecutors chose not to pay attention to their business activities.

of an independent judiciary, such formal legalism does not constitute the rule *of* law, but rather the rule *by* law. Instead of the supremacy of legal principles over political and economic interests, the autocratic regulatory states use law as an instrument of self-enrichment, clientelistic rent-creation, and legitimation of their power.

In 2005, Putin laughed at a journalist's question about corruption inside the Kremlin (*Lenpravda*, 2005). Ozhegov's dictionary of the Russian language—the go-to reference for Russian speakers—defines corruption as "a moral decay of public officials or politicians, expressed in illegal enrichment, bribery, embezzlement and merger with mafia structures." Putin laughed at the question because being above the law, he has ensured that the activities of Kremlin insiders have been legalized even when leading to embezzlement, dealings with criminals, and public harm.[171] Through exercising control over legislative and administrative processes, autocrats legalize discriminatory economic arrangements and grant licenses for private enrichment through control of state assets, while shielding the special interests from market-related risks. There could not be any corruption in the Kremlin because the Kremlin has a monopoly on defining what is permissible and what is corrupt. Kremlin insiders, therefore, are also immune to the anti-corruption campaigns. This is also the case in Akorda, the citadel of power of Kazakh authoritarianism.

This immunity can help explain why corruption-ridden regimes can also be effective in fighting low-level corruption. Although the Transparency International Corruption Perception Index continues to place Russia and Kazakhstan at the bottom of the world's anticorruption ranking—in 2020 the countries were ranked 119th and 94th in the world, respectively, in terms of their control of corruption—survey research documents that citizens are becoming more satisfied with the official anti-corruption measures. Starting in 2005, the Russian Public Opinion Research Center (Russian acronym VCIOM) published the anticorruption index based on the popular responses to the following closed-ended question: "The country's leadership keeps talking about anti-corruption efforts. Have you noticed any results of these efforts over the recent year?"[172] Measured as a sum of percentages of positive

---

[171] Dawisha (2014), for example, describes how Putin, after assuming the leadership of the country, purged the criminal investigation archives and eliminated key witnesses to his associates' legal transgressions.

[172] The question was part of the VCIOM stratified random-sample household surveys and VCIOM-Sputnik telephone random-sample survey based on a complete list of landline and mobile phone numbers operating in Russia. The Control of Corruption Index is not designed to capture the

and negative answers, which can vary from −100 to 100, the index stood at −35 points in 2005, climbed to −14 between 2006 and 2008, further improved to −6 in 2012, and even rose to a positive value of 3 points in 2015. After sliding back to −12 in 2016, it gained 29 points over the next two years and stood at +17 in 2018, the last year for which it was published (VCIOM, 2018).

According to Levada Center, 73 percent of Russian respondents reported encountering no opportunities for bribery payments in 2000, and 76 percent of those surveyed in 2005 and 2007 reported zero bribery payments. The subsequent surveys recorded an increase in bribery in 2010, with only 69 percent of respondents facing no corruption, but then 73 percent of respondents reporting no bribery in 2012, 76 percent in 2015, and 78 percent in 2017.[173] With a modest decrease in low-level corruption, the attitudes towards bribery also became less tolerant. Between 2005 and 2017, Levada Center reports a 5-percentage-point increase in respondents who believe bribe givers and bribe takers share the responsibility for corruption. When it comes to high-level corruption, between 2001 and 2014, most Russians (between 54 percent and 64 percent) believed that "there has been approximately the same amount of stealing and corruption in the country's leadership since Vladimir Putin's election as a President." In 2015, Levada dropped the reference to Putin in that question and asked about "today as compared to the early 2000s." Consequently, the percentage of respondents reporting things stayed the same dropped to 46 percent in 2015 and 43 percent in 2017, while those reporting an increase in stealing and bribery increased from the teens to 30–32 percent. Although the majority of Russians (52 percent in 2000 and 58 percent in 2017) believed the extent of corruption and bribery can be significantly reduced, between 2012 and 2017, 10 percent more Russians (an increase from 35 percent agreeing with this statement to 45 percent) subscribed to the opinion that "Putin will attempt to fight corruption, but real success is unlikely, as corruption in Russia is incurable" (Levada Center, 2017).

---

extent of corruption, but rather the perception of whether the government's anticorruption efforts are effective. This is arguably a better measure of state effectiveness.

[173] Percentages are based on the "none of the above" responses to the following question: In the past three years, have you, your close friends, or relatives had occasion to give or be solicited for bribes, gifts, or other services when you had to?" followed by the list of common public services provided by state officials. Of those respondents who reported violating the rules of the road and being detained by traffic police, however, 47 percent reported facing the opportunity of or being solicited for bribes in 2013 and 42 percent in 2017.

The World Values Survey, conducted in Kazakhstan in 2018, asked a representative sample of 1,276 respondents to express their views on corruption on a 10-point scale, where 1 means "there is no corruption in my country" and 10 means "there is abundant corruption." The mean response value was 6.98 points. However, when asked about the propensity of different groups of people to be involved in corruption, 55.4 percent of respondents believed none or few public officials were involved in corruption. The same percentage of respondents saw civil service providers (police, judiciary, civil servants, doctors, teachers) as not being prone to corruption. Business executives and local authorities received lower probity scores: 50.7 percent and 50.9 percent of respondents respectively believed none or few people in these groups are corrupt. Respondents rated the press as the least corrupt institution, with nearly 60 percent of respondents believing none or few journalists were corrupt. Unfortunately, it is hard to verify the validity of these estimates because few reputable opinion surveys ask sensitive questions about corruption.

In 2017–2018, the Russian public's longing for the rule of law crystalized in a series of blog posts and media publications contrasting the rule of law with the "rule of understandings" (*po poniatiiam*), a phrase that in criminal jargon means informal code of conduct. The public discussion made explicit connection to the criminal-business networks of the 1990s and the mid-2010s predominance of *siloviki* (the state officials with law enforcement and security services backgrounds), who also are known to use the same criminal jargon. One publicist, citing unfair legal norms, posed a rhetorical question "Who is to blame that 'by law' turns out worse than 'by understandings'?" (Novitskii, 2017).

The development of a law-based formal regulatory environment means that more resources travel through the official channels. Nowadays, Russians and Kazakhs pay fees and taxes through e-government internet portals and prefer debit card to cash transactions. Formal contracts replace handshake agreements, and electronic registries replace paper-based accounting books. Citizens and businesses follow more clearly defined and consistently enforced rules regulating their private and economic lives. They might have fewer face-to-face encounters with tax and customs officials, but they have a track record of electronic documentation and receipts, along with more procedural clarity when it comes to the legally binding rules and regulations they have to follow. These rules, however, are not necessarily written to protect average citizens and their property from state encroachment or the interests of powerful corporations owned by the close associates of the rule-writing officials. The average person might find the legal system to be unfair and abusive not because the rules are broken and laws are not enforced, but because the official rules are rigged in favor of those who hold power. The rise of the formal regulatory state should not be confused with the establishment of the rule of law.

Institutional Capacity

In the twenty-first century, the leading international development institutions have focused on state capacity, and more generally institutional capacity, as one of the developmental priorities. State capacity has been linked to better economic outcomes: professional, purpose-oriented, and resourceful institutions are the necessary tools of effective governance and statesmanship. Contributing to the growing literature on state capacity, Chapter 4 of this book showed that bureaucratic resources and regulatory specificity interact in influencing economic outcomes.[174] My examination of subnational variation in the level of bureaucratic regulatory specificity and the size of the bureaucracy across regions of the Russian Federation reveals that the way in which rule-based bureaucratic constraints affect economic outcomes largely depends on the underlying resources of state institutions to provide public services and enforce their own rules. I argued that bureaucratic discretion affects economic outcomes differentially in resourceful and resource-deprived institutions of governance. The rule-constrained executive agencies are the most beneficial when they are well-staffed and well-supplied with resources. When bureaucratic agencies are understaffed and deprived of resources, extensive bureaucratic regulatory specificity may be counterproductive. Bureaucratic constraint should be understood as one of the many consequential components of a high-capacity state.

One possible objection to the theory of the autocratic regulatory state is posed by the notion of state weakness and portrayals of Russia and Kazakhstan as weak states. Their rulers, one might argue, are not able to effectively curtail subversive bureaucrats. Corruption, spotty regulatory enforcement, official predation, and discrepancies between policy and enforcement

---

[174] This finding is in line with the literature that links better economic performance to resourceful bureaucracies (Rauch and Evans, 1999; Brown et al., 2009).

practices could be seen as both the symptoms and consequences of state weakness. In fact, much of the literature on corruption focuses on the lack of state resources or enforcement as the reason for corruption. With the growing record of Eurasian autocrats' effective persecution of their political foes and society, this interpretation however, loses traction. The 2011 Zhanaozen massacre of protestors in the Western oil-producing region of Kazakhstan, the 2012 mass arrest in Bolotnaya square in Moscow, Russia's intervention in Georgia and Ukraine, and the brutal repression of the 2021 and 2022 protests in Russia and Kazakhstan should caution against treating inconsistent policy application as evidence of state weakness or institutional decay.

The argument that authoritarian states might engage in formal regulatory institution-building for the sake of strengthening an autocrat's power casts doubt on the normative dimension of state capacity. Capacity and effectiveness have replaced democracy and freedom as internationally recognized developmental objectives. This book's account of autocratic regulatory state-building, however, clearly shows that institutional capacity development should not be treated as a normative good. The stronger state institutions in Russia and Kazakhstan might decrease the amount of unpredictability, promote order, and at times enhance their public goods provision. Still, the primary objective for such capacity-enhancing institutional developments is to serve the autocrats who effectively and efficiently suppress freedoms, plunder national resources, prosecute their opponents, and expropriate private property.

Growth and Development

Theory on the regulatory state casts an interesting light on Russia's and Kazakhstan's developmental outlooks. Neopatrimonial, crony capitalist states, whose leaders take ownership of vast economic resources and whose state officials dominate the distribution of private rents, are believed to have poor developmental prospects (Kohli, 2004). Russia and Kazakhstan, however, despite their continuing concentration of political and economic power, increasing state control over the private sector, and distribution of access to economic resources on the basis of nepotism and personal connections, have been quite successful not only in building institutional capacity, but also in maintaining positive economic growth. Both have been able to expand their economies, integrate into world markets, and modernize some industries. Neopatrimonialism can account for the failures of becoming "normal" industrialized capitalist countries, including the lack of fair access to economic opportunities, absence of the rule of law, and persistent favoritism of special interests over public interests. Still, the analyzed post-Soviet autocracies preserve pockets of efficiency and, despite fluctuations in oil prices and international sanctions, continue to grow their economies.

Russia's record of regulatory reforms in the era of economic sanctions and inward-looking economic policy suggests that in that country, reforms are not introduced as "short-term signals that require developing countries attain and retain external support and legitimacy" (Andrews, 2013, p. 3), but are driven by internal political-economic dynamics. As the study of economic policy reforms and their developmental consequences has shifted from the search for the "right" institutional framework to the analysis of incentives and structural components of governance (Rodrik, 2007; Evans and Harris, 2004; Grindle, 2004; Goldsmith, 2012), this book contributes to exploring specific formal institutions of state governance that structure those incentives. Policies change, sometimes radically, but the frameworks for designing regulations and implementing them most often transcend the content of specific economic policies. In this book I traced the institutional development of regulatory state institutions, rather than the adoption of specific economic policies.

Chapters 3 and 4 of this book argued that the lack of formal regulatory constraints and the resulting capricious policy enforcement have a strong negative effect on investment, revenue, and business formation—factors reflective of the health of the private economy as well as the general wellbeing of society. My quantitative analysis of regional variation in economic performance in Russia and Kazakhstan has linked formal aspects of regulatory regimes to the economic performance indicators carefully selected to avoid biases associated with economic rents and state-orchestrated development projects. I analyzed the dynamics of regional enterprises' decisions to reinvest their profits and the growth of the number and cumulative profits of small and medium enterprises.[175] My analysis showed that both statutory and administrative-level constraints are consequential for the bottom-up aspects of economic performance. In Russian regions and Kazakh provinces,

---

[175] These are defined as companies employing fewer than 50 people in Kazakhstan and fewer than 250 people in Russia, or generating an annual revenue that does not exceed $75,000 in Kazakhstan or $27 million in Russia.

more detailed statutory regulations and bylaws enacted by subnational executive agencies lead to higher rates of investment and a healthier small business sector.

This finding casts strong doubts on the popular notion that business growth is stifled by too many rules and regulations. Unlike in countries with public-serving regulatory state agencies, fewer and shorter regulatory documents do not entice post-Soviet public servants to use their flexibility for the sake of improving regional economic performance, effective implementation of economic policy, or betterment of the business climate. Quite the opposite, a lengthier regulatory corpus was associated with better regional economic performance. Finding these effects in unitary Kazakhstan, a country with a very high concentration of political and administrative controls at the hands of the central government, is rather remarkable. Central control, constant personnel reshuffles, and dependence on the centrally allocated budgets rule out bureaucratic, organizational, and human resources as alternative explanatory factors linking regulatory quality to economic outcomes.

Political Limitation of Autocratic Regulatory States

In 2006, Douglass North, John Joseph Wallis, and Barry Weingast proposed that most historical and contemporary human societies "provide order by using the political system to limit economic entry to create rents, and then using the rents to stabilize the political system and limit violence" (North et al., 2006). The authors call this arrangement a natural state, or "limited access order." Their integrated theory of politics and economics highlights the fact that the combination of economic freedom and democratic politics—the one that the authors call an "open access order"—is not the norm, but rather a rare social arrangement.

This book has explored a specific contemporary institutional arrangement that structures a limited access political-economic order in a way that allows autocratic rulers to balance the predatory interests of patronage-bound economic elites with the growth-focused economic policy. The regulatory states I described in this book crafted a policy enforcement arrangement that allows the rulers to balance the elites' demands for monopolistic access to private wealth with the needs for maintaining public goods provision. The latter are in fact essential for authoritarian survival because they help maintain the complacency of a critical mass of ordinary citizens *and* to ensure the continuing economic expansion to sustain future rents. I explored how the creation of authoritarian regulatory states has strengthened the "limited-access orders" by the formal regulatory institutions built to both enable and constrain informal practices of nepotism, corruption, and patronage by allowing the rulers to control the "length of the leash" they use for keeping the predatory cronies happy but under control.

The single most important limitation of the regimes relying on the political support of a state bureaucracy stems from the political tradeoff potentially leading to overregulation. The more restrictive the economic order, the costlier the regulations for economic actors, and the more resources can be potentially channeled to the regime insiders and bureaucrats through preferentialism and corruption. Regime survival in Kazakhstan from the early days of independence and in Russia increasingly from the early 2000s has relied upon the ability of the central government to win or install the support of state bureaucracy.[176] This necessitated that the state bureaucracies—specialized agencies and regional governments—retain and expand their control over potentially extractable economic resources. Costly regulations, however, tend to undermine economic performance, which is also essential for politicians' survival in office.

Even though the autocratic governments are not defined by their policy objectives, authoritarian regimes can clearly be linked to the specific institutional logic underlying the way they build institutions of regulatory enforcement. That logic accounts for the intermittent tolerance of corruption and probity initiatives, terror and violence against insiders and opponents coinciding with the state backing and pestering other private sector elites, and the recurring episodes of cryptic shifts from ruler's wrath to benevolence. These schizophrenic shifts, however, are quite logical and consistent from the vantage point of the authoritarian regulatory state. They reflect the balancing between the public good and parochial interests. What might seem to be the defects of institutional reforms of economic development are in fact the optimal outcomes from the regime survival standpoint, which requires combining clientelism with state efficiency.

The oscillating priorities in state-economy relations, nevertheless, pose an important limitation: an inconsistent, stop-and-go developmental trajectory. Economic downturns are likely to erode the autocrats' popular

---

[176] The relationships between the federal and regional authorities in Russia illustrate the importance of this support quite clearly.

legitimacy, leading to the reinvigoration of the state's developmental agenda. Resumption of economic growth, however, might lessen the popular pressures but intensify the elite's demands for rent creation. This necessarily undermines the long-term developmental outlook of the autocratic regulatory states.

Yet another limitation imposed by the authoritarian regulatory state lies in the international political dimension. Although the growth of formal mechanisms of the regulatory state has strengthened the authoritarian regimes, the logic of regime survival imposes constraints on countries' international political choices. In a 2008 article, Marcin Kaczmarski, referring to the independent political power of Russia's *siloviki*, suggested that "The growth of Putin's winning coalition has broadened the scope of Russia's international preferences" (Kaczmarski, 2008, p. 385). Citing the parochial domestic interests' ability to alter the final outcomes of foreign policy in the process of policy implementation, Kaczmarski concluded that the domestic political-economic arrangements have empowered bureaucratic elites to influence Moscow's foreign policy in Asia to favor their parochial economic interests. In their investigation of the People's Republic of China, Jones and Hameiri (2021) presented a similar argument. They documented how China's state agencies and powerful corporate interests have subverted the central government's foreign policy in such strategically important areas as the South China Sea, cross-border trade in narcotics, and international development financing. Clearly, lax policy enforcement—the core mechanism for autocratic regulatory state-building—poses important limitations not only on domestic but also on international policy implementation.

The growing complexity of economic processes, including production technologies, distribution networks, infrastructural requirements, and financial instruments, creates yet another limitation on the authoritarian regulatory state. Research shows that politicians are more likely to grant administrative authorities considerable discretionary powers when regulatory activities require highly specialized and technical knowledge (Wilson-Sokhey, 2017). Technological sophistication that requires specialized knowledge puts technical barriers on the use of ex ante control mechanisms. Legislators and high-level political appointees might lack the necessary skills for designing specific regulatory mechanisms in those specialized areas, which means the autocratic regulatory states will necessarily be less effective compared to countries with a system of open society-based feedback on legislation and administration. The only potential remedy to this limitation is the development of more professional legislatures and high-level political administrative appointees. The access to independent professional or technical expertise at the rulemaking echelons of power is limited, however, by the kleptocratic, clientele-building logic of authoritarian survival.

In light of these major limitations of autocratic regulatory states, the 2022 Russian war in Ukraine raises a pressing question about the future of Russian authoritarianism. Russia's military ineptitude and unexpectedly heavy losses (Beardsworth, 2022) further highlight the autocratic state-building paradox of institutional efficiency and corrupt cronyism. Despite its expensive and much celebrated modernization, the Russian military machine had shown itself to be inept and incompetent (Dobson, 2022; Schake, 2022). While the economic difficulties, military failures, and popular protests against partial military mobilization have been interpreted as clear signs of Putin's weakness and imminent decline (Laruelle, 2022), we should not underestimate the resilience of Russia's autocratic regime and its well-institutionalized state. The internal logics of authoritarian regulatory states are likely to last beyond Putin's personal autocratic rule the same way the Kazakh regulatory authoritarian state outlasted the rule of Nursultan Nazarbayev. The war economy and military mobilization necessitate rebalancing the autocrat's priorities over elite and mass interests, which factor prominently in the autocrats' dilemma. The series of mysterious deaths of Russian oligarchs point to the growing importance of popular support and de-prioritizing elite rents (Kottasova, 2022). The war might also necessitate more repressive mechanisms of regime survival. Ratcheting up repression and stumping political criticisms, however, will further reduce ex ante mechanisms for disciplining unruly and corrupt public officials and make ex ante formal mechanisms of controlling official discretion even more important for maintaining a functioning autocratic state.

Formal Argument

This appendix presents a formal account of strategic interactions under regulatory arrangements characterized by discretionary and limited bureaucratic powers. A variant of this model first appeared in Duvanova (2012). The model has three players: a firm F, a low-level bureaucrat B, and his political principal P. All are assumed to be rational utility maximizers. Following a standard assumption, the private sector's decisions to invest in new production, all other things held constant, respond negatively to the expected costs of doing business (Krueger, 1974; Acemoglu and Verdier, 2000). Business climate, therefore, is a negative function of a firms' expected costs (c). The firm maximizes the difference between revenues and costs: $I_F = r - c$, where I_F is income, r is total revenue, and c is total cost, and operates under the total budget constraint set by $0 \leq I_F = r - c$. Following the discussions in the chapter, the cost c is disaggregated into production cost c_p and regulatory cost c_r.

Regulatory costs are imposed by the political authority P (legislators or the autocrat) whose utility function reflects the internalized costs of production externalities, revenue generated by regulatory involvement (taxes, tariffs, and licensing fees), and social welfare produced by the firms' reinvested profits.[177] In line with the standard neoliberal expectation of positive regulatory cost, increase in c_r reduces a firm's expected profit and leads to lower levels of investment or business activity.[178]

Discretionary Power

Politicians' political or economic considerations may prompt them to vest bureaucrats with discretionary powers. Let d represent the amount of discretion the politician delegates to the bureaucrat, so that d ranges from 0 (no discretion) to 1 (the entire regulatory cost is subject to discretionary application). High regulatory costs may reduce profits for some firms, potentially hurting powerful economic interests. By selectively lowering the cost of regulatory compliance to $c_r^* = c_r - dc_r$ the bureaucrat may ensure these interests are protected. Discretionary policy application also allows bureaucrats to impose greater regulatory pressure on select firms that generate higher revenues, produce negative externalities, or have no exit options. By setting $c_r^* = c_r + dc_r$ bureaucrats can target these firms. Discretionary power, hence, can be applied selectively either to lower or to increase the cost of regulatory compliance.[179]

---

[177] This political utility function is consistent with Margaret Levi's revenue maximization objective of the ruler (Levi, 1988).

[178] This assumes the regulatory regimes are exogenous to the private sector's preferences, costs, and profits. This is a more realistic assumption for some authoritarian regimes than others. In Chapter 6 I relax this assumption to consider the political dynamics behind the choice of regulatory regimes under authoritarianism.

[179] Notice that in this formulation a unit of discretion does not have a fixed cost. Instead, the effects of discretion are greater under a more burdensome regulatory regime.

Private sector actors may face a lot of uncertainty in predicting the direction of bureaucratic regulatory bias. In evaluating the expected effects of discretionary policy application, nevertheless, it is important to weigh the expected benefits of discretionary policy implementation by the probability of favorable treatment, $p \in [0; 1]$:

$$-p(c_r - d \times c_r) - (1 - p)(c_r + d \times c_r) = -c_r - dc_r(1 - 2p) \qquad (1)$$

Depending on the probability that discretionary policy application yields a positive outcome for the regulated business, three scenarios are possible. First, when the bureaucrats are more likely to use their discretionary powers favorably, to reduce the official cost of compliance ($p > .5$), discretionary powers should have a positive effect on a firm's perception of business climate and, by extension, lead to greater rates of investment and business activity, $(-dc_r(1 - 2p)) > 0$. This expectation is in line with arguments emphasizing positive economic effects of discretionary bureaucratic powers.

Second, when probabilities of favorable and unfavorable treatment are identical, discretionary power, in expectation, has no effect on the cost of doing business, $dc_r(1 - 2p) = 0$. This expectation effectively justifies ignoring the regulatory implementation dimension in empirical applications.

Third, when the probability of unfavorable treatment is greater than the probability of favorable treatment ($p < .5$), bureaucratic discretion enters the firm's utility function with a negative sign, $(-dc_r(1 - 2p)) < 0$, meaning it increases the expected cost of doing business. This is consistent with the empirical expectation that bureaucratic discretion suppresses business activity. Because this formulation does not make restrictive assumptions about the direction of discretionary bias, the model does not impose *a priori* assumptions about economic effects of bureaucratic discretion and leaves these effects open to empirical tests.

Given the expected cost of regulations set up by (1), the firm chooses between complying with regulations, evading regulatory compliance through illicit deals with regulatory authorities, or exiting the formal markets.[180] Consider the ways in which the discretion given to bureaucratic agencies to implement regulations affects a firm's regulatory compliance decisions.

Regulatory Compliance under Constrained Bureaucracy

Assume no discretionary power over policy implementation is delegated by politicians to the regulatory agencies ($d = 0$). In other words, the regulatory costs are set at the policy-formulation stage, and there is no red tape. The firm may choose to *comply* with

---

[180] The firm's total profit constraint means that if the cost of regulatory compliance exceeds a firm's revenue, minus the cost of production, and other strategies are not available, the firm might be forced to exit the market or operate illegally. Operating outside the formal sector, the firm runs the risk of being prosecuted, thus private protection mechanisms, including mafia-type organizations, are going to ensure firms' continuing operation in the informal sector. The firm's activity per se is not illegal—it might continue producing legal products and providing legal services. What makes the firm's operations illegal is that it exits regular regulatory relations with the state, such as paying taxes, obtaining permits and licenses, and submitting its practices and products to state control and protection. Such strategy, however, goes beyond the scope of this investigation. For the analysis of entrance into the unofficial economy, see Hibbs and Piculescu (2010).

the existing regulations at a cost of c_r or bribe the bureaucrat and pay b instead of c_r.[181] Under these two strategies available to the firm, it maximizes income I_F as defined below:

$$I_F(comply) = r - c_p - c_r$$
$$I_F(bribe) = r - c_p - b - qf,$$

where b is bribe, and qf is the expected cost of punishment for bribery.

The bureaucrat's income is supplemented by any bribe b he/she might receive from the firm in exchange for overlooking regulatory violations. This "service" is assumed to be costless to the bureaucrat. If the bureaucrat chooses to be *corrupt*, she sets the amount of bribe b. If the firm and the bureaucrat engage in corrupt behavior, both face a chance of being fined f with probability q. The composition of anticorruption measures qf is set by the politician. The bureaucrat maximizes income I_B where s is salary:

$$I_B(honest) = s$$
$$I_B(corrupt) = s + b - qf$$

All variables are assumed to be non-negative and $q \in [0; 1]$. The politician announces regulatory regime and anticorruption measures, and the bureaucrat proposes a bribe b. The firm chooses *comply* or *bribe*. Compliance will be chosen over bribery if and only if $c_r < b + qf$. The bureaucrat is corrupt whenever $I_B(corrupt) > I_B(honest)$, or

$$b > qf \tag{2}$$

To entice the firm into corrupt behavior, the bureaucrat must offer a bribe such that $I_F(bribe) > I_F(comply)$, or

$$b < c_r - qf \tag{3}$$

If there is such c_r that satisfies $c_r < qf$, then the necessary and sufficient condition for the firm to bribe rather than comply is $b < 0$. The bureaucrat, however, will be honest rather than offer a negative bribe, and so for $c_r < pf$, the firm complies, and the bureaucrat is honest. Combining (2) and (3), we find that in the absence of discretionary bureaucratic power, b will never exceed c_r. Under a constrained bureaucracy, the cost of regulations c_r increases the cost of bribery. Quite intuitively, anticorruption measures qf reduce the cost of bribery and promote compliance.

---

[181] This follows Shleifer and Vishny's (1993) "corruption with theft" type. Bribery allows firms to forgo the cost of compliance altogether. When a firm chooses to bribe, it pays no regulatory cost. To simplify the presentation, I assume that on any given issue the firm either bribes or complies. This does not mean that the firms cannot pursue a mixed strategy over a range of issues.

Regulatory Compliance under Discretionary Bureaucracy

When the bureaucratic agencies can influence the cost of regulatory compliance through discretionary enforcement practices, red-tape creation, and extortion, the firm faces the following choice of alternative regulatory compliance strategies:

$$I_F(comply) = r - c_p - c_r - dc_r(1 - 2p)$$
$$I_F(bribe) = r - c_p - b - qf$$

This means that the bribe the bureaucrat can charge for turning a blind eye on a firm's failure to comply with regulations has to satisfy the following condition:

$$b' < c_r + dc_r(1 - 2p) - qf \tag{4}$$

When $dc_r(1 - 2p)$ is greater than zero ($p < .5$), the bribe charged under the discretionary regulatory regime (4) is larger than in the absence of regulatory discretion (2). Regimes with discretionary policy application allow the bureaucrat to augment the initial regulatory regime imposed by the politician c_r by creating red tape $\tau = f(d, p), \tau \in [0; d]$. To entice corruption the bureaucrat then chooses τ, which only applies to the portion of regulatory cost subject to bureaucrats' discretion dc_r. Since the increase in b' comes from the dc_r term, the bureaucrat's expected utility from bribery, therefore, is maximized by $\tau = d, p = 0$. Under such conditions the politician cannot deter bribery by $pf > c_r$ because the firm's utility function now depends on $c_r + dc_r(1 - 2p)$. To deter bribery, the politician has to set $pf \geq c_r + dc_r(1 - 2p)$, which, given the corrupt bureaucrat's incentive to maximize τ (subject to the firm's total profit constraint), translates to $pf > c_r + dc_r$. This means that to be effective against discretionary bureaucracy, the anticorruption measures have to be more certain and/or punitive compared to those effective in the limited bureaucracy settings.

Unlike the case of a constrained bureaucracy, corruption under discretionary policy application does not necessarily entail the choice between bribery ($b - qf$) and compliance with the official regulations (c_r). When the total costs of regulations consist of the official regulatory burden and the bureaucrat-imposed red tape, bribery may become the mechanism for cutting the red tape. Assuming the red tape is being created ($dc_r(1 - 2p) > 0$), bribery might not entail forgone compliance:

$$I_F(bribe) = r - c_p - c_r - b - qf$$

When graft reduces the red tape (the so-called unofficial "speed" or "facilitation" fees), the equilibrium bribe has to satisfy the following condition:

$$b'' < dc_r - qf, \tag{5}$$

so that $b'' < b < b'$. Still, as long as $b'' > pq$, the bureaucrats have incentives to supplement their incomes with bribery.[182] One reason the bureaucrat who has some discretionary

---

[182] This falls into the "corruption without theft" category, in which the state agent collects appropriate taxes and enforces official regulatory norms, but charges regulated entities extra unofficial fees for doing it effectively, without costly delays and unnecessary paperwork.

Table 17 Summary of Theoretical Expectations

Bureaucratic Authority	Conditions for Corruption	Bribe Size and Red-Tape Creation
Bureaucratic constraint	Compliance if $qf \geq c_r$	No red tape
	Corruption if $qf < c_r$	$b = c_r - pf, \frac{\Delta b}{\Delta c_r} > 0$
	Predatory Bureaucrat	
	Compliance if $qf \geq c_r + dc_r(1 - 2p)$	Red tape
	Corruption if $qf < c_r + dc_r(1 - 2p)$	$b' = c_r + dc_r - qf$
Bureaucratic discretion	*Business-Friendly Bureaucrat*	
	Compliance if $qf \geq dc_r(1 - 2p)$	Red tape
	Corruption if $qf < dc_r(1 - 2p)$	$b'' = dc_r - qf$

power might prefer b'' over b' is because she is motivated to deliver the expected level of regulatory compliance (c_r);[183] the other reason is that the agency contract might link the bureaucrats' monetary or career incentives to the achievement of certain levels of regulatory compliance.[184]

Extending this logic, even when the bureaucrat is inclined to treat the firm favorably—when $dc_r(1 - 2p)$ is greater than zero—the bureaucrat may benefit from the red-tape creation. If the bureaucrat's discretionary policy application is driven by her independent preferences over c_r, red tape offers additional leverage in channeling bureaucratic resources towards the firm targeted for preferential treatment. By creating additional hurdles for the firm's competitors, the bureaucrat enhances the unfair advantage of the favored firm without compromising the official regulatory policy.[185] Hence, under discretionary policy application, the bureaucrat does not need to engage in bribery to have an incentive to create the red tape. Table 17 summarizes theoretical expectations for high and low levels of bureaucratic discretion.

---

[183] The bureaucrat's preferences over optimal levels of c_r might align with those of the politician.

[184] The bureaucrat's salary s and the probability of being investigated and/or prosecuted for corruption q might depend on how well the regulatory policy is being enforced. This further assumes there exists some observable indicators of the actual levels of regulatory compliance.

[185] In other words, red-tape creation allows the bureaucrat to pursue her policy or rent-seeking objectives without undermining the official regulatory norms.

Results of Vector Autoregressions

Table 18 Russian Regulatory Documents and Good Governance Indicators, Vector Autoregressive Models

	Control Corruption		Government Effectiveness		Regulatory Quality	
	coef.	s.e.	coef.	s.e.	coef.	s.e.
All Regulations, 1,000 documents	.085*	017	.068*	.018	.035	.021
Statutory Regulations, 1,000 documents	1.572*	.401	.663	.459	1.227*	.271
Clarifying Instructions, 1,000 documents	.131*	.035	.135*	.028	.035	.038
All Regulations, million words	.144*	035	.121*	.032	.054	.037
Statutory Regulations, million words	−.491	.367	.313	.355	.094	.280
Clarifying Instructions, million words	.235*	.062	.239*	.050	.065	.067

Note: GARANT data. Exogenous covariates: oil rents, government size, and GDP per capita.
*significant at .001 level or better.

Sample Regulatory Document

TOMSK CITY ADMINISTRATION
EXECUTIVE ORDER
September 15, 2010 No. R1284

ON APPROVAL OF THE PROVISION ON THE RULES AND PROCEDURE FOR
THE PREPARATION OF LONG-TERM MUNICIPAL CONTRACTS FOR
MUNICIPAL NEEDS OF THE MUNICIPAL ENTITY "TOMSK CITY" AND
MUNICIPAL CUSTOMERS FOR THE PERFORMANCE OF WORKS (PROVISION
OF SERVICES) WITH A LONG PRODUCTION CYCLE

In accordance with Part 3, Article 72 of the Budget Code of the Russian Federation and the Decree of the Government of the Russian Federation of December 29, 2007 N 978 "On approval of the rules for concluding long-term state (municipal) contracts for the performance of work (rendering of services) with a long production cycle."

1. To approve the provision of the rules and procedure for making decisions on concluding long-term municipal contracts for municipal needs of the municipal entity "City of Tomsk" and municipal customers for the performance of work (provision of services) with a long production cycle in accordance with the appendix to this order.

2. Assign to the Deputy Mayor for Economics and Finance of the City of Tomsk A.P. Abramov the control over the execution of this order.

Mayor of Tomsk
N.A. Nikolaychuk
[signed]

Appendix to the executive order of Tomsk city administration
September 15, 2010 No. R1284

PROVISION ON THE RULES AND PROCEDURE FOR THE CONCLUSION OF
LONG-TERM MUNICIPAL CONTRACTS FOR MUNICIPAL NEEDS OF THE
MUNICIPAL ENTITY "TOMSK CITY" AND MUNICIPAL CUSTOMERS FOR THE
PERFORMANCE OF WORKS (PROVISION OF SERVICES) WITH A LONG
PRODUCTION CYCLE

1. These Provisions determine the rules and procedure for making decisions on concluding long-term municipal contracts for the performance of work (rendering of services) for the municipal needs of the municipal entity "City of Tomsk" and municipal contractors, the duration of the production cycle of fulfillment (provision) of which exceeds the period of the approved limits of budgetary cycle.

2. The decision to conclude a long-term municipal contract for municipal needs of the municipal entity "City of Tomsk" and municipal customers is taken by the administration of the City of Tomsk in the form of a municipal legal act of the administration of the City of Tomsk.

3. Municipal customers are entitled to conclude long-term municipal contracts:

3.1. within the limits of funds established for the relevant purposes by the city long-term target programs for the period of implementation of these programs;

3.2. for a period and within the limits of funds stipulated by regulatory municipal legal acts of the administration of the City of Tomsk on budget investments in capital construction projects of municipal property not included in urban long-term target programs;

3.3. for a period and within the limits of funds established by the municipal legal act of the administration of the City of Tomsk. The specified municipal legal act approves:

- the planned results of the performance of work (rendering of services);
- description of the scope of work (services);
- deadline for the performance of work (provision of services), taking into account the time required to place an order;
- the maximum amount of funds for the implementation of a long-term municipal contract by year.

4. The draft municipal legal act on the conclusion of long-term municipal contracts is developed by municipal customers and, after the review by the Department of Finance of the Administration of the City of Tomsk and the Department of Economic Development and Municipal Property Management of the Administration of the City of Tomsk, is sent by them to the Administration of the City of Tomsk.

5. The financial and economic substantiation of the project and an explanatory note are attached to the draft municipal legal act on the conclusion of long-term contracts. The explanatory note to the draft regulation should contain:

a) justification of the need to achieve the planned results of work (services); b) substantiation of the deadline for the performance of work (rendering of services), taking into account the duration and continuity of the production cycle in the context of technologies adopted in industries and approved by technical regulatory documents, as well as legislative requirements and regulatory legal documents (including the time required to place an order);

c) substantiation of the maximum amount of funds for the implementation of a long-term municipal contract by year and price calculation taking into account the inflation rate;

d) the planned results of the performance of work (rendering of services);

e) a description of the scope of work (services);

f) the deadline for the performance of work (provision of services), taking into account the time required to place an order;

g) the maximum amount of funds for the implementation of a long-term municipal contract by year.

6. The Department of Finance of the Administration of the City of Tomsk and the Department of Economic Development and Municipal Property Management of the Administration of the City of Tomsk within a period not exceeding 15 days from the receipt date of a draft municipal legal act of the administration of the City of Tomsk, financial and economic justification and an explanatory note to it, determine whether the specified project meets the following conditions:

- compliance of the proposed long-term municipal contract with the 'expenditure obligations register';
- compliance of the maximum budgetary allocations of a long-term municipal contract for municipal needs of the municipal entity "City of Tomsk" in the current financial

year and remaining planned period with the budgetary allocations stipulated for the fulfillment of the corresponding expenditure obligation in the City Budget approved by the City Council of Tomsk;

- not exceeding the annual maximum amount of funds provided for the payment of a long-term municipal contract for the needs of the municipal entity "City of Tomsk" and municipal customers outside the planning period, over the maximum annual amount of budgetary allocations provided for paying the specified contract within the planning period (in the current financial year).

7. The conclusion of long-term municipal contracts is carried out based on the results of placing orders in the manner prescribed by the July 21, 2005 Federal Law #94-FZ "On Placing Orders for the Supply of Goods, Performance of Work for State and Municipal Needs."

Validity of the Empirical Measure
of Regulatory Specificity

If the proposed measure of regulatory specificity of statutory regulations adequately captures the concept of regulatory constraint, it should correlate with other indicators of regulatory quality and governance. My theoretical framework suggests that discretion-limiting formal constraints should be positively correlated with regulatory efficiency. To check if this is the case, I model the World Bank World Governance indicators of Regulatory Quality, Control of Corruption, and Government Effectiveness as a first-order vector autoregressive process with some measures of formal regulatory constraint, growth, and GDP per capita as the exogenous covariates. I find that the number of regulatory documents that were in force in a given year, as well as the total number of words across these documents, are positively correlated with Control of Corruption, Regulatory Quality, and Government Effectiveness estimates. The second-order autoregressive models produce similar results.

Table 19 Kazakh Regulatory Documents and Good Governance Indicators, Vector Autoregressive Models

	Regulatory Quality		Control Corruption		Gov. Effectiveness	
	coef.	s.e.	coef.	s.e.	coef.	s.e.
Number Economic Regulations	.00007**	.00003	.00002**	1.00e–05	.00006**	.00003
Length Economic Regulations	1.14e–07**	4.73e–08	3.90e–08**	1.73e–08	1.02e–07**	4.82e–08
Number Executive Business Regulations	.0002**	.0001	.00007*	.00004	.0002	.00012
Length Executive Business Regulations	4.10e–07**	1.95e–07	.1.17e–07*	6.75e–08	2.93e–07	1.96e–07
Number Ministerial Financial Regulations	.0004***	.0001	.0001**	.00006	.00037**	.00016
Length Ministerial Financial Regulations	7.11e–07***	2.14e–07	2.08e–07**	9.24e–08	5.83e–07**	2.57e–07

Note: Republican Center for Legal Information (RCLI) Data. *, **, *** significant at .05, .01, .001 level or better.

Modeling Independent and Interactive Effects of Discretion on Business Climate

Country Panel

To test Hypothesis 1, I analyze an unbalanced country panel. Some countries contribute just one observation, hence, I use random effects panel analysis models. Theoretical arguments suggest the following regression specification:

$$Y_{it+1} = \beta_0 + \beta_1 audit_{it} + \beta_2 reg_{it} + \beta_3(audit_{it} \times reg_{it}) + \beta_4 GDP/cap_{it} + C_i + u_{it} \quad (6)$$

where Y_{it} is the dependent variable (business climate) for $i = 1, \ldots, 102$ countries; $audit_{it}$ is a dummy for low discretion; reg_{it} stands for the number of official regulations (of market entry) that vary across countries and time; $\beta_4 GDP/cap_{it}$ is the control for the level of development; C_i are country random effects; and u_{it} is a stochastic element. The independent variables are measured with one-year lags. To facilitate the interpretation of regression coefficients, interactive variable regressions include a binary variable for low and high discretion. Substantive results, however, do not change when a continuous measure of audit effectiveness is used instead.

Note that if $audit = 0$, then

$$Y_{it} = \beta_0 + \beta_2 reg_{it} + \cdots + u_{it} \quad (7)$$

If $audit = 1$,

$$Y_{it} = \beta_0 + \beta_1 audit_{it} + (\beta_2 + \beta_3) reg_{it} + \cdots + u_{it} \quad (8)$$

This means that by comparing β_2 and $(\beta_2 + \beta_3)$ we can directly assess how regulations impact the business climate under low- and high-discretion settings.

All regression models control for the level of economic development using GDP per capita data from the Penn World Table (Heston et al., 2009). Facing strong multi-collinearity among attributes of good governance, I strived for the most parsimonious model. As with much of the extant cross-sectional analysis, there is a tradeoff between omitted variables and multi-collinearity. The omitted variable concern, however, is mitigated by the fact that the key explanatory variables exhibit variation across income groups, political regimes, economic openness, and stability. The results of empirical analysis are not sensitive to the inclusion of the political regime variables (e.g., Polity IV, Freedom House, and Voice and Accountability Index). Ultimately, the relatively small sample size renders many standard control variables insignificant in predicting the outcome.

Table 20, models 1–3, present the results of the above regression specifications and the baseline models. Model 1 and 2 regress the original interval and dummy variables measuring discretion and the number of entry procedures from the World Bank (WB) "Doing Business" project on GCI, but omit the interaction term. Model 4 re-estimates model 3, substituting entry regulations with the count of regulatory procedures required for property registration, construction permits, contract enforcement, paying taxes, obtaining electricity, and trading across borders. Model 5 uses HF index of business freedom as the dependent variable.

Models 6–8 test Hypothesis 2, postulating bureaucratic corruption as a causal mechanism connecting bureaucratic discretion to the discrepancy between regulatory intervention and business environment. I test the following model specification:

$$Corruption_{it+1} = \beta_0 + \beta_1 audit_{it} + \beta_2 reg_{it} + \beta_3(audit_{it} \times reg_{it}) + \sum \beta_{k_{it}} + C_i + u_{it} \quad (9)$$

Corruption is operationalized using the Control of Corruption indicator from the WB World Governance Indicators database. This variable is available for $i = 1, \ldots, 119$ countries; $audit_{it}$ is a dummy for low discretion based on the GI audit effectiveness index; reg_{it} stands for the number of official regulations of entry, property registration, construction, contract enforcement, paying taxes, obtaining electricity, and trading across borders; $\beta_k x_{k_{it}}$ is a vector of control variables; C_i are country random effects; and u_{it} is a stochastic element. Again, if $audit = 0$, then the effect of regulations is given by $\beta_2 reg_{it}$; if $audit = 1$, the effect of regulation is given by $(\beta_2 + \beta_3)reg_{it}$. The results of the baseline and interactive models with lagged dependent variable and GDP per capita as a sole control variable. These results are robust to the inclusion of other standard controls and the WB Rule of Law indicator.

Business Survey Data Analysis

Columns 1 and 2 in Table 21 present the fixed effects panel regression results operationalizing official regulatory burden in terms of the number of entry procedures. Columns 3 and 4 substitute the number of procedures with the number of days it takes an average firm to register. Columns 1 and 3 report the base-level models, and Columns 2 and 4 contain the results of the interacted variable regression specifications. I report the country-clustered standard errors. All models include identical control variables (coefficients not reported in the table). Robustness checks using an alternative dependent variable are in Columns 5 and 6. Column 5 contains the results of the baseline model. Column 6 reports the results of the interacted variables' regression specification. These analyses use country-level random effects.

Table 20 Effects of Regulations on Business Climate and Corruption as Conditioned by Discretion

	Global Competitiveness Index				HF	Control Corruption		
	Entry Regulations				All Regulations			
	(1)	(2)	(3)	(4)	(5)	(6)	(7)	(8)
Discretion Low Supreme audit index	.001 (.0009)*					.002 (.0006)***		
Discretion Low Supreme audit dummy		.021 (.030)	.235 (.088)**	−.176 (.082)**	3.779 (1.106)***		.052 (.019)***	.170 (.049)***
Regulations	−.022 (.006)***	−.021 (.006)***	−.008 (.008)	.0006 (.0005)	.010 (.006)	−.0005 (.0002)***	−.0005 (.0002)**	−.00002 (.0003)
Number procedures, lagged								
Regulation × Discretion			−.021 (.008)**	.002 (.001)**	−.030 (.009)**			−.001 (.0003)
$\beta_2 + \beta_3$			−.029 (.007)***	.002 (.0004)***	−.020 (.007)***		−.001	−.001 (.0004)**
GDP per Capita 100 current USD	.003 (.0001)***	.003 (.0001)***	.003 (.0001)***	.004 (.0001)***	.036 (.005)***	.003 (.0003)***	.002 (.0003)***	.003 (.0003)***
Const.	3.763 (.088)***	3.840 (.077)***	3.718 (.090)***	3.577 (.077)***	54.44 (1.014)***	−.645 (.069)***	−.519 (.062)***	−.582 (.065)***
Obs.	337	337	337	337	438	455	455	455
Groups	102	102	102	102	112	119	119	119
R^2 within	.125	.13	.15	.20	.020	.004	.001	.003
R^2 between	.589	.57	.58	.58	.38	.60	.57	.57
R^2 overall	.545	.53	.54	.45	.29	.48	.46	.45
σ_u	.339	.348	.347	.351	6.08	.490	.516	.511
σ_e	.160	.160	.159	.153	2.59	.104	.104	.104
ρ	.819	.827	.827	.840	.846	.957	.961	.960

Note: *, **, *** significant at .05, .01, .001 level or better. Standard errors are in parentheses.

Table 21 Entry Regulations, Regulatory Time, and Corruption: Fixed Effects in Country, Sector, and Survey

	Managerial Time Spent Dealing with Regulations				Regulations Are a Major Problem	
	(1)	(2)	(3)	(4)	(5)	(6)
Discretion High		1.314		1.139		1.353
		(.799)*		(.631)*		(.412)***
Entry Procedures	.223	.252			.117	.152
	(.086)***	(.114)**			(.071)*	(.073)**
EntryProc. × Discretion		−.122				−.065
		(.074)*				(.030)**
$x_1 = 1, \beta_2 + \beta_3$		.130				.087
		(.101)				(.075)
StartTime (days)			.056	.064		
			(.025)**	(.025)**		
StartTime × Discretion				−.031		
				(.012)***		
$x_1 = 1, \beta_2 + \beta_3$				.033		
				(.023)		
Const.	30.707	32.131	27.465	35.010	19.557	18.940
	(18.832)	(20.168)	(41.871)	(42.571)	(5.648)***	(5.619)***
Within R^2	.069	.068	.032	.033	.056	.065
Between R^2	.004	.002	.037	.008	.349	.313
Overall R^2	.012	.015	.007	.009	.081	.086
F (df)	55.26/19	42.9/21	61.74/18	54.86/20	–	–
ρ (Variance due to u_i)	.305	.259	.108	.100	–	–
Obs.	14344	12420	11622	10783	3663	3502
N countries	24	24	24	24	16	16
Survey Installments	3	3	2	2	1	1
Country	FE	FE	FE	FE	RE	RE

Note: *, **, *** significant at .05, .01, .001 level or better. Standard errors are in parentheses.

References

Acemoglu, Daron, Johnson, Simon, Querubin, Pablo, and Robinson, James A. (2008). When does policy reform work: The case of central bank independence. *Brookings Papers on Economic Activity*, **1**, 351–418.

Acemoglu, Daron and Verdier, Thierry A. (2000). The choice between market failures and corruption. *American Economic Review*, **90**, 194–211.

Aidis, Ruta and Adachi, Yuko (2007). Russia: Firm entry and survival barrier. *Economic Systems*, **31**(4), 391–411.

Akhmetkali, Aibarshyn (2022). Samruk kazyna sovereign wealth fund undergoes corporate restructuring and reforms. *The Astana Times*, **January 25**.

Akorda.kz (*n. d.*) Strategies and programs. Official Website of the President of the Republic of Kazakhstan. https://www.akorda.kz/en/ official_documents/strategies_ and_programs.

Akorda.kz (2017). The third modernization of Kazakhstan: Global competitiveness. Official Website of the President of the Republic of Kazakhstan.

Alesina, Alberto, Ardagna, Silvia, Nicoletti, Giuseppe, and Schiantarelli, Fabio (2005, June). Regulation and investment. *Journal of the European Economic Association*, **3**(4), 791–825.

Aljazeera. (2020, July 9). Russia arrests governor on suspicion of ordering murders. **July 9**.

Alkhabayev, Shokan (2021). Krushenie samolieta bekair: osudili chinovnikov i rieltora. *Tengrinews*, **May 12**.

Analiticheskii tsentr pri pravitel'stve RF (2019). Reformy KND. Sait reformy kontrol'noi i nadzornoi deiatel'nosti.

Andreeva, Daria (2014). Zemlia obetovannaia: V Krymu sniat maratorii na vydachu zemli i privatizatsiiu gossobstvennosti. *Rosinformbiuro*, **May 21**.

Andrews, Matt (2013). *Limits of Institutional Reform in Development: Changing Rules for Realistic Solutions*. Cambridge University Press, New York, NY.

Ashimbaev, Daniiar (2008). Putevoditel' po administrativnoi reforme Kazakhstana. *Kazakhstan*, **July 8**.

Aslund, Anders (1995). *How Russia Became a Market Economy*. Brookings Institution Press, Washington, DC.

Aslund, Anders (2007). *Russia's Capitalist Revolution: Why Market Reforms Succeeded and Democracy Failed*. Peterson Institute for International Economics, Washington, DC.

Aslund, Anders (2019). *Russia's Crony Capitalism: The Path from Market Economy to Kleptocracy*. Yale University Press, New Haven, CT.

Aslund, Anders (2020). Responses to the COVID-19 crisis in Russia, Ukraine, and Belarus. *Eurasian Geography and Economics*, **61**(4–5), 532–545.

Aslund, Anders and Commander, Simon (2016). Russia's gloomy prospects. *Project Syndicate*, **May 9**.

Astakhova, Anastasiia and Grozovskii, Boris (2009). Reforma tekhnicheskogo regulirovaniia i ee proval. Nauchno-Issledovatel'skii Portal IQ. Vysshaiia Shkola Ekonomiki.

Astana Times (2017). 60 percent of privatisation programme completed, says Samruk Kazyna chair. **August 28**.

Aubakirova, G. M. (2020). Transformational change in the economy of Kazakhstan. *Studies on Russian Economic Development*, **31**, 113–119.

Auriol, Emmanuelle, Flochel, Thomas, and Straub, Stephane (2016). Public procurement and rent-seeking: The case of Paraguay. *World Development*, **77**, 395–407.

Bandiera, Oriana, Best, Michael Carlos, Khan, Adnan Qadir, and Prat, Andrea (2019). The allocation of authority in organizations: A field experiment with bureaucrats. NBER Working Paper #26733.

Bardhan, Pranab and Mookherjee, Dilip (2006). Decentralization, corruption and government accountability. In *International Handbook on the Economics of Corruption, Volume I* (ed. S. Rose-Ackerman), pp. 161–188. Edward Elgar, Cheltenham, UK.

Bassanini, Andrea and Brunello, Giorgio (2007). Barriers to entry, deregulation and workplace training. IZA Discussion Paper Series.

Bates, Robert (2010). *Prosperity and Violence: The Political Economy of Development*. Norton, New York, NY.

Baum, Jeeyang Rhee (2007). Presidents have problems too: The logic of intra-branch delegation in East Asian democracies. *British Journal of Political Science*, **37**, 659–684.

BBC News (2018). Russia Kemerovo fire: How party turned into nightmare. **March 26**.

BBC News. (2021). Kemerovo fire: Jail terms for bosses over Russian mall disaster. **October 29**.

Beardsworth, James (2022). Tank losses in Ukraine raise strategic questions for Russia. *The Moscow Times*, **July 18**.

Beazer, Quintin H. (2012). Bureaucratic discretion, business investment, and uncertainty. *Journal of Politics*, **74**(3), 637–653.

Berenson, Marc P. (2018). *Taxes and Trust: From Coercion to Compliance in Poland, Russia, and Ukraine*. Cambridge University Press, Cambridge, UK.

Berry (1998). Strategic planning in small high tech companies. *Long Range Planning*, **31**(3), 455–466.

Berwick, Elissa and Christia, Fotini (2018). State capacity redux: Integrating classical and experimental contributions to an enduring debate. *Annual Review of Political Science*, **21**, 71–91.

Besley, Timothy and Persson, Torsten (2009). The origins of state capacity: Property rights, taxation, and politics. *American Economic Review*, **99**(4), 1218–1233.

Bessinger, Mark (1988). *Scientific Management, Socialist Discipline, and Soviet Power*. Harvard University Press, Cambridge, MA.

Best, Michael Carlos, Hjort, Jonas, and Szakonyi, David (2017). Individuals and organizations as sources of state effectiveness. NBER Working Paper #23350.

Bhuiyan, Shahjahan H. (2010). Decentralization and local governance in Kazakhstan. *International Journal of Public Administration*, **33**(12–13), 658–672.

Bhuiyan, Shahjahan H. and Amagoh, Francis (2011). Public sector reform in Kazakhstan: Issues and perspectives. *International Journal of Public Sector Management*, **24**(3), 227–249.

Bland, Stephen M. (2018). The case of the Khrapunovs: International institutions fail to measure up to the task of tackling globalized financial crime. *The Diplomat*, **July 18**.

Boies, D. B. and Bortz, S. (1965). Economical and effective deicing agents for use on highway structures. National Research Council. NCHRP Report #19.

Bosio, Erica, Djankov, Simeon, Glaeser, Edward, and Shleifer, Andrei (2020). Public procurement in law and practice. The World Bank Discussion Paper #798.

Boycko, M., Shleifer, A., and Vishny, R. (1995). *Privatizing Russia*. MIT Press, Cambridge, MA.

Bratton, Michael (1994). Peasant-state relations in post-colonial Africa: Patterns of engagement and disengagement. In *State Power and Social Forces: Domination and Transformation in the Third World* (eds. J. S. Migdal, A. Kohli, and V. Shue), pp. 231–254. Cambridge University Press, Cambridge, UK.

Bremmer, Ian (2009, May-June). State capitalism comes of age: The end of the free market? *Foreign Affairs*, **88**(3), 40–55.

Broadman, Harry G. (2001). Competition and business entry in Russia. IMF External Relations Department: Finance and Development.

Brown, David J., Earle, John S., and Gehlbach, Scott (2009). Helping hand or grabbing hand? State bureaucracy and privatization effectiveness. *American Political Science Review*, **103**, 264–283.

Bueno de Mesquita, B. and Smith, A. (2012). *The Politics of Authoritarian Rule*. Cambridge University Press, New York, NY.

Bunce, Valerie (1999). *Subversive Institutions: The Design and the Destruction of Socialism and the State*. Cambridge University Press, Cambridge, UK.

Burkhardt, Fabian and Libman, Alexander (2018). The tail wagging the dog? Top-down and bottom-up explanations for bureaucratic appointments in authoritarian regimes. *Russian Politics*, **3**, 239–259.

Burrell, Ian (2011). Goga Ashkenazi: By royal ascent. *The Independent*, **12 March**.

Busygina, Irina (2017). State-building in Russia and the choice for coercion in external relations. In *Russia–EU Relations and the Common Neighborhood*. Routledge, Abingdon, UK.

Busygina, I. M. and Filippov, M. G. (2013). Ogranichit' korruptsiiu: naiti novykh liudei ili izmenit' motivatsii? [Restrict corruption: Find new people or change incentives?]. *Polis–Political Studies*, **1**, 50–71.

Campos, Nauro F. and Giovannoni, Francesco (2008). Lobbying, corruption, and other banes. SSRN Working Paper Series.

Cárdenas, Mauricio, Eslava, Marcela, and Ramírez, Santiago (2010). *Revisiting the Effects of Conflict on State Capacity: A Panel Data Approach*. Brookings Institution, Washington, DC.

Chaisty, Paul (2006). *Legislative Politics and Economic Power in Russia*. Palgrave MacMillan, London, UK.

Chaney, Carole K. and Saltzstein, Grace H. (1998). Democratic control and bureaucratic responsiveness: The police and domestic violence. *American Journal of Political Science*, **42**, 745–768.

Chazan, Guy (2002). Russia's small-business reforms backfire by increasing red tape. *The Wall Street Journal*, **July 26**.

Chazan, Guy (2004). In Russia's courts, a judge speaks up–and gets fired. *The Wall Street Journal*, **August 5**.

Chebankova, Elena (2006). The unintended consequences of gubernatorial appointments in Russia, 2005–2006. *Journal of Communist Studies and Transition Politics*, **22**(4), 457–484.

Chebankova, Elena (2008). Adaptive federalism and federation in Putin's Russia. *Europe-Asia Studies*, **60**(6), 989–1009.

Chebotarev, Andrey (2018). V Kazakhstane nachalas' podgotovka k tranzitu vlasti. *Forbes Kazakhstan*, **February 7**.

Chubanov, Vadim (1995). Mer Cherepovtsa Viacheslav Pozgalev: 'prakticheski legche odin raz stat' sil'nym, chem vse vremia byt' slabym'. *Rossiiskii obosrevatel'*, **July**(1), 78–85.

Cincera, M. and Galgau, O. (2005). Impact of market entry and exit on EU productivity and growth performance. European Commission, Directorate General Economic and Financial Affairs.

Connolly, Richard (2018). *Russia's Response to Sanctions: How Western Economic Statecraft Is Reshaping Political Economy in Russia*. Cambridge University Press, Cambridge, UK; New York, NY.

CNN (2015). Slalom house: Ski slope on top of an apartment block. **December 14**.

Cooley, Alexander and Heathershaw, John (2017). *Dictators without Borders: Power and Money in Central Asia*. Yale University Press, New Haven, CT.

Cooley, Alexander and Snyder, Jack (eds.) (2015). *Ranking the World: Grading States as a Tool of Global Governance*. Cambridge University Press, Cambridge, UK.

Crowley, Stephenn (2021). *Putin's Labor Dilemma: Russian Politics between Stability and Stagnation*. Cornell University Press, Ithaca, NY.

Dal Bo, Ernesto, Bo, Pedro Dal, and Tella, Rafael Di (2006). 'Plata o plomo?': Bribe and punishment in a theory of political influence. *American Political Science Review*, **100**, 41–53.

Damgaard, Erik and Jensen, Henrik (2006). Assessing strength and weakness in legislatures: The case of Denmark. *Journal of Legislative Studies*, **12**(3/4), 426–442.

Dawisha, Karen (2014). *Putin's Kleptocracy: Who Owns Russia?* Simon and Shuster, New York, NY.

De Carbonnel, Alissa (2013). Billions stolen in Sochi Olympics preparations—Russian opposition. *Reuters*, **May 30**.

De Soto, Hernando (1990). *The Other Path: The Invisible Revolution in the Third World*. Harper and Row, New York.

Decarolis, Francesco, Giuffrid, Leonardo M., Iossa, Elisabetta, Mollisi, Vincenzo, and Spagnolo, Giancarlo (2019). Bureaucratic competence and procurement outcomes. NBER Working Paper #24201.

Dellepiane-Avellaneda, Sebastian (2010). Review article: Good governance, institutions and economic development: Beyond the conventional wisdom. *British Journal of Political Science*, **40**, 195–224.

Deutshe Welle Russia (2021). Politikov sgubila zhadnost': Gromkie korruptsionnye skandaly v Rossii i FRG. **March 2**.

Di Bella, Gabriel, Dynnikova, Oksana, and Slavov, Slavi (2019). The Russian state's size and its footprint: Have they increased? International Monetary Fund Working Paper #19/53.

Djankov, Simeon, Georgieva, Dorina Peteva, and Ramalho, Rita (2018). Business regulations and poverty. *Economic Letters*, **165**, 82–87.

Djankov, Simeon, La Porta, Rafael, Lopez-De-Silanes, Florencio, and Shleifer, Andrei (2002). The regulation of entry. *The Quarterly Journal of Economics*, **117**(1), 1–37.

Dobson, John (2022). Why are Russian armed forces performing so badly? *Sunday Guardian*, **April 9**.

d-Russia.ru (2016). Ministr informtekhnologii Rostovskoi oblasti: elektronnye uslugi ustraniaiut pochvu dlia korruptsii. **July 21**.

Duvanova, Dinissa (2012). Bureaucratic discretion and the regulatory burden: Business environments under alternative regulatory regimes. *British Journal of Political Science*, **42**, 481–509.

Duvanova, Dinissa (2013). *Building Business in Post-Communist Russia, Eastern Europe, and Eurasia: Collective Goods, Selective Incentives, and Predatory States*. Cambridge University Press, New York, NY.

Duvanova, Dinissa (2014). Economic regulation, red tape, and bureaucratic corruption in post-communist economies. *World Development*, **59**, 298–312.

Dye, Kenneth M. (2007). Corruption and fraud detection by supreme audit institutions. In *Performance Accountability and Combatting Corruption* (ed. A. Shah), pp. 299–331. World Bank, Washington, DC.

Easson, A. J. (2004). *Tax Incentives for Foreign Direct Investment*. Kluwer Law International, The Hague, NL; New York, NY.

Easter, Gerald (2012). *Capital, Coercion, and Postcommunist States*. Cornell University Press, Ithaca, NY.

EBRD (1999). *Transition Report*. European Bank for Reconstruction and Development, London, UK.

Egorov, Georgy, Guriev, Sergei, and Sonin, Konstantin (2009). Why resource-poor dictators allow freer media: A theory and evidence from panel data. *American Political Science Review*, **103**, 645–668.

Egorov, G. and Sonin, Konstantin (2011). Dictators and their viziers: Endogenizing the loyalty-competence trade-off. *Journal of European Economic Association*, **9**(5), 903–930.

Eisner, Marc Allen (2000). *Regulatory Politics in Transition*. Johns Hopkins University Press, Baltimore, MD.

elbasy.kz (2021). Sovet bezopasnosti respubliki Kazakhstan. https://elbasy.kz/en. Official website of the First President of the Republic of Kazakhstan.

Engvall, Johan (2016). *The State as Investment Market: Kyrgyzstan in Comparative Perspective*. University of Pittsburg Press, Pittsburgh, PA.

Enriquez, Elaine and Centeno, Miguel Angel (2012). State capacity: Utilization, durability, and the role of wealth vs. history. *International and Multidisciplinary Journal of Social Sciences*, **1**(2), 130–162.

Ericson, Claes (2012). *The Oligarchs: Money and Power in Capitalist Russia*. Stockholm Text; English Edition, Stockholm, SE.

Esquire.kz (2021). 'Skolko korov nuzhno prinesti v zhertvu, chtoby dostroit' LRT?' Chto kazakhstantsy dumaiut o stolichnom dolgostroe. **June 18**.

Evans, Alastair (2008). The role of supreme audit institutions in combating corruption. Transparency International.

Evans, Peter (1992). The state as problem and solution: Predation, embedded autonomy, and structural change. In *The Politics of Economic Adjustment* (eds. S. Haggard and R. Kaufman), pp. 139–181. Princeton University Press, Princeton, NJ.

Evans, Peter B. (1995). *Embedded Autonomy: States and Industrial Transformation*. Princeton University Press, Princeton, NJ.

Evans, Peter B., Rueschemeyer, Dietrich, and Skocpol, Theda (ed.) (1985). *Bringing the State Back In*. Cambridge University Press, Cambridge, UK.

Evans, Tony and Harris, John (2004). Street-level bureaucracy, social work and the (exaggerated) death of discretion. *British Journal of Social Work*, **34**(6), 871–895.

Feldman, Daniel L. (2017). *Administrative Law: The Sources and Limits of Government Agency Power*. CQ Press, Washington, DC.

Fisman, Raymond and Svensson, Jacob (2007). Are corruption and taxation really harmful to growth? Firm level evidence. *Journal of Development Economics*, **83**, 63–75.

Forbes.kz (2017). Top chastnykh kompanii Kazakhstana. **January**.

Forbes.ru (2021). Dvesti krupneishikh chastnykh kompanii Rossii. **September 29**.

Fortescue, Stephen (2020). Russia's civil service: Professional or patrimonial? Executive-level officials in five federal ministries. *Post-Soviet Affairs*, **36**, 1–24.

Fortin, Jessica (2010). A tool to evaluate state capacity in post-communist countries, 1989–2000. *European Journal of Political Research*, **49**(5), 654–686.

Francis, John G. (1993). *The Politics of Regulation: A Comparative Perspective*. Blackwell, Oxford, England.

Freinkman, Lev and Yakovlev, Andrei (2015). Institutional frameworks to support regulatory reform in middle-income economies: Lessons from Russia's recent experience. *Post-Communist Economies*, **27**(3), 354–369.

Fremer, Iana (2022). Kazakhstan: Newly adopted constitutional amendments introduce new governance model and strengthen role of parliament. *Global Legal Monitor*, **7**(135).

Frye, Timothy (2002). Private protection in Russia and Poland. *American Journal of Political Science*, **46**(3), 572–584.

Frye, Timothy (2004). Credible commitment and property rights: Evidence from Russia. *American Political Science Review*, **98**(3), 453–466.

Frye, Timohy (2006). Original sin, good works, and property rights in Russia. *World Politics*, **58**(July), 479–504.

Frye, Timothy (2017). *Property Rights and Property Wrongs*. Cambridge University Press, Cambridge, UK.

Frye, Timothy (2021). *Weak Strongman: The Limits of Power in Putin's Russia*. Princeton University Press, Princeton, NJ.

Frye, Timothy and Shleifer, Andrei (1997). The invisible hand and the grabbing hand. *American Economic Review*, **87**(2), 354–358.

Frye, Timothy and Zhuravskaya, Ekatherina (2000). Rackets, regulation and the rule of law. *The Journal of Law, Economics, and Organization*, **16**(2), 478–502.

Fukuyama, Francis (2004). *State-Building: Governance and World Order in the 21st Century*. Cornell University Press, Ithaca, NY.

Fukuyama, Francis (2013). What is governance? *Governance*, **26**(3), 347–368.

Galbraith, C. S. (1985). High technology location and development: The case of Orange County. *California Management Review*, **28**(1), 98–109.

Galle, Brian (2015). In praise of ex ante regulation. *Vanderbilt Law Review*, **68**, 1715–.

Gandhi, Jennifer and Przeworski, Adam (2006). Cooperation, cooptation, and rebellion under dictatorships. *Economics and Politics*, **18**(1), 1–26.

Gans-Morse, Jordan (2017a). Demand for law and the security of property rights: The case of post-Soviet Russia. *American Political Science Review*, **11**(1), 338–359.

Gans-Morse, Jordan (2017b). *Property Rights in Post-Soviet Russia: Violence, Corruption, and the Demand for Law*. Cambridge University Press, Cambridge, UK.

Gazeta.ru (2011). Medvedev vnes v Gosdumu popravki o stokratnom shtrafe za vziatki i kommercheskii podkup. **February 16**.

Geddes, Barbara (1994). *Politician's Dilemma: Building State Capacity in Latin America*. University of California Press, Berkeley, CA.

Gehlbach, Scott (2008). What is a big bureaucracy? Reflections on rebuilding leviathan and runaway state-building. *Czech Sociological Review*, **44**(6), 1189–1197.

Gehlbach, Scott and Keefer, Philip (2011). Investment without democracy: Ruling-party institutionalization and credible commitment in autocracies. *Journal of Comparative Economics*, **39**(2), 123–139.

Gehlbach, Scott and Keefer, Philip (2012). Private investment and the institutionalization of collective action in autocracies: Ruling parties and legislatures. *Journal of Politics*, **74**(2), 621–635.

Gehlbach, Scott, Sonin, Konstantin, and Zhuravskaya, Ekaterina (2010). Businessman candidates. *American Journal of Political Science*, **54**(3), 718–736.

Gel'man, Vladimir (2016). The vicious circle of post-Soviet neopatrimonialism in Russia. *Post-Soviet Affairs*, **32**(5), 455–473.

Gel'man, Vladimir (2017a). Political foundations of bad governance in post-Soviet Eurasia: Towards a research agenda. *East European Politics*, **33**(4), 496–516.

Gel'man, Vladimir (2017b). *Politics versus policy: Tekhnokraticheskie lovushki postsovetskikh preobrazovanii.* Izdatel'stvo Evropeiskogo universiteta v Sankt-Peterburge, Saint Petersburg, RUS.

Gel'man, Vladimir and Starodubtsev, A. V. (2014). *Vozmozhnosti i ogranicheniia avtoritarnoi modernizatsii: Rossiiskie reformy 2000-kh godov.* Izdatel'stvo Evropeiskogo universiteta v Sankt-Peterburge, Saint Petersburg, RUS.

Gimpelson, Vladimir, Magun, Vladimir, and Brym, Robert (2009). Hiring and promoting young civil servants: Weberian ideals versus Russian reality. In *Russian Bureaucracy and the State: Officialdom from Alexander III to Vladimir Putin* (eds. D. K. Rowney and E. Huskey), pp. 231–252.

Gin, Kira (2019). Chto takoe reguliatornaia gil'otina? https://www.buhgalteria.ru/article/chto-takoe-regulyatornaya-gilotina-.

Glaeser, Edward L., La Porta, Rafael, Lopez-de Silanes, Florencio, and Shleifer, Andrei (2004). Do institutions cause growth? *Journal of Economic Growth*, **9**, 271–303.

Goldsmith, Arthur (1999). Africa's overgrown state reconsidered: Bureaucracy and economic growth. *World Politics*, **51**(4), 520–546.

Goldsmith, Arthur A. (2012). Is governance reform a catalyst for development? In *Is Good Governance Good for Development?* (eds. J. K. Sundaram and A. Chowdhury). Bloomsbury Academic.

Gordeev, Vladislav (2020). SMI uznali o planakh minfina sokratit' chislo goskompanii v 1,5 raza. *rbk.ru*, **July 24**.

Gordon, Sanford C. and Hafer, Catherine (2005). Flexing muscle: Corporate political expenditures as signals to the bureaucracy. *American Political Science Review*, **99**(2), 245–61.

Gorgulu, Nisan, Sharafutdinova, Gulnaz, and Steinbuks, Jevgenijs (2020). Political dividends of digital participatory governance: Evidence from Moscow pothole management. World Bank Group Policy Research Working Paper #9445. Washington, DC.

Grindle, Merilee S. (1996). *Challenging the State: Crisis and Innovation in Latin America and Africa.* Cambridge University Press, Cambridge, UK.

Grindle, Merilee S. (2004). Good enough governance: Poverty reduction and reform in developing countries. *Governance*, **17**(4), 525–548.

Grzymala-Busse, Anna and Jones Luong, Pauline (2002). Reconceptualizing the state: Lessons from post-communism. *Politics and Society*, **30**(4), 259–554.

Guriev, Sergei (2004). Red tape and corruption. *Journal of Development Economics*, **73**(2), 489–504.

Guriev, Sergei and Rachinsky, Andrei (2005). The role of oligarchs in Russian capitalism. *Journal of Economic Perspectives*, **19**(1), 131–150.

Gurvich, Evsei and Prilepskii, Il'ia (2015). The impact of fnancial sanctions on the Russian economy. *Russian Journal of Economics*, **1**(4), 359–385.

Hale, Henry (2014). *Patronal Politics: Eurasian Regime Dynamics in Comparative Perspective*. Cambridge University Press, Cambridge, UK.

Hallerberg, Mark, Strauch, Rolf R., and von Hagen, Jurgen (2010). *Fiscal Governance in Europe*. Cambridge University Press, Cambridge, UK.

Hallward-Driemeier, Mary, Khun-Jush, Gita, and Pritchett, Lant (2010). Deals versus rules: What is policy uncertainty and why do firms hate it? NBER Working Paper #16001.

Hanson, Jonathan K. and Sigman, Rachel (2021). Leviathan's latent dimensions: Measuring state capacity for comparative political research. *Journal of Politics*, **83**(4), 1495–1510.

Hanson, Steve (2018). State capacity and the resilience of electoral authoritarianism: Conceptualizing and measuring the institutional underpinnings of autocratic power. *International Political Science Review*, **39**(1), 17–32.

Harding, Luke (2010). Russian president sacks Moscow mayor. *The Guardian*, **September 28**.

Hellman, Joel S. (1998). Winners take all: The politics of partial reform in post-communist transitions. *World Politics*, **50**(2), 203–234.

Hellman, Joel S., Jones, Geraint, and Kaufmann, Daniel (2000). Seize the state, seize the day: State capture, corruption, and influence in transition. World Bank Policy Research Working Paper #2444.

Helmke, Gretchen and Levitsky, Steven (2004). Informal institutions and comparative politics: A research agenda. *Perspectives on Politics*, **2**(4), 725–740.

Heston, Alan, Summers, Robert, and Aten, Bettina (2009). Penn World Table version 6.3. Database, Center for International Comparisons of Production, Income and Prices at the University of Pennsylvania.

Hibbs, Douglas A. and Piculescu, Violeta (2010). Tax toleration and tax compliance: How government affects the propensity of firms to enter the unofficial economy. *American Journal of Political Science*, **54**(1), 18–33.

Higashijima, Masaaki (2022). *The Dictator's Dilemma at the Ballot Box: Electoral Manipulation, Economic Maneuvering, and Political Order in Autocracies*. University of Michigan Press, Ann Arbor, MI.

Holmes, Leslie (2006). *Rotten States: Corruption, Post-Communism, and Neoliberalism*. Duke University Press, Durham, NC.

Hood, Christopher and Dunsire, Andrew (1981). *Bureaumetrics: The Quantitative Comparison of British Central Government Agencies*. Ashgate Publishing Group, Farnham, UK.

Huber, John D. and McCarty, Nolan (2004). Bureaucratic capacity, delegation, and political reform. *American Political Science Review*, **98**(3), 481–494.

Huber, John D. and Shipan, Charles R. (2002). *Deliberate Discretion: The Institutional Foundations of Bureaucratic Autonomy*. Cambridge University Press, New York.

Huber, John D., Shipan, Charles R., and Pfahler, M. (2001). Legislatures and statutory control of the bureaucracy. *American Journal of Political Science*, **45**(2), 330–345.

Huen, Eustacia (2016). Inside the world's first residential building with a 1,000-foot ski slope. *Forbes*, **January 31**.

Huntington, Samuel P. (1968). *Political Order in Changing Societies*. Yale University Press, New Haven, CT.

Informatsionnyi portal stroitelnoi otrasli Kryma (2017). V Krymu prodlili maratorii na dooformlenie zemelnykh uchastkov. http://stroy-krim.org/encyclopedia/news/v-krymu-prodlili-moratoriy-na-dooformlenie-zemelnyh-uchastkov.

Informburo (2010). Ostorozhno: u vas snimaiut. **August 16**.

Informburo (2021). Kulginov o vozobnovlenii stroitel'stva LRT: Aktivnaia rabota budet prodolzhena po mere postupleniia sredstv. **June 30**.

Informburo (2022). Akimat otsudil zemliu u avtora proekta "Dom-slalom" v Nur-Sultane. **May 20**.

Institute National de la Statistigue at des Etudeseconomiques (2021). In 2020, employment increased by .6% in the French civil service. Report #332.

Isaacs, Rico (2014). Neopatrimonialism and beyond: Reassessing the formal and informal in the study of Central Asian politics. *Contemporary Politics*, **20**(2), 229–245.

ITAR-TASS (2021). Bor'ba s koruptsiei. https://tass.ru/borba-s-korruciey.

Izotin (2008). O nekotoryh osobennostiakh nachal'nigo etapa v deiatel'nosti Cherepovetskoi gorodskoi Dumy. In *Stanovlenie mestnogo samoupravleniya v Vologodskoi oblasti* (ed. L. I. Antonova), pp. 71–73. Drevnosti Severa, Vologda, RUS.

Jenkins, Rob (2007). The role of political institutions in promoting accountability. In *Performance Accountability and Combatting Corruption* (ed. A. Shah), pp. 299–331. World Bank, Washington, DC.

Jensen, Bradford J., Bernard, Andrew B., and Schott, Peter K. (2006). Trade costs, firms, and productivity. *Journal of Monetary Economics*, **53**(5), 917–937.

Johnson, Chalmers A. (1982). *MITI and the Japanese Miracle: The Growth of Industrial Policy, 1925–1975*. Stanford University Press, Stanford, CA.

Johnson, Simon, Kaufmann, Daniel, and Shleifer, Andrei (1998). The unofficial economy in transition. *Brookings Papers on Economic Activity*, **2**, 159–239.

Jones, Lee and Hameiri, Shahar (2021). *Fractured China: How State Transformation Is Shaping China's Rise*. Cambridge University Press, Cambridge, UK.

Kaczmarski, Marcin (2008). Domestic power relations and Russia's foreign policy. *Problems of Post-Communism*, **55**(5), 383–409.

Kalgin, Alexander (2012). Upravlenie po rezul'tatam na regional'nom urovne: kontrol' ili rezul'tativnost'? *Voprosy gosudarstvennogo i munitsipal'nogo upravleniia*, **3**, 35–60.

Kalgin, Alexander (2016). Implementation of performance management in regional government in Russia: Evidence of data manipulation. *Public Management Review*, **18**(1), 110–138.

Kalinin, Aleksey (2019). On the reform of the executive power and the structures of the executive bodies in the Russian Federation. *Obshchestvo i ekonomika*, **5**, 78–86.

Kapital.kz (2022). Utilizatsionnyi sbor: Podborka materialov. https://kapital.kz/info/utilizatsionnyy-sbor.

Karas, Alexei, Pyle, William, and Schoor, Koen (2015, May). A 'de Soto effect' in industry: Evidence from the Russian Federation. *Journal of Law and Economics*, **58**(2), 451–480.

Kaufmann, Daniel, Kraay, Aart, and Mastruzzi, Massimo (2009). *Governance Matters VIII: Aggregate and Individual Governance Indicators 1996–2008*. The World Bank.

Kazakhstan2.0 (2021). How they set up Kanat Sultanbekov. *KZ.expert*, **September 30**.

Keeler, Theodore (1984). Theories of regulation and the deregulation movement. *Public Choice*, **44**(1), 103–145.

Kiselyova, Maria and Tetrault-Farber, Gabrielle (2021). Belarus jails Lukashenko foe Babariko for 14 years in 'sham' trial. *Reuters*, **July 6**.

Klimenko, A. V. (2014). Desiatiletie administrativnoi reformy: rezul'taty i novye vyzovy. *Voprosy gosudarstvennogo i munitsipal'nogo upravleniia* (1), 8–51.

Klitgaard, Robert E. (1988). *Controlling Corruption*. University of California Press, Berkeley, CA.

Klitgaard, Robert E., MacLean-Abaroa, Ronald, and Parris, Lindsey H. (2000). *Corrupt Cities: A Practical Guide to Cure and Prevention*. World Bank, Washington, DC.

Knack, Stephen and Keefer, Philip (1995). Institutions and economic performance: Cross-country tests using alternative institutional measures. *Economics and Politics*, 7(3), 207–227.

Kohli, Atul (2004). *State-Directed Development: Political Power and Industrialization in the Global Periphery*. Cambridge University Press, Cambridge, UK.

Kohli, Atul (2010). State capacity for development. Human Sciences Research Council (HSRC).

Kosenov, Aldiiar (2016). Avtor proekta "dom-slalom" v Astane nagrazhden premiei International Quality Summit. *Tengrinews*, **June 1**.

Koskina, Ainur (2019). Astana LRT: A project or a scam? *Central Asian Bureau for Analytical Reporting (CABAR)*, **December 24**.

Kottasova, Ivana (2022). At least eight Russian businessmen have died in apparent suicide or accidents in just six months. *CNN*, **September 2**.

Kozhakhmetov, Asylbek (2007). Reforma gosudarstvennogo upravleniia. Report.

Kramer, Andrew E. (2007). Moscow presses BP to sell a big gas field to Gazprom. *The New York Times*, **June 23**.

Kriukovskie Vedomosti (2015). Sobianin: elektronnye gosuslugi—profilaktika korruptsii. **June 30**.

Kriuchkova, Polina (2007). Otsenka sotsial'no-economicheskikh posledstvii priniatiia tehnicheskih reglamentov. In *Modernizatsiia ekonomiki i obshchestvennoe razvitie* (ed. E. G. Yasin), Volume 1, pp. 347–356. VIII Mezhdunarodnaia nauchnaia konferentsiia: GU-VShE.

Krueger, A. (1974). Political economy of rent-seeking society. *American Economic Review*, 64(3), 291–303.

Kudaibergenova, Diana (2015). The ideology of development and legitimation: Beyond Kazakhstan 2030. *Central Asian Survey*, 34(4), 440–455.

Kumenov, Almaz and Lillis, Joanna (2022). Kazakhstan explainer: Why did fuel prices spike, bringing protesters out onto the streets? *Eurazianet*, **January 4**.

Kunicova, Jana (2006). Democratic institutions and corruption: Incentives and constraints in politics. In *International Handbook on the Economics of Corruption, Volume I* (ed. S. Rose-Ackerman), pp. 140–160. Edward Elgar, Cheltenham, UK.

Kun.kz (2021). Kak ostanovit' bezzakonie v zemel'nykh otnosheniyah. Podcast.

Kurtz, Marcus and Schrank, Andrew (2007). Growth and governance: Models, measures, and mechanisms. *Journal of Politics*, 69(2), 538–554.

Kuz'minov, Yaroslav and Mau, Vladimir (2012). Itogovyi doklad o rezul'tatakh ekspertnoi raboty po aktual'nym problemam sotsial'no-ekonomicheskoi strategii Rossii na period do 2020 goda 'Strategiia 2020: Novaia model' rosta–novaia sotsial'naia politika'. Government Report.

Kydland, Finn E. and Prescott, Edward C. (1977). Rules rather than discretion—Inconsistency of optimal plans. *Journal of Political Economy*, 85(3), 473–91.

Kyzylkulova, Aliia (2007). Nyneshniaia reforma usilivaet kontrol' nazarbaeva. *Nachnem s Ponedel'nika*, **July 13–16**.

Lambsdorff, Johann Graf and Cornelius, Peter K. (2000). Corruption, foreign investment, and growth. In *The Africa Competitiveness Report 2000/2001* (eds. K. Schwab, L. Cook, P. Cornelius, J. D. Sachs, S. Sievers, and A. Warner), pp. 70–78. Oxford University Press, Oxford, UK.

Lankina, Tomila and Tertytchnaya, Katerina (2019). Protest in electoral autocracies: A new dataset. *Post-Soviet Affairs*, **36**(1), 20–36.

Lankina, Tomila and Voznaya, Alisa (2015). New data on protest trends in Russia's regions. *Europe-Asia Studies*, **67**(2), 327–342.

Laruelle, Marlene (2022). Putin is in trouble. *New York Times*, **September 22**.

Ledeneva, Alena V. (1998). *Russia's Economy of Favours: Blat, Networking and Informal Exchange*. Cambridge University Press, Cambridge, UK.

Ledeneva, Alena (2006). *How Russia Really Works: The Informal Practices that Shaped Post-Soviet Politics and Business*. Cornell University Press, Ithaca, NY.

Ledeneva, Alena (2013). *Can Russia Modernise? Sistema, Power Networks and Informal Governance*. Cambridge University Press, Cambridge, UK.

Leff, Nathaniel H. (1964). Economic development through bureaucratic corruption. *American Behavioral Scientist*, **8**(3), 8–14.

Lehmbruch, Gerhard (1992). The institutional framework of German regulation. In *The Politics of German Regulation* (ed. K. Dyson), pp. 29–52. Dartmouth Pub., Cambridge.

Lenpravda (2005). Putina nasmeshil vopros of korruptsii. **June 9**.

Lessmann, Christian and Markwardt, Gunther (2010). One size fits all? Decentralization, corruption, and the monitoring of bureaucrats. *World Development*, **38**(4), 631–646.

Levada Center (2017). Corruption: Press-releases. https://www.levada.ru/en/2017/04/21/corruption/.

Levi, Margaret (1988). *Of Rule and Revenue*. University of California Press, Berkeley, CA.

Li, Quan (2006). Democracy, autocracy, and tax incentives to foreign direct investors: A cross-national analysis. *Journal of Politics*, **68**(1), 62–74.

Li, Shiqiang (2013). Delegation in organizations under incomplete contracts: A literature survey. SSRN eLibrary.

Libman, Alexander and Rochlitz, Michael (2019). *Federalism in China and Russia*. Edward Elgar Publishing, Cheltenham, UK.

Loayza, Norman V., Oviedo, Ana Maria, and Serven, Luis (2009). Regulation and microeconomic dynamics. In *Business Regulation and Economic Performance* (eds. N. Loayza and L. Serven). World Bank, Washington, DC.

Lomskaia, Tatiana, Nikol'skii, Aleksei, and Mukhamedshina, Elena (2017). Tretii srok Putina: Chto bylo obeschano i chto sdelano. *Vedomosti*, **December 8**.

Lopez-Claros, Augusto (2006). Executive summary. In *The Global Competitiveness Report 2006* (ed. K. Schwab and M. E. Porter), p. xiii. World Economic Forum, Geneva, CH.

Luechinger, Simon, Meier, Stephan, and Stutzer, Alois (2008). Bureaucratic rents and life satisfaction. *Journal of Law, Economics, and Organization*, **24**(2), 476–488.

Makhmutova, Meruert (2001). Local government in Kazakhstan. In *Developing New Rules in the Old Environment: Local Governments in Eastern Europe, in the Caucasus and Central Asia* (eds. I. Munteanu and V. Popa), pp. 408–468. Central European University Press, Budapest, HU.

Malkov, K. B. (2010). *Upravlenie po resul'tatam v organakh gosudarstvennoi vlasti*. MGU Press, Moscow, RUS.

Manion, Melanie (1996). Corruption by design: Bribery in Chinese enterprise licensing. *Journal of Law, Economics, and Organization*, **12**(1), 167–195.

Mann, Michael (1988). The autonomous power of the state: Its origins, mechanisms and results. In *States, War and History* (ed. M. Mann). Blackwell Publishers, Oxford, UK.

Mann, Michael (2008). Infrastructural power revisited. *Studies in Comparative International Development*, **43**(3), 355–365.

Markus, Stanislav (2016). *Property, Predation, and Protection: Piranha Capitalism in Russia and Ukraine*. Cambridge University Press, Cambridge, UK.

Mashaev, Askar and Veliev, Farid (2021). Predstavlen reiting 100 krupneishikh kompanii Kazakhstana po ob'emu vyruchki. *Kursiv.kz*, **December 29**.

Masters, Jonathan (2014). Why the Crimean referendum is illegitimate. Interview by John B. Bellinger III. *Council of Foreign Relations*, **March 16**.

Mauro, Paolo (1995). Corruption and growth. *Quarterly Journal of Economics*, **110**(3), 681–712.

MBKhMedia (2020). Kto Bol'she? Samye gromkie korruptsionnye dela v sovremennoi Rossii. **December 9**.

McChesney, Fred S. (1997). *Money for Nothing: Politicians, Rent Extraction, and Political Extortion*. Harvard University Press, Cambridge, MA.

McCubbins, Mathew D., Noll, Roger G., and Weingast, Barry R. (1987). Administrative procedures as instruments of political control. *Journal of Law, Economics, and Organization*, 3(2), 243–277.

McCubbins, Mathew D. and Schwartz, Thomas (1984). Congressional oversight overlooked: Police patrols versus fire alarms. *American Journal of Political Science*, **28**(1), 165–179.

McIntyre, Robert J. (2003). The complex ecology of small enterprise systems. In *Small and Medium Enterprises in Transitional Economies (Studies in Development Economics and Policy)* (eds. R. McIntyre and B. Dallago), pp. 18–35. Palgrave MacMillan, London, UK.

McMann, Kelly M. (2014). *Corruption as a Last Resort*. Cornell University Press, Ithaca, NY.

Mendez, Fabio and Sepulveda, Facundo (2010). What do we talk about when we talk about corruption? *Journal of Law, Economics, and Organization*, **26**(3), 493–514.

Meon, Pierre-Guillaume and Weill, Laurent (2010). Is corruption an efficient grease? *World Development*, **38**(3), 244–259.

Migdal, Joel S. (1988). *Strong Societies and Weak States: State-Society Relations and State Capabilities in the Third World*. Princeton University Press, Princeton, NJ.

Mikhailova, K. (2006). Chernaia igra. *Megapolis*, **15**(279).

Miles, Paul (2015). The unbuilt residential towers with a view to the future. *The Financial Times*, **October 23**.

Ministerstvo Ekonomicheskogo Razvitiia RF (2021). Mekhanizm reguliatornoi gil'otiny. economy.gov.ru.

Mishra, Ajit (2006). Corruption, hierarchies and bureaucratic structure. In *International Handbook on the Economics of Corruption, Volume I* (ed. S. Rose-Ackerman), pp. 189–215. Edward Elgar, Cheltenham, UK.

Moldabekov, Daniyar (2020). Rekonstruktsii, propaganda gospolitiki i konferentsii: Na chto tratili den'gi akimaty s nachala epidemii. *Vlast.kz*, **July 10**.

Moran, Michael (2002). Review article: Understanding the regulatory state. *British Journal of Political Science*, **32**(2), 391–413.

Moscow Times (2020). After decline and stagnation, Russian income growth hits six-year high. **January 29**.

Moses, Joel C. (2014a). The political resurrection of Russian governors. *Europe-Asia Studies*, **66**(9), 1395–1424.

Moses, Joel C. (2014b). Putin and Russian subnational politics in 2014. *Demokratizatsiya: The Journal of Post-Soviet Democratization*, **23**(2), 181–203.

Murray, Matthew (1999). Small business: A response to corruption in Russia. U. S. House of Representatives, Committee on International Relations, Testimony.

Myagkov, Mikhail, Ordeshook, Peter C., and Shakin, Dmitri (2009). *The Forensics of Election Fraud: Russia and Ukraine*. Cambridge University Press, New York, NY.

Nastoiashchee Vremia (2019). Rasstrel v Zhanaozene—16 dekabria 2011 goda. **December 16**.

Navalny, Alexey (2011). Suhoi ostatok. Interview on Finam FM.

Nechepurenko, Ivan (2021). The Russian private sector today: Challenges and prospects in a post-pandemic world. IRInsider.org, NYU.

Neto, Octavio A. and Santos, Fabiano (2003). The inefficient secret revisited: The legislative input and output of Brazilian deputies. *Legislative Studies Quarterly*, **28**(4), 449–479.

Nicoletti, Giuseppe and Scarpetta, Stefano (2003). Regulation, productivity, and growth: OECD evidence. *Economic Policy*, **18**(36), 9–72.

Noll, Roger G. (1989). Economic perspectives on the politics of regulation. In *Handbook of Industrial Organization* (eds. R. Schmalensee and R. D. Willing), pp. 1253–1287. Elsevier Science Publishers, New York, NY.

Noll, Roger G. and Owen, Bruce M. (1983). *The Political Economy of Deregulation: Interest Groups in the Regulatory Process*. American Enterprise Institute for Public Policy, Washington, DC.

North, Douglass C. (1990). *Institutions, Institutional Change, and Economic Performance*. Cambridge University Press, Cambridge, UK.

North, Douglass C., Wallis, John Joseph, and Weingast, Barry R. (2006). A conceptual framework for interpreting recorded human history. NBER Working Paper #12795.

North, Douglass C., Wallis, John Joseph, and Weingast, Barry R. (2009). *Violence and Social Orders: A Conceptual Framework for Interpreting Recorded Human History*. Cambridge University Press, Cambridge, UK.

Noss, O. (ed.) (2010). *Za chto Luzhkovu dali po kepke? 'Glavnyi Vziatok'*. Eksimo, Moscow, RUS.

Novaia Gazeta (2002). Strana trekh kitov: korruptsii, kriminala i kaznokratstva. Stenogramma zakrytogo zasedaniia komiteta GD po bezopasnosti. **June 29**(54).

Novitskii, Viacheslav (2017). Vam po zakonu ili po poniatiam? *Echo of Moscow*, **May 28**.

Novokmet, Filip, Piketty, Thomas, and Zucman, Gabriel (2018). From Soviets to oligarchs: Inequality and property in Russia 1905–2016. *The Journal of Economic Inequality*, **16**(2), 189–223.

Nye, Joseph S. (1969). Corruption and political development: A cost-benefit analysis. In *Political Corruption: A Handbook*, pp. 963–984. Transaction Publishers, Piscataway, NJ.

Obolonsky, Alexander (1999). The modern Russian administration in the time of transition: New challenges versus old nomenclature legacy. *International Review of Administrative Sciences*, **65**(4), 569–577.

OECD (2005). *Russia: Building Rules for the Market (OECD Review of Regulatory Reform)*. OECD, Paris, France.

OECD (2020). *Government at a Glance: Latin America and the Caribbean 2020*. OECD Publishing, Paris, France.

OECD and Asian Development Bank (2019). *Government at a Glance: Southeast Asia 2019*. OECD Publishing, Paris, France.

Olcott, Martha Brill (2002). *Kazakhstan: Unfulfilled Promise?* Carnegie Endowment for International Peace, Washington, DC.

Olson, Mancur (2000). *Power and Prosperity: Outgrowing Communist and Capitalist Dictatorships*. Basic Books, New York, NY.

Ordabaiev, Sh. N. (2016). Global'nyi indeks konkurentosposobnosti: na puti v 30-ku konkurentosposobnykh stran. *Zakon.kz*, **December 2**.

Owen, Catherine (2020). Participatory authoritarianism: From bureaucratic transformation to civic participation in Russia and China. *Review of International Studies*, **46**(4), 415–434.

Palmer, David A. (1987). Formates as alternative deicers. *Transportation Research Record*, **1127**, 34–36.

Pearson, Margaret (2005). The business of governing business in China: Institutions and norms of the emerging regulatory state. *World Politics*, **57**(2), 296–322.

Pei, Minxin (2016). *China's Crony Capitalism: The Dynamics of Regime Decay*. Harvard University Press, Cambridge, MA.

Peltzman, Sam (1976). Toward a more general theory of regulation. *Journal of Law and Economics*, **19**(2), 211–240.

Piore, Michael Joseph (2011). Beyond markets: Sociology, street-level bureaucracy, and the management of the public sector. *Regulation and Governance*, **5**(1), 145–164.

Pis'mennaia, Evgeniia (2013). *Sistema Kudrina: Istoriia kliuchevogo ekonomista putinskoi Rossii*. Mann, Ivanov i Ferber, Moscow, RUS.

Poliakova, Viktoriia (2020). Putin zayavil o korobiashchikh ego vysokikh zarplatakh glav goskompanii. *rbc.ru*, **March 13**.

Potter, Joshua D. and Tavits, Margit (2011). Curbing corruption with political institutions. In *International Handbook on the Economics of Corruption, Volume II* (eds. S. Rose-Ackerman and T. Soreide), pp. 299–331. Edward Elgar, Cheltenham, UK.

Pravitel'stvo Rossii (2018). Natsional'nye proekty. http://government.ru/rugovclassifier/section/2641/.

PRS Group (2010). International country risk guide. http://www.prsgroup.com/ICRG.aspx.

Pyle, William (2011). Organized business, political competition, and property rights: Evidence from the Russian Federation. *Journal of Law, Economics, and Organization*, **27**(1), 2–31.

Radaev, Vadim (1998). Formirovaniye novykh rossiiskikh rynkov: transaktsionnye izderzhki, formy kontrolya i delovaya etika (Formation of new Russian markets: Transaction costs, forms of control and business ethics). Moscow: Center for Political Technologies.

Radaev, Vadim (2000). Corruption and violence in Russian business in the late 1990s. In *Economic Crime in Russia* (eds. A. Ledeneva and M. Kurkchiyan). Kluwer Law International, Alphen ann den Rjin, NL.

Radaev, Vadim (2010). Administrirovaniye rynochnykh pravil (kak razrobatyvalsia zakon o torgovle). *Voprosy gosudarstvennogo i munitsipal'nogo upravleniia* (3), 5–35.

Radaev, Vadim (2018). Rise of state activism in a competitive industry: The case of Russian retail trade law of 2009. *Communist and Post-Communist Studies*, **51**(1), 27–37.

Randazzo, Kirk A., Waterman, Richard W., and Fine, Jeffrey A. (2006). Checking the federal courts: The impact of congressional statutes on judicial behavior. *Journal of Politics*, **68**(4), 1006–1017.

Randazzo, Kirk A., Waterman, Richard W., and Fix, Michael P. (2011). State supreme courts and the effects of statutory constraint: A test of the model of contingent discretion. *Political Research Quarterly*, **64**(4), 779–789.

Rasul, Imran and Rogger, Daniel (2016). Management of bureaucrats and public service delivery: Evidence from the Nigerian civil service. *The Economic Journal*, **128**(608), 413–446.

Rauch, James E. and Evans, Peter (1999). Bureaucracy and growth: A cross-national analysis of the effects of Weberian state structures on economic growth. *American Sociological Review*, **64**(5), 748–765.

Reuter, Ora John (2017). *The Origins of Dominant Parties: Building Authoritarian Institutions in Post-Soviet Russia*. Cambridge University Press, New York, NY.

Reuter, O. J., Buckley, N., Shubenkova, A., and Garifullina, G. (2016). Local elections in authoritarian regimes: An elite-based theory with evidence from Russian mayoral elections. *Comparative Political Studies*, **49**(5), 682–697.

Reuter, O. J. and Robertson, G. B. (2012). Subnational appointments in authoritarian regimes: Evidence from Russian gubernatorial appointments. *The Journal of Politics*, **74**(4), 1023–1037.

RFE/RL's Kazakh Service (2022). Kazakhstan rocked by third day of protests over energy price hike. *Radio Free Europe—Radio Liberty*, **January 4**.

RIA Novosti (2014). Moratorii na pereprodazhu zemli vvedut v Krymu (2014b). **November 6**.

RIA Novosti (2014a). Busines-ombudsmen RF zaiavil o povyshennom interese investorov v Krymu. **November 5**.

RIA Novosti (2019). Plan privatizatsii na 2020–2022 gody vkliuchaet 293 predpriiatiia. **December 25**.

RIA Press (2019). Desiat' samykh kruptykh ugolovno-korruptsionnykh skandalov 2019 goda. **December 28**.

Roberts, Cynthia and Sherlock, Thomas (1999). Bringing the Russian state back in: Explanations of the derailed transition to market democracy. *Comparative Politics*, **31**(4), 477–498.

Robinson, James A. (2003). Politician-proof policy? Paper prepared as a background paper to the World Bank's 2004 World Development Report.

Robinson, Neil (2011). Russian patrimonial capitalism and the international financial crisis. *Journal of Communist Studies and Transition Politics*, **27**(3–4), 434–455.

Robinson, Neil (2013). Russia's response to crisis: The paradox of success. *Europe-Asia Studies*, **65**(3), 450–472.

Rochlitz, Michael (2014). Corporate raiding and the role of the state in Russia. *Post-Soviet Affairs*, **30**(2–3), 89–114.

Rodrik, Dani (2007). *One Economics, Many Recipes: Globalization, Institutions, and Economic Growth*. Princeton University Press, Princeton, NJ.

Rogov, K. (2010). O sovetnikakh i begemote. *Novaia Gazeta*, **June 7**.

Rosbizneskonsalting (2021). RBK Pro predstavliaet reiting krupneishikh po vyruchku companii Rossii. https://pro.rbc.ru/rbc500.

Rose-Ackerman, Susan (1999). *Corruption and Government*. Cambridge University Press, Cambridge, UK.

Rourke, Alison and Roth, Andrew (2019). Kazakhstan plane crash: 12 killed as Bek Air flight crashes near Almaty airport. *The Guardian*, **December 27**.

Ruiz, Rebecca R. and Schwirtz, Michael (2016). Russian insider says state-run doping fueled Olympic gold. *The New York Times*, **May 12**.

Rutland, Peter (2008). Putin's economic record: Is the oil boom sustainable? *Europe-Asia Studies*, **60**(6), 1051–1072.

Rutland, Peter (2009). *The Politics of Economic Stagnation in the Soviet Union: The Role of Local Party Organs in Economic Management* (2nd ed.). Cambridge Russian, Soviet, and Post-Soviet Studies Series. Cambridge University Press, Cambridge, UK.

Rutland, Peter (2023). The contradictions in Putin's economic nationalism: From Western partner to fortress Russia, *Russian Politics*, **8**(1), 24–47.

Sakenov, Salim (2018). K 2025 godu Kazakhstan narastit torgovyi flot do 20 sudov. *kursiv.kz*, **February 7**.

Sakwa, Richard (2014). *Putin and the Oligarch: The Khodorkovsky—Yukos Affair*. I. B. Tauris, London, UK.

Salikov, Marat S. (2005). O tekotorykh problemakh razgranicheniia zakonodatel'nykh polnomochii v rossiiskoi federativnoi sisteme. *Rossiiskoe pravo: obrazovanie, praktika, nauka* (1), 24–25.

Santoni, M. and Zucchini, F. (2006). Legislative output and the constitutional court in Italy. *Constitutional Political Economy*, **17**(3), 165–187.

Satubaldina, Asel (2022). Share of SMEs in Kazakhstan reaches 34.7 percent. *The Astana Times*, **April 20**.

Schake, Kori (2022). Russia's military is incompetent. That makes it more dangerous. *Washington Post*, **March 17**.

Schimpfössl, Elisabeth (2017). *Rich Russians: From Oligarchs to Bourgeoisie*. Oxford University Press, Oxford, UK.

Scholz, J. T. and Wang, C. L. (2006). Cooptation of transformation? Local policy networks and federal regulatory enforcement. *American Journal of Political Science*, **50**(1), 81–97.

Schueth, Sam (2015). Winning the rankings game: The republic of Georgia, USAID, and the Doing Business project. In *Ranking the World: Grading States as a Tool of Global Governance* (eds. A. Cooley and J. Snyder), pp. 151–177. Cambridge University Press, Cambridge, UK.

Schumpeter, Joseph A. (1942). *Capitalism, Socialism, and Democracy*. Harper, New York, NY.

Schwab, Klaus (ed.) (2010). *The Global Competitiveness Report*. World Economic Forum, Geneva, CH.

Scott, James C. (1998). *Seeing Like a State: How Certain Schemes to Improve the Human Condition Have Failed*. Yale University Press, New Haven, CT.

Shah, Anwar (ed.) (2007). *Performance Accountability and Combating Corruption*. World Bank, Washington, DC.

Shalal, Andrea (2021). World Bank aims to replace canceled 'Doing Business' report in two years. *Reuters*, **November 10**.

Sharafutdinova, Gulnaz (2009). Subnational governance in Russia: How Putin changed the contract with his agents and the problems it created for Medvedev. *Publius: The Journal of Federalism*, **40**(4), 672–696.

Sharafutdinova, Gulnaz (2013). Gestalt switch in Russian federalism: The decline in regional power under Putin. *Comparative Politics*, **45**(3), 357–376.

Sharafutdinova, Gulnaz (2021). *The Red Mirror: Putin's Leadership and Russia's Insecure Identity*. Oxford University Press, New York.

Sharafutdinova, Gulnaz and Dawisha, Karen (2017). The escape from institution-building in a globalized world: Lessons from Russia. *Perspectives on Politics*, **15**(2), 361–378.

Sharafutdinova, Gulnaz and Lokshin, Michael (2020). Hide and protect: A role of global financial secrecy in shaping domestic institutions. World Bank Policy Research Working Paper #9348.

Sharipova, Dina (2018). *State-Building in Kazakhstan: Continuity and Transformation of Informal Institutions*. Lexington Books, New York, NY.

Shchetinin, Oleg, Zamulin, Oleg, Zhuravskaya, Ekaterina, and Yakovlev, Evgeny (2005). Monitoring the administrative barriers to small business development in Russia: 5th round. Center for Economic and Financial Research at New Economic School (CEFIR) Policy Paper #22.

Shevchenko, Iulia and Golosov, Grigorii (2001). Legislative activism of Russian Duma deputies, 1996–1999. *Europe-Asia Studies*, **53**(2), 239–261.

Shkel, Stanislav (2019). Neo-patrimonial practices and sustainability of authoritarian regimes in Eurasia. *Communist and Post-Communist Studies*, **52**(2), 169–76.

Shlapentokh, Vladimir (2013). Corruption, the power of state and big business in Soviet and post-Soviet regimes. *Communist and Post-Communist Studies*, **46**(1), 147–158.

Shleifer, Andrei and Treisman, Daniel (2000). *Without a Map: Political Tactics and Economic Reform in Russia*. MIT Press, Cambridge, MA.

Shleifer, Anrei and Vishny, Robert W. (1993). Corruption. *Quarterly Journal of Economics*, **108**(3), 599–617.

Shleifer, Andrei and Vishny, Robert W. (1998). *The Grabbing Hand: Government Pathologies and Their Cures*. Harvard University Press, Cambridge, MA.

Sputnik Kazakhstan (2021). Shumnyi sosed: Skandal vokrug muzeia Kasteeva prokomentirovaly v Minkultury. **July 14**.

Shwab, Klaus and Zahidi, Saadia (2020). *Global Competitiveness Report 2020: How Countries Are Performing on the Road to Recovery*. World Economic Forum, Geneva, CH.

Smith-Spark, Laura (2015). Boris Nemtsov: Opposition figure who took on Vladimir Putin. *CNN*, **February 28**.

Solash, Richard (2010). After seven years, 'Kazakhgate' scandal ends with minor indictment. *Radio Free Europe/Radio Liberty*, **August 10**.

Soldatkin, Vladimir and Callus, Andrew (2013). Rosneft pays out in historic TNK-BP deal completion. *Reuters*, **March 22**.

Sorbello, Paolo (2021). Kazakhstan's light rail corruption case drags on the capital's light rail might never be built, and the corrupt officials that stole public funds might never be convicted. *The Diplomat*, **October 16**.

Spechler, Martin C., Ahrens, Joachim, and Hoen, Herman W. (2017). *State Capitalism in Eurasia*. World Scientific Publishing Company, SG.

Statistisches Bundesamt (Federal Statistical Office of Germany) (2021). Government: Public service. Online database.

Stigler, George J. (1971). Theory of economic regulation. *Bell Journal of Economics and Management Science*, **2**(1), 3–21.

Stiglitz, Joseph E. (1999). Whither reform? Ten years of the transition. In *World Bank Annual Conference on Development Economics*, Washington, DC., pp. 1–32.

Storey, David J. (1994). *Understanding the Small Business Sector.* Routledge, London, UK.

Sukonkina, Iuliia (2018). Pochemu v Krymu posle sniatiia moratoriia liudi ne mogut dooformit' uchastki. *RG.ru,* **July 26.**

Sun, Yan and Johnston, Michael (2010). Does democracy check corruption? Insights from China and India. *Comparative Politics,* **42**(1), 1–19.

Svensson, Jacob (2005). Eight questions about corruption. *Journal of Economic Perspectives,* **19**(3), 19–42.

Svolik, Milan W. (2012). *The Politics of Authoritarian Rule.* Cambridge University Press, New York, NY.

Szakonyi, David (2018). Businesspeople in elected office: Identifying private benefits from firm-level returns. *American Political Science Review,* **112**(2), 322–338.

Szakonyi, David (2019). Princelings in the private sector: The value of nepotism. *Quarterly Journal of Political Science,* **14**(4), 349–381.

Szakonyi, David (2020). *Politics for Profit: Business, Elections, and Policymaking in Russia.* Cambridge University Press, Cambridge, UK.

Szakonyi, David (2021). Private sector policy making: Business background and politicians' behavior in office. *Journal of Politics,* **53**(1), 260–276.

Tanzi, Vito and Davoodi, Hamid R. (2000). Corruption, growth, and public finances. IMF Working Paper #2000/182.

TASS News Agency (2020). Twenty questions with Putin. Televised Interview.

Taylor, Brian D. (2011). *State Building in Putin's Russia.* Cambridge University Press, New York, NY.

Taylor, Brian D. (2018). *The Code of Putinism.* Oxford University Press, New York, NY.

The Guardian (2015). Kazakh Leader's Ex-son-in-law Rakhat Aliyev found dead in Austrian jail. **February 24.**

Tilly, Charles (1993). *Coercion, Capital, and European States: 1990–1992.* Blackwell Publishing, Cambridge, MA.

Ting, Michael M. (2003). A strategic theory of bureaucratic redundancy. *American Journal of Political Science,* **47**(2), 274–292.

Tokayev, Kassym-Jomart (2022). Speech at the Mazhilis. *Forbs.kz,* **January 11.**

Toyken, Saniiash (2021). 'My pogibali ot ruk palachei.' Vospolinaniia ochevidtsev Zhanaozenskikh sobytii. *Radio Azattyk,* **December 16.**

Transparency International (2012). Business and anti-corruption: Snapshot of the Kazakhstan country profile. https://www.transparency.org.

Treisman, Daniel (2000). The causes of corruption: A cross-national study. *Journal of Public Economics,* **76**(3), 399–457.

Treisman, Daniel (2001). *After a Deluge: Regional Crises and Political Consolidation in Russia.* The University of Michigan Press, Ann Arbor, MI.

Treisman, Daniel (2011). Presidential popularity in a hybrid regime. *American Journal of Political Science,* **55**(3), 590–609.

Treisman, Daniel (2018). Introduction: Rethinking Putin's political order. In *The New Autocracy: Information, Politics, and Policy in Putin's Russia* (ed. D. Treisman), pp. 1–28. Brookings Institution Press, Washington, DC.

Turisbekov, Zautbek (2006). The main directions of the civil service's reforming. Keynote report by the Chairman of The Agency for Civil Service Affairs, International Practical Conference "International Trends of Effective State Governance."

Tutumlu, Assel and Rustemov, Ilyas (2019). The paradox of authoritarian power: Bureaucratic games and information asymmetry: The case of Nazarbayev's Kazakhstan. *Problems of Post-Communism*, **68**(2), 1–11.

TASS News (2020). V Rossii vvoditsia 'reguliatornaia gil'otina'. **December 31**.

Vaal, Tamara (2021). Appeliatsionnyi sud stolitsy otmenil prigovor figurantam po delu o hishchenii sredstv LRT. *Vlast.kz*, **October 7**.

VCIOM (2018). Corruption in Russia. https://wciom.com/press-release/corruption-in-Russia.

Vogel, David and Kagan, Robert A. (2004). *Dynamics of Regulatory Change: How Globalization Affects National Regulatory Policies*. University of California Press, Berkeley, CA.

Voronov, Konstantin (2020). 'Zimniuiu vishniu' proveriat na korruptsiiu. *Kommersant*, **February 18**.

Wade, Robert (1990). *Governing the Market: Economic Theory and the Role of Government in East Asian Industrialization*. Princeton University Press, Princeton, NJ.

Way, Lucan (2015). *Pluralism by Default: Weak Autocrats and the Rise of Competitive Politics*. John Hopkins University Press, Baltimore, MD.

Weber, Max (1946). Bureaucracy. In *From Max Weber: Essays in Sociology* (eds. H. H. Gerth and W. Mills), pp. 196–244. Oxford University Press, New York, NY.

Weingast, Barry R. (1981). Regulation, reregulation, and deregulation: The political foundations of agency clientele relationships. *Law and Contemporary Problems*, **44**(1), 147–177.

Weinthal, Erika and Luong, Pauline Jones (2001). Energy wealth and tax reform in Russia and Kazakhstan. *Resources Policy*, **27**(4), 215–223.

Welter, Friederike and Smallbone, David (2003). Entrepreneurship and enterprise strategies in transition economies: An institutional perspective. In *Small Firms and Economic Development in Developed and Transition Economies* (eds. David A. Kirby and Anna Watson), pp. 95–114. Ashgate Publishing, Farnham, UK.

Whitmore, Brian (2010). Russia arrests whistleblowing 'YouTube cop'. *Radio Free Europe/Radio Liberty*, **22 January**.

Wienekea, Axel and Gries, Thomas (2011). SME performance in transition economies: The financial regulation and firm-level corruption nexus. *Journal of Comparative Economics*, **39**(2), 221–229.

Wilson-Sokhey, Sarah (2017). *The Political Economy of Pension Policy Reversal in Post-Communist Countries*. Cambridge University Press, Cambridge, UK.

Wood, Tony (2018). *Russia Without Putin: Money, Power and the Myths of the New Cold War*. Verso, New York, NY.

World Bank (2020a). *Doing Business 2020: Comparing Business Regulation in 190 Economies*. World Bank, Washington, DC.

World Bank (2020b). Enterprise surveys. https://www.enterprisesurveys.org.

Wright, Joseph (2008). Do authoritarian institutions constrain? How legislatures affect economic growth and investment. *American Journal of Political Science*, **52**(2), 322–343.

Yakovlev, Andrey (2006). The evolution of business—state interaction in Russia: From state capture to business capture? *Europe-Asia Studies*, **58**(7), 1033–1056.

Yakovlev, Evgeny and Zhuravskaya, Ekaterina (2013). The unequal enforcement of liberalization: Evidence from Russia's reform of business regulation. *Journal of the European Economic Association*, **11**(4), 808–838.

Zakon.kz (2012). Shtrafy za narusheniia PDD mozhno oplatit' cherez bankomat ili s pomoshchiu mobil'nogo telefona. **September 18**.

Zakon.kz (2013). Po indikatoru 'bremia tamozhennykh protsedur' Kazakhstan uluchshil pokazateli na rekordnye 25 pozitsii. **July 23**.

Zaloznaya, Marina (2017). *The Politics of Bureaucratic Corruption in Post-Transitional Eastern Europe*. Cambridge University Press, Cambridge, UK.

Zhang, Jun (2010). *Transformation of the Chinese Enterprise*. Cengage Learning, Andover, MA.

Index

Printed in the USA/Agawam, MA
October 19, 2023

853407.005